Maharshi Dayananda Sarasvati's

Sanskāravidhi

संस्कारविधि

[A Process for the Transformation of a Human Being]

Sanskrit Text, Roman Transliteration and English Translation

By

Prof. Dr. Ravi Prakash Arya

Chair Professor
Maharshi Dayanand Saraswati Chair
Maharshi Dayanad University, Rohtak

Amazon Books, USA

In Association with

Indian Foundation for Vedic Science

1051, Sector-1, Rohtak, Haryana, India-124001
Contact Nos. 09313033917; 09650183260
email: vedicsience@rediffmail.com; vedicscience@gmail.com
website : https://vedic-sciences.com

First Edition

Kali era: 5124 (c. 2023)

Kalpa era: 1,97,29,49,124

Brahma era: 15,55,21,97,29,49,124

ISBN 9789394724624

Contents

Scheme of Transliteration

When transliterating the Vedic mantras into Roman script, the internationally accepted scheme was followed. This will help English-knowing readers pronounce the mantras correctly.

Vowels			Consonants		
अ	a	क्	k	प्	p
आ	ā	ख्	kh	फ्	ph
इ	i	ग्	g	ब्	b
ई	ī	घ्	gh	भ्	bh
उ	u	ङ्	ṅ	म्	m
ऊ	ū	च्	ch	य्	y
ऋ	ṛ	छ्	chh	र्	r
ए	e	ज्	j	ल्	l
ऐ	ai	झ्	jh	व्	v
ओ	o	ञ्	ñ	श्	ś
औ	au	ट्	ṭ	ष्	ṣ
अं	aṁ	ठ्	ṭh	स्	s
अः	aḥ	ड्	ḍ	ह्	h
लृ	ḷ	ढ्	ḍh	क्ष्	kṣ
ऽ	'	ण्	ṇ	त्र्	tr
꣌	꣌	त्	t	ज्ञ्	jñ
꣦ (Veda) ṃ		थ्	th	ळ	ḻ
(꣦) in Hindi ṅ		द्	d	ळह	ḻh
		ध्	dh		
		न्	n		

Abbreviations

<table>
<tr><td colspan="2">Hindi</td><td colspan="2">English</td></tr>
<tr><td>अ, अथर्व.</td><td>अथर्ववेद</td><td>AV.</td><td>Atharvaveda</td></tr>
<tr><td>आ.</td><td>आरण्यक</td><td>Aśv.</td><td>Āśvalāyana</td></tr>
<tr><td>आश्व०</td><td>आश्वलायन</td><td>Br.</td><td>Brāhmaṇa</td></tr>
<tr><td>ऋ.</td><td>ऋग्वेद</td><td>GS.</td><td>Gṛhya Sūtra</td></tr>
<tr><td>उप.</td><td>उपनिषद</td><td>Go.</td><td>Gobhila</td></tr>
<tr><td>खिल.</td><td>खिलपाठ</td><td>Kh.</td><td>Khila Pāṭha</td></tr>
<tr><td>गृसू, गृह्य सू.</td><td>गृह्य सूत्र</td><td>Man.</td><td>Mantra</td></tr>
<tr><td>गो०, गोभिल</td><td>गोभिल</td><td>Manu.</td><td>Manusmṛti</td></tr>
<tr><td>तैआ.</td><td>तैत्तिरीय आरण्यक</td><td>Pār.</td><td>Pāraskara</td></tr>
<tr><td>पार.</td><td>पारस्कर</td><td>RV.</td><td>Ṛgveda</td></tr>
<tr><td>ब्रा.</td><td>ब्राह्मण</td><td>SV.</td><td>Sāmaveda</td></tr>
<tr><td>मंब्रा, मन्त्रब्रा.</td><td>मन्त्र ब्राह्मण</td><td>Sām.</td><td>Sāma</td></tr>
<tr><td>मनु.</td><td>मनुस्मृति</td><td>Ś.Br.</td><td>Śatapatha Brāhmaṇa</td></tr>
<tr><td>यजु.</td><td>यजुर्वेद</td><td>TĀr.</td><td>Taittirīya Āraṇyaka</td></tr>
<tr><td>शब्रा.</td><td>शतपथ ब्राह्मण</td><td>Up.</td><td>Upaniṣad</td></tr>
<tr><td>सा.</td><td>सामवेद</td><td>YV.</td><td>Yajurveda</td></tr>
<tr><td>श्रौत सू.</td><td>श्रौत सूत्र</td><td></td><td></td></tr>
<tr><td>सुश्रुत०</td><td>सुश्रुत संहिता</td><td></td><td></td></tr>
</table>

Preface

The modern age is the age of Science. Science has played a vital role in the making of modern society by way of developing technological know-how. In the other words, the main thrust of modern science has been toward the sanskāras of material things. The modern technique of refinement, modification, purification and processing the material things is known in Vedic science as sanskāras. Charaka defines the term sanskāras as under:

संस्कारो हि गुणान्तरधानमुच्यते ।

samskāro hi guṇāntaradhānamuchyate ।

Samskāras means transformation of human being.

Thus we can say that modern science has given stress upon the samskāras of material things and developed a technology to promote the convenience and comfort of human beings. Here there is a basic difference between the concept of Vedic Science and modern science. Vedic science gave more thrust to the samskāras of human beings as compared to material things. According to Vedic science, a human being who has not undergone through a certain process of samskāras remains in his crude form and is recognized as no better than an animal. As such a human being is not considered to be an actual social being. In material things also we can see, that so long as they are in their crude form, they cannot have their practical application. For their practical application, the material things have to undergo particular samskāras or processing. For instance, oil in its crude form cannot be used to operate cars, buses, and airplanes, but after undergoing the process of refinement it becomes usable. Thus the conversion of oil from its crude form to the refined form is known as Science. However, in the race for processing or refining material things, modern science has totally ignored the need for saṁskāras **of human beings for whom the entire technological know-how is being developed.** That is why in the present age of machinery, human beings are also considered to be machines. They are considered on a similar plane as lifeless things and so there is always a talk of 'human resource development' and never of 'human development'. The concept of human resource development receives its strength in considering humans as resources just like other natural resources. Natural resources are often exploited for the benefit of humankind and so are human beings. However, there is a basic difference between the exploitation of natural sources and the exploitation of human beings. The exploitation of natural resources is done by human beings; on the other hand exploitation of human beings is done by human beings. This exploitation results usually in the exploitation of certain helpless and poor human beings for the larger interest of a certain resourceful, powerful and opulent group of human beings.

As far as the Vedas are concerned, the primary object of science is not only the sanskāras of material things but the saṁskāras of human beings. Vedic seers never considered human beings as the means or resources. For them, human beings are not the means but ends. Everything was directed toward the development and elevation of human beings.

Vedic seers had a humanitarian and ethical approach while handling human problems. Their main aim was to relieve human beings permanently of the suffering, deprivation, and all other problems that haunted them.

Modern Science has though developed so many aids for the comfort of human beings, yet it has a limited approach. Its approach is not universal. Modern science has no moral, ethical or humanitarian foundation. It is founded on the laws of survival of the fittest in the struggle that ensues among human beings around the globe. Modern science wants to define and describe everything in the light of struggle. It has no remedy to put an end to this struggle. Contrary to this, the main aim of Vedic science is to put an end to this struggle and prepare a stage for friendship, fraternity, and co-existence of each and every human being on Earth. It clears a stage for co-existence of each and every human-being by giving a call for accepting the principles of mutual understanding and co-operation among human beings.

सह नौ भुनक्तु सह वीर्यं करवावहै ।
तेजस्विनावधितमस्तु मा विद्विषावहै । ।
saha nau bhunaktu saha vīryan karvāvahai
tejasvināvadhitamastu, mā vidviṣāvahai.

Let there be mutual co-operation in eating and gaining power. Let each one of us become illumined with knowledge. Let us not envy or struggle with each other."

Since modern science has its foundation laid out on the laws of struggle, it talks about the exploitation of natural resources as well as human beings and aims at the comfort of those who are able to survive the struggle around the globe. We can see that in spite of high advancement in the area of technology and production of each and everything, the benefits are not reaching each and every human being on the globe due solely to the absence of moral and humanitarian values. We have more than sufficient amount of food grains piled up in our stocks, still, poverty, misery and hunger looms large around the globe. At one hand, the excess food grains are being disposed off in the sea, on the other hand, human beings in various parts of the globe are reduced to skeletal for want of food. Science has blessed modern humanity with great prosperity, yet more than 50% of human beings on the globe are below the poverty line and suffering from hunger, thirst, and malnutrition, phenomenon of coldness and hotness, and the dearth of essential things for their survival. One can say unhesitatingly that modern science has failed in doing saṁskāras of human beings. It could develop and produce material things but not real human beings.

Everything has been commercialized and in the race of commercialization moral values have been given a goodbye. Money has become the basis of material advancement and replaced moral values which are the real basis of the advancement of humanity around the globe. These moral values are called by Vedic seers as Dharma. *Dhāraṇāt Dharma prāhuḥ* i.e. since these values are sustaining humanity around the globe, they are called Dharma. Following moral values are said to be the constituents of dharma.

Dhṛti (patience), kṣmā (forgiveness), damaḥ (to have control over one's mind), asteya (non-stealing), śauca (inner and outer cleanliness), indrīya nigraha (to have control over one's sensual desires) dhi (use of intellect, rationale) vidyā (education) satya (seeking truth) and krodha (calmness, i.e absence of anger).

Today we see Dharma is applied in an altered sense. Different sects or schools propagating and fanning fundamentalism are known as religion, which is not dharma in the real sense of terms.

The sanśkāras of human beings take place by inculcating the above components of Dharma.

There is clear-cut observation in the Vedic philosophy that every human being is born as śudra (devoid of sanskaras of education etc.) from the womb of his/her mother. When subjected to sanskaras of moral ethical values and education, a human being becomes dvija (twice-born).

जन्मना जायते शूद्रः, संस्कारैर्द्विज उच्यते ।

janmanā jāyate śūdraḥ, saṁskārairdvija uchyate

That is, by birth all human beings are born as Śudra (illetrate). When subjected to Sanskaras (inculcation of moral values and education) a human being attains second birth and becomes a real human being called dvij.

We can say that mere biological birth is not sufficient to make human-being a real human being; rather at this stage, he is no better than an animal. To become an actual human being he has to take second birth, i.e. in addition to his biological birth from the mother's womb, he has to take birth from Āchārya's womb. Āchārya is a person who educates him and helps inculcate moral and ethical values.

आचार्य कस्मात् आचिनोति अर्थान् । आचारं ग्राहयतीति सतः ।

āchārya kasmāt āchinoti arthān | āchāraṁ grāhayatīti satah

Just as a child stay for nine months in his/her mother's womb, similarly he/she has to stay with Acharya in Gurukula for years together to be born again as a perfect, knowledgeable human being. The stay of a child with Achārya is called his/her antaḥvāsa and the child observing antaḥvāsa (staying in the womb of Achārya) is known as antaḥvāsī. Just as in developing a certain instrument or machine, several types of processing are required, similarly, in developing a perfect human being, the Vedic sages stressed the need for sixteen main saṁskāras right from the birth to death of an individual.

Here it is also important to understand the term

sanskāra and its role in shaping the life of human beings in the next life as humans, animals, birds, insects, or plants. What is Sanskāra? Sanskāra is information of our actions, and thoughts imprinted on our subtle mind (subconscious mind). They act as a seed for attaining a species in the next life. Vedanta Darśana says:

संस्कारबीजात् सृष्टिः ।

saṁskārabījāt sṛṣṭiḥ

Seeds of Sanskāras are instrumental behind the future species of human beings. It depends upon your Sanskāras what type of species you have destined for you, as Sanskāras of human being leads one to the birth of a human being. With feminine sanskāras, one is born as a woman, and with masculine sanskāras one is born as a man. Animal, insect, and plant like Sanskāras lead one to be born as animal, insect, and plant respectively. Patanjali says:

संस्कारसाक्षात्करणात् पूर्वजाति ज्ञानम् ।

saṁskārasākṣātkaraṇāt pūrvajñāti jñānam.

Realisation of the sanskāras of human being enables one to know about his past species.

To explain this phenomenon further, our present life is the result of our past sanskāras. As per Vedic philosophy, a human being also carries along with him āyu (life span), vidyā (education), yaśa (name, fame and prosperity) and bala (physical health) in the present life due to sanskāras accumulated in the past life. That is why, Bharatiya sages suggested that if one wants to prolong his life span, add to his knowledge, seek name and fame and maintain a healthy body, he/she take care of elderly persons.

अभिवादनशीलस्य नित्यं वृद्धोपसेविनः ।
चत्वारि तस्य वर्धन्ते आयुर्विद्यायशोबलम् ॥

abhivādanaśīlasya nityaṁ vṛddhopasevinaḥ;
chatvāri tasya vardhante āyurvidyāyaśobalam.

So it is necessary to inculcate good sanskāras so that either a human being is transformed into Deva or attains the species of a human being maintaining a status quo and not revert back to *naraka loka,* i.e. animal or plant life. To understand the concept of Svarga and Naraka and the process of progression and regression of the life of a human being, we need to understand the theory of five koṣas. The entire creation of living beings is distributed over to the five koṣas. The body of human beings also consists of five koṣas. Hereunder is explained this mystery.

There are five koṣas:

1. Annamaya Koṣa

2. Prāṇamaya Koṣa

3. Manomaya Koṣa

4. Vijñānamaya Koṣa

5. Ānandamaya Koṣa

The development of the above-mentioned five-koṣas is visible in a physical body. Similarly, various species of living beings develop according to the dominance of one of the above five koṣas.

For instance, skin, flesh, fat, bones and filth of the physical body are composed of Annamaya Koṣa. Annamaya Koṣa is nourished by food and acts as the foodstuff for living beings. At this level consciousness remains dormant or say consciousness remains unconscious or in the state of deep sleep. All plants, herbs, shrubs, grains and vegetation may be categorised to have developed at this level and so are considered as the best foodstuffs for human beings.

The prāṇic system, sense organs and organs of action of the body are formed of prāṇamaya kośa. The prāṇic system is constituted of five types of prāṇa vāyus.

1. Prāna vāyu controls the breathing system.

2. Apāna vāyu controls excretory system

3. Vyāna controls the circulatory system

4. Samāna controls the digestive system, and

5. Udāna controls the vocal system or sound production mechanism of the body.

At this level consciousness remains in the state of dream and it can be identified with the feeling of a sensation. All small insects have developed at this level. They are attributed with sensation.

We find further development of consciousness at manomaya kośa. The mind of a living being is composed of manomaya kośa. What is Mind? This question has often vexed scholiasts and psychologists. While discussing the subject of the origin of the human body and mind or citta, the thinking power or conscious mind has been perceived in Yogavāsiṣtha (Chapter 91) as the cause of all things in course of time, and the source of all its pleasurable and painful feelings, which develop and diminish in itself and never grow without it.

अविनाभाविनीनित्यं काल कांक्षिक्रमे तथा ।

सर्वमुत्पादयत्येतच्चित्तकः संविदात्मकः ॥ 5.91.51

avinābhāvinīnityaṁ kāla kāṁkṣikrame tathā;
sarvamutpādayatyetachchittakaḥ saṁvidātmakaḥ.

[Meaning] The conscious mind is the cause of all

things in the course of time and the source of all its pleasure and pain which rise and fall in itself and never grow without it.

At the same time concept of sensation and citta or mind has also been defined as the union of the prāṇa vāyu (breath of life) in the company of sense organs with desire, the origin of citta or mind takes place.

यथा प्राणेन्द्रियानन्दमानन्दपवनावुभौ ।

चित्तस्योत्पादिके सार्धं यदैत वासने तदा ॥ 5.91.52

yathā prāṇendriyānandamānandapavanāvubhau;
chittasyotpādike sārdhaṁ yadaita vāsane tadā.

[Meaning] As the union of the breath of life with the sense organs produces sensations, so these being united with desire are productive of the citta or mind.

All animals and birds who have an urge or desire are said to have developed at this level. All sensitive insects and plants which are devoid of desire are devoid of mind also. In this course, it may be stated that the end of desire, is the end of mind, and the end of mind is tantamount to the end of the birth-death cycle which is known in philosophical terms as emancipation. But this is possible when a living being is endowed with the power of intellect.

Consciousness' further development is traced to vijñānmaya koṣa. The development of human intellect can be attributed to the vijñānamaya koṣa. Rationality and the ability to decide and discriminate between right and wrong is the attributive of intellect. All human beings are considered to be born at the level of vijñānmaya koṣa.

The highest stage of development of consciousness is seen at ānanda-maya koṣa. This is the stage of complete bliss. Only human beings developed at vijñānamaya koṣa can attain this stage.

Let me here clarify that vijñānamaya koṣa is known as Manuṣya Loka in the language of Vedic philosophy. The lower koṣas, viz. annamaya koṣa, prāṇamaya koṣa and manomaya koṣa are known as Naraka Lokas and higher koṣa, viz. ānanda-maya koṣa is known as Svarga Loka. We can understand it the other way round. If an individual soul is born after death in the species developed at the level of annamaya koṣa, prāṇamaya koṣa and manomaya koṣa, it is said to be suffering under Naraka Loka. If an individual soul takes birth after death as a human being, it is said to have maintained the status quo, i.e. human birth. If a human being elevates himself or herself to the level of superhuman being or a yogī and becomes Jivana Mukta he is said to have upsurged at ānanda-maya koṣa or Svarga Loka. A Jīvana Mukta after his death becomes liberated permanently and enjoys Svarga Loka till the next creation cycle. So Manuṣya Loka is a level playing field where all human beings are provided an opportunity either to progress to the ānandamaya koṣa, i.e. Svarga Loka, or to regress to the lower koṣas, i.e. Naraka Loka. As such suffering Naraka or enjoying Svarga is within the ambit of human beings and depends upon the sanskāras stored by them in their subtle body (Sukṣma Śarīra) by dint of his or her acts and thoughts. As whatever act a person performs, whatever a person thinks and whatever he or she eats and drinks, that is coded in our mind as sanskāra which are instrumental behind attaining the life hereafter.

Since sanskāras play an important role in shaping the life of an individual, so the Vedic culture has given the utmost emphasis on the sanskaras. An individual is supposed to undergo the process of at least 16 Sanskaras even before birth till death for being trasformed into a perfect human being. This process starts even before the birth of a child.

Modern Science has no provision of the sanskāra of a human being although it has a provision of the sanskara of material things. Its advancement is lop-sided. It has played a pivotal role towards developing perfect material things as an aid to the human beings but miserably failed to develop perfect human beings for want of which there is terrorism, blood shed all around.

Here it may not be out of context to inform that sanskāra is a psychological genes that reflects into the biological genes (DNA,RNA) of an individual or say the biology of a living being is shaped by its psychology (sanskāras). So sanskāra (psychological genes) and biological genes (DNA, RNA) are interrelated or interdependent. Modification at the level of sanskāras will result in modification at the biological level (DNA, RNA level) or modification of genes will lead to the modification of sanskāras.

Hereunder we shall give a scientific explanation and detailed description of the 16 sanskāras (except three sanskāras of Gṛhyāśram, Vānaprasthāśrama and Saṁnyāśāśram) as explained and eluciated by Maharshi Dayanand Saraswati in his Sanskāra Vidhi. All mantras quoted by Maharshi Dayanand Saraswati in his SanskāraVidhi have been rendered with Sanskrit text and Roman transliteration with Engish translation by the author of present lines for easy understanding of readers, researchers and chaplains. These sanskāras are laid down in the Vedic culture as a process for transformation of himan beings. This book is brought out for the lovers of Vedic knowledge system as a part of celebration of 2nd birth centenary of Maharshi Dayanand Saraswati (1824-1883) who was a great social reformer of India in 19th century, known as Indian Renaissance Rishi and embodiment of Vedic life and thought. Hope the readers and researchers both would be benefitted by this publication.

Prof. Ravi Prakash Arya
Chair Professor
Maharshi Dayanand Saraswati Chair (UGC)
Maharshi Dayanand University, Rohtak

अथ संस्कारविधिं वक्ष्यामः

Introduction

ओं सह नाववतु। सह नौ भुनक्तु। सह वीर्य्यं करवावहै। तेजस्वि नावधीतमस्तु। मा विद्विषावहै॥ ओं शान्तिः शान्तिः शान्तिः॥

तैत्तिरीय आरण्यक 8.1

Oṁ saha nāvavatu, saha nau bhunaktu, saha vīryyaṁ karavāvahai, tejasvi nāvadhītamastu, mā vidviṣāvahai. Oṁ śāntiḥ śāntiḥ śāntiḥ ǁ Taittirīya Āraṇyaka, 8.1

Now, we will describe the procedure of sanskāras.

Let us both, the teacher and taught, preserve the standard of education together, eat together, resort to endeavour and exertion together, and let whatever we have learnt is sound and fruitful.

सर्वात्मा सच्चिदानन्दो विश्वादिर्विश्वकृद्विभुः।
भूयात्तमां सहायो नस्सर्वेशो न्यायकृच्छुचिः॥1॥

sarvātmā sachchidānando viśvādirviśvakṛdvibhuḥ,
bhūyāttamāṁ sahāyo nassarveśo nyāyakṛchchhu-chiḥ ǁ1 ǁ

May God who is the spirit of all, who is Existent, Conscious and All-bliss, who is the Creator of the universe, who is the first cause of the universe, who is All pervading, who is the Master of all, who is Holy by nature and who is the Dispenser of justice, be our helpful guide.

गर्भाद्या मृत्युपर्य्यन्ताः संस्काराः षोडशैव हि।
वक्ष्यन्ते तं नस्कृत्यानन्तविद्यं परेश्वरम्॥2॥

garbhādyā mṛtyuparyyantāḥ saṁskārāḥ ṣoḍaśaiva hi,
vakṣayante taṁ naskṛtyānantavidyaṁ pareśvaram ǁ2 ǁ

The sixteeen sanskāras beginning with Garbhādhāna (impregnation) and ending with Antyeṣṭi (death) will be described by us, after paying our homage to Him who is the paramount Lord and Possessor of infinite knowledge.

वेदादिशास्त्रसिद्धान्तमाध्याय परमादरात् ।
आर्यैतिह्यं पुरस्कृत्य शरीरात्मविशुद्धये ॥3 ॥

vedādiśāstrasiddhāntamādhyāya paramādarāt,
āryaitihyaṁ puraskṛtya śarīrātmaviśuddhaye ॥3 ॥

These sanskāras will be described by us for the purification of the body and the soul by giving full consideration to the principles of the Śāstras of which the first is this Veda, with due respect and mindful of the history of the Aryas.

संस्कारैस्संस्कृतं यन्मेध्यमत्र तदुत्तमम् ।
असंस्कृतं तु यल्लोकं तदमेध्यं प्रकीर्त्यते ॥4 ॥

saṁskāraissaṁskṛtaṁ yanmedhyamatra taduttamam,
asaṁskṛtaṁ tu yallokaṁ tadamedhyaṁ prakīrtyate ॥4 ॥

Whatever is purified and refined through the process of sanskāras in this world, is pure and excellent and whatever is not thus purified and refined is described impure in this world.

अतः सस्कारकरणे क्रियतामुद्यमो बुधैः ।
शिक्षयौषधिभिर्नित्यं सर्वथा सुखवर्द्धनः ॥5 ॥

ataḥ saskārakaraṇe kriyatāmudyamo budhaiḥ,
śikṣayauṣadhibhirnnityaṁ sarvathā sukhavarddhanaḥ ॥5 ॥

Therefore, always an endeavour should be made in performing the sanskāras, by the learned men as per norms with the help of herbs and plants altogether.

कृतानीह विधानानि ग्रन्थग्रन्थनतत्परैः ।
वेदविज्ञानविरहैः स्वार्थिभिः परिमोहितैः ॥6 ॥

kṛtānīha vidhānāni granthagranthanatatparaiḥ,
vedavijñānavirahaiḥ svārthibhiḥ parimohitaiḥ ॥6 ॥

In this regard procedures of performing various sanskāras have been laid down by various persons who remain engaged in compiling books, but are bereft of the knowledge of the Veda and have selfish motives and are totally confused.

प्रमाणैस्तान्यनाद‍त्य क्रियते वेदमानतः ।
जनानां सुखबोधाय संस्कारविधिरुत्तमः ॥7॥

pramāṇaistānyanādṛtya kriyate vedamānataḥ,
janānāṁ sukhabodhāya saṁskāravidhiruttamaḥ. ॥7॥

Setting their views asie with proofs, authorities and reasons, this excellent book of sanskāras is being written by me according to the dicta and dictates of the Veda for the easy understanding of the people.

बहुभिः सज्जनैस्सम्यङ् मानवप्रियकारकैः ।
प्रवृत्तो ग्रन्थकरणे क्रमशोऽहं नियोजितः ॥8॥

bahubhiḥ sajjanaissamyaṅ mānavapriyakārakaiḥ,
pravṛtto granthakaraṇe kramaśo'haṁ niyojitaḥ. ॥8॥

On having been persuaded from time to time by many gentlemen devoted to the good of the people. I took up the work of writing this book.

दयाया आनन्दो विलसति परो ब्रह्मविदितः
सरस्वत्यस्याग्रे निवसति मुदा सत्यनिलया ।
इयं ख्यातिर्यस्य प्रततसुगुणा हीशशरणाऽ-
स्त्यनेनायं ग्रन्थो रचित इति बोद्धव्यमनघाः ॥9॥

dayāyā ānando vilasati paro brahmaviditaḥ
sarasvatyasyāgre nivasati mudā satyanilayā,
iyaṁ khyātiryasya pratatasuguṇā hīśaśaraṇā-
styanenāyaṁ grantho rachita iti boddhavyamana-ghāḥ ॥9॥

O pious persons! let it be known to you that this book (the Sanskārvidhi) is written by this author in whose name the word 'Ānand', which is found in Brahman, the Supreme Being, occurs after the word 'Dayā' the word 'Sarasvati' who resides in truth gets its place thereafter i.e. after Ānand, and thus whose name is

Dayanand Sarasvati.

चक्षूरामाङ्कचन्द्रेऽब्दे कार्तिकस्यान्तिमे दले ।
अमायां शनिवारेऽयं ग्रन्थारम्भः कृतो मया ॥10 ॥

chakṣūrāmāṅkachandre'bde kārtikasyāntime dale,
amāyāṁ śanivāre'yaṁ granthārambhaḥ kṛto mayā ॥10 ॥

This book is started in the middle of Kārtika month on Saturday, the day of Amāvasya in the Vikrama year 1932 (1875 AD).

बिन्दुवेदाङ्कचन्द्रेऽब्दे शुचौ मासेऽसिते दले ।
त्रयोदश्यां रवौ वारे पुनः संस्करणं कृतम् ॥11 ॥

binduvedāṅkachandre'bde śuchau māse'site dale,
trayodaśyāṁ ravau vāre punaḥ saṁskaraṇaṁ kṛtam ॥11 ॥

The amended editon of this book was prepared again on Sunday, the 13th day of dark half of the month Āṣāḍha in the Vikrama year 1940 (1883 AD).

At the beginning of all the sanskāras, one should chant the following mantras for eulogy, prayer and worship of God with the meaning thereof and thus meditate on God with a concentrated mind. Others present should listen attentively and ponder the chanting of mantras and their meanings.

अथेश्वर-स्तुति-प्रार्थनोपासनामन्त्राः

Mantras for Eulogy, Prayer and Worship of Īśvara

ओं विश्वानि देव सवितर्दुरितानि परा सुव । यद् भद्रं तन्न आ सुव ॥

यजु. 30.3

Oṁ viśvāni deva savitar duritāni parāsuva. yad bhadraṁ tanna āsuva.

O God, O Radiant Divinity, Creator of the Universe, Pure, Bestower of happiness and bliss, may You keep us away from all vices, misfortune and distress; confer upon us all that is beneficial by virtue of its properties, nature and action.

ओं हिरण्यगर्भः समवर्त्तताग्रे भूतस्य जातः पतिरेक आसीत् । स दाधार पृथिवीं द्यामुतेमां कस्मै देवाय हविषा विधेम ॥ ऋ. 10.121.1; यजु. 13.4

Oṁ hiraṇyagarbhaḥ samavarttatāgre bhūtasya jātaḥ patireka āsīt. sa dādhāra pṛthivīṁ dyām utemāṁ kasmai devāya haviṣā vidhema.

Unto him, who, like energy, existed even before the origin of this visible universe; unto him, who was the single Master of all originated world; unto him who sustains this observer space and light space, do we offer worship, in love and through the practice of Yoga.

ओं य आत्मदा बलदा यस्य विश्व उपासते प्रशिषं यस्य देवाः । यस्यच्छायाऽमृतं यस्य मृत्युः कस्मै देवाय हविषा विधेम ॥ यजु. 25.13

Oṁ ya ātmadā baladā yasya viśva upāsate praśiṣaṁ yasya devāḥ. yasyacchāyā'mṛtaṁ yasya mṛtyuḥ kasmai devāya haviṣā vidhema.

Unto Him, who releases ātmans at the beginning of the creation to take birth according to their karmas; who activates the energy for the creation of the material world; unto Him, whose commands, directions and justice are worshipped, adored and obeyed by all scholars; unto Him, whose refuge provides emancipation, and desertion causes mortality; unto Him, the Blissful One and All-knowing, do we offer our worship from the core of our heart and soul.

ओं यः प्राणतो निमिषतो महित्वैक इद्राजा जगतो बभूव। य ईशे अस्य द्विपदश्चतुष्पदः कस्मै देवाय हविषा विधेम ॥ यजु. 23.3

Oṁ yaḥ prāṇato nimiṣato mahitvaika idrājā jagato babhūva. ya īśe asya dvipadaś catuṣpadaḥ kasmai devāya haviṣā vidhema.

Unto Him, who, in His infinite capacity, is the single Lord of all things, living and non-living; unto Him, who Rules this biped and quadruped creation; unto Him, the Blissful One, do we offer our worship from the core of our heart and soul.

ओं येन द्यौरुग्रा पृथिवी च दृढा येन स्वः स्तभितं येन नाकः। यो अन्तरिक्षे रजसो विमानः कस्मै देवाय हविषा विधेम ॥ यजु. 32.6

Oṁ yena dyaur ugrā pṛthivī ca dṛdhā yena svaḥ stabhitaṁ yena nākaḥ. yo antarikṣe rajaso vimānaḥ kasmai devāya haviṣā vidhema.

Unto Him, who created the light space and stabilized the turbulent state of observer space; unto Him who distinguished between happiness and Moksha; unto Him, who creates all matter particles, anti-particles and heavenly bodies in observer space and rotates them like flying birds; unto Him, the Blissful One, do we offer our worship from the core of our hearts and souls.

ओं प्रजापते न त्वदेतान्यन्यो विश्वा जातानि परि ता बभूव। यत्कामास्ते जुहुमस्तन्नो अस्तु वयं स्याम पतयो रयीणाम् ॥ ऋ. 10.121.10

Oṁ prajāpate na tvadetānyanyo viśvā jātāni pari tā bahūva.

yat kāmāste juhumas tanno astu vayaṁ syāma patayo rayīṇām.

O Master of all Beings, no one but You can surpass this living and non-living world. You are supreme. Grant us wishes that we desire while offering oblations in Your name. May we, by your grace, be the masters of all earthly and heavenly riches.

ओं स नो बन्धुर्जनिता स विधाता धामानि वेद भुवनानि विश्वा। यत्र देवा अमृतमानशानास्तृतीये धामन्नध्यैरयन्त॥ यजु. 32.10

Oṁ sa no bandhur janitā sa vidhātā dhāmāni veda bhuvanāni viśvā. yatra devā amṛtam ānaśānās tṛtīye dhāmann adhyair yanta.

He is a benefactor like our brother, the One Creator, the One Who makes the constitution of this creation. He knows all the 14 worlds and three spaces, of which the third one, the light space, holds various matter particles in their immortal form, i.e. energy.

ओम् अग्ने नय सुपथा रायेऽअस्मान् विश्वानि देव वयुनानि विद्वान्। युयोध्यस्मज्जुहुराणमेनो भूयिष्ठां ते नम उक्तिं विधेम॥ यजु. 40.16

Om agne naya supathā rāye asmān viśvāni deva vayunāni vidvān. Yuyodhyasmaj juhurāṇam eno bhūyiṣṭhāṁ te nama uktiaṁ vidhema.

O Self-effulgent, the embodiment of knowledge and illuminator of the whole universe, lead us unto the Path of wise and righteous people so that we may excel in scientific pursuits and be blessed with earthly and heavenly riches. You are keeping a close vigil on our activities, so keep us away from all immoral and criminal acts. Let us offer plentiful prayers and live a life of bliss.

अथ स्वस्तिवाचनम्

Prayer for Well-being

ओम् अग्निमीळे पुरोहितं यज्ञस्य देवमृत्विजम् । होतारं रत्नधातमम् ॥

ऋ. 1.1.1

Om agnim īḷe purohitaṁ yajñasya devam ṛtvijam.
hotāraṁ ratna-dhātamam.

Spiritual meaning: I invoke Agni (Almighty God), who is the forerunner of entire process of creation, highly effulgent, creator of different things at different times, presenter or provider of several facilities and the possessor of precious traits.

Scientific meaning: I appreciate geothermal energy, which is the forerunner of the entire creation process on Earth, and act as hotā priest who performs the creation yajña on the Earth at the proper time. Due to this geothermal energy, the Earth holds many precious stones in her womb.

ओं स नः पितेव सूनवेऽग्ने सूपायनो भव । सचस्वा नः स्वस्तये ॥ ऋ. 1.1.9

Oṁ sa naḥ piteva sūnave'gne sūpāyano bhava.
sacasvā naḥ svastaye.

Agni (God), be easy to access for us, as is father to his son; bless us for our good.

ओं स्वस्ति नो मिमीतामश्विना भगः स्वस्ति देव्यदितिरनर्वणः । स्वस्ति पूषा असुरो दधातु नः स्वस्ति द्यावापृथिवी सुचेतुना ॥ ऋ. 5.51.11

Oṁ svasti no mimītāmaśvinā bhagaḥ svasti devyaditi-ranarvaṇaḥ. svasti pūṣā asuro dadhātu naḥ svasti dyāvāpṛthivī sucetunā.

May the rising and setting sun benefit us; may the dawn period be useful to us; may the solar energy by nature bring us benefits; may the moon nourish us. May the earth and the sun bring us well-being with benevolence.

ओं स्वस्तये वायुमुपब्रवामहै सोमं स्वस्ति भुवनस्य यस्पतिः । बृहस्पतिं सर्वगणं स्वस्तये स्वस्तय आदित्यासो भवन्तु नः ॥ ऋ. 5.51.12

Om svastaye vāyum upabravāmahai somam svasti bhuvanasya yaspatiḥ. bṛhaspatim sarvagaṇam svastaye svastaya ādityāso bhavantu naḥ.

We appreciate the function of the magnetosphere of the earth, which shields us from the solar winds, and moon. May the protector of this universe be our benefactor. May the expanding universe along with all its components be useful for us. May the sun of various 12 months be beneficial to us.

ओं विश्वे देवा नो अद्या स्वस्तये वैश्वानरो वसुरग्निः स्वस्तये। देवा अवन्त्वृभवः स्वस्तये स्वस्ति नो रुद्रः पात्वंहसः ॥ ऋ. 5.51.13

Om viśvedevā no adyā svastaye vaiśvānaro vasuragniḥ svastaye. devā avant vṛbhavaḥ svastaye svasti no rudraḥ pātvam hasaḥ.

May all the forms of energy protect us. May the energy abiding all objects shield us. The charged particles coming from the magnetosphere of the earth do not harm us and the radiation of the universe be beneficial to us and protect us from all its harmful effects.

ओं स्वस्ति मित्रावरुणा स्वस्ति पथ्ये रेवति । स्वस्ति न इन्द्रश्चाग्निश्च स्वस्ति नो अदिते कृधि ॥ ऋ. 5.51.14

Om svasti mitrāvarūṇā svasti pathye revati.
svasti na indraścāgniścha svāsti no adite kṛdhi.

The Prāṇa and Apāna air bring us health and happiness. The welfare route leads us to prosperity. A healthy mind and body are blessings for us because a person with a disturbed mind and sick body suffers from fear and pain. Let spiritual power also bless us with happiness.

ओं स्वस्ति पन्थामनुचरेम सूर्याचन्द्रमसाविव।
पुनर्ददताघ्नता जानता संगमेमहि ॥ ऋ. 5.51.15

Oṁ svasti panthāmanu carema sūryacandramasāviva.
punardadatāghnatā jānatā saṁgamemahi.

May we walk the path of welfare like the Sun and the Moon. May we have a friendship with a scholar who habitually shares knowledge with others and abstains from criminal and violent activities.

ओं ये देवानां यज्ञिया यज्ञियानां मनोर्यजत्रा अमृता ऋतज्ञाः। ते नो रासन्तामुरुगायमद्य यूयं पात स्वस्तिभिः सदा नः ॥ ऋ. 7.35.15

Oṁ ye devānāṁ yajñiyā yajñiyānāṁ manoryajatrā amṛtā ṛtajñāḥ te no rāsantāmurugāyam adya yūyaṁ pāta svastibhiḥ sadā naḥ.

Let the living liberated scholars who are most worshipped among worshipable, great thinkers, worthy of friendship and excel in the knowledge of valid laws and principles governing nature, impart to us this knowledge which has been ferociously discussed and debated among scholars. May all scholars save us from being led astray by virtue of their valuable guidance and preachings.

ओं येभ्यो माता मधुमत्पिन्वते पयः पीयूषं द्यौरदितिरद्रिबर्हाः। उक्थशुष्मान् वृषभरान्त्स्वप्रसस्ताँ आदित्याँ अनुमदा स्वस्तये ॥ ऋ. 10.63.3

Oṁ yebhyo mātā madhumat pinvate payaḥ pīyūṣaṁ dyauraditiradribarhāḥ. ukthaśuṣmān vṛṣabharānt svapnasastāṁ ādityāṁ anumadā svastaye.

Provide for our happiness solar winds from the sun, full of lustre and charged particles. By virtue of these sun rays, which help mother Earth produce various flavours, the sky remains overcast with clouds, and celestial provides light on the Earth in the form of nectar.

ओं नृचक्षसो अनिमिषन्तो अर्हणा बृहद् देवासो अमृतत्वमानशुः। ज्योतीरथा अहिमाया अनागसो दिवो वर्ष्माणं वसते स्वस्तये ॥ ऋ. 10.63.4

Om nṛcakṣaso animiṣanto arhaṇā bṛhad devāso amṛtatvm ānaśuḥ. jyotīrathā ahimāyā anāgaso divo varṣmāṇaṁ vasate svastaye.

Various forms of light energy [radio waves, microwaves, infrared, ultraviolet, x-rays and gamma rays] known to humans are at work, day and night, in nature, as per their capacity. They are immortalised in the space of Brahman [Chidākāśa], i.e. they are located in Chidākāśa in the inactive or dark form. The transformation of active energy into inactive energy [dark energy] is known as the immortality of devas in Vedas. All these various forms of light energy ride on the chariot of light. They are sustained by themselves in Chidākāśa to maintain this universe.

ओं सम्राजो ये सुवृधो यज्ञमाययुरपरिह्वृता दधिरे दिवि क्षयम्। ताँ आ विवास नमसा सुवृक्तिभिर्महो आदित्याँ अदितिं स्वस्तये ॥ ऋ. 10.63.5

Om samrājo ye suvṛdho yajñam āyayura parihvṛtā dadhire divi kṣayam. tāṁ ā vivāsa namasā suvṛktibhir maho āditayāṁ aditiṁ svastaye.

The radiant energy particles, located in the Chidākāśa, accelerate the creation process in Bhūtākāśa [space known to modern physics] when activated by Brahman. To maintain creation in Bhūtākāśa, the energy of the Chidākāśa had to take refuge in the Bhūtākāśa in active form.

NB: According to the Veda, the creation in Bhūtākāśa starts when Brahman activates energy. Before activation, inactive energy remains in dark [tamas] form in

Chidākāśa. It is also called the equilibrium of sattva (light), rajas (motion) and tamas (matter/inertia) guṇas. Activation entails motion, which can also be called the origin of rajas. Thus, with the origin of rajoguṇa, the equilibrium of sattva and tamas guṇa also gets disturbed, and the active energy appears in its two forms— massless and mass forms. Masslessness is the property of sattva guṇa, and mass is the property of tamoguṇa. Rajoguṇa is the motion that breaks the equilibrium or harmony of the sattva and tamoguṇa. A particle under the dominance of sattvaguṇa remains massless and is called the light particle. Sattvaguṇa is also called prakāśātmaka (a form of light in terms of physics). Tamoguṇā is called sthityātmaka (mass or inertia in terms of physics). So, a light particle is massless, and a matter particles have mass. When the energy is activated by the power of saṅkalpa of Brahman in Chidākāsa [Svarāṭ], it creates the field and a Bhūtākāśa is formed within the Chidākāsa, and one-fourth of energy participate as active energy and three-fourth remains in dark form.

ओं को वः स्तोमं राधति यं जुजोषथ विश्वे देवासो मनुषो यति छन । को वोऽध्वरं तुविजाता अरं करद्यो नः पर्षदत्यंहः स्वस्तये ॥ ऋ. 10.63.6

Oṁ ko vaḥ stomaṁ rādhati yaṁ jujoṣatha viśve devāso manuṣo yati ṣṭhana. kovo'dhvaraṁ tuvijātā araṁ karadyo naḥ parṣadatyaṁhaḥ svastaye.

O famous energy particles! who creates those waves, you transform in? O transformable energy particles, who amongst you accelerate the process of creation. This Yajña of creation protects us from the destructive powers for our wellbeing.

NB: According to the above mantra of Veda, inactive energy transforms into active energy in the Bhūtākāśa. Under this transformation process, opposite powers are defeated leading to the formation of universe.

ओं येभ्यो होत्रां प्रथमामायेजे मनुः समिद्धाग्निर्मनसा सप्तहोतृभिः । त आदित्या अभयं शर्म यच्छत सुगा नः कर्त सुपथा स्वस्तये ॥ ऋ. 10.63.7

Oṁ yebhyo hotrāṁ prathamāmāyeje manuḥ samiddhāgnir manasā saptahotṛbhiḥ. ta ādityā abhayaṁ śarma yachchhata sugā naḥ karta supathā svastaye.

Let those Āditya Brahmacharī-s bring us happiness and make for us the path leading to our welfare, unto whom the scholars or experts of Jñāna Yajña carried out jñāna yajña with the help of seven priests, i.e. mind, intellect and five sense organs on account of their will power.

ओं य ईशिरे भुवनस्य प्रचेतसो विश्वस्य स्थातुर्जगतश्च मन्तवः । ते नः कृतादकृतादेनसस्पर्यद्या देवासः पिपृता स्वस्तये ॥ ऋ. 10.63.8

Oṁ ya īśire bhuvanasya pracetaso viśvasya sthāturjagataśca mantavaḥ. te naḥ kṛtādakṛtādenasasparyadyā devāsaḥ pipṛtā svastaye.

The wise and thoughtful persons who can comprehend the entire creation of living beings and non-living things protect us from criminal acts committed or not committed by us for our well-being in this life.

ओं भरेष्विन्द्रं सुहवं हवामहेंऽहोमुचं सुकृतं दैव्यं जनम् । अग्निं मित्रं वरुणं सातये भगं द्यावापृथिवी मरुतः स्वस्तये ॥ ऋ. 10.63.9

Oṁ bhareṣvindraṁ suhavaṁ havāmaheṁ'homucaṁ sukṛtaṁ daivyaṁ janam. agniṁ mitraṁ varuṇaṁ sātaye bhagaŠ dyāvāpṛthivī marutaḥ svastaye.

We invoke the electric force for the protection of protons and electrons and newly formed matter particles in Bhūtākāsa. It is often invoked during wars between Indra (expanding power) and Vṛtra (contracting power of the Universe), Devas and Asuras (annihilation process between matter and anti-matter particles). It protects us from Vṛtra, the surface tension or contracting force of the Universe, and performs the best function of creation. It is generated from the charged matter particles. Let the solar region, earth, and pessure belts in atmosphere do us no harm.

ओं सुत्रामाणं पृथिवीं द्यामनेहसं सुशर्माणमदितिं सुप्रणीतिम्। दैवीं नावं स्वरित्रामनागसमस्रवन्ती- मारुहेमा स्वस्तये ॥ ऋ. 10.63.10

Oṁ sutrāmāṇaṁ pṛthivīṁ dyāmanehasaṁ suśarmāṇam aditiṁ supraṇītim. daivīṁ nāvaṁ svaritrām anāgasam asravantīmā ruhemā svastaye.

Let us embark upon a natural boat made by God with the earth and solar region for our wellbeing. This boat has all the safety features. It is hassle-free, adequately built, equipped with all fine-looking accessories, leak-proof, well-rowed and free from all construction flaws.

ओं विश्वे यजत्रा अधि वोचतोतये त्रायध्वं नो दुरेवाया अभिह्रुतः। सत्यया वो देवहूत्या हुवेम श्रृण्वतो देवा अवसे स्वस्तये॥ ऋ. 10.63.11

Oṁ viśve yajatrā adhi vocatotaye trāyadhvaṁ no durevāyā abhihrutaḥ. satyayā vo devahūtyā huvema sṛṇvato devā avase svastaye.

O salutation-worthy scholars! Enlighten us on all safety and security measures to save us from violence and miseries. For our safety and happiness, we invite you, since you concede to our request, through an invitation worthy to be extended to true scholars.

ओम् अपामीवामप विश्वामनाहुतिमपारातिं दुर्विदत्रामघायतः। आरे देवा द्वेषो अस्मद्युयोतनोरु णः शर्म यच्छता स्वस्तये ॥ ऋ. 10.63.12

Om apāmīvāmapa viśvām anāhutim apārātiṁ durvidatrām aghāyataḥ. āre devā dveṣo asmad yuyotanoru ṇaḥ śarma yachchhatā svastaye.

O, Learned people, keep us away from problems and diseases; remove from us whatever is non-Vedic or does not conform to the standards of yajñīya life. Inspire us to contribute to our society and nation and make good sense prevail. Ward us off the enmity and wicked will of the viciously inclined enemies. Bless us with a blissful life.

ओम् अरिष्टः स मर्त्तो विश्व एधते प्र प्रजाभिर्जायते धर्मणस्परि । यमादित्यासो नयथा सुनीतिभिरति विश्वानि दुरिता स्वस्तये ॥ ऋ. 10.63.13

Om ariṣṭaḥ sa martto viśva edhate pra prajābhir jāyate dharmaṇaspari. yam ādityāso nayathā sunītibhir ati viśvāni duritā svastaye.

O Learned scholars leading a celibate life commensurate with the standard of Āditya Brahmachārī! Should you divert a person from the wrong path and evils towards the good path and virtues by virtue of your good policies for his wellbeing, he progresses in his life by leaps and bounds, evading all sufferings and miseries and prospers along with his family engaging himself in dharmic activities.

ओं यं देवासोऽवथ वाजसातौ यं शूरसाता मरुतो हिते धने । प्रातर्यावाणं रथमिन्द्र सानसिमरिष्यन्तमा रुहेमा स्वस्तये ॥ ऋ. 10.63.14

Oṁ yaṁ devāso'vatha vājasātau yaṁ śūrasātā maruto hite dhane. prātaryāvāṇaṁ ratham-indraṁ sānasim ariṣyantamā ruhemā svastaye.

O Indra (the electric force of the universe) and Maruts (the radiation pressure of the universe)! To protect mass-energy in the Universe, you keep fighting the war with Vṛtra, the surface tension of the universe, like those of brave soldiers. We ride the same chariot of the universe, which brings prosperity and happiness, starts its journey at dawn and is relatively harmless. You safeguarded the same for our well-being and prosperity.

NB: The war between Indra and Vṛtra is a continuous

process in the universe. Vṛtra represents the universe's surface tension, and Indra is the electric force in the universe. Maruts are radiation pressure. The surface tension of the universe forces the universe, causing its collapse. However, the electric force and radiation pressure neutralise the effect of surface tension and save it from contraction, which is necessary for its existence and continuation.

ओं स्वस्ति नः पथ्यासु धन्वसु स्वस्त्यप्सु वृजने स्ववति । स्वस्ति नः पुत्रकृथेषु योनिषु स्वस्ति राये मरुतो दधातन ॥ ऋ. 10.63.15

Oṁ svasti naḥ pathyāsu dhanvasu svastyapsu vṛjane svarvati. svasti naḥ putra-kṛtheṣu yoniṣu svasti rāye maruto dadhātana.

O radiation pressure of universe! May this creation is not harmful to us. May the midsphere not be harmful to us; may the union of matter and anti-matter particles be not harmful to us. May the war between Indra and Vṛtra bring us well-being. May the inactive energy of Chidākāśa transforming into the active energy in Bhūtākāśa uphold the element of well-being in it so that the active energy of Bhūtākāśa may also be diffused for our benefit.

NB: Maruts and Rudras are co-deities of Indra abiding in the intermediate space.

ओं स्वस्तिरिद्धि प्रपथे श्रेष्ठा रेक्णस्वत्यभि या वाममेति । सा नो अमा सो अरणे निपातु स्वावेशा भवतु देवगोपा ॥ ऋ. 10.63.16

Oṁ svastiriddhi prapathe śreṣṭhā rekṇasvastyabhi yā vāmameti. sā no amāso araṇe nipātu svāveśā bhavatu devagopā.

May those be blessed here with happiness who tread the path of bliss. She, the best and most glorious, may be our life partner. May she stand by us in household affairs and in hours of need. May our household life be happy and protected from all natural catastrophes.

ओम् इषे त्वोर्जे त्वा वायव स्थ देवो वः सविता प्रार्पयतु श्रेष्ठतमाय कर्मण आप्यायध्वमघ्या इन्द्राय भागं प्रजावतीरनमीवा अयक्ष्मा मा वस्तेन ईशत माघशꣳसो ध्रुवा अस्मिन् गोपतौ स्यात बह्वीर्यजमानस्य पशून् पाहि ॥ यजु. 1.1

Om iṣe tvorje tvā vāyavastha devo vaḥ savitā prārpayatu śreṣṭhatamāya karmaṇa āpyāyadhvam aghnyā indrāya bhāgaṁ prajāvatīr anamīvā ayakṣmā mā vas tena īśata māghaśaṁso dhruvā asmin gopatau syāta bahvīr yajamānasya pasūn pāhi

O Creator of all! We depend on you for energy and food. You instil life into living beings. O creator, you inspire people to undertake noble endeavours. May you all prosper. Milch animals like cows, etc., should not be killed. You all are supposed to contribute your mite to the development and prosperity of the nation. Everybody be blessed with progeny. Let all be hale and hearty. Let corrupt rulers and officials not govern you. Let the protectors of cows be blessed with happiness and comforts of all types. May you safeguard the property of Yajamāna (host of yajña).

ओम् आ नो भद्राः क्रतवो यन्तु विश्वतोऽदब्धासो अपरीतास उद्भिदः । देवा नो यथा सदमिद् वृधे असन्नप्रायुवो रक्षितारो दिवेदिवे ॥ यजु. 25.14

Om ā no bhadrāḥ kratvao yantu viśvato'dabdhāso aparītāsa udbhidaḥ. devā no yathā sadamid vṛdhe asanna prāyuvo rakṣitāro dive dive.

May noble thoughts devoid of violence and bringing salvation from sufferings come to us from all sides. The scholars enjoying long life and warden of knowledge should behave in such a manner as to expand our assemblies day by day.

ओं देवानां भद्रा सुमतिर्ऋजूयतां देवानाꣳ रातिरभि नो निवर्त्तताम् । देवानाꣳ सख्यमुपसेदिमा वयं देवा न आयुः प्रतिरन्तु जीवसे ॥ यजु. 25.15

Oṁ devānāṁ bhadrā sumatiṛrjūyatām devānāḥ rātirabhi no nivarttatām। devānāḥ sakhyamupasedimā vayaṁ devā na āyuḥ pratirantu jīvase.

May we be endowed with the benevolent wisdom of the scholars; may we achieve perfection in knowledge because of the tendency to share knowledge with others. May we be blessed with their friendship. Let them educate us to live a long life.

ओं तमीशानं जगतस्तस्थुषस्पतिं धियञ्जिन्वमवसे हूमहे वयम्। पूषा नो यथा वेदसामसद्वृद्धे रक्षिता पायुरदब्ध: स्वस्तये ॥ यजु. 25.18

Oṁ tamīśānaṁ jagatas tasthuṣas patiṁ dhiyañ jinvam avase hūmahe vayam. pūṣā no yathā vedasām asad vṛdhe rakṣītā pāyur adabdhaḥ svastaye.

We invoke God for our safety and security. He is a custodian of the stationary and the moving universe. He is a sharpener of wisdom and Omnipotent. He is responsible for increasing, nourishing, and protecting our riches. May God bless us all with happiness and comfort and not curse us with misery.

ओं स्वस्ति न इन्द्रो वृद्धश्रवा: स्वस्ति न: पूषा विश्ववेदा:। स्वस्ति नस्ताक्ष्र्यो अरिष्टनेमि: स्वस्ति नो बृहस्पतिर्दधातु ॥ यजु. 25.19

Oṁ svasti na indro vṛddhaśravāḥ svasti na pūṣā viśvavedāḥ. svasti nas tārkṣyo ariṣṭanemiḥ svasti no bṛhaspatir dadhātu.

May the Supreme power, who has been highly eulogised and the sole mighty Lord, be for our well-being. He who is the source of all knowledge, i.e. the Veda and the cosmic force, sustains well-being for us like the sun and air. May the master of all natural powers be for our well-being.

ओं भद्रं कर्णेभि: श‍ृणुयाम देवा भद्रं पश्येमाक्षभिर्यजत्रा:। स्थिरैरङ्गैस्तुष्टुवाꣳ सस्तनूभिर्व्यशेमहि देवहितं यदायु: ॥ यजु. 25.21

Oṁ bhadraṁ karṇebhiḥ śrṇuyāma devā bhadraṁ paśyemākṣabhir yajatrāḥ. sthirair aṅgais tuṣṭuvāṁ sastanūbhir vyaśemahi devahitaṁ yadāyuḥ.

O scholars, the performer of Jñāna Yajña, may we, in your good company, hear with our ears only that which is truthful; may we, being sanctified, see with our eyes only that which is benevolent. Endowed with steady limbs and bodies, ever eulogising and contemplating the Supreme, may we enjoy the life-span as enjoyed by the scholars.

ओम् अग्न आ याहि वीतये गृणानो हव्यदातये । नि होता सत्सि बर्हिषि ॥

सा. 1.1

*Om agna ā yāhi vītaye grṇāno havya dātaye.
ni hotā satsi barhiṣi.*

Come, O God, the embodiment of knowledge, for the sake of dispelling ignorance and having conceded to our prayer, be seated with us as the priest on the sanctum of Jñāna yajña to offer oblations in Jñāna Yajña.

ओं त्वमग्ने यज्ञानां होता विश्वेषां हितः । देवेभिर्मानुषे जने ॥ सा. 1.2

*Oṁ tvamagne yajñānāṁ hotā viśveṣāṁ hitaḥ.
devebhir mānuṣe jane.*

O the embodiment of knowledge, you are the priest of all types of Yajñas. The scholars have made you established (well known) amongst human beings.

ओं ये त्रिषप्ताः परियन्ति विश्वा रूपाणि बिभ्रतः ।
वाचस्पतिर्बला तेषां तन्वो अद्य दधातु मे ॥ अ. 1.1.1

Oṁ ye triṣaptāḥ pariyanti viśvā rūpāṇi bibhrataḥ. vācaspatir balā teṣāṁ tanvo adya dadhātu me.

The three (sattva, rajas, tamas qualities) multiplied by seven (mahat, ahankāra, and five tanmātrās) have prevailed in the universe, manifesting in all cosmic forms. May God bless me with the power of the group of twenty-one.

इति स्वस्तिवाचनम्

अथ शान्तिकरणम्
Prayer for peace

ओं शं न इन्द्राग्री भवतामवोभिः शं न इन्द्रावरुणा रातहव्या। शमिन्द्रासोमा सुविताय शं योः शं न इन्द्रापूषणा वाजसातौ ॥ ऋ. 7.35.1

Oṁ śaṁ na indrāgnī bhavatām avobhiḥ śaṁ na indrāvaruṇā rātahavyā. śamindrāsomā suvitāya śaṁ yoḥ śaṁ na indrāpūṣaṇā vājasātau.

May, O Supreme One, cosmic energy and electric force benefit us. May electron and their electric force benefit us. May the electric force and electric charge help us increase our comfort and prosperity. May the electric force and the set of particles work as the protective shield for us in the war between Indra and Vṛtra and devas (particles) and asuras (anti-particles) and bless us with happiness.

NB: The continuation of the universe takes place due to two wars. The first war is known as Indra-Vṛtrāsura saṅgrāma, i.e. a war between Indra (electric force) and Vṛtra (the skin of the universe, which may be called as the surface tension of the universe). Indra is the electric force of the universe, and Vṛtra is the skin of the universe, which may also be called the surface tension of the universe. Indra is the electric repulsive force that causes the expansion of the universe. On the other hand, Vṛtra causes the universe's contraction, ultimately leading it to collapse. In this war between Indra and Vṛtra, Indra emerges victorious.

The second war is known as devāsura-saṅgrāma, the

annihilation of particles (devas) and anti-particles (asuras). Here, devas represent particles, and asuras represent anti-particles. When particles annihilate their anti-particles, the power of Indra increases, i.e., the electric force is added to the universe. In this process, particles increase over anti-particles, resulting in the universe's continuity

ओं शं नो भगः शमु नः शंसो अस्तु शं नः पुरन्धिः शमु सन्तु रायः। शं नः सत्यस्य सुयमस्य शंसः शं नो अर्यमा पुरुजातो अस्तु ॥ ऋ. 7.35.2

Om śaṁ no bhagaḥ śamu naḥ śaṁso astu śaṁ naḥ purandhiḥ śamu santu rāyaḥ. śaṁ naḥ satyasya suyamasya śaṁsaḥ śaṁ no aryamā purujāto astu.

May the source of particles be beneficial to us; may the sustainer of particles be beneficial to us, just as the word of praise makes us feel better and elated. Just as wealth comforts us, similarly, appreciation of truth, rules and regulations is for our betterment. May the famous neutron be for our benefit.

ओं शं नो धाता शमु धर्ता नो अस्तु शं न उरूची भवतु स्वधाभिः। शं रोदसी बृहती शं नो अद्रिः शं नो देवानां सुहवानि सन्तु ॥ ऋ. 7.35.3

Om śaṁ no dhātā śamu dhartā no astu śaṁ na urūcī bhavatu svadhābhiḥ. śaṁ rodasī bṛhatī śaṁ no adriḥ śaṁ no devānāṁ suhavāni santu.

May the sun grant us peace; may the gravitational force be for our benefit; may the earth, along with her self-sustaining power, stand for our benefit. May the vast celestial sphere and earth benefit us, and the universe's surface stand in peace. May our invocations of the natural powers bring peace and harmony.

ओं शं नो अग्निर्ज्योतिरनीको अस्तु शं नो मित्रावरुणावश्विना शम्। शं नः सुकृतां सुकृतानि सन्तु शं न इषिरो अभि वातु वातः ॥ ऋ. 7.35.4

Om śaṁ no agnir jyotir anīko astu śaṁ no

*mitrāvaruṇāvasvinā śam. śaṁ naḥ sukṛtāṁ sukṛtāni santu śaṁ
na iṣiro abhi vātu vātaḥ.*

May geothermal energy be peaceful; may the solar light bring us peace. May twilight hours marked by sunrise and sunset grant us peace. May the noble deeds of noble persons grant us peace. May the swift-blowing breeze blow for our peace.

ओं शं नो द्यावापृथिवी पूर्वहूतौ शमन्तरिक्षं दृशये नो अस्तु। शं न ओषधीर्वनिनो भवन्तु शं नो रजसस्पतिरस्तु जिष्णुः ॥ ऋ. 7.35.5

Oṁ śaṁ no dyāvāpṛthivī pūrvahūtau śam antarikṣaṁ dṛśaye no astu. śaṁ na oṣadhīr vanino bhavantu śaṁ no rajasas patirastu jiṣṇuḥ.

May the first ever born solar region and earth bring peace; may the intermediate space be peaceful to our vision. May the herbs and shrubs of the forest bring us peace, and may the victorious Lord of our planets be in peace for us.

ओं शं न इन्द्रो वसुभिर्देवो अस्तु शमादित्येभिर्वरुणः सुशंसः। शं नो रुद्रो रुद्रेभिर्जलाषः शं नस्त्वष्टा ग्राभिरिह श्रृणोतु ॥ ऋ. 7.35.6

Oṁ śaṁ na indro vasubhir devo astu śam ādityebhir varuṇaḥ suśaṁsaḥ. śaṁ no rūdro rūdrebhir jalāṣaḥ śaṁ nastvaṣṭā gnābhir iha sṛṇotu.

May the rainy waters along with other vasus [factors helping in sustenance of life on the earth] - like earth, agni, vāyu, antarikṣa, dyau, moon and constellations, bring peace unto us; may the 12 months that are invoked with the sun bring peace unto us; soul along with other ten prāṇas (vital airs) bring us peace, and may we hear the news of happiness in the thunder sound of cloud.

ओं शं नः सोमो भवतु ब्रह्म शं नः शं नो ग्रावाणः शमु सन्तु यज्ञाः। शं नः स्वरूणां मितयो भवन्तु शं नः प्रस्वः शम्वस्तु वेदिः ॥ ऋ. 7.35.7

Oṁ śaṁ naḥ somo bhavatu brahma śaṁ naḥ śaṁ no gravāṇaḥ śamu santu yajñāḥ. śaṁ naḥ svarūṇāṁ mitayo bhavantu śaṁ naḥ prasvaḥ śamvastu vediḥ.

May the cosmic electric charge be peaceful; the whole universe gives us peace. May the boundary of the universe be peaceful. May various creations be peaceful. May the pillars of cosmic altars be peaceful. May the manifested universe bring us peace. May this universe, the altar of cosmic yajña, be peaceful.

ओं शं नः सूर्य उरुचक्षा उदेतु शं नश्चतस्रः प्रदिशो भवन्तु। शं नः पर्वता ध्रुवयो भवन्तु शं नः सिन्धवः शमु सन्त्वापः ॥ ऋ. 7.35.8

Oṁ śaṁ naḥ sūrya uruchakṣā udetu śaṁ naścatasrah pradiśo bhavantu. śaṁ naḥ parvatā dhruvayo bhavantu śaṁ naḥ sindhavaḥ śamu santvāpaḥ.

May the sun, the eye of millions of people, rise in peace; may the four cardinal directions (east, west, north and south) be peaceful unto us; may the steady mountains be in peace and may the rivers flow in peace and water be for our peace.

ओं शं नो अदितिर्भवतु व्रतेभिः शं नो भवन्तु मरुतः स्वर्काः। शं नो विष्णुः शमु पूषा नो अस्तु शं नो भवित्रं शम्वस्तु वायुः ॥ ऋ. 7.35.9

Oṁ śaṁ no aditir bhavatu vratebhiḥ śaṁ no bhavantu marutaḥsvarkāḥ. śaṁ no viṣṇuḥ śamu pūṣā no astu śaṁ no bhavitraṁ śamvastu vāyuḥ.

May the magnetosphere of the earth grant us peace through its rule of protecting. Radiation pressure, with its fantastic radiation, be peaceful to us. May the process of creation extended into three spaces be peaceful to us. May the set of particles bring us peace. May providence be peaceful to us and the intermediate space be peaceful too.

ओं शं नो देवः सविता त्रायमाणः शं नो भवन्तूषसो विभातीः। शं नः पर्जन्यो

भवतु प्रजाभ्यः शं नः क्षेत्रस्य पतिरस्तु शम्भुः ॥ ऋ. 7.35.10

Oṁ śaṁ no devaḥ savitā trāyamāṇaḥ śaṁ no bhavantūṣaso vibhātīḥ. śaṁ naḥ parjanyo bhavatu prajābhyaḥ śaṁ naḥ kṣetrasya patirastu śambhuḥ.

May the solar energy, the saviour of creation on earth, give us peace; may the glorious light of dawn be peaceful, and may the clouds be peaceful for us. May the cosmic radiation be peaceful to us.

ओं शं नो देवा विश्वदेवा भवन्तु शं सरस्वती सह धीभिरस्तु। शमभिषाचः शमुरातिषाचः शं नो दिव्याः पार्थिवाः शं नो अप्याः ॥ ऋ. 7.35.11

Oṁ śaṁ no devā viśvadevā bhavantu śaṁ sarasvatī saha dhībhir astu. śam abhiṣācaḥ śamu rātiṣācaḥ śaṁ no divyāḥ pārthivāḥ śaṁ no apyāḥ.

May all forms of light be peaceful unto us. May the energy of midspace, along with rainy waters, be in peace. May all associated forces of creation be for our peace, and may all energy-gifting forces be in peace. May the energy of the celestial sphere, midspace and earth be peaceful.

ओं शं नः सत्यस्य पतयो भवन्तु शं नो अर्वन्तः शमु सन्तु गावः । शं न ऋभवः सुकृतः सुहस्ताः शं नो भवन्तु पितरो हवेषु ॥ ऋ. 7.35.12

Oṁ śaṁ naḥ satyasya patayo bhavantu śaṁ no arvantaḥ śamu santu gāvaḥ. śaṁ na ṛbhavaḥ sukṛtaḥ suhastāḥ śaṁ no bhavantu pitaro haveṣu.

May the rules and principles governing the creation be in peace for us. May solar energy bring us peace. May the geothermal energy bring us peace. May cosmic rays be peaceful. May the particles participating in the noble cause of creation be peaceful in the creation process.

ओं शं नो अज एकपाद् देवो अस्तु शं नोऽहिर्बुध्न्यः शं समुद्रः। शं नो अपांनपात् पेरुरस्तु शं नः पृश्निर्भवतु देवगोपा ॥ ऋ. 7.35.13

Om̐ śam̐ no aja ekapād devo astu śam̐ no'hirbudhnyaḥ śam̐ samudraḥ. śam̐ no apām̐ napāt perūrastu śam̐ naḥ pṛśnir bhavatu devagopā.

May the single-footed energy give us peace. May the surface tension enveloping the universe bring us peace. May the intermediate space be peaceful. May the source of subatomic particles lead us to peace. May space, the custodian of various energy forces, ive us peace.

NB: Energy in the Chidākāśa is known as one-footed. Upon its transfer to intermediate space, it becomes two-footed, but its final transfer to Bhūtākāśa makes it four-footed.

ओम् इन्द्रो विश्वस्य राजति । शं नो अस्तु द्विपदे शं चतुष्पदे ॥ यजु. 36.8

Om indro viśvasya rājati.
śam̐ no astu dvipade śam̐ catuṣpade.

Indra (the electric force) is one of the most powerful, fundamental forces in the universe. The particles manifested under two feet and four feet may be peaceful to us.

ओं शं नो वातः पवताऽ शं नस्तपतु सूर्य्यः ।
शं नः कनिक्रदद् देवः पर्जन्यो अभि वर्षतु ॥ यजु. 36.10

Om̐ śam̐ no vātaḥ pavatām̐ śam̐ nas tapatu sūryaḥ.
śaŠ naḥ kanikradad devaḥ parjanyo abhi varṣatu.

May the breezes blow peacefully for us; may the sun shine peacefully. May the clouds in atmosphere burst forth and send rain for our peace.

ओम् अहानि शं भवन्तु नः शऽ रात्रीः प्रति धीयताम् । शं न इन्द्राग्री भवतामवोभिः शं न इन्द्रावरुणा रातहव्या । शं न इन्द्रापूषणा वाजसातौ शमिन्द्रासोमा सुविताय शं योः ॥ यजु. 36.11

Om ahāni śam̐ bhavantu naḥ śam̐ rātrīḥ prati dhīyatām.
śam̐ na indrāgnī bhavatāmavobhiḥ śam̐ na indrāvaruṇa

rātahavyā. śaṁ na indrā pūṣaṇā vājasātau śamindrā somā suvitāya śaṁ yoḥ.

May the creation of particles be for our peace. May the annihilation of particles be for our peace. The electric force associated with the energy of observer space brings us peace. May the electric force associated with electrons be peaceful for us. May the electric force associated with the electric charge bring us peace. May the electric force associated with the set of charged particles be peaceful. May this electric force and charged particles act as a protective shield for us in the battle between Indra (repulsive electric force) and vṛtra (surface tension of universe), where matter particles and their anti-particles annihilate each other.

ओं शं नो देवीरभिष्टय आपो भवन्तु पीतये । शंयोरभि स्रवन्तु नः ॥

यजु. 36.42

Oṁ śaṁ no devīr abhiṣṭaye āpo bhavantu pītaye.
śaṁyor abhi-sravantu naḥ.

May God these rainy waters fulfil our needs and desires and be calm, tranquil and potable. Let all these waters flow for our happiness and prosperity, i.e. should not cause any catastrophe through floods, etc.

ओं द्यौः शान्तिरन्तरिक्षꣲ शान्तिः पृथिवी शान्तिरापः शान्तिरोषधयः शान्तिः । वनस्पतयः शान्तिर्विश्वे देवाः शान्तिर्ब्रह्म शान्तिः सर्वꣲ शान्तिः शान्तिरेव शान्तिः सा मा शान्तिरेधि ॥ यजु. 36.17

Oṁ dyauḥ śāntirantarikṣaꣲ śāntiḥ pṛthivī śāntirāpaḥ śāntiroṣadhayaḥ śāntiḥ; vanaspatayaḥ śāntirviśve devāḥ śāntirbrahma śāntiḥ sarvaꣲ śāntiḥ śāntireva śāntiḥ sā mā śāntiredhi

May there be peace in the solar region, the mid-region, and the earth. May the waters flow peacefully. May the herbs and shrubs, with powers of healing, grow peacefully. May all natural forces bring us peace. Knowledge grants us peace. Everything should bring us peace, and peace be peace in the true sense. Let that peace come to me.

ओं तच्चक्षुर्देवहितं पुरस्ताच्छुक्रमुच्चरत् । पश्येम शरदः शतं जीवेम शरदः शतꣳ श्रृणुयाम शरदः शतं प्र ब्रवाम शरदः शतमदीनाः स्याम शरदः शतं भूयश्च शरदः शतात् ॥ यजु. 36.24

Oṁ taccakṣur deva-hitaṁ purastāc chukram uccarat. paśyema śaradaḥ śataṁ jīvema śaradaḥ śataꣳ sṛṇuyāma śaradaḥ śataṁ pra bravāma śaradaḥ śatam adīnāḥ syāma śaradaḥ śataṁ bhūyaśca śaradaḥ śatāt.

That light energy is the eye of the universe. It embodies in itself all energy particles. This shining light energy rises in the east. Having endowed with that energy, may we see for a hundred autumn seasons; may we hear Śāstras for a hundred autumn seasons; may we speak, teach and preach for a hundred autumn seasons; may we be unsubdued for a hundred autumn seasons, may we do so even more than a hundred autumn seasons.

ओं यज्जाग्रतो दूरमुदैति दैवं तदु सुप्तस्य तथैवैति । दूरङ्गमं ज्योतिषां ज्योतिरेकं तन्मे मनः शिवसंकल्पमस्तु ॥ यजु. 34.1

Oṁ yaj jāgrato dūram udaiti daivaṁ tadu suptasya tathaivaiti. dūraṅgamaṁ jyotiṣāṁ jyotir ekaṁ tanme manaḥ śiva-saṁkalpam astu.

The far-going and lightest mind, which is the instrument of the soul, flies to distances in one's wakeful state and even so in one's sleep. May the mind, an instrument of the soul, be filled with beautiful, benevolent thoughts.

NB: In this regard, Maharṣi Vātsyāyana holds that sense organs are the external receptors. They receive information from the outside world and pass it on to the mind. The mind passes it on to the intellect, and knowledge takes place when the intellect comes into contact with the soul.

ओं येन कर्माण्यपसो मनीषिणो यज्ञे कृण्वन्ति विदथेषु धीराः। यदपूर्वं यक्षमन्तः प्रजानां तन्मे मनः शिवसंकल्पमस्तु ॥ यजु. 34.2

Oṁ yena karmāṇyapaso manīṣiṇo yajñe kṛṇvanti vidatheṣu dhīrāḥ. yad apūrvaṁ yakṣam antaḥ prajānāṁ tanme manaḥ śiva-saṁkalpam astu.

That, by which the wise ones, who are expert in rituals and observe self-restraint, perform their various rituals in the Śrauta yajñas (somayāga etc. yajñas described in Śrauta Sūtras), which allegorically represent the process of creation; that which plays an exceptional role in the pursuit of knowledge and science; that which exists as an inner sense of creatures; may that my mind be filled with beautiful and benevolent thoughts.

ओं यत्प्रज्ञानमुत चेतो धृतिश्च यज्ज्योतिरन्तरमृतं प्रजासु। यस्मान्न ऋते किंचन कर्म क्रियते तन्मे मनः शिवसंकल्पमस्तु ॥ यजु. 34.3

Oṁ yat prajñānam uta ceto dhṛtiśca yaj jyotir antar amṛtaṁ prajāsu. yasmānna ṛte kiṁ cana karma kriyate tanme manaḥ śiva-saṁkalpam astu.

That, which is the means of cognition, that which is the means of memory, that which is patience and causes one to feel ashamed, that which is located like immortal light inside human beings, that without which no action is performed, may that my mind be filled with beautiful and benevolent thoughts.

ओं येनेदं भूतं भुवनं भविष्यत्परिगृहीतममृतेन सर्वम्। येन यज्ञस्तायते सप्तहोता तन्मे मनः शिवसंकल्पमस्तु ॥ यजु. 34.4

Oṁ yenedaṁ bhūtam bhuvanaṁ bhaviṣyat parigṛhītam amṛtena sarvam. yena yajñas tāyate saptahotā tanme manaḥ śiva saṅkalpam astu.

That immortal one, by which is held all the news of past, present and future; that by which the *ātma yajña* consisting of the seven priests (mind, intellect and five sense organs) is carried out, may that my mind be filled with beautiful and benevolent thoughts.

ओं यस्मिन्नृचः साम यजू꣱षि यस्मिन् प्रतिष्ठिता रथनाभाविवाराः । यस्मिंश्चित्त꣱ सर्वमोतं प्रजानां तन्मे मनः शिवसंकल्पमस्तु ॥ यजु. 34.5

Oṁ yasminnṛchaḥ sāma yajū꣱ṣi yasmin pratiṣṭhitā rathanābhāvivārāḥ; yasimnśchittaꣳ sarvamotaṁ prajānāṁ tanme manaḥ śivasaṁkalpamastu.

That, by which are secured the verses of the *Ṛgveda*, the *Yajurveda*, and the *Sāmaveda* like the spokes are secured in the hub of a wheel; that into which rest all types of knowledge, may that my mind be filled with beautiful and benevolent thoughts.

ओं सुषारथिरश्वानिव यन्मनुष्यान्नेनीयतेऽभीशुभिर्वाजिन इव । हृत्प्रतिष्ठं यदजिरं जविष्ठं तन्मे मनः शिवसंकल्पमस्तु ॥ यजु. 34.6

Oṁ suṣārathir aśvān iva yan manuṣyān nenīyate'bhīśubhir vājina iva. hṛt pratiṣṭhaṁ yad ajiraṁ javiṣṭhaṁ tanme manaḥ śiva-saṁkalpam astu.

That which, like an expert charioteer controlling the horses with the reins held fast, ever leads men; that which is heart-abiding, ever-moving, and speediest of all forces, may that my mind be filled with beautiful and benevolent thoughts.

ओं स नः पवस्व शं गवे शं जनाय शमर्वते ।
शं राजन्नोषधीभ्यः ॥ सा.उ. 1.3 (653); ऋ.9.11.3

Oṁ sa naḥ pavasva śaṁ gave śaṁ janāya śamarvate. śaṁ rājann oṣadhībhyaḥ.

Purify us, O Shining electric charge, be quietly

distributed over Gau, Aśva and other particles, as well as over other charged particles.

NB: Here, the mantras state that electric charge remains distributed over different types of charged particles.

ओम् अभयं नः करत्यन्तरिक्षमभयं द्यावापृथिवी उभे इमे। अभयं पश्चादभयं पुरास्तादुत्तरादधरादभयं नो अस्तु॥ अथर्व. 19.15.5

Om abhayaṁ naḥ karatyantarikṣam abhayaṁ dyāvāpṛthivī ubhe ime. abhayaṁ paścād abhayaṁ purastād-uttrād-adharād-abhayaṁ no astu.

May the intermediate space cause us no fear, no fear from the sun and on the earth. May there be no fear from behind and from the front, and may there be no fear from above and below.

ओम् अभयं मित्रादभयممित्रादभयं ज्ञातादभयं पुरो यः। अभयं नक्तमभयं दिवा नः सर्वा आशा मम मित्रं भवन्तु॥ अथर्व. 19.15.6

Om abhayaṁ mitrād abhayam amitrād abhayaṁ jñātād abhayaṁ puro yaḥ. abhayaṁ naktam abhayaṁ divā naḥ sarvā āśā mama mitraṁ bhavantu.

No fear from the friend, no fear from the foe, no fear from what is known to us, and no fear of what is in front of us. No fear in the night and no fear in the day. May all directions be friends to us.

इति शान्तिकरणम्

अथ सामान्यप्रकरणम्

Common Procedure

The procedure given below should be followed in all the sanskāras. Any specific procedure will be indicated separately. Whatever more or less is to be conducted will be instructed at the proper place.

The Place of Yajña: The place of Yajña should be neat and clean. It should be located where there is no pollution or disturbance.

Yajñaśālā: This is also called Yajñamaṇḍapa. It should be a maximum 16 hasta (24 sq.ft.) square and a minimum eight hasta (12 sq. ft) square. If the soil is dirty, then Yajñaśālā should be made by digging the ground two ft., the dirty soil should be removed, and the pit should be filled up with pure and clean soil if Yajñaśālā is made of 8 square yards. There should be twenty pillars; if four square yards, the number of the pillars may be twelve. There should be a roof on the pillars over the whole area.

The height of the roof of yajñaśālā should be at least 15 sq. ft.; there should be four entrances on all four sides of it. There should be flags fixed on all corners. It should be decorated with leaves etc. The Yajñaśālā should be cleaned every day. It should be anointed with cow dung and pure water and decorated with lines and drawings of saffron, turmeric and powder of wheat or rice. It is mandatory on the part of all persons to offer prayer to the almighty through yajña for the well-being of all. The oblations should be of sweat-smelling or fragrant dravyas (material).

Dimension of the Yajñakuṇḍa: If one lakh oblations are to be offered, then the dimension of the yajñakuṇḍa should be four hasta square (6 sq.ft.). It should be four hast square (6 square feet) deep, but at the bottom, it should be 1/4 of the upper surface, i.e. one hast square (1.5 sq. ft.). In this manner, the dimension of the kuṇḍa should be according to the number of the oblations to be offered in the fire of yajña. If more oblations are to be offered, then the size of the kuṇḍa should be increased proportionately to the increase of the oblations.

Suppose only 50,000 oblations are to be offered. In that case, there should be one hast square (1.5 sq. ft.) decrease in the parameters of kuṇḍa (altar), i.e. kuṇḍa should be three hasta square (4.5 sq. ft) in width. Its depth should be three hasta (4.5ft), and the bottom should be 1.15 sq. ft. If 25,000 oblations are to be offered, the kuṇḍa should be two hast sq. (3 sq. ft) in width and to the same extent deep, but the bottom should be 1/2 hast sq. (0.75 sq. ft). Up to 10,000 oblations, the same parameter of yajñakuṇḍa may be maintained. If the number of oblations is reduced to 5,000, the kuṇḍa should have a width of 1.5 hast sq. (2.25 sq. ft) and, to the same extent deep, its bottom should be 8.5 aṅgulas (9 sq. inch).

The above parameters of kuṇḍa are only for specific oblations of ghee. Suppose the oblations of *mohanbhoga* or *khira* are to be offered to the tune of 2,500 and also of ghee to the tune of 2,500 in addition to that. In that case, the parameters of kuṇḍa should be two hast sq. (3 sq. ft) width and two hasta sq. (3 sq. ft) deep with 1/2 hasta sq. (0.75 sq. ft) hasta bottom. If only 1,000 oblations of ghee are to be offered, the kuṇḍa should not be less than 1.25 hasta sq. in width and depth; its bottom should be 1/4 of the upper surface. In all these kuṇḍas, there should be three girdles of 15 inches and 5 inches in height. These three girdles should be constructed from the surface of the yajñaśāla raised upward. The first three girdles should be five inches high and five inches wide. The same should be the scale of the second and third girdle.

Samidhās (woods) Prescribed for Yajña: Palāśa (Butra Frondosa), Śami (Momosa Suma), Peeple (Ficus Religiosa), Banyan, Gular (Ficus glomerata), Āmra (Mango tree), Bilva (Aegle Marmelos) are the woods prescribed as samidhās for the yajña. The samidhās should be secured after cutting them into pieces in proportions of the area of yajñakuṇḍa. It should be ensured that the samidhās are not infected with worms and should not be produced in dirty places and spoiled with dirty things. These should be examined thoroughly and arranged squarely in the middle of yajñakuṇḍa.

Four kinds of Āhuti material for Yajña:

1. The first kind of āhuti material consists of sweat-smelling/fragrant dravyas like Kasturi (musk), Keśara (Rotileria Tinctoria) Agara (Aquilaria Agellocha), Tagar (Tebernamutan Caronaria), Śveta Chandana (white sandalwood or powder) Ilāyachi (Feronia Elphantum), Jāyaphala (Nutmeg) and Jāvitrī (Mace) etc.

2. The second kind of āhuti dravyas consists of nourishing drvayas like ghee, milk, fruits, herbaceous roots, cereals, rice, wheat and urad (Phaseolus radiatus).

3. Third kind of Āhutī drvayas consists of sweeteners like sugar, date, dried grapes, etc..

4. The fourth kind of āhutī dravyas consists of medicinal herbs like Somalatā, i.e. Giloya (Cocculus cordifolius) and other herbs.

Sthālīpaka, the Dish for Yajña:

Following delicious preparations of rice, khichadi (rice cooked with cereal), khira, laddoo, mohanabhoga (a kind of sweat meal made of flour, ghee and sugar) should be prepared in the following manner.

ओ३म्। देवस्त्वा सविता पुनत्वच्छिद्रेण पवित्रेण वसोः सूर्यस्य रश्मिभिः ॥

O3m, devastvā savitā punatvachchhidreṇa pavitreṇa vasoḥ sūryasya raśmibhiḥ.

The purpose of this mantra is that things to be prepared for the oblations should be entirely cleaned. These should be carefully examined and sieved. After mixing them in proper proportion, the dish should be made, e.g., if mohanabhoga is to be prepared in 1 kg. of ghee, 0.1 gm of musk, one 0.9 gm. of Kesar (saffron), 1.8 gm. jāyphala (Tinctoria) and jāvitrī (Nutmeg) and 1.2 kg sugar be mixed. In the same manner, sweat rice, khira, khichadi, modaka (round small laddoo) prepared in ghee with a grain powder should be prepared for the yajña.

The recipe for preparing Charu (Dish):

ओम् अग्नये त्वा जुष्टं निर्वपामि) आश्व॰ गृ॰ 1.10.6

Om agnaye tvā juṣṭaṁ nirvapāmi) Āśva. Gṛ. 1.10.6

That is 16 gm of rice etc. for each of the oblation according to the numbers of oblations should be taken and by reciting the mantra.

ओम् अग्नये त्वा जुष्टं प्रोक्षामि। आश्व॰ गृ॰ 1.10.7

Om agnaye tvā juṣṭaṁ prokṣāmi. Āśv. Gṛ 1.10.7

It should be washed and cleaned with water. The same should be put in a pan and cooked. It should be secured in a separate vessel for the sake of yajña, and molten ghee should be poured on it.

Yajñapātra: The pots of yajña should be specifically made of silver, gold or wood; they should be as follows:

अथ पात्रलक्षणान्युच्यन्ते-बाहुमात्र्यः पाणिमात्रपुष्करा:, षडङ्गुलखातास्त्वग्बिला

हंसमुखप्रसेकाः, मूलदण्डाश्चतस्रः स्रुचो भवन्ति। तत्र पालाशी जुहूः, आश्वत्थ्युपभृत् वैकङ्कती ध्रुवा, अग्निहोत्रहवणी च।

अरत्निमात्रः खादिरः स्रुवः, अङ्गुष्ठपर्वमात्रपुष्करः। तथाविधो द्वितीयो वैकङ्कतः स्रुवः।

वारणं बाहुमात्रं मकराकारमग्निहोत्रहवणीनिधानार्थं कूर्चम्। अरत्निमात्रं खादिरं खड्गाकृति वज्रम्॥ वारणान्यहोमसंयुक्तानि। तत्रोलूखलं नाभिमात्रम्, मुसलं शिरोमात्रम् अथवा मुसलोलूखले वार्क्ष्ये सारदारुमये शुभे इच्छाप्रमाणे भवतः। तथा- खादिरं मुसलं कार्यं पालाशः स्यादुलूखलः।

यद्वोभौ वारणौ कार्यौ तदभावेऽन्यवृक्षजौ।

शूर्पं वैणवमेव वा, ऐषीकं नलमयं वाऽवचर्मबद्धम्।

प्रादेशमात्री वारणी शम्या। कृष्णाजिनमखण्डम्।

दृषदुपले अश्ममये। वारणीं 24 हस्तमात्रीं, 22 अरत्निमात्रीं खातमध्यां मध्यसंगृहीतामिडापात्रीम्।

अरत्निमात्राणि ब्रह्मयजमानहोतृपत्न्यासनानि।

मुंजमयं त्रिवृतं व्याममात्रं योक्त्रम्।

प्रादेशदीर्घे अष्टाङ्गुलायते षडङ्गुलखातमण्डलमध्ये पुरोडाशपात्र्यौ।

प्रादेशमात्रं द्व्यङ्गुलपरीणाहं तीक्ष्णाग्रं श्रृतावदानम्। आदर्शकारे चतुरस्रे वा प्राशित्रहरणे। तयोरेकमीषत्खातमध्यम्।

षडङ्गुलं कङ्कतिकाकारमुभयतः खातं षडवत्तम्।

द्वादशाङ्गुलमर्धचन्द्राकारमष्टाङ्गुलोत्सेधमन्तर्धानिकटम्।

उपवेशोऽरत्निमात्रः। मुंजमयी रज्जुः।

खादिरान् द्वादशाङ्गुलदीर्घान् चतुरङ्गुलमस्तकान् तीक्ष्णाग्रान् शङ्कून्। यजमानपूर्णपात्रं पत्नीपूर्णपात्रं च द्वादशाङ्गुलदीर्घं चतुरङ्गुलविस्तारं चतुरङ्गुलखातम्।

तथा प्रणीतापात्रं च। आज्यस्थाली द्वादशाङ्गुलविस्तृता प्रादेशोच्चा।

तथैव चरुस्थाली। अन्वाहार्यपात्रं पुरुषचतुष्ट्याहारपाकपर्याप्तम्।

समिदिध्मार्थं पलाशशाखामयम्। कौशं बर्हिः।

ऋत्विग्वरणार्थं कुण्डलाङ्गुलीयकवासांसि।

पत्नीयजमानपरिधानार्थं क्षौमवासश्चतुष्टयम्।

अग्न्याधेयदक्षिणार्थं चतुर्विंशतिपक्षे एकोनपंचाशद् गावः, द्वादशपक्षे पंचविंशतिः, षद्पक्षे त्रयोदश, सर्वेषु पक्षेषु आदित्येष्टौ धेनुः। वरार्थं चतस्रो गावः॥

atha   pātralakṣaṇānyuchyante-bāhumātrayaḥ pāṇimātrapuṣkarāḥ,   ṣaḍaṅgulakhātāstvagbilā haṁsamukhaprasekāḥ, mūladaṇḍāśchatasraḥ srucho bhavanti, tatra pālāśī juhūḥ, āśvatthyupabhṛt vaikaṅkatī dhruvā, agnihotrahavaṇī cha,

aratnimātraḥ   khādiraḥ   sruvaḥ, aṅguṣṭhaparvamātrapuṣkaraḥ, tathāvidho dvitīyo vaikaṅkataḥ sruvaḥ,

vāraṇaṁ   bāhumātram makarākāramagnihotrahavaṇīnidhānārtha kūrcham,

aratnimātraṁ khādiraṁ khaḍgākṛti vajram.

vāraṇānyahomasaṁyuktāni, tatrolūkhalaṁ nābhimātram, musalaṁ śiromātram athavā musalolūkhale

vārkṣaye sāradārumaye śubhe ichchhāpramāṇe bhavataḥ, tathā-

khādiraṁ musalaṁ kāryaṁ pālāśaḥ syādulūkhalaḥ,

yadvobhau vāraṇau kāryau tadabhāve'nyavṛkṣajau,

śūrpaṁ   vaiṇavameva   vā,   aiṣīkaṁ   nalamayaṁ vā'vacharmabaddham,

prādeśamātrī vāraṇī śamyā,

kṛṣṇājinamakhaṇḍam,

dṛṣadupale aśmamaye, vāraṇīṁ 24 hastamātrīṁ, 22 aratnimātrīṁ khātamadhyāṁ madhyasaṁgṛhītāmiḍāpātrīm,

aratnimātrāṇi brahmayajamānahotṛpatnyāsanāni,

muṁjamayaṁ trivṛtaṁ vyāmamātraṁ yoktram,

prādeśadīrghe   aṣṭāṅgulāyate ṣaḍaṅgulakhātamaṇḍalamadhye puroḍāśapātrayau,

prādeśamātraṁ   dvyaṅgulapariṇāhaṁ   tīkṣaṇāgraṁ śṛtāvadānam, ādarśakāre chaturasre vā prāśitraharaṇe, tayorekamīṣatkhātamadhyam,

ṣaḍaṅgulaṁ kaṅkatikākāramubhayataḥ khātaṁ ṣaḍavattam,

dvādaśāṅgulamarddhachandrākāramaṣṭāṅgulotsedhamantar ddhānakaṭam,

upaveśo'ratnimātraḥ,

muṁjamayī rajjuḥ,

khādirān dvādaśāṅguladīrghān chaturaṅgulamastakān tīkṣaṇāgrān śaṅkūn,

yajamānapūrṇapātraṁ patnīpūrṇapātraṁ cha dvādaśāṅguladīrghaṁ chaturaṅgulavistāraṁ chaturaṅgulakhātam,

tathā praṇītāpātraṁ cha,

ājyasthālī dvādaśāṅgulavistṛtā prādeśochchā,

tathaiva charusthālī,

anvāhāryapātraṁ puruṣachatuṣṭayāhārapākaparyāptam,

samididhmārthaṁ palāśaśākhāmayam,

kauśaṁ barhiḥ,

ṛtvigvaraṇārthaṁ kuṇḍalāṅgulīyakavāsāṁsi,

patnīyajamānaparidhānārthaṁ kṣaumavāsaśchatuṣṭayam,

agnyādheyadakṣiṇārthaṁ chaturviśatipakṣe ēkonapaṁchāśad gāvaḥ, dvādaśapakṣe paṁchaviṁśatiḥ, ṣaṭpakṣe trayodaśa, sarveṣu pakṣeṣu ādityeṣṭau dhenuḥ, varārthaṁ chatasro gāvaḥ.

ऋत्विग्वरण

Selection and Appointment of Ṛtvik (Yajñapriests)

Request by the Yajñmāna (host)

ओमावसोः सदने सीद। गोभिल गृसू॰ 1.6.5

Omāvasoḥ sadane sīda. Go. Gṛ. 1.6.5

[Meaning] In the name of Om, I request you to take your seat in the yajña till the completion of it.

Chanting the above mantra, the host should request the priest to conduct the yajña.

Acceptance by the priest

ओं सीदामि।

Oṁ sīdāmi,

[Meaning] I take my seat in the name of Om.

Pronouncing this, the priest should take seat fixed for him. The host says:

अहमद्योक्तकर्मकरणाय भवन्तं वृणे।

ahamadyoktakarmakaraṇāya bhavantaṁ vṛṇe.

The priest says:

वृतोऽस्मि।

vṛto'smi,

I accept it.

The qualifications of a Priest

A Priest should be a learned person who is well versed in Vedas, dharma, content, expert in conducting the rituals required in yajña, uncovetous, benevolent, free from bad habits, belonging to a good family, having good character, believer in Vedic life and thought. The host may select 1, 2, 3 or 4 priests.

If the priest is one, he will be called a Purohita; if they are two, they will be called Ritvik and Purohita; if three, they will be called Ritvik, Purohita and Adhyakṣa and if they are four, their titles will be Hotā, Adhvaryu, Udgātā and Brahmā. The seats of these priests should be arranged on the four sides of the yajñakuṇḍa in the manner that hotā be in the west facing east, adhvarhu is in the north facing south, udgātā is in the east facing west, and brahmā is in the south facing north. Yajamān (host) will take his/her seat in the west facing east or south facing north. These priests should be allowed to sit with due respect and honour. They should take their seats gladly, and none of them should do anything except conduct the procedure of sanskāra/yajña which they are entrusted with.

अथ आचमन-मन्त्राः

Mantras for sipping waters

1. ओम् अमृतोपस्तरणमसि स्वाहा ॥ तैत्तिरीय आ. 10.32.1

Om amṛtopastaraṇam asi svāhā.

O Immortalized energy [prakṛti], you act as the bedspread (First Sip)

2. ओम् अमृतापिधानमसि स्वाहा ॥ तैत्तिरीय आ. 10.35.1

Om amṛtāpidhānam asi svāhā.

O Immortalized energy [prakṛti], you act as the protective shield like that of a shawl. (Second Sip)

3. ओं सत्यं यशः श्रीर्मयि श्रीः श्रयतां स्वाहा ॥ आपस्तम्ब गृह्य सू.1.24.29

Oṁ satyaṁ yaśāḥ śrīr mayi śrīḥ śrayatāṁ svāhā.

May, the truth, fame and spiritual wealth and prosperity ever be with us. (Third Sip)

अथ अंगस्पर्शमन्त्राः

Mantras for consecrating body parts

1. ओं वाङ्म आस्येऽस्तु ॥

Oṁ vāṅma āsye'stu.

Let there be the power of speech in my mouth. (Touch lips)

2. ओं नसोर्मे प्राणोऽस्तु ॥

Oṁ nasor me prāṇo'stu.

Let there be breath in my nostrils (Touch nostrils)

3. ओम् अक्ष्णोर्मे चक्षुरस्तु ॥

Om akṣṇor me cakṣur astu.

Let there be the sight in my eyes. (Touch eyes)

4. ओं कर्णयोर्मे श्रोत्रमस्तु ॥

Oṁ ṇyor me śrotram astu.

Let there be hearing power in my ears. (Touch ears)

5. ओं बाह्वोर्मे बलमस्तु ॥

Oṁ bāhvor me balam astu.

Let there be prowess in my arms. (Touch arms)

6. ओम् ऊर्वोर्म ओजोऽस्तु ॥

Om ūrvor ma ojo'stu.

Let there be power in my thighs. (Touch thighs)

7. ओम् अरिष्टानि मेऽङ्गानि तनूस्तन्वा मे सह सन्तु ॥ पारस्कर गृह्य सू. 1.3. 25

Om ariṣṭāni me'ṅgāni tanūs tanvā me saha santu.

Let all the parts of my body be healthy and lasting.

(Sprinkle water on all parts of the body)

अथ अग्न्याधानमन्त्राः

Mantras for Placing fire

Havan represents creation yajña. Creation yajña starts with the placement of energy in Bhūloka [Bhūtākāśa].

Warning: Never use foreign-made camphor. It is heard that it is a mixture of impure articles. It is better to kindle fire with the help of Samidhās (wooden sticks) dipped in ghṛta (clarified butter).

ओं भूर्भुवः स्वः ॥ गोभिल गृह्य सू. 1.1.11

Oṁ bhūr bhuvaḥ svaḥ.

Agni [energy] exists in active form in Bhūloka [Bhūtākāśa], intermediate space and in dark form in Brahmaloka [Brahmākāśa or Chidākāśa]

Instruction: Now, light a wick soaked in ghee or camphor in a spoon and place it in the havana-kuṇḍa (fire-altar), wherein arranged pieces of wood are smeared in ghee. [Note: Fire altar represents Bhūloka [earth and Bhūtākāśa] Chant the following mantras—

ओं भूर्भुवः स्वर्द्यौरिव भूम्ना पृथिवीव वरिम्णा । तस्यास्ते पृथिवि देवयजनि पृष्ठेऽग्निमन्नादमन्नाद्यायादधे ॥ यजु. 3.5

Oṁ bhūr bhuvaḥ svar dyaur iva bhūmnā pṛthivīva varimṇā. tasyās te pṛthivi devayajani pṛṣṭhe" gnim annādam annādyāyādadhe.

Energy exists in all three spaces—earth or Bhūtākāśa, midspace and solar region or Brahmaloka [Chidākāśa]. This energy is famous for its pervading power in the solar region or Chidākāśa and expansion on earth or Bhūtākāśa. Do I place this agni [energy], the consumer of anna, at thy back, O earth, for consuming oblations given in the fire of yajña [and Bhutākāśa for consuming particles, as particles are the food of energy]?

NB: This mantra talks about annihilating matter particles into energy in observer space. Energy or fire is called annāda; anna means the pair of matter particles and anti-matter particles, and their consumption means a change of particles and antiparticles into energy following their collision. Here, it may be known that there is a continuous interaction between light space and observer space, with energy changing into particles and particles into energy, thus causing the expansion of devayaja (creation of particles) in the observer space. The particles and antiparticles continue to change into energy following the annihilation process.

ओम् उद् बुध्यस्वाग्ने प्रतिजागृहि त्वमिष्टापूर्ते सꣳसृजेथामयं च। अस्मिन्त्सधस्थे अध्युत्तरस्मिन् विश्वे देवा यजमानश्च सीदत ॥ यजु. 15.54

Om ud budhyasvāgne pratijāgṛhi tvamiṣṭ-āpūrte saṁsṛjethāmayaṁ ca. asmintsadhasthe adhyuttarasmin viśve devā yajamānaśca sīdata.

Let the energy appear in the Bhūtākāśa [and earth]. O energy, you ensure the supply of those things required for the universe's creation. Let all the light and matter particles reside in the Bhūtākāśa, and this dark energy, the host of creation, resides in Brahmaloka [Chidākāśa].

NB: This mantra says that the abode of dark energy or inactive energy is Brahmaloka [Brahma-space], and on being activated, it transfers its abode to Bhūtākāśa, also known as Brahmāṇḍa

अथ समिधाधानमन्त्राः

Mantras for Placing of Samidhā in the Fire Altar

The scientific significance of the below-given mantras is the creation of geothermal energy of earth [or energy of Bhūtākāśa/Brahmāṇḍa]. The samidhā is the means of creation of geothermal energy of the earth [or Bhūtākāśa]. There is a provision of offering three samidhā-s in the Havana to be performed daily, which symbolises that mass-energy is created three times daily at the surface of the universe [Brahmāṇḍa].

Take three pieces of wood, each about eight fingers (6 inches) long, dip them in the ghee and place each in the fire of havan kuṇḍa (fire-altar) one by one, reciting the following Mantras.

ओम् अयन्त इध्म आत्मा जातवेदस्तेनेध्यस्व वर्द्धस्व चेद्ध वर्द्धय चास्मान् प्रजया पशुभिर्ब्रह्मवर्चसेनान्नाद्येन समेधय स्वाहा । इदमग्नये जातवेदसे इदन्न मम ॥

आश्वलायन गृह्य सू.1.10.12

Om ayanta idhma ātmā jātavedas tenedhyasva varddhasva ceddha varddhaya cāsmān prajayā paśubhir brahma-varcasenānnādyena samedhaya svāhā. Idam agnaye jātavedase idanna mama.

First meaning in the context of Bhūtākāśa/Brahmāṇḍa: O Agni [energy] of Bhūtākāśa, this samidhā [gamma-rays bursts] acts as a soul to generate the energy of Bhūtākāśa, pervading in all objects born in Bhūtākāśa. Get kindled with this samidhā [gamma-ray bursts] and increase, having enriched with offshoots, matter particles, an effulgence, and abundance of mass-energy, and so do prosper us and lead us on the path of progress. Thus do I make this offering; it is intended for the energy of Bhūtākāśa/Brahmāṇḍa [agni] pervading all objects of Brahmāṇḍa and not for me.

NB: Here, Samidhā represents digdāha, literally meaning glow at the surface of the universe, which is nothing but the creation of energy at the surface of the universe. The phenomenon of digdāha can be compared to gamma-ray bursts occurring daily in our universe from unknown locations billions of light years away from Earth.

Second meaning in the context of Earth: This samidhā [fission process in the Earth] acts as a soul to generate geothermal energy of the Earth, O fire [energy] of creation yajña, pervading in all objects born on the Earth. Get kindled with this samidhā (fission process) and increase, having enriched with offshoots, domestic animals and progeny, intelligence, and abundance of crops and grains, and so do prosper us and lead us on the path of progress. Thus, do I make this offering; it is intended for geothermal energy [agni] pervading all objects of the Earth and not for me.

Third meaning in the context of conventional fire of yajñā: This samidhā [wooden stick] acts as a soul to kindle fire in the fire-altar, O fire of yajña. Get enkindled with this samidhā (wooden stick) and increase, having enriched with offshoots, domestic animals and progeny, intelligence, and abundance of crops and grains, and so do prosper us and lead us on the path of progress. Thus do I make this offering; it is intended for geothermal energy [agni] pervading all objects of the Earth and not for me.

Instruction: Place the first piece of wood (samidhā) dipped in ghee onto the fire.

दूसरी समिधा
Second Samidhā

ओं समिधाग्निं दुवस्यत धृतैर्बोधयतातिथिम् आस्मिन् हव्या जुहोतन स्वाहा ॥
इदमग्रये इदन्न मम ॥ यजु. 3.1

Oṁ smidhāgniṁ duvasyata ghṛtair bodhayatātithim. āsmin havyā juhotana svāhā. idam agnaye idanna mama.

Samidhā, as already pointed out above, represents the natural phenomenon of digdāha (gamma-ray bursts) in the context of the generation of energy in Bhūtākāśa and nuclear fission reaction in the core of the Earth in the context of the generation of geothermal energy and wooden stick for kindling conventional fire in the yajña.

The First meaning in the context of Bhūtākāśa/Brahmāṇḍa: Samidhā (gamma rays bursts) cause the creation of energy on the surface of the universe. Let the gamma-ray bursts generate the energy. Make the offerings of suitable things for the progress and success of the process of creation in Bhūtākāśa. Thus do I make this offering; it is intended for kindling energy and not for me.

The Second meaning in the context of Earth: Samidhā (nuclear fission reaction in the Earth) causes the creation of geothermal energy. Let the fission reaction generate the energy. Make the offerings of suitable things for the progress and success of the creation process on Earth. Thus do I make this offering; it is intended for kindling energy and not for me.

Third meaning in the context of conventional fire of yajña: Samidhā (wooden stick) causes the kindling of fire in the fire-altar. Let these wooden sticks generate the fire. Make the offerings of suitable things for the progress and success of this yajña. Thus, do I make this offering; it is intended for kindling energy and not for me.

ओं सुसमिद्धाय शोचिषे घृतं तीव्रं जुहोतन। अग्नये जातवेदसे स्वाहा॥ इदमग्नये जातवेदसे इदन्न मम॥ यजु. 3.2

Oṁ susmiddhāya śociṣe ghṛtaṁ tīvraṁ juhotana. agnaye jātavedase svāhā. idamagnaye jātavedase idanna mama.

Meaning in the context of conventional fire of yajña: To obtain a good amount of fire, offer the oblation of ghṛta. Thus do I make this offering for agni pervading all earthly objects; it is intended for agni pervading all earthly objects of and not for me.

Instruction: Place the second piece of wood (samidhā) dipped in ghee onto the fire in the firealtar.

तीसरी समिधा

Third Samidhā

ओं तन्त्वा समिद्धिरङ्गिरो घृतेन वर्द्धयामसि। बृहच्छोचा यविष्ठय स्वाहा। इदमग्नयेऽङ्गिरसे इदन्न मम॥ यजु. 3.3

Oṁ tantvā samidbhir aṅgiro ghṛtena varddhayāmasi. bṛhacchocā yaviṣṭhya svāhā. idam agnaye"ṅgirase idanna mama.

Meaning in the context of conventional fire of yajña: We increase you by ghṛta (clarified butter) charged particles and radiation. O ever-youthful Agni energy, let you kindle properly. Thus do I make this offering; it is intended for energy residing in charged matter particles and not for me.

Instruction: Now place the third piece of wood (samidhā) dipped in ghee on to the fire.

अथ घृताहुतिमन्त्राः
पांच आहुति घी की

Five Ghee Offerings

Ghee is the symbol of energy. Energy is needed for the extension of creation on the earth. Hence, offering of Ghee is prescribed here. The following *mantra* should be recited five times followed by an oblation of a spoonful of ghee offered on the fire. The residue of each oblation should be collected in a utensil full of water and the same may be applied on face after the conclusion of Yajña.

ओम् अयन्त इध्म आत्मा जातवेदस्तेनेध्यस्व वर्द्धस्व चेद्ध वर्द्धय चास्मान् प्रजया पशुभिर्ब्रह्मवर्चसेनान्नाद्येन समेधय स्वाहा । इदमग्नये जातवेदसे इदन्न मम ॥

आश्वलायन गृह्य सू.1.10.12

Om ayanta idhma ātmā jātavedas tenedhyasva varddhasva ceddha varddhaya cāsmān prajayā paśubhir brahma-varcasenānnādyena samedhaya svāhā. Idam agnaye jātavedase idanna mama.

The first meaning in the context of Bhūtākāśa/Brahmāṇḍa: O Agni [energy] of Bhūtākāśa, this samidhā [gamma-rays bursts] acts as a soul to generate the energy of Bhūtākāśa, pervading in all objects born in Bhūtākāśa. Get kindled with this samidhā [gamma-ray bursts] and increase, having enriched with offshoots, matter particles, an effulgence, and abundance of mass-energy, and so do prosper us and lead us on the path of progress. Thus do I make this offering; it is intended for the energy of Bhūtākāśa/Brahmāṇḍa [agni] pervading all objects of Brahmāṇḍa and not for me.

NB: Here, Samidhā represents digdāha, literally

meaning glow at the surface of the universe, which is nothing but the creation of energy at the surface of the universe. The phenomenon of digdāha can be compared to gamma-ray bursts occurring daily in our universe from unknown locations billions of light years away from Earth.

The second meaning in the context of Earth: This samidhā [fission process in the Earth] acts as a soul to generate geothermal energy of the Earth, O fire [energy] of creation yajña, pervading in all objects born on the Earth. Get kindled with this samidhā (fission process) and increase, having enriched with offshoots, domestic animals and progeny, intelligence, and abundance of crops and grains, and so do prosper us and lead us on the path of progress. Thus do I make this offering; it is intended for geothermal energy [agni] pervading all objects of the Earth and not for me.

The third meaning in the context of conventional fire of yajñā: This samidhā [wooden stick] acts as a soul to kindle fire in the fire-altar, O fire of yajña. Get enkindled with this samidhā (wooden stick) and increase, having enriched with offshoots, domestic animals and progeny, intelligence, and abundance of crops and grains, and so do prosper us and lead us on the path of progress. Thus do I make this offering; it is intended for geothermal energy [agni] pervading all objects of the Earth and not for me.

अथ जलप्रसेचनमन्त्राः

Mantras for puring water

Take water in a utensil meant for it and pour it all around the kuṇḍ, as directed, after each *Mantra*.

In the east—

ओम् अदितेऽनुमन्यस्व ॥ गोभिल गृह्य सू. 1.3.1

Om adite'numanyasva.

O the sun-lit part of earth, permit me to perform this yajña.

In the west—

ओम् अनुमतेऽनुमन्यस्व ॥ गोभिल गृह्य सू. 1.3.2

Om anumate'numanyasva.

O the moon-lit part of earth, permit me to perform this yajña.

In the north—

ओं सरस्वत्यनुमन्यस्व ॥ गोभिल गृह्य सू. 1.3.3

Oṁ sarasvatyanumanyasva.

O hydrosphere the earth, permit me to perform this yajña.

All four sides—

ओं देव सवितः प्रसुव यज्ञं प्रसुव यज्ञपतिं भगाय । दिव्यो गन्धर्वः केतपूः केतं नः पुनातु वाचस्पतिर्वाचं नः स्वदतु ॥ यजु. 30.1

Oṁ deva savitaḥ prasuva yajñaṁ prasuva yajñapatiṁ bhagāya. divyo gandharvaḥ ketapūḥ ketaṁ naḥ punātu vācaspatir vācaṁ naḥ svadatu.

First meaning in the context of Bhūtākāśa/Brahmāṇḍa: O energy, the material cause of creation, performs yajña of creation and stirs the creation-promoting elements towards transforming energy into matter particles. This energy, the material cause of creation, resides in dyauloka [Brahmākāśa] and sustains Bhūtākāśa. This energy impels intelligence into the universe. So, let it also sharpen our intelligence. May

God, the Governor of this cosmic energy, make good use of this energy in our interest.

The Second meaning in the context of Earth: O solar rays energy performs yajña of creation on Earth and stirs the creation-promoting elements. This energy, causing creation on Earth, resides in dyauloka [sun] and sustains life on the Earth. This solar energy impels intelligence on the Earth. So, let it also sharpen our intelligence. May God, the Governor of the energy, make this energy for our good use.

अथ आघारावाज्याहुतिमन्त्राः
Mantras for Ghee Offerings

Here, the word 'Ājya' is used to denote ghee. Ājya means 'that which pertains to Ajā', and the apparent meaning of Ajā is goat. So, naturally, some scholars argue that in Havana, ghee obtained from goats must be used instead of cows. However, the tradition gives us the understanding that only cow ghee can be used in Agnihotra. So, here the question arises as to why the word 'Ajā' is used to denote 'cow ghee'. The answer is simple. In the Vedas, the intended meaning of 'Ajā' is 'that which is 'unborn'. So, energy particles that have not transformed into matter particles are called Ajā.

On the other hand, solar energy that has not reached the earth to participate in or sustain creation is also known as Ajā. The energy of Chidākāśa that has not been activated to form Bhūtākāśa is also Ajā. Cow ghee symbolises energy because cow ghee has a golden hue, which is the hue of energy.

So, offer the oblation of ghee by chanting the following mantras. With the chanting of the first mantra, offer ahuti/oblation in the east direction, as agni is the governor of the east direction. Earth rotates from west to east; the sun also rises in the east, thus allowing energy to enter from the east direction.

In the east:

ओम् अग्रये स्वाहा । इदमग्रये इदन्न मम ॥ 1 ॥

Om agnaye svāhā. Idam agnaye idanna mama.

[Chanting below given mantra, ahuti be offered in the north direction of the fire altar, as earth's magnetism exists in the north direction].

In the north:

ओं सोमाय स्वाहा । इदं सोमाय इदन्न मम ॥ 2 ॥

Om somāya svāhā. idam somāya idanna mama.

I offer the oblation to enhance the power of soma [+ve elements of universe]. This offering is for soma and not for me.

अथ आज्य-भागाहुति मन्त्राः
Mantras for Ājya-bhāga Offering

Offer oblation in the centre of fire altar and chant following mantras:

ओं प्रजापतये स्वाहा । इदं प्रजापतये इदन्न मम ॥ 1 ॥

Om prajāpataye svāhā. idam prajāpataye idanna mama.

This oblation is offered to Prajapati Parameśvara. This offering is intended for Prajapati Parameśvara and not for me.

ओम् इन्द्राय स्वाहा । इदमिन्द्राय इदन्न मम ।

Om indrāya svāhā. idam indrāya. idanna mama.

This oblation is offered to the electric force of the universe. This offering is intended for electric force and not for me.

अथ व्याहति-आहुतिमन्त्राः
Mantras for Vyāhṛti-offerings

The whole universe has a three-tier arrangement - Bhūloka [Bhūtākāśa or Brahmāṇḍa], Dyauloka [Chidākāśa or Brahmaloka] and Antarikṣa [intervening space]. So far as our universe is concerned, it also has three three-tier systems: the sun [dyauloka], the earth [bhūloka] and the mid-space or magnetosphere [antarikṣa]. These three levels of the universe are known as three Vyāhṛtis.

ओं भूरग्रये स्वाहा । इदमग्रये इदन्न मम ॥ 1 ॥

Oṁ bhūr agnaye svāhā. Idam agnaye idanna mama.

This oblation is offered to kindle geothermal energy. This offering is intended for the geothermal energy of Bhūloka and not for me.

ओं भुवर्वायवे स्वाहा । इदं वायवे इदन्न मम ॥ 2 ॥.

Oṁ bhuvar vāyave svāhā. idaṁ vāyave idanna mama.

This oblation is offered to field energy of intermediate space. This offering is intended for field energy and not for me.

ओं स्वरादित्याय स्वाहा । इदमादित्याय इदन्न मम ।

Oṁ svar ādityāya svāhā. Idam ādityāya idanna mama.

This oblation is offered to the energy of svarloka [Brahmaloka and Sun]. This offering is intended for the energy of svarloka and not for me.

ओं भूभुर्वः स्वरग्निवाय्वादित्येभ्यः स्वाहा । इदमग्निवाय्वादित्येभ्यः इदन्न मम ॥

Oṁ bhūr bhuvaḥ svar agni-vāyv-ādityebhyaḥ svāhā. Idam agni-vāyvādityebhyaḥ idanna mama.

This oblation is offered combinedly to the energy of Bhūloka [earth and Bhūtākāsa], Antarikṣa [intermediate sphere] and Brahmaloka [Chidākāśa or Svarloka]. This offering is specially intended for the energy of all the three spaces and not for me.

अथ स्विष्टकृत्-आहुतिमन्त्रः

Mantra for offering of sweet

The *sviṣṭa-kṛt āhuti* should be offered with ghee and some sweets.

ओं यदस्य कर्मणोऽत्यरीरिचं यद्वा न्यूनमिहाकरम्। अग्रिष्टत् स्विष्टकृद् विद्यात् सर्वं स्विष्टं सुहुतं करोतु मे। अग्नये स्विष्टकृते सुहुतहुते सर्वप्रायश्चित्ताहुतीनां कामानां समर्द्धयित्रे सर्वान्नः कामान्त्समर्द्धय स्वाहा। इदमग्रये स्विष्टकृते इदन्न मम॥

आश्वलायन गृह्य सू. 1.10.12

Oṁ yadasya karmaṇo'tyarīricaṁ yadvā nyūnam ihākaram. agniṣṭat sviṣṭakṛd vidyāt sarvaṁ sviṣṭaṁ suhutaṁ karotu me. Agnaye sviṣṭakṛte suhuta-hute sarvaprāyaścitt-āhutīnāṁ kāmānāṁ samarddhayitre sarvānnaḥ kāmānt samarddhaya svāhā. idam agnaye sviṣṭakṛte idanna mama.

Whatever in my performance of yajña, I have done extra or less than required, may the Parameśvara, who fulfils all desires, who knows all our good desires, make up the difference of the oblations offered. This oblation is offered to Parameśvara, who fulfils all good desires, makes all offerings a success, and salvages offerings given in repentance towards fulfilling one's wishes. May Parameśvara fulfil all my desires. This offering is intended for Parameśvara, the fulfiller of all desires causing spiritual upliftment and not for me.

अथ प्राजापत्याहुतिमन्त्रः

Mantra for offering to Prajāpati

Silently meditate on this *mantra* and make offering.

ओं प्रजापतये स्वाहा । इदं प्रजापतये इदन्न मम ॥ यजु. 18.28

Om prajāpataye svāhā. idam prajāpataye idanna mama.

This oblation is offered to Prajāpati Parameśvara. This offering is intended for Prajāpati Parameśvara and not for me.

अथ आज्याहुतिमन्त्राः

Mantras for Ghee-offerings

प्रधान होम सम्बन्धी

Associated with Main Homa

Give four Ghee offerings, one with each of the following mantras.

ओं भूर्भुवः स्वः । अग्न आयूंषि पवस आ सुवोर्जमिषं च नः । आरे बाधस्व दुच्छुनां स्वाहा । इदमग्नये पवमानाय इदन्न मम ॥ ऋ. 9.66.19

Om bhūr bhuvaḥ svaḥ. agna āyūṁṣi pavasa ā suvorjam iṣaṁ ca naḥ. āre bādhasva ducchunāṁ svāhā. idamagnaye pavamānāya idanna mama.

The energy is located in all three spaces- as agni in Bhūtākāśa/Bhūloka or earth, as vāyu in intermediate space and as āditya in Brahmaloka and Sun. O energy of the Bhūtākāśa/Bhūloka or earth, bring life in the Bhūtākāśa/Bhūloka or earth and grant us food grains and power. Remove all our hurdles. So, is made this offering. This offering is for energy that brings life and not for me.

ओं भूर्भुवः स्वः । अग्निऋर्षिः पवमानः पाञ्चजन्यः पुरोहितः । तमीमहे महागयं

स्वाहा । इदमग्नये पवमानाय इदन्न मम ॥ ऋ. 9.66.20

Oṁ bhūr bhuvaḥ svaḥ. agnir ṛṣiḥ pavamānaḥ pāñcajanyaḥ purohitaḥ. tamīmahe mahāgayaṁ svāhā. idam agnaye pavamānāya idaṁ na mama.

The energy is located in all three spaces- as agni in Bhūtākāśa/Bhūloka or earth, as vāyu in intermediate space and as āditya in Brahmaloka and Sun. The geothermal energy of earth [and energy of Bhūtākāśa/Bhūloka] is the life principle of creation. It brings life to Bhūtākāśa/Bhūloka or earth. It creates five elements —Pṛthivī, Jala, Agni, Vāyu and Ākāśa. It is the precursor of creation. We wish to have energy that finds a big house in Bhūtākāśa/Bhūloka or earth, intermediate space and Brahmaloka and Sun. This offering is for energy that brings life and not for me.

ओं भूर्भुवः स्वः । अग्ने पवस्व स्वपा अस्मे वर्चः सुवीर्यम् ॥ दधद्रयिं मयि पोषं स्वाहा ॥ इदमग्नये पवमानाय इदन्न मम ॥ ऋ. 9.66.21

Oṁ bhūr bhuvaḥ svaḥ. agne pavasva svapā asme varcaḥ suvīryam. dadhad rayiṁ mayi poṣam svāhā. idam agnaye pavamānāya idanna mama.

The energy is located in all three spaces- as agni in Bhūtākāśa/Bhūloka or earth, as vāyu in intermediate space and as āditya in Brahmaloka and Sun. O geothermal energy, you perform the beautiful act of purifying the earth. Bring life to it. Provide it with (*rayim*) natural prosperity and (*poṣam*) nourishment. This offering is made to strengthen geothermal energy. This offering is for geothermal energy that brings life and not for me.

Finally, a āhuti is offered to Prajāpati Parameśvara, Who is the efficient cause of this creation, with the following *mantra*.

ओं भूर्भुवः स्वः। प्रजापते न त्वदेतान्यन्यो विश्वा जातानि परिता बभूव। यत्कामास्ते जुहुमस्तन्नो अस्तु वयं स्याम पतयो रयीणां स्वाहा। इदं प्रजापतये इदन्न मम ॥ ऋ. 10.121.10

Oṁ bhūr bhuvaḥ svaḥ. prajāpate na tvad etānyanyo viśvā jātāni paritā babhūva. yat kāmās te juhumas tanno astu vayaṁ syāma patayo rayīṇāṁ svāhā. idaṁ prajāpataye idanna mama.

Prajāpati Parmeśvara pervades all the three spaces- Bhūloka, Antarikṣa loka [intermediate space] and Brahmākāśa. O Lord of all people, none except Thee can surpass all animate and inanimate beings born in this universe. When we invoke you for our desired object, let it be ours. Let us be the possessor of all wealth. This offering is for the Lord of the universe and not for me.

अथ अष्टाज्याहुतिमन्त्राः

Mantras for eight Ghee-offerings

Offer eight oblations of *Ghee* with the following *mantras*.

ओं त्वन्नोऽग्ने वरुणस्य विद्वान् देवस्य हेळोऽव यासिसीष्ठाः। यजिष्ठो वह्नितमः शोशुचानो विश्वा द्वेषांसि प्रमुमुग्ध्यस्मत् स्वाहा ॥ इदमग्निवरुणाभ्याम् इदन्न मम ॥

ऋ. 4.1.4

Oṁ tvanno'gne varuṇasaya vidvān devasya heḷo'ava yāsisīṣṭhāḥ. yajiṣṭho vahnitamaḥ śośucāno viśvā dveṣāṁsi pra mumugdhyasmat svāhā. Idam agnivaruṇābhyām idanna mama.

O Pramameśvara, you know the adverse effects of Prakṛti, so keep us away from them. You create this universe repeatedly; you are the greatest energy source. You are the most glorious. Remove all elements that impede the process of creation. Hence, this offering. This offering is intended for Puruṣa and Prakṛti and not for me.

ओं स त्वन्नो अग्नेऽवमो भवोती नेदिष्ठो अस्या उषसो व्युष्टौ । अव यक्ष्व नो
वरुणं रराणो वीहि मृळीकं सुहवो न एधि स्वाहा । इदमग्निवरुणाभ्याम् इदन्न मम ॥

ऋ. 4.1.5

Oṁ sa tvanno agne'vamo bhvotī nediṣṭho asyā uṣaso vyuṣṭau. ava yakṣva no varuṇaṁ rarāṇo vīhi mṛḷīkaṁ suhavo na edhi svāhā. idam agnivaruṇābhyām idanna mama.

Do you, Puruṣa, the embodiment of Agni, be our protector and most nigh to us with your protection? When this energy is utilized, activate more of it (because if it is not activated, the creation process will stall). Please provide us with such energy as is beneficial to us. Reach us in our invocations. So is given this offering. This offering is for Puruṣa and Prakṛti and not for me.

ओम् इमं मे वरुण श्रुधि हवमद्या च मृळय । त्वामवस्युराचके स्वाहा । इदं
वरुणाय इदन्न मम ॥ ऋ. 1.25.19

Om imaṁ me varuṇa śrudhi havam adyā ca mṛḷaya. tvām avasyur ācake svāhā. idaṁ varuṇāya idanna mama.

O Prakṛti, the material cause of creation, hear this call of mine, be gracious. I propitiate you from all sides for the protection of this creation. That is why this oblation is offered. This offering is for Prakṛti and not for me.

NB: According to the Veda, Prakṛti is the material cause of creation. The *Mahābhārata* (12.318.39), while propounding the Sāṅkhya system of philosophy, interprets the Vedic God Mitra as "Puruṣa" and Varuṇa as "Prakṛti".

ओम् तत्त्वा यामि ब्रह्मणा वन्दमानस्तदाशास्ते यजमानो हविर्भिः । अहेळमानो
वरुणेह बोध्युरुशंस मा न आयुः प्र मोषीः स्वाहा । इदं वरुणाय इदन्न मम ॥

ऋ. 1.24.11

Oṁ tattvā yāmi brahmaṇā vandamānastadāśāste yajamāno havirbhiḥ. aheḷmāno varuṇeha bodhyurūśaṁsa mā na āyuḥ pramoṣīḥ svāhā. idaṁ varuṇāya idanna mama.

O Prakṛti, the material cause of creation, I pray you to give a lease of life to this creation. This universe expansion is nothing but a prayer of adoration unto you. The creator performing the yajña of creation also wishes this universe to live its lifespan through His oblations. O thou of wide reputation, don't disrespect His wish and cut short the life of this universe. That is why this oblation is offered. This offering is for Prakṛti and not for me.

ओं ये ते शतं वरुण ये सहस्रं यज्ञियाः पाशा वितता महान्तः। तेभिर्नोऽद्य सवितोत विष्णुर्विश्वे मुञ्चन्तु मरुतः स्वर्काः स्वाहा। इदं वरुणाय सवित्रे विष्णवे विश्वेभ्यो देवेभ्यो मरुद्भ्यः स्वर्केभ्यः इदन्न मम ॥ कात्यायन श्रौत सू. 25.1.11

Oṁ ye te śataṁ varuṇa ye sahasraṁ yajñiyāḥ pāśā vitatā mahāntaḥ. tebhir no'dya savitota viṣṇur viśve muñchantu marūtaḥ svarkāḥ svāhā. idaṁ varuṇāya savitre viṣṇave viśvebhyo devebhyo marudbhyaḥ svarkebhyaḥ idanna mama.

O Prakṛti, the material cause of creation, you have a vast network of hundreds and thousands of nooses in the form of Savitā (solar energy with the power of creation), Viṣṇu (The universe), Viśvedevāḥ (all natural forces), Maruts (radiation pressure of universe), and svarkas (charged matter particles). Kindly liberate us from them so that we may not have to be entangled in the natural cycle of life and death. That is why this oblation is offered. This offering is for Prakṛti and its various forms like Savitā, Viṣṇu, Viśvedevāḥ, Maruts, and svarkas; and not for me.

NB: This all-side prevailing network of Prakṛti is the nooses of Varuṇa. Savitā is energy material for creation. Viṣṇu is three tier universe. Viśvedeva refers here to all natural forces. The term svarkāḥ refers here to charged matter particles. In this mantra, liberation from the clutches of Prakṛti is prayed for.

ओम् अयाश्चाग्रेऽस्यनभिशस्तिपाश्च सत्यमित्त्वमयासि। अया नो यज्ञं वहास्यया नो धेहि भेषजꣳ स्वाहा। इदमग्नये अयसे इदन्न मम ॥ कात्यायन श्रौतसू. 25.1.11

Om ayāś cāgne'sy anabhiśastipāśca satyam ittvamayāsi. ayā no yajñam vahāsyayā no dhehi bheṣajam svāhā. Idam agnaye ayase idanna mama.

O Puruṣa, possessed of energy in your womb, thou art performer of creation yajña and protector of such elements as do not violate this creation process. You are undoubtedly a performer of creation yajña in this Bhūtākāśa. Sustain this creation of ours. Bless us with happiness. That is why this oblation is offered. This offering is for the performer of creation yajña and not for me.

ओम् उदुत्तमं वरुण पाशमस्मदवाधमं वि मध्यमं श्रथाय। अथा वयमादित्य व्रते तवानागसो अदितये स्याम स्वाहा। इदं वरुणायादित्यायादितये च इदन्न मम ॥

ऋ.1.24.15

Om uduttamam varuṇa pāśam asmad avādhamam vi madhyamam srathāya. athā vayam āditya vrate tavānāgaso aditaye syāma svāhā. idam varuṇāy ādityāyāditaye ca idanna mama.

O Prakṛti, the material cause of creation, you keep us away from your trap of higher space [solar region], lower space [earth] and mid-space so that we may attain mokṣa, as a person trapped in prakṛti cannot attain mokṣa. After that, may we not become instrumental in breaking thy vow for undisturbed Brahmacharya, O Āditya Brahmachārī. That is why this oblation is offered. This offering is for Prakṛti, Āditya Brahmacharī, and for the undisturbed vow of Brahmacharya and not for me.

NB: The mantra suggests that one can achieve Mokṣa by staying away from natural attractions and observing the vow of Āditya Brahmacharya, i.e. living a celibate life for 48 years attaining knowledge.

ओं भवतं नः समनसौ सचेतसावरेपसौ । मा यज्ञꣳ हिꣳसिष्टं मा यज्ञपतिं जातवेदसौ शिवौ भवतमद्य नः स्वाहा । इदं जातवेदोभ्याम् इदन्न मम ॥ यजु. 5.3

Oṁ bhavataṁ naḥ samanasau sacetasā-varepasau. mā yajñaṁ hinsiṣṭaṁ mā yajñapatiṁ jātavedasau śivau bhavatam adya naḥ svāhā. idaṁ jātavedobhyām idanna mama.

According to the Veda, the sun is the abode of energy. It percolates down from the solar region to the earth's magnetosphere and, after that, to the earth, which is the cause of creation on the earth. This mantra talks about the harmony between solar energy and geothermal energy.

O solar and geothermal energies, you be harmonious and give us the desired fruit. Do not oppose each other to harm the yajña of creation and the objective of the host of creation (Paramātmā). Be kind to us now and forever. That is why this oblation is offered. This offering is for the energy of intermediate space and earth and not for me.

पूर्णाहुति

Pūrṇāhuti : Completing the procedure of Āhutis

Filling the spoon with ghee, yajamāna should perform pūrṇāhuti with the following mantra recited thrice

ओं सर्वं वै पूर्णꣳ स्वाहा।

Oṁ sarvaṁ vai pūrṇaṁ svāhā.

This offering is intended to make up all other offerings.

मंगलकार्य

Maṅgalakārya (Auspicious Act)

The following vāmdevyagāna of Sāmaveda should be performed positively in the sankāras starting from Garbhādhāna ending with Saṁnyāsa.

ओं भूर्भुवः स्वः। कया नश्चित्र आ भुवदूती सदावृधः सखा।
कया शचिष्ठया वृता॥

Oṁ bhūrbhuvaḥ svaḥ, kayā naśchitra ā bhuvadūtī sadāvṛdhaḥ sakhā. kayā sachiṣṭhayā vṛtā.

[Meaning] God is existent, conscious all-blissful. He is mature, unique and friend of all. May he come to our help with his power of protection intelligently.

ओं भूर्भुवः स्वः। कस्त्वा सत्यो मदानां मꣳ हिष्ठो मत्सदन्धसः।
दृढा चिदारुजे वसु॥

Oṁ bhūrbhuvaḥ svaḥ, kastvā satyo madānāṁ maṁ̮hiṣṭho matsadandhasaḥ, dṛḍhā chidāruje vasu.

[Meaning] Brahman is Existent, Conscious, All-bliss. Brahman, the greatest processor of blessedness, is True and All-beatitude. O All human beings! He may make you happy and give you the power to overcome external and internal enemies.

ओं भूर्भुवः स्वः। अभी षु णः सखीनामविता जरितृणाम्। शतं भवास्यूतये॥

Om bhūrbhuvaḥ svaḥ, abhī ṣu ṇaḥ sakhīnāmavitā jaritṝṇām, śatam bhavāsyūtaye.

[Meaning] O God, you protect your devotees who have attained great intimacy with you. Please always protect us.

Mahāvāmdevyam

काऽ5या। नश्चा3 इत्रा3 आभुवात्। ऊ। तो सदाबधः स। खा। औ3 इत्रा3 आभुवात्। ऊ। ती सदाबधः स। खा। औ3होहाइ। कया २ ३ शचाइ। छयौहो3। हुम्मा२। वार्ता3ऽ5हाठ॥1॥

काऽ5स्वा। सत्यो3मा3दानाम्। मा। हिष्ठो मात्सादन्ध। सा। औ3होहाइ। दृढा २ ३ चिदा। रुजौहो3। हुम्मा२। वाऽ3सो3ऽ5 हायि॥2॥

kā'5yā, naśchā3 itrā3 ābhuvāt, ū, to sadābadhaḥ sa, khā, au3 itrā3 ābhuvāt, ū, tī sadābadhaḥ sa, khā, au3hohāi, kayā 2 3 śachāi, ṣṭhayauho3, hummā2, vā2rtā3'5hāṭha ॥1॥

kā'5stvā, satyo3mā3dānām, mā, hiṣṭho mātsādandha, sā, au3hohāi, dṛdhā 2 3 chidā, rujauho3, hummā2, vā'3so3'5 hāyi ॥2॥

आऽ5भी। षु णा3 साऽ3खीनाम्। आ। विता जरायितृ। णाम्। औ3 हो हायि। शता २ ३ म्भवा। सियोहो3। हुम्मा२। ताऽ2 यो3ऽ5 हायि॥ ३

ā'5bhī, ṣu ṇā3ḥ sā3khīnām, ā, vitā jarāyitṝ, ṇām, au3 ho hāyi, śatā 2 3 mbhavā, siyoho3, hummā2, tā'2 yo3'5 hāyi ॥ 3

After the performance Trance of Vāmdevyamgāna concludes, householders (men and women), volunteers, righteous, prominent gentlemen, scholars, and impartial saṁnyāsīs who are constantly engaged in the proliferation of knowledge and altruistic welfare of society should be given due respect by entertaining them with kneels clothes money and gift according to the capacity of the host.

Those who have participated as observers should also be seen off respectfully. Those who desire to watch the conduct of saṁskāras should take their seats separately and keep quiet without indulging in any whisper. All should be attentive and look happy. The priest should discharge their duties peacefully according to the procedure. This standard procedure may be followed in the performance of all Sanskāras.

इति सामान्यप्रकरणम् ॥

iti sāmānyaprakaraṇam

Here ends the standard procedure.

अथ गर्भाधानसंस्कारः
Garabhādhāna Sanskāra

Garbhādāna Sanskāra is about conceiving a child. Here, it is pertinent to know that two factors play an essential part in the transmigration of souls. The first important factor, as discussed above, is Sanskāra. It determines the species a soul is entitled to transmigrate after death. Whether a soul will take birth to a man, a woman, an animal, a bird, an insect or a plant is determined by the Sanskāras held by the soul in its subtle body as a result of its karmas, thoughts, eating and drinking habits. The second prominent factor is 'moha', i.e. attachment. Attachment is a biological instinct that attracts two or more living beings together. The attachment factor is responsible for the placement of a soul after death. It determines the place, family, or surroundings where a soul is destined to reach after death, according to the Sanskāras.

So Garbhādāna is planning for the newcomer. The newcomer's fate is decided by his/her Sanskāras and attachment instinct. The newcomer is not free to make a choice but is bound by the factor of Sanskāra and attachment inherited by him or her from the previous life. The Garbhādāna is an attempt to provide a conducive atmosphere or conditions for some good soul to come into the family, as a new soul is born to the parents having Sanskāras corresponding to them. In other words, we can say that parents with a particular Sanskāra will attract the child of the corresponding Sanskāra. So it is up to the parents what type of child they want to welcome to their family; accordingly, they shall have to plan. Here, I may cite Yāska (kali 400, i.e. c. 2701 BC), who quotes Gobhila Gṛhya Sūtra (2.8.21) in his Nirukta (3.4) and observes thus:

अंगादंगात्संभवसि हृदयादधि जायसे।

आत्मा वै पुत्र नामासि स जीव शरदः शतम्।।

amgādamgātsambhavasi hrdayādadhi jāyase ।

ātmā vai putra nāmāsi sa jīva śaradaḥ śatam ।।

[Meaning] You are produced from every limb. You are engendered from the heart itself. Verily, you are the very soul named son; as such, live a hundred autumns.

From the above quote, it is clear that a child is born to the parents who hold genes corresponding to him. In other words, a child inherits the genes of his parents. At another place, it is observed:

यस्य यस्य हि अंगावयस्य बीजे बीजभागः उपतप्तो भवति तस्य तस्य हि अंगावयवस्य विकृतिरूपजायते, नोपजायते चानुपतापात्, तस्मात् उपयोपपत्ति।

yasya yasya hi amgāvayasya bīje bījabhāgaḥ upatapto bhavati tasya tasya hi amgāvayavasya vikṛtirūpajāyate, nopajāyate chānupatāpāt, tasmāt upayopapatti.

[Meaning] If parents suffer from genetic defects or disorders, their children generally inherit the same. If they are not suffering from any genetic defect at any level, the children also do not inherit the same.

Because of the above fact, it has been proposed to the woman in the family way that she must let the same Sanskāra dominate in herself as she expects from her future child.

तन्मना बींज गृह्णीयात्।

tanmanā bīmja gṛhṇīyāt ।

Thus, it is clear that a soul seeks favourable conditions as per its Sanskāras for taking its birth. It cannot take birth in adverse conditions. So the parents can plan a baby of their choice.

Let me narrate here the history of Madālasā. She was desirous to seek her children to grow into Brahmarṣis. So, during her pregnancy, she used to think about the following sentence:

शुद्धोसि बुद्धोसि निरंजनोसि संसारमाया परिवर्जितोसि।

śuddhosi buddhosi niraṁjanosi saṁsāramāyā parivarjitosi।

[Meaning] O my son! You are pure, enlightened, void of passions and emotions and unfazed by worldly allurement.

History informs that due to the Sanskāras of the above thought, all her eight children achieved the state of Brahmarṣis.

Now, the question arises about how to get a child of one's own choice. In this regard, Suśruta Samhitā has laid down a particular procedure. Accordingly,

ध्रुवं चतुर्णां सान्निध्यात् गर्भः स्याद्विधिपूर्वकम्।
ऋतु-क्षेत्राम्बुबीजानां संयोगात् अंकुरो यथा॥

dhruvaṁ chaturṇāṁ sānnidhyāt garbhaḥ syādvidhipūrvakam।
ṛtu-kṣetrāmbubījānāṁ saṁyogāt aṁkuro yathā॥

[Meaning] Just as the combination of Ṛtu (proper season), Kṣetra (fertile land), Ambu (water) and Bīja (seed) is essential for the growth of a sapling, similarly the presence of **Ṛtu** (time after menstruation), **Kṣetra** (Ovary/ovum), **Ambu** (Semen/sperm) and **Bija** (Sanskāra) is essential for the growth of foetus in human being.

Here, some explanation is necessary regarding the above-cited four factors.

1. Ṛtu: Here ṛtu menas menstrual period in females. According to Ayurveda, the golden period for begetting a progeny is from the fifth day after the onset of the menstrual period till the 16th day. So, couples wanting a progeny can have sex during these 12 days. If the female partner conceives during this period, the future child will enjoy sound health, long life, prosperity, good fortune, physical prowess, effulgence and excellent sensory organs. If a mother conceives after the expiry of this golden period, it may adversely impact a child's health and physique, and the child will be destined with a short life span. It is said that the life span of a child is impacted proportionately by the period of conception after the golden period. So, from the 17th to the 26th days after the onset of menstruation should be known as a bad period for conception. The child conceived during this period will be attributed with poor health, physique and short life span.

तासु उत्तरोत्तरमायुः आरोग्यैश्वर्यसौभाग्यबलवर्णेन्द्रिय सम्पत् अपत्यस्य भवति ।
अतः परं तु उत्तरोत्तरमेव आयुरादीनां ह्रासः ।

*tāsu   uttarottaramāyuḥ   ārogyaiśvaryasaubhāgyabala-
varṇendriya sampat apatyasya bhavati. ataḥ paraṁ tu
uttarottarameva āyurādīnāṁ hrāsaḥ.*

2. Kṣetra: The second component is Kṣetra, or the ovary of the female partner. The ovaries are an essential part of the female reproductive system. Their job is twofold. They produce the hormones, including estrogen, that trigger menstruation. They also release at least one egg each month for possible fertilization. The menstruation purifies the ovary and makes it capable of ovulation. That is why it is said:

रसः प्रसेकात् नारीणां मासि मासि विशुध्यति..........तस्मान्न प्रमेहन्ति स्त्रियः ।

*rasaḥ   prasekāt   nārīṇāṁ   māsi   māsi
viśudhyati..........tasmānna pramehanti striyaḥ*

So, a healthy ovum (egg) is necessary for a baby's healthy growth.

3. Ambu: The third component is Ambu or the semen of the male partner. Semen quality is a measure of the ability of semen to accomplish fertilization. Thus, it is a measure of fertility in a man. It is the sperm in the semen that is important; therefore, semen quality involves both sperm quantity and quality. Decreased semen quality is a significant factor in male infertility.

4. Bīja: The fourth component is the Bīja. Bīja is the set of Sanskāras travelling with the soul through a subtle body. When egg cells are fertilized with sperm, the soul enters the egg cells, giving way to developing a new organism. *Charaka* (*Śārīra Sthāna*, 3.3) sheds ample good light on the factors responsible for the origin and development of the foetus and the process leading to it.

पुरुषस्य अनुपहतरेतसः स्त्रियाश्च अप्रदुष्टयोनि-शोणित-गर्भायाः यदा भवति संसर्गः ऋतुकाले यदा च अनयोः तथा युक्ते संसर्गे शुक्र-शोणितसंसर्गमन्तगर्भाशयगतं जीवः अवक्रामति सत्त्वसंप्रयोगात् तदा गर्भो अभिनिवर्तते। स सात्म्यरसोपयोगात् अरोगो भवति अभिवर्धते सम्यक् उपचारश्चोपचार्यमाणः।

puruṣasya anupahataretasaḥ striyāścha apraduṣṭayoni-śoṇita-garbhāyāḥ yadā bhavati saṁsargaḥ ṛtukāle yadā cha anayoḥ tathā yukte saṁsarge śukra-śoṇitasaṁsargamantagarbhāśayagataṁ jīvaḥ avakrāmati sattvasaṁprayogāt tadāā garbho abhinivartate। sa sātmyarasopayogāt arogo bhavati abhivardhate samyak upachāraśchopachāryamāṇāḥ.

If a male partner, possessing healthy semen, conducts sexual intercourse with his female partner having a healthy ovum and devoid of disorders of the genital tract and uterus during the opportune period (i.e. starting from the 4th day of menstruation and ending with the

16th day). In this process, the sperm of the male partner gets fused with the ovum of the female partner. When the soul impelled by sattva (sanskāras) descends into the zygote in the uterus, the embryo is formed. For the healthy growth of the fetus, it is essential to have a healthy and sāttvika nourishment suitable to the mother's body and proper management, devoid of abnormality.

Then, it enters the uterus at the proper time, resulting in embryo development.

Thus, Garbhādāna Sanskāra is essential for begetting high-quality progeny.

अथ गर्भाधानविधिं वक्ष्यामः

Procedure of Garabhādhāna Sanskāra

Now the procedure of Garbhādhāna Sanskāra will be explained

निषेकादिश्मशानान्तो मन्त्रैर्यस्योदितो विधिः ॥ मनुस्मृति 2.16

niṣekādiśmaśānānto mantrairyasyodito vidhiḥ. Manu. 2.16

For the fitness and sound health (physical, mental, spiritual) of the people, sixteen sanskāras were prescribed beginning from Garabhādhān (impregnation) to the Antyeṣṭi (last journey). The body's birth occurs with Garabhādhāna sanskāra and ends with the cremation. The Garabhādhāna is the first sanskāra. Garabhādhāna is the act of impregnation to ensure conception. As the robust crop is grown in fertile land, healthy couples can give birth to healthy progeny. Therefore, to fulfil the conditions of this sanskāra, the female spouse should be at least sixteen years of age, have full bloom youth, practise celibacy and complete her education. The male spouse should be at least 25 years of age or more than this. A female below the age of sixteen is not mature enough to conceive a child and for the proper development of the foetus; similarly, a male cannot attain the power of proper procreation until and unless he crosses the age of 25 years. In this connection, medical science observes as follows:

पंचविंशे ततो वर्षे पुमान्नारी तु षोडशे ।
समत्वागतवीर्यौ तौ जानीयात् कुशलो भिषक् ॥ सुश्रुत 35.13

paṁchaviṁśe tato varṣe pumānnārī tu ṣoḍaśe,
samatvāgatavīryau tau jānīyāt kuśalo bhiṣak. Suśruta 35.13

[Meaning] An intelligent physician should know that that a male of 25 years of age and a female of 16 years of age develops capability of procreation and not beofre this age.

ऊनषोडशवर्षायामप्राप्तः पंचविंशतिम् ।
यद्याधत्ते पुमान् गर्भं कुक्षिस्थः स विपद्यते ॥ सुश्रुत० 10.54

ūnaṣoḍaśavarṣāyāmaprāptaḥ paṁchaviṁśatim,
yadyādhatte pumān garbhaṁ kukṣisthaḥ sa vipadyate.

Suśruta, 10.54

[Meaning] Should a female below 16 years and a male below 25 years go for procreation, the fetus in the womb of mother face problems.

जातो वा नि चिरं जीवेज्जीवेद्वा दुर्बलेन्द्रियः ।
तस्मादत्यन्तबालायां गर्भाधानं न कारयेत् ॥ सुश्रुत० 10.55

jāto vā ni chiraṁ jīvejjīvedvā durbalendriyaḥ,
tasmādatyantabālāyāṁ garbhādhānaṁ na kārayet.

Suśruta, 10.55

[Meaning] Either the child born of such a couple will have a short life span or will live an unhealthy life. So, do not make a girl at a young age conceived.

The above-cited ślokas are registered in the Suśruta (a treatise on ancient Indian medical sciences). The procedure of growth, declination, maturity and immaturity of the body described in the Āyurveda has no match elsewhere. The fundamental principles of Āyurveda in this connection, which could be written in the Vedārambha sanskāra, include the idea and details of growth and degeneration, maturity and immaturity of the essential ingredients of the body corresponding with its age. Therefore, it is necessary to take exceptional help from the Āyuvedic texts in conducting the sanskāras of Garabhādhāna, etc.

Here, it may be pointed out that the authority of the Suśruta is unchallenged and accepted by all. According to him, the minimum age for marriage of a girl should be sixteen years and a boy 25 years. A female of sixteen years and a male of 25 years are fit for marriage and bearing a child. Whatever capacity and physical fitness is acquired by a female at sixteen years, the same capacity and fitness is acquired by a male at 25 years. That is why the Āyurveda treat both at par for their physical fitness. If a male below 25 impregnates a female below sixteen, the foetus will be unhealthy, and there is a likelihood of abortion. If any baby is born with this type of impregnation, it may not live long; if it manages to survive, it could be physically and mentally weak. Therefore, the couple must not procreate if they have not attained the proper age limit. At another place, the Suśrut has observed as:

चतस्रोऽवस्थाः शरीरस्य वृद्धियौवनं संपूर्णता किंचित् परिहाणिश्चेति। आषोडशाद्वृद्धिराचतुर्विंशतेयौंवनमाचत्वारिंशतः सम्पूर्णता ततः किंचित्परिहाणिश्चेति ॥ सुश्रूत सूत्रस्थान 35.29

chatasro'vasthāḥ śarīrasya vṛddhiyauvanaṁ sampūrṇatā kiṁchit parihāṇiścheti, āṣoḍaśādvṛddhirāchaturviṁśateryauvanamā-chatvāriṁśataḥ sampūrṇatā tataḥ kiṁchitparihāṇiścheti.

Suśrūta Sūtrasthāna 35.29

From the age of sixteen onwards, all the body's tissues

grow, and youth begins at the age of 25th year, and it completes at the age of 40th year. At this age, the youth fully develops, and all body tissues mature. Afterwards, seminal fluid starts weakening. That is, at the 40-years of age, all the limbs and organs of the body are perfectly developed. Afterwards, the semen produced from diet takes a turn towards loss.

Therefore, it is proved that marriage should be solemnized only when the girl attains the age of 16 years, and the boy is 25 years old or the girl is 20 years old and the boy is 40 years. It is the middle course; the excellent marriage period is when the girl is 24 years old, and the boy attains the age of 48 years.

Those who desire the superior family line, superior progeny endowed with good physical, mental and spiritual health, long life, accomplished in knowledge, wise and prosperous should not under any circumstances do the betrothal ceremony of their girls attaining the age less than 16 years and the boy attaining the age less than 25 years. It is the act leading to progress, reform and prosperity. People should ensure that their children get a good education observing celibacy so that the family may be blessed with superior quality progeny in future.

ऋतुदान का काल

The time for insemination

ऋतुकालाभिगामी स्यात्सवदारनिरतस्सदा ।
पर्ववर्जं व्रजेच्चैनां तद्व्रतो रतिकाम्यया ॥ मनु. 3.45

ṛtukālābhigāmī syātsavadāraniratassadā,

parvavarjaṁ vrajechchaināṁ tadvrato ratikāmyayā.

Manu. 3.45

[Meaning] A married man who is contented with his own wife and approaches her in her monthly course, i.e. from the 5th day after the onset of the menstrual period

till the 16th day (According to Ayurveda), is as better as a
Brahmachārī.

ऋतुः स्वाभाविकः स्त्रीणां रात्रयः षोडश स्मृताः ।
चतुर्भिरितरैः सार्द्धमहोभिः सद्विगर्हितैः ॥ मनु. 3.46

ṛtuḥ svābhāvikaḥ strīṇāṁ rātrayaḥ ṣoḍaśa smṛtāḥ,
chaturbhiritaraiḥ sārddhamahobhiḥ sadvigarhitaiḥ.

Manu. 3.46

[Meaning] Here ṛtu menas menstrual period in
females. The human menstrual cycle is of 27 or 28 days.
Sixteen days and nights in each menstrual period, i.e.
from the 17th to the 26th or 27th days period after the
onset of the menstrual cycle (12 days) plus the first four
days of the onset of the next menstrual cycle are
prohibited and considered as the bad period for
conception, and so prohibited for begetting a child.
According to Ayurveda, from the fifth day after the onset
of the menstrual cycle till the 16th day, this period of 12
days is a golden period or natural season for women to
begetting a child.

So, couples wanting a progeny can have sex during
these 12 days. If the female partner conceives during this
period, the future child will enjoy sound health, long
life, prosperity, good fortune, physical prowess,
effulgence and excellent sensory organs. If a mother
conceives after the expiry of this golden period, it may
adversely impact a child's health and physique, and the
child will be destined with a short life span. It is said that
a child's life span is impacted proportionately to
conception after the golden period. So, from the 17th to
the 26th, days after the onset of menstruation, it should
be known as a bad period for conception. The child
conceived during this period will be attributed with poor
health, physique and short life span.

तासामाद्याश्चतस्रस्तु निन्दितैकादशी च या ।

त्रयोदशी च शेषास्तु प्रशस्ता दश रात्रयः ॥ मनु. 3.47

tāsāmādyāśchatasrastu ninditaikādasī cha yā,
trayodasī cha śeṣāstu prasastā dasa rātrayaḥ. Manu. 3.47

[Meaning] But among these, the first four days after the onset of menstruation and the eleventh and the thirteenth are declared to be bad periods for conception; the remaining nights from the 5th to 16th after the onset of menstruation are recommended for conception.

युग्मासु पुत्रा जायन्ते स्त्रियोऽयुग्मासु रात्रिषु ।
तस्माद्युग्मासु पुत्रार्थी संविशेदार्त्तवे स्त्रियम् ॥ मनु. 3.48

yugmāsu putrā jāyante striyo'yugmāsu rātriṣu,
tasmādyugmāsu putrārthī saṁviśedārttave striyam.

Manu. 3.48

[Meaning] Male babies are generally conceived on even nights, from the fifth day of menstruation to the 16th. Similarly, female babies are conceived on uneven nights; hence, a couple who desires to have sons should approach each other on the even (nights) after the 5th day of menstruation till the 16th day and not after that.

पुमान् पुंसोऽधिके शुक्रे स्त्री भवत्यधिके स्त्रियाः ।
समे पुमान् पुंस्त्रियौ वा क्षीणेऽल्पे च विपर्ययः ॥ मनु. 3.49

pumān puṁso'dhike śukre strī bhavatyadhike striyāḥ,
same pumān puṁstriyau vā kṣīṇe'lpe cha viparyayaḥ.

Manu. 3.49

[Meaning] A male child is produced if the sperm is healthier and its count is higher than the ovum (female egg cell). Similarly, a female child is produced if the ovum is healthier and its count is higher than the sperm. If both are equal or equally healthy, a hermaphrodite (genderless) baby is produced. If (both are) weak or deficient in quantity, conception failure occurs.

The health or count of sperm or ovum depends on

diet and other physical exercises. As such, a couple desiring a particular type of baby can prepare themselves accordingly and perform Puṁsvana Sanskāra. According to Yājñavalkya, the amount of cow ghee is important in improving or reducing health. The greater the amount of ghee, the better the health. Lesser the amount of ghee, slim and trim the human being.

निन्द्यास्वष्टासु चान्यासु स्त्रियो रात्रिषु वर्जयन् ।
ब्रह्मचार्य्येव भवति यत्र तत्राश्रमे वसन् ॥ मनु, 3.50

nindyāsvaṣṭāsu chānyāsu striyo rātriṣu varjayan,
brahmachāryyeva bhavati yatra tatrāśrame vasan.

Manu, 3.50

[Meaning] He who avoids women on the eight forbidden nights (first four days after the onset of menstruation, 11th, 13th, 17th and 18th day) and eight others (18th to 26th), is equal in chastity to a Brahmachārī, in whichever Āśrama he may live.

In this way, the seers like Manu, etc., have decidedly prescribed the time of insemination and rules for married couples.

उपनिषदि गर्भलम्भनम्० ॥ आश्व. गृ. 1.13.2

upaniṣadi garbhalambhanam. Āśva. Gṛ. 1.13.2

It is the statement of the Āśvalāyana Gṛhyasūtra. The insemination procedure should conform to the procedure laid down in the Upaniṣad. The Upaniṣad endorses the abovementioned procedure regarding the marriage between a female of 16 years and a male of 25 years.

अथ गर्भाधानँ स्त्रियाः । पुष्पवत्याश्चतुरहादूर्ध्वँ स्नात्वा विरुजायास्तस्मिन्नेव दिवा आदित्यं गर्भमिति ॥

atha   garbhādhānaṁ   striyāḥ,
puṣpavatyāśchaturahādūrdhvaṁ   snātvā   virujāyāstasminneva

divā ādityaṁ garbhamiti.

It is the statement of the Pāraskara Gṛhyasūtra. The Gobhilīya and Śaunakīya Gṛhyasūtras have similar views. From the 5th day onward, after the onset of the menstrual period, till the 16th day, when the man and woman desire to have a conception, the ceremony should be held reciting the mantra:

आदित्यं गर्भमिति ।

ādityaṁ garbhamiti.

The yajña, according to Common Procedure, should be performed with the odoriferous things prescribed for the purpose, and the oblations with the following verses should be offered. The wife should sit on the left side of her husband, and the husband should sit in the east direction of the Vedī, keeping his face in the west, south or north directions as per his suitability. The priests should sit in four directions of the Vedī as per their convenience.

ओं अग्ने प्रायश्चित्ते त्वं देवानां प्रायश्चित्तिरसि ब्राह्मणस्त्वा नाथकाम उपधावामि यास्याः पापी लक्ष्मीस्तनूस्तामस्या अपजहि स्वाहा । इदमग्नये-इदन्न मम ॥

गोभिल गृसू० 2.5.2

Oṁ agne prāyaśchitte tvaṁ devānāṁ prāyaśchittirasi brāhmaṇastvā nāthakāma upadhāvāmi yāsyāḥ pāpī lakṣamīstanūstāmasyā apajahi svāhā. idamagnaye-idanna mama.
Go. Gṛ. Sū. 2.5.2

[Meaning] O Agni! you are the purifier of the environment. The scholars approach you for the fulfilment of their desires. Let this Agni remove the bad ideas from the mind of this lady. This oblation is meant for Agni and not for me.

ओं वायो प्रायश्चित्ते त्वं देवानां प्रायश्चित्तिरसि ब्राह्मणस्त्वा नाथकाम उपधावामि यास्याः पापी लक्ष्मीस्तनूस्तामस्या अपजहि स्वाहा ॥ इद्र वायवे-इदन्न मम ॥

गोभिल गृसू॰ 2.5.3

Oṁ vāyo prāyaśchitte tvaṁ devānāṁ prāyaśchittirasi brāhmaṇastvā nāthakāma upadhāvāmi yāsyāḥ pāpī lakṣamīstanūstāmasyā apajahi svāhā. idra vāyave-idanna mama.

Go. Gṛ. Sū. 2.5.3

[Meaning] O Vāyu! you are the purifier of the environment. The scholars approach you for the fulfilment of their desires. Let this Vāyu remove the bad ideas from the mind of this lady. This oblation is meant for Vāyu and not for me.

ओं चन्द्र प्रायश्चित्ते त्वं देवानां प्रायश्चित्तिरसि ब्राह्मणस्त्वा नाथकाम उपधावामि यास्याः पापी लक्ष्मीस्तनूस्तामस्या अपजहि स्वाहा ॥ इद्र चन्द्राय-इदन्न मम ॥

गोभिल गृसू॰ 2.5.4

Oṁ chandra prāyaśchitte tvaṁ devānāṁ prāyaśchittirasi brāhmaṇastvā nāthakāma upadhāvāmi yāsyāḥ pāpī lakṣamīstanūstāmasyā apajahi svāhā. idra chandrāya-idanna mama. Go. Gṛ. Sū. 2.5.4

[Meaning] O Chandra! you are the pacifier of mind and environment. The scholars approach you for the fulfilment of their desires. Let this Chandra remove the disturbance from the mind of this lady. This oblation is meant for Chandra and not for me.

ओं सूर्य प्रायश्चित्ते त्वं देवानां प्रायश्चित्तिरसि ब्राह्मणस्त्वा नाथकाम उपधावामि यास्याः पापी लक्ष्मीस्तनूस्तामस्या अपजहि स्वाहा ॥ इदं सूर्याय-इदन्न मम ॥

गोभिल गृसू॰ 2.5.5

Oṁ sūrya prāyaśchitte tvaṁ devānāṁ prāyaśchittirasi brāhmaṇastvā nāthakāma upadhāvāmi yāsyāḥ pāpī lakṣamīstanūstāmasyā apajahi svāhā. idaṁ sūryāya-idanna mama. Go. Gṛ. Sū. 2.5.5

[Meaning] O Sūrya! You are the purifier of the environment. The scholars approach you for the fulfilment of their desires. Let the Sūrya remove the bad ideas from the mind of this lady. This oblation is meant for Sūrya and not for me.

ओं अग्निवायुचन्द्रसूर्य्याः प्रायश्चित्तयो यूयं देवानां प्रायश्चित्तयः स्थ ब्राह्मणो वो नाथकाम उपधावामि यास्याः पापी लक्ष्मीस्तनूस्तामस्या अपहत स्वाहा ॥ इदमग्निवायुचन्द्रसूर्येभ्यः-इदन्न मम ॥ गोभिल गृसू० 2.5.6

Oṁ agnivāyuchandrasūryyāḥ prāyaśchittayo yūyaṁ devānāṁ prāyaśchittayaḥ stha brāhmaṇo vo nāthakāma upadhāvāmi yāsyāḥ pāpī lakṣamīstanūstāmasyā apahata svāhā. idamagnivāyuchandrasūryebhyaḥ-idanna mama.

Go. Gṛ. Sū. 2.5.6

[Meaning] O Agni, Vāyu and Sūrya! you combinedly purify the atmosphere. The scholars approach you for the fulfilment of their desires. Let these Agni, Vāyu and Sūrya remove the bad ideas from this lady's mind. This oblation is meant for Agni, Vāyu and Sūrya and not for me.

ओं अग्ने प्रायश्चित्ते त्वं देवानां प्रायश्चित्तिरसि ब्राह्मणस्त्वा नाथकाम उपधावामि यास्याः पतिघ्नी तनूस्तामस्या अपजहि स्वाहा ॥ इदमग्नये-इदन्न मम ॥

पार गृसू० 1.11.1

Oṁ agne prāyaśchitte tvaṁ devānāṁ prāyaśchittirasi brāhmaṇastvā nāthakāma upadhāvāmi yāsyāḥ patighnī tanūstāmasyā apajahi svāhā. idamagnaye-idanna mama.

Pār. Gṛ. Sū. 1.11.1

[Meaning] O Agni, the best natural purifier, you are the purifier of the atmosphere. In my Brahmāchārya life, I approached (used) you to fulfil my desires. Let this Agni remove the bad ideas about her husband from this lady. The oblation is meant for Agni and not for me.

ओं वायो प्रायश्चित्ते त्वं देवानां प्रायश्चित्तिरसि ब्राह्मणस्त्वा नाथकाम उपधावामि यास्याः पतिघ्नी तनूस्तामस्या अपजहि स्वाहा ॥ इदं वायवे-इदन्न मम ॥

पार गृसू० 1.11.2

Oṁ vāyo prāyaśchitte tvaṁ devānāṁ prāyaśchittirasi

brāhmaṇastvā nāthakāma upadhāvāmi yāsyāḥ patighnī tanūstāmasyā apajahi svāhā. idaṁ vāyave-idanna mama.

Pār. Gṛ. Sū. 1.11.2

[Meaning] O Vāyu, the best natural purifier, you are the purifier of the atmosphere. In my Brahmāchārya life, I approached (used) you to fulfil my desires. Let this Vāyu remove the bad ideas about her husband from this lady. The oblation is meant for Vāyu and not for me.

ओं चन्द्र प्रायश्चित्ते त्वं देवानां प्रायश्चित्तिरसि ब्राह्मणस्त्वा नाथकाम उपधावामि यास्याः पतिघ्नी तनूस्तामस्या अपजहि स्वाहा ॥ इदं चन्द्राय-इदन्न मम ॥

मन्त्रब्राह्मण 1.4.1

Oṁ chandra prāyaśchitte tvaṁ devānāṁ prāyaśchittirasi brāhmaṇastvā nāthakāma upadhāvāmi yāsyāḥ patighnī tanūstāmasyā apajahi svāhā. idaṁ chandrāya-idanna mama.

Mantra Br. 1.4.1

[Meaning] O Chandra, the best natural pacifier, bring peace and calmness to the atmosphere. In my Brahmāchārya life, I approached (used) your beams to fulfil my desires. Let Chandra help control the bad ideas about her husband from this lady. The oblation is meant for Chandra and not for me.

ओं सूर्य प्रायश्चित्ते त्वं देवानां प्रायश्चित्तिरसि ब्राह्मणस्त्वा नाथकाम उपधावामि यास्याः पतिघ्नी तनूस्तामस्या अपजहि स्वाहा ॥ इद्र सूर्य्याय-इदन्न मम ॥

मन्त्रब्राह्मण 1.4.2

Oṁ sūrya prāyaśchitte tvaṁ devānāṁ prāyaśchittirasi brāhmaṇastvā nāthakāma upadhāvāmi yāsyāḥ patighnī tanūstāmasyā apajahi svāhā. idra sūryyāya-idanna mama.

Mantra Br. 1.4.2

[Meaning] O Sūrya, the best natural purifier, you are the purifier of the atmosphere. In my Brahmacharya life, I approached (used) you to fulfil my desires. Let this Sūrya burn the bad ideas about her husband from this lady. The oblation is meant for Sūrya and not for me.

ओं अग्निवायुचन्द्रसूर्य्याः पांयश्चित्तयो यूयं देवानां प्रायश्चित्तयः स्थ ब्राह्मणो वो नाथकाम उपधावामि यास्याः पतिघ्नी तनूस्तामस्या अपहत स्वाहा ॥ इदमग्निवायुचन्द्रसूर्येभ्यः:-इदन्न मम ॥ मन्त्रब्राह्मण 1.4.3

Oṁ agnivāyuchandrasūryyāḥ pāṁyaśchittayo yūyaṁ devānāṁ prayaśchittayaḥ stha brāhmaṇo vo nāthakāma upadhāvāmi yāsyāḥ patighnī tanūstāmasyā apahata svāhā. idamagnivāyuchandrasūryebhyaḥ-idanna mama.

Mantra Br. 1.4.3

[Meaning] O Agni, Vāyu, Chandra and Sūrya, the best natural purifier, you are the purifier of the atmosphere. In my Brahmacharya life, I approached (used) you to fulfil my desires. Let these Agni, Vāyu, Chandra and Sūrya remove the bad ideas about her husband from this lady. The oblation is meant for Agni, Vāyu, Chandra and Sūrya and not for me.

ओं अग्ने प्रायश्चित्ते त्वं देवानां प्रायश्चित्तिरसि ब्राह्मणस्त्वा नाथकाम उपधावामि यास्या अपुत्र्या तनूस्तामस्या अपजहि स्वाहा ॥ इदमग्नये-इदन्न मम ॥

मन्त्रब्राह्मण 1.4.4

Oṁ agne prāyaśchitte tvaṁ devānāṁ prāyaśchittirasi brāhmaṇastvā nāthakāma upadhāvāmi yāsyā aputrayā tanūstāmasyā apajahi svāhā. idamagnaye-idanna mama.

Mantra Br. 1.4.4

[Meaning] O Agni, the best natural purifier, you are the purifier of the atmosphere. In my BrahmAchārya life, I approached (used) you to fulfil my desires. Let this Agni remove the imperfections from this lady. The oblation is meant for Agni and not for me.

ओं वायो प्रायश्चित्ते त्वं देवानां प्रायश्चित्तिरसि ब्राह्मणस्त्वा नाथकाम उपधावामि यास्या अपुत्र्या तनूस्तामस्या अपजहि स्वाहा ॥ इदं वायवे-इदन्न मम ॥

मन्त्रब्राह्मण 1.4.5

Oṁ vāyo prāyaśchite tvaṁ devānāṁ prāyaśchittirasi brāhmaṇastvā nāthakāma upadhāvāmi yāsyā aputrayā tanūstāmasyā apajahi svāhā. idaṁ vāyave-idanna mama.

Mantra Br. 1.4.5

[Meaning] O Vāyu, the best natural purifier, you are the cleaner of the atmosphere. In my Brahmacharya life, I approached (used) you to fulfil my desires. Let this Vāyu remove the imperfections from this lady. The oblation is meant for Vāyu and not for me.

ओं चन्द्र प्रायश्चित्ते त्वं देवानां प्रायश्चित्तिरसि ब्राह्मणस्त्वा नाथकाम उपधावामि यास्या अपुत्र्या तनूस्तामस्या अपजहि स्वाहा ॥ इदं चन्द्राय-इदन्न मम ॥

Om chandra prāyaśchite tvam devānām prāyaśchittirasi brāhmaṇastvā nāthakāma upadhāvāmi yāsyā aputrayā tanūstāmasyā apajahi svāhā. idam chandrāya-idanna mama.

[Meaning] O Chandra, the best natural pacifier, bring peace and calmness to the atmosphere. In my Brahmacharya life, I approached (used) you to fulfil my desires. Let this Chandra remove the imperfections from this lady. The oblation is meant for Chandra and not for me.

ओं सूर्य प्रायश्चित्ते त्वं देवानां प्रायश्चित्तिरसि ब्राह्मणस्त्वा नाथकाम उपधावामि यास्या अपुत्र्या तनूस्तामस्या अपजहि स्वाहा ॥ इदं सूर्याय-इदन्न मम ॥

Om sūrya prāyaśchitte tvam devānām prāyaśchittirasi brāhmaṇastvā nāthakāma upadhāvāmi yāsyā aputrayā tanūstāmasyā apajahi svāhā. idam sūryāya-idanna mama.

[Meaning] O Sūrya, the best natural purifier, you are the purifier of the atmosphere. In my Brahmacharya life, I approached (used) you to fulfil my desires. Let this Sūrya remove the imperfections from this lady. The oblation is meant for Sūrya and not for me.

ओं अग्निवायुचन्द्रसूर्याः प्रायश्चित्तयो यूयं देवानां प्रायश्चित्तयः स्थ ब्राह्मणो वो नाथकाम उपधावामि यास्या अपुत्र्या तनूस्तामस्या अपहत स्वाहा ॥ इदमग्निवायुचन्द्रसूर्येभ्यः-इदन्न मम ॥

Om agnivāyuchandrasūryāḥ prāyaśchittayo yūyam devānām prāyaśchittayaḥ stha brāhmaṇo vo nāthakāma

upadhāvāmi yāsyā aputrayā tanūstāmasyā apahata svāhā.
idamagnivāyuchandrasūryebhyaḥ-idanna mama.

[Meaning] O Agni, Vāyu, Chandra and Sūrya, the best natural purifier, you are the purifier of the atmosphere. In my Brahmacharya life, I approached (used) you to fulfil my desires. Let these Agni, Vāyu, Chandra and Sūrya remove the imperfections from this lady. The oblation is meant for Agni, Vāyu, Chandra and Sūrya and not for me.

ओं अग्रे प्रायश्चित्ते त्वं देवानां प्रायश्चित्तिरसि ब्राह्मणस्त्वा नाथकाम उपधावामि यास्याः अपसव्या तनूस्तामस्या अपजहि स्वाहा ॥ इदमग्रये-इदन्न मम ॥

Oṁ agne prāyaśchitte tvaṁ devānāṁ prāyaśchittirasi brāhmaṇastvā nāthakāma upadhāvāmi yāsyāḥ apasavyā tanūstāmasyā apajahi svāhā. idamagnaye-idanna mama.

[Meaning] O Agni, the best natural purifier, you are the purifier of the atmosphere. In my Brahmacharya life, I approached (used) you to fulfil my desires. Let this Agni remove the deficiencies from this lady's body. The oblation is meant for Agni and not for me.

ओं वायो प्रायश्चित्ते त्वं देवानां प्रायश्चित्तिरसि ब्राह्मणस्त्वा नाथकाम उपधावामि यास्या अपसव्या तनूस्तामस्या अपजहि स्वाहा ॥ इदं वायवे-इदन्न मम ॥

Oṁ vāyo prāyaśchitte tvaṁ devānāṁ prāyaśchittirasi brāhmaṇastvā nāthakāma upadhāvāmi yāsyā apasavyā tanūstāmasyā apajahi svāhā. idaṁ vāyave-idanna mama.

[Meaning] O Vāyu, the best natural purifier, you are the purifier of the atmosphere. In my Brahmāchārya life, I approached (used) you to fulfil my desires. Let this Vāyu remove the deficiencies from the body of this lady. The oblation is meant for Vāyu and not for me.

ओं चन्द्र प्रायश्चित्ते त्वं देवानां प्रायश्चित्तिरसि ब्राह्मणस्त्वा नाथकाम उपधावामि यास्या अपसव्या तनस्तामस्या अपजहि स्वाहा ॥ इदं चन्द्राय-इदन्न मम ॥

Oṁ chandra prayaśchitte tvaṁ devānāṁ prayaśchittirasi brāhmaṇastvā nāthakāma upadhāvāmi yāsyā apasavyā tanastāmasyā apajahi svāhā. idaṁ chandrāya-idanna mama.

[Meaning] O Chandra, the best natural purifier, you are the purifier of the atmosphere. In my Brahmacharya life, I approached (used) you to fulfil my desires. Let this Chandra remove the deficiencies from the body of this lady. The oblation is meant for Chandra and not for me.

ओं सूर्यं प्रायश्चिते लं देवानां प्रायश्चित्तिरसि ब्राह्मणस्त्वा नाथकाम उपधावामि यास्या अपसव्या तनूस्तामस्या अपजहि स्वाहा ॥ इदं सूर्याय-इदन्न मम ॥

Oṁ sūryaṁ prāyaśchite tvaṁ devānāṁ prāyaśchittirasi brāhmaṇastvā nāthakāma upadhāvāmi yāsyā apasavyā tanūstāmasyā apajahi svāhā. idaṁ sūryāya-idanna mama.

[Meaning] O Sūrya, the best natural purifier, you are the purifier of the atmosphere. In my Brahmāchārya life, I approached (used) you to fulfil my desires. Let this Sūrya remove the deficiencies from the body of this lady. The oblation is meant for Sūrya and not for me.

ओं अग्निवायुचन्द्रसूर्याः प्रायश्चित्तयो यूयं देवानां प्रायश्चित्तयः स्थ ब्राह्मणो वो नाथकाम उपधावामि यास्या अपसव्या तनूस्तामस्या अपहत स्वाहा ॥ इदमग्निवायुचन्द्रसूर्येभ्यः-इदन्न मम ॥

Oṁ agnivāyuchandrasūryāḥ prāyaśchittayo yūyaṁ devānāṁ prāyaśchittayaḥ stha brāhmaṇo vo nāthakāma upadhāvāmi yāsyā apasavyā tanūstāmasyā apahata svāhā. idamagnivāyuchandrasūryebhyaḥ-idanna mama.

[Meaning] O Agni, Vāyu, Chandra and Sūrya, the best natural purifier, you are the purifier of the atmosphere. In my Brahmacharya life, I approached (used) you to fulfil my desires. Let these Agni, Vāyu, Chandra and Sūrya remove the deficiencies from this lady's body. The oblation is meant for Agni, Vāyu, Chandra and Sūrya and not for me.

The twenty oblations should be offered with each of the above-cited twenty mantras. The leftover ghee should be kept safe and covered in a pot of bronze.

Note: While offering these Āhutis, the wife should touch the right shoulder of her husband with her right hand.

After that, this procedure should be followed to offer the oblations of the cooked rice. The cooked rice should be kept in one pot of silver or bronze for some time after mixing ghee, milk and sugar. When they combine perfectly, offer an oblation of this mixture with each of the mantras cited below, and the leftover oblation in the spoon should be dropped into the bronze pot containing water.

ओं अग्नये पवमानाय स्वाहा ॥ इदमग्नये पवमानाय इदन्न मम ॥

Oṁ agnaye pavamānāya svāhā. idamagnaye pavamānāya idanna mama.

[Meaning] I offer oblation to Agni, the purifier, This oblation is meant for Agni, the purifier and not for me.

ओं अग्नये पावकाय स्वाहा ॥ इदमग्नये पावकाय इदन्न मम ॥

Oṁ agnaye pāvakāya svāhā. idamagnaye pāvakāya idanna mama.

[Meaning] I offer oblation to Agni, the disinfectant agent. This oblation is meant for Agni, the disinfectant and not for me.

ओं अग्नये शुचये स्वाहा ॥ इदमग्नये शुचये-इदन्न मम ॥

Oṁ agnaye śuchaye svāhā. idamagnaye śuchaye-idanna mama.

[Meaning] I offer oblation to the bright and clean Agni. This oblation is meant for bright and clean Agni and not for me.

ओं अदित्यै स्वाहा ॥ इदमदित्यै-इदन्न मम ॥ पार.गृ.सू. 1.2.7

Oṁ adityai svāhā. idamadityai-idanna mama.

Pār.Gṛ.Sū. 1.2.7

[Meaning] I offer oblation to the Aditi, the indivisible energy. This oblation is meant for Aditi and not for me.

ओं प्रजापतये स्वाहा ॥ इदं प्रजापतये-इदन्न मम ॥ पार.गृ.सू. 1.11.3

Oṁ prajāpataye svāhā. idaṁ prajāpataye-idanna mama.

Pār.Gṛ.Sū. 1.11.3

[Meaning] I offer oblation to the Prajāpati, Hiraṇyagarbha (solar nebula). This oblation is meant for Prajāpati and not for me.

ओं यदस्य कर्मणोऽत्यरीरिचं यद्वा न्यूनमिहाकरम्। अग्निष्टत्स्विष्टकृद्विद्यात्सर्व स्विष्टं सुहुतं करोतु मे। अग्नये स्विष्टकृते सुहुतहुते सर्वप्रायश्चित्ताहुतीनां कामानां समर्धयित्रे सर्वान्नः कामान्त्समर्धय स्वाहा ॥ इदमग्नये स्विष्टकृते-इदन्न मम ॥

आश्व.गृ.सू. 1.10.22

Oṁ yadasya karmaṇo'tyarīrichaṁ yadvā nyūnamihākaram, agniṣṭatsviṣṭakṛdvidyātsarvaṁ sviṣṭaṁ suhutaṁ karotu me, agnaye sviṣṭakṛte suhutahute sarvaprāyaśchittāhutīnāṁ kāmānāṁ samardhayitre sarvānnaḥ kāmāntsamardhaya svāhā. idamagnaye sviṣṭakṛte-idanna mama. Āśv.Gṛ.Sū. 1.10.22

[Meaning] Whatever in my performance of yajña, I have done extra or less than required, may the God, who fulfils all desires, who knows all our good desires, make up the difference of the oblations offered. This oblation is offered to God, who fulfils all good desires, makes all offerings a success, and salvages offerings given in repentance towards fulfilling one's wishes. May God fulfil all my desires. This offering is intended for God, the fulfiller of all auspicious desires and not for me.

With these six mantras cited above, the oblations of cooked rice should be offered. Afterwards, eight oblations should be offered with the eight mantras of

Eight Ājya Āhutis written in the Samānya Prakaraṇa (Common Procedure). In addition to the eight oblations with those eight mantras, one Ājya Āhuti (oblation) each be offered with the following mantras:

विष्णुर्योनिं कल्पयतु त्वष्टा रूपाणि पिंशतु।
आ सिंचतु प्रजापतिर्धाता गर्भं दधातु ते स्वाहा ॥

ऋ. 10.184.1; गोभि गृसू॰ 2.5.9

viṣṇuryoniṁ kalpayatu tvaṣṭā rūpāṇi piṁśatu,
ā siṁchatu prajāpatirdhātā garbhaṁ dadhātu te svāhā ||1 ||

RV. 10.184.1; Go. Gṛ. Sū. 2.5.9

[Meaning] O lady! let Viṣṇu make your uterus healthy suitable for conception; let Tvaṣṭā help in formation of healthy embryo; let Prajāpati give life and envigoration to it; let Dhātā perserve the embryo.

गर्भं धेहि सिनीवालि गर्भं धेहि सरस्वति।
गर्भं ते अश्विनौ देवावा धत्तां पुष्करस्रजा स्वाहा ॥

ऋ. 10.184.2; गोभि गृसू॰ 2.5.10

garbhaṁ dhehi sinīvāli garbhaṁ dhehi sarasvati,
garbhaṁ te aśvinau devāvā dhattāṁ puṣkarasrajā svāhā.

RV. 10.184.2; Go. Gṛ. Sū 2.5.10

[Meaning] O Moon like beautiful lady! Let you be conceived. O learned wife! Let you be pregnant and let Aśvinau, the Prāṇa and apāna, which are present in space preserve and protect your embryo.

हिरण्ययीं अरणी यं निर्मन्थतो अश्विना।
तं ते गर्भं हवामहे दशमे मासि सूतवे स्वाहा ॥ ऋ॰ 10.184.3

hiraṇyayīṁ araṇī yaṁ nirmanthato aśvinā,
taṁ te garbhaṁ havāmahe daśame māsi sūtave svāhā.

RV. 10.184.3

[Meaning] We desire the child in your womb which is strengthened by Aśvinau, the Prāṇa and Apāna, that is pure like gold and pervading the body. We invoke the foetus coming from the womb in the tenth lunar sidereal month.

Note: Lunar sidereal month has 27 days. The Veda considers the sidereal month. Infact human menstrual cycle phisiology is influenced by the moon. The 10th lunar sidereal month is equal to 270 days which is equal to nine solar months.

रेतो मूत्रं वि जहाति योनिं प्रविशदिन्द्रियम् ।
गर्भो जरायुणावृत उल्बं जहाति जन्मना ।
ऋतेन सत्यमिन्द्रियं विपानꣳ शुक्रमन्धस
इन्द्रस्येन्द्रियमिदं पयोऽमृतं मधु स्वाहा ॥ यजु॰ 19.76

reto mūtram̐ vi jahāti yonim̐ praviśadindriyam,

garbho jarāyuṇāvṛta ulbam̐ jahāti janmanā,

ṛtena satyamindriyam̐ vipānam̐ śukramandhasa

indrasyendriyamidam̐ payo'mṛtam̐ madhu svāhā.

YV. 19.76

[Meaning] The male organ entering into the organ of female releases semen in preference of urine. The semen develops in the form of embryo in uterus and leaves the membrane surrounding at birth. The embryo gains strength through the breathings of mother and her diet and drinks composed of milk and honey.

यत्ते सुसीमे हृदयं दिवि चन्द्रमसि श्रितम् । वेदाहं तन्मां तद्विद्यात् पश्येम शरदः शतं जीवेम शरदः शतꣳ श्रृणुयाम शरदः शतं प्र ब्रवाम शरदः शतमदीनाः स्याम शरदः शतं भूयश्च शरदः शतात् स्वाहा ॥ पारस्कर गृसू. 1.11.9

yatte susīme hṛdayam̐ divi chandramasi śritam, vedāham̐ tanmām̐ tadvidyāt paśyema śaradaḥ śatam̐ jīvema śaradaḥ śatam̐ śṛṇuyāma śaradaḥ śatam̐ pra bravāma śaradaḥ śatamadīnāḥ syāma śaradaḥ śatam̐ bhūyaścha śaradaḥ śatāt svāhā. Pār.Gṛ. Sū. 1.11.9

[Meaning] O well-dressed wife! I know your mind is influenced by the moon located in the sky. Let you know my mind also. (Let there be mutual understanding between us). May we both vision in our eyes for a hundred autumns (years); may we both live for a hundred autumns; may we both hear for a hundred autumns; may we both have the power of speech for a hundred autumns; may we both enjoy freedom for hundred autumns; and if we attain a life longer than this, may all these privileges be granted further.

यथेयं पृथिवी मही भूतानां गर्भंमादधे।
एवा ते ध्रियतां गर्भो अनु सूतुं सवितवे स्वाहा॥

yatheyaṁ pṛthivī mahī bhūtānāṁ garbhaṁmādadhe;
ēvā te dhriyatāṁ garbho anu sūtuṁ savitave svāhā.

[Meaning] O wife, as this mighty earth bears the germ of creatures in her womb, so may your womb bear a progeny to deliver it in appropriate time.

यथेयं पृथिवी मही दाधारेमान् वनस्पतीन्।
एवा ते ध्रियतां गर्भो अनु सूतुं सवितवे स्वाहा॥

yatheyaṁ pṛthivī mahī dādhāremān vanaspatīn;
ēvā te dhriyatāṁ garbho anu sūtuṁ savitave svāhā.

[Meaning] As this mighty earth bears vegetations and trees, so may your womb bear a progeny to deliver it in appropriate time.

यथेयं पृथिवी मही दाधार पर्वतान् गिरीन्।
एवा ते ध्रियतां गर्भो अनु सूतुं सवितवे स्वाहा॥

yatheyaṁ pṛthivī mahī dādhāra parvatān girīn,
ēvā te dhriyatāṁ garbho anu sūtuṁ savitave svāhā.

[Meaning] As this mighty earth bears mountains and hills, so may your womb bear a progeny to deliver it in appropriate time

यथेयं पृथिवी मही दाधार विष्ठितं जगत्।
एवा ते ध्रियतां गर्भो अनु सूतुं सवितवे स्वाहा॥ अथर्व० 6.17.14

yatheyaṁ pṛthivī mahī dādhāra viṣṭhitaṁ jagat,

ēvā te dhriyatāṁ garbho anu sūtuṁ savitave svāhā.

AV. 6.17.14

[Meaning] As this mighty earth supports the moving world, so may your womb bear a progeny to deliver it in the appropriate time

After offering nine oblations of the *ghee* and *Mohanabhoga* with the above-cited mantras, the four oblations of *ghee* should be offered with the following mantras:

ओं भूरग्नये स्वाहा ॥ इदमग्नये इदन्न मम ॥

Oṁ bhūragnaye svāhā. idamagnaye-idanna mama.

[Meaning] This oblation is offered to strengthen the earth's geothermal energy. This offering is intended for geothermal energy and not for me.

ओं भुवर्वायवे स्वाहा ॥ इदं वायवे इदन्न मम ॥

Oṁ bhuvarvāyave svāhā. idaṁ vāyave-idanna mama.

[Meaning] This oblation is offered to strengthen the earth's magnetosphere. This offering is intended for the magnetosphere and not for me.

ओं स्वरादित्याय स्वाहा ॥ इदमादित्याय इदन्न मम ॥

Oṁ svarādityāya svāhā. idamādityāya-idanna mama.

[Meaning] This oblation is offered to strengthen the energy of the sun. This offering is intended for the energy of the sun and not for me.

ओम् अग्निवाय्वादित्येभ्यः प्राणपानव्यानेभ्यः स्वाहा ॥
इदमग्निवाय्वादित्येभ्यः प्राणापानव्यानेभ्यः इदन्न मम ॥ गोभि० गृसू 1.8.15

Om agnivāyvādityebhyaḥ prāṇapānavyānebhyaḥ svāhā;
idamagnivāyvādityebhyaḥ prāṇāpānavyānebhyaḥ-idanna
mama. Go.Gṛ.Sū 1.8.15

[Meaning] I offer this oblation to enhance the power

of energies of earth, magnetosphere and the sun called as prāṇa, apāna and vyāna respectively. This offering is intended for energies energies of earth, magnetosphere and the sun called as prāṇa, apāna and vyāna respectively and not for me.

ओम् अयास्यग्रेर्वषट्कृतं यत्कर्मणोऽत्यरीरिचं देवा गातुविदः स्वाहा ॥ इदं देवेभ्यो गातुविद्भ्यः इदन्न मम ॥ पार.गृ.सू. 1.2.11

Om ayāsyagnervaṣaṭkṛtaṁ yatkarmaṇo'tyarīricaṁ devā gātuvidaḥ svāhā. idaṁ devebhyo gātuvidbhyaḥ idanna mama.

Pār.Gṛ.Sū. 1.2.11

[Meaning] O expert of yajña! Let the Havana perform in the fire; whatever has been overperformed, let it be permanent.

ओं प्रजापत्तये स्वाहा । इदं प्रजापतये-इदन्न मम ॥ पार.गृ.सू. 1.11.3

Oṁ prajāpattaye svāhā, idra prajāpataye-idanna mama.

Pār.Gṛ.Sū. 1.11.3

[Meaning] This oblation is offered to Prajapati Parameśvara. This offering is intended for Prajapati Parameśvara and not for me.

After this performance one sviṣṭakṛt oblation of ghee be offered with the mantra यदस्य कर्मणोऽत्यरीरिचं.. *yadasya karmaṇo'tyarīricaṁ..*

The wife should take the ghee left over from oblations and gather it in the waterpot made of bronze. She should go to the bathroom and rub it on her body from the foot to head and take a bath. She should wipe her body with a clean towel and wear neat and clean outfits. After that, she should come to the Yajña-kuṇḍa. The wife and husband both should circumambulate the kuṇḍa and have a glimpse of the sun. Looking at the sun, they should recite the following mantras and meditate on God.

ओं आदित्यं गर्भं पयसा समङ्धि सहस्रस्य प्रतिमां विश्वरूपम् । परिवृङ्धि हरसा

माभि मꣳस्थाः शतायुषं कृणुहि चीयमानः ॥ यजु॰ 13.41

Oṁ ādityaṁ garbhaṁ payasā samaṅgdhi sahasrasya pratimāṁ viśvarūpam, parivṛṅdhi harasā mābhi maꣳsthāḥ śatāyuṣaṁ kṛṇuhi chīyamānaḥ. YV. 13.41

[Meaning] O Almighty power! Energize the embryo in the womb with the milk and juices of the fruits and herbs eaten by the mother. The child in the womb is the model of the universe. Please remove the obstacles in its way by your power and save it from infliction. Make the daily growing embryo live a life of hundred years.

सूर्यो नो दिवस्पातु वातो अन्तरिक्षात् ।
अग्निर्नः पार्थिवेभ्यः ॥ ऋ॰ 10.158.1

*sūryo no divaspātu vāto antarikṣāt;
agnirnaḥ pārthivebhyaḥ. RV. 10.158.1*

[Meaning] O God! By your grace, may the solar radiation protect us from the celestial sphere; may the earth's magnetosphere save us from the midsphere and may the geothermal energy save us from the earth.

जोषा सवितर्यस्य ते हरः शतं सवाँ अर्हति ।
पाहि नो दिद्युत पतन्त्याः ॥ ऋ॰ 10.158.2

*joṣā savitaryasya te haraḥ śataṁ savāṁ arhati;
pāhi no didyuta patantyāḥ. RV 10.158.2*

[Meaning] O All-creating God! Be kind to us. May your energy, which creates and sustains this universe for 100 Brāhma years (311 Trillion years), protect us. Save us from the adverse effect of the thunderbolt of Indra (lightning) falling from the clouds.

चक्षुर्नो देवः सविता चक्षुर्न उत पर्वतः ।
चक्षुर्धाता दधातु न ॥ ऋ॰ 10.158.3

*chakṣurno devaḥ savitā chakṣurna uta parvataḥ;
chakṣurdhātā dadhātu na. RV. 10.158.3*

[Meaning] Let the sun located in celestial sphere be our eyes and let the cloud be eye-opener to us and let the life sustaining forces provide us the vision of life.

चक्षुर्नो धेहि चक्षुषे चक्षुर्विख्यै तनूभ्यः ।
सं चेदं वि च पश्येम ॥ ऋ० 10.158.4

chakṣurno dhehi chakṣuṣe chakṣurvikhyai tanūbhyaḥ;
saṁ chedaṁ vi cha paśyema. RV.10.158.4

[Meaning] O God! Please grant us a vision to see things in their true nature and grant our children an eye of knowledge so that we may identify the reality of self and the outside world.

सुसंदृशं त्वा वयं प्रति पश्येम सूर्य ।
वि पश्येम नृचक्षसः ॥ ऋ० 10.158.5

susaṁdṛśaṁ tvā vayaṁ prati paśyema sūrya;
vi paśyema nṛchakṣasaḥ. RV 10.158.5

[Meaning] O All-inspiring God! May we, who are busy seeing the objects of the outside world, see you inside our souls. By your grace, we may see all things worthy to be seen by a human being.

Meditating God with above cited mantras the wife should recite:

ओं अमुक गोत्रा शुभदा, अमुक नाम्नी अहं भो भवन्तमभिवादयामि ॥

गोभिलगृ.सू. 2.4.11

Oṁ amuka gotrā śubhadā, amuka nāmnī ahaṁ bho bhavantamabhivādayāmi. Go.Gṛ.Sū. 2.4.11

She should say namaste to her husband. Afterwards, she should offer her best compliments to her father-in-law, grandfather-in-law etc. and respectable men. She should also pay respect to her mother-in-law and elderly women of other family members present there.

Thus, after having tied in the nuptial knot, the

husband and wife should sit on a nice seat in the west of the Vedī, keeping their faces eastward and should recite the Vāmadevyagāna.

After that, both should take their prescribed meals and see the priests and other guests off after entertaining them with food.

Afterwards, at a fixed time in the night when the body of both (the wife and husband) is in sound health, they feel exceedingly happy and find themselves in a state of exuberant love; they should conduct sexual intercourse. The time of impregnation may be fixed at any time between the period after three hours of commencement of night and three hours before the end of night. The wife and husband ought to keep their bodies stable, their face delighted, their mouths facing each other, and their noses and whole bodies straight. The husband should deposit sperm in the reproductive organs of the wife. The wife realizing that the sperm has been deposited in her organ, should contract the bottom of her rectum, uterus and vagina upward and force the sperm towards her uterus (womb).

After some break, they should take a bath. In the winter season, they should first take milk heated with Keśar (Musk), Kasturī (Nutmeg), Jāyaphala (Mace), Jāvitrī and Feronia Elephantum (Elaichi) and sleep separately. Suppose the couple is assured that the conception has taken place. In that case, they should give oblations in the yajña on the second day of conception. If they are not assured of pregnancy, then after a month at the time of mensuration, they will get the confirmation of pregnancy when the menstrual cycle is missed.

In both cases on the second day of conception or second day of the beginning of the second month, wife and husband should offer the oblations in the yajña with following mantras.

यथा वातः पुष्करिणी समिङ्गयति सर्वतः ।
एवा ते गर्भ एजतु निरैतु दशमास्यः स्वाहा ॥ ऋ.5.78.7

yathā vātaḥ puṣkariṇī samiṅgayati sarvataḥ,
ēvā te garbhaṁ ējatu niraitu daśamāsyaḥ svāhā. RV.5.78.7

[Meaning] O bride! As the wind moves water in waterbodies, so move your embryo and come out from the womb after 10 sidereal months.

यथा वातो यथा वनं यथा समुद्र एजति ।
एवा त्वं दशमास्य सहावेहि जरायुणा स्वाहा ॥ ऋ.5.78.8

yathā vāto yathā vanaṁ yathā samudra ējati,
ēvā tvaṁ daśamāsya sahāvehi jarāyuṇā svāhā. RV.5.78.8

[Meaning] O ten month old soul in the womb! As the wind freely moves, as the forest freely flourishes, and as the ocean moves without obstruction, so you take birth out of the womb with membrane surrounding you.

दश मासांछशयानः कुमारो अधि मातरि ।
निरैतु जीवो अज्ञतो जीवो जीवन्त्या अधि स्वाहा ॥ ऋ० 5.78.9

daśa māsāṁchhaśayānaḥ kumāro adhi mātari,
niraitu jīvo ajñato jīvo jīvantyā adhi svāhā. RV 5.78.9

O Lord of Universe! May the embodied soul, to be called Kumar, sleeping in the womb of the mother for ten sidereal months come out of the womb of the mother without any defects and problems.

एजतु दशमास्यो गर्भो जरायुणा सह ।
यथायं वायुरेजति यथा समुद्र एजति ।
एवायं दशमास्यो अस्रज्जरायुणा सह स्वाहा ॥ यजु० 8.28

ējatu daśamāsyo garbho jarāyuṇā saha;
yathāyaṁ vāyurejati yathā samudra ējati;
ēvāyaṁ daśamāsyo asrajjarāyuṇā saha svāhā. YV. 8.28.

[Meaning] May the embryo of ten months move and grow with his membrane. As the wind moves without any obstructions and the ocean remains undisturbed, so this ten months old embryo take birth without obstructions and any disturbance.

यस्यै ते यज्ञियो गर्भो यस्यै योनिर्हिरण्ययी।
अङ्गान्यहुता यस्य तं मात्रा समजीगमꣳ स्वाहा ॥ यजु॰ 8.29

yasyai te yajñiyo garbho yasyai yonirhiraṇyayī,
aṅgānyahnutā yasya taṁ mātrā samajīgamaꣳ svāhā.

YV. 8. 29

[Meaning] O fortunate lady! The embryo that you have in your womb has the sanskāras of performing yajña, knowledge and moral act, your womb is also healthy. May I, the husband, receive that embryo whose limbs are free from all kinds of infirmities. I offer oblation with the above intention.

पुमाँसौ मित्रावरुणौ पुमाँसावश्विनावुभौ।
पुमानग्निश्च वायुश्च पुमान् गर्भस्तवोदरे स्वाहा ॥ सामवेद मन्त्रब्रा.1.4.7

pumāṁsau mitrāvaruṇau pumāṁsāvaśvināvubhau,
pumānagniścha vāyuścha pumān garbhastavodare svāhā.

Sām.Man. Br.1.4,7

[Meaning] The Mitra (prāṇa) and Varuṇa (apāna) give you the power to conceive a child; Aśvinau (right and left nostrils) give you the power to conceive a child. Agni dhātu (a constituent) of the body gives you the power to conceive a child; the air you inhale gives you the power to conceive a child; may the embryo in your womb be healthy. I offer oblation with the above intention.

पुमानग्निः पुमानिन्द्रः पुमान्देवा बृहस्पतिः।
पुमाँसं पुत्रं विन्दस्व तं पुमाननु जायतां स्वाहा ॥ सामवेद मन्त्रब्रा. 1.4,9

pumānagniḥ pumānindraḥ pumāndevā bṛhaspatiḥ,
pumāṁsaṁ putraṁ vindasva taṁ pumānanu jāyatāṁ svāhā.

Sām.Man. Br. 1.4,9

[Meaning] O Devī! Let the agni dhātu of your body be powerful; let your mind be strong enough to bear a child; let other senses and your intellect be healthy; may you beget a healthy child and the child succeeding this child also be healthy. I offer oblation so that the above wish may come true.

Having offered the oblations with the above-cited mantras and also the oblations with mantras prescribed in the Common Procedure (Sāmānya Prakaraṇa) for peace and tranquillity, they should complete the process of Purṇāhutī as prescribed in the Common Procedure (Sāmānya Prakaraṇa).

A proper dietary regimen for a pregnant lady should be laid down. Any intoxicant purgatives like Terminalia Chubula (Haritki), dishes containing excessive salt, pungent or sour tastes, dry grain, chillies, etc., should always be avoided by her. Nevertheless, she should take ghee, milk, sweet, Somalata, i.e. Guḍuchī, etc. herbs; rice, sweet curd, wheat, urad dal (black gram), moong dal (green gram), jawar, etc. grains; and the energetic vegetables. In these dishes, she should mix the spices according to seasons. In the summer season, she should take Fronia Elephantum (Elāyachī), etc. and in the cold season, the saffron, musk, etc. She should always follow the dietary regimen prescribed for her. The woman in the time of pregnancy should mainly use dry ginger and Brāhmī in the milk. So that the child to be born is intelligent, healthy and endowed with good qualities, actions and temperament.

Here ends the procedure of Garbhādhāna Sanskāra.

पुंसवन संस्कार परिचय
Introduction to the Puṁsavana Sanskāra

According to modern medical science, the male has both X and Y chromosomes, but a female has only X chromosomes. Any of the two types of sperm of a male can fertilize the egg. If a Y-bearing sperm fertilizes the egg, the zygote has the 44 + XY composition, and the resulting embryo becomes a boy. When an X-bearing sperm fertilizes the egg, the resulting zygote has the 44 + XX composition. This embryo develops into a girl. All the children inherit one X chromosome from the mother.

However, the Vedic scientist knew that human sex is not genetically determined. The rate of metabolism and food quality may determine sex in humans, overriding the genetic basis. In the *Mahābhārata*, we have an example of Durvāsā, a visionary sage, who solved this puzzle during his experiments on Kuntī by suggesting her regimen to be followed by her during her pregnancy.

It may also be noted that environmental conditions such as temperature around the developing embryo may determine sex in some animals. Such conditions may override the genetic basis. Some animals, such as snails, can even change their sex, showing that their sex is not genetically determined.

Therefore, Vedic science says that couples can choose a particular baby, male or female. This Sanskāra is performed by those parents who desire a particular baby, e.g. male or female. This Sanskāra is performed when the first signs of conception are visible.

On the issue of begetting a male or female

baby, *Manusmṛti* (3.48) says:

युग्मासु पुत्रा जायन्ते स्त्रियोऽयुग्मासु रात्रिषु ।
तस्माद् युग्मासु पुत्रार्थी संविशेदार्तवे स्त्रियम् ॥

yugmāsu putrā jāyante striyo'yugmāsu rātriṣu;
tasmād yugmāsu putrārthī saṁviśedārtave striyam.

[Meaning] Male babies are generally conceived on even nights, from the 5th day of menstruation to the 16th day. Similarly, female babies are conceived on uneven nights; hence, a couple who desires to have sons should approach each other on the even (nights) after the 5th day of menstruation till the 16th day and not after that.

One more opinion has been expressed there itself (*Manusmṛti*, 3.49). Accordingly,

पुमान् पुंसोऽधिके शुक्रे स्त्री भवत्यधिके स्त्रियाः ।
समेऽपुमान् पुंस्त्रियौ वा क्षीणेऽल्पे च विपर्ययः ॥

pumān puṁso'dhike śukre strī bhavatyadhike striyāḥ;
same'pumān puṁstriyau vā kṣīṇe'lpe cha viparyayaḥ.

[Meaning] A male child is produced if the sperm count is healthier and sperm count is higher than the ovum (female egg cell). Similarly, a female child is produced if the ovum is healthier than the sperm and its count is higher than the sperm. If both are equal or equally healthy, a hermaphrodite (genderless) baby is produced. If (both are) weak or deficient in quantity, conception failure occurs.

The health or count of sperm or ovum depends on diet and other physical exercises. As such, a couple desiring a particular type of baby can prepare themselves accordingly and perform Puṁsvana Sanskāra. According to Yājñavalkya, the amount of cow ghee is essential in improving or reducing health. The greater the amount of ghee, the better the health. The smaller the amount, the slim and trim the human being.

क्षामता च तस्मिन् काले रजस्वला व्रतेन भवति। अथ चेन्न भवति तदा कर्त्तव्या क्षामता। पुत्रेत्पत्यर्थं अल्पस्निग्ध भोजनादिना।

kṣāmatā cha tasmin kāle rajasvalā vratena bhavati. atha chenna bhavati tadā karttavyā kṣāmatā. putretpatyarthaṁ alpasnigdha bhojanādinā.

[Meaning] Menstruation makes women slim and trim. If it does not, a woman can live on a diet with less fat.

So, Puṁsvana Sanskāra was performed to have a desired progeny. Also, by way of this Sanskāra, the pregnant lady is told about precautions so that she may give birth to a baby of her choice.

अथ पुंसवनम्

Puṁsvana Sanskāra

Here begins the Sanskāra of procreating a child.

The time of Punsvana Sanskāra should be fixed in the second or third month from the period when it is known that pregnancy has been assured. The sanskāra should be performed when one gets the benefit of manly vigour. Unless two months after the child's birth have elapsed, the husband should preserve his virility and observe celibacy. He should conduct the affairs of eating, clothing, sleeping and awaking not to waste his virility, which may help make other progeny of superior quality.

अत्र प्रमाणानि

atra pramāṇāni

Here are the scriptural authorities:

पुमाꣳसौ मित्रावरुणौ पुमाꣳसावश्विनावुभौ।

पुमानग्निश्च वायुश्च पुमान् गर्भस्तवोदरे ॥ सामवेद 1.4.8

pumāṁsau mitrāvaruṇau pumāṁsāvaśvināvubhau,
pumānagniścha vāyuścha pumān garbhastavodare. SV. 1.4.8

[Meaning] The Mitra (prāṇa) and Varuṇa (apāna) give your power to conceive a child; Aśvinau (right and left nostrils) give you the power to conceive a child. Agni dhātu (a constituent) of the body gives you the power to conceive a child; the air you inhale gives you the power to conceive a child; may the embryo in your womb be healthy. I offer oblation with the above intention.

पुमानग्निः पुमानिन्द्रः पुमान् देवी बृहस्पतिः ।
पुमाꣳसं पुत्रं विन्दस्व तं पुमाननु जायताम् ॥ सामवेद 1.4.9

pumānagniḥ pumānindraḥ pumān devī bṛhaspatiḥ,
pumāṁsam putraṁ vindasva taṁ pumānanu jāyatām.

SV. 1.4.9

[Meaning] O Devī! Let the agni dhātu of your body be powerful; let your mind be strong enough to bear a child; let other senses and your intellect be healthy; may you beget a healthy child and the child succeeding this child also be healthy. I offer oblation so that the above wish may come true.

शमीमश्वत्थ आरूढस्तत्र पुंसवनं कृतम् ।
तद्वै पुत्रस्य वेदनं तत्स्त्रीष्वा भरामसि ॥ अथर्व 6.11.1

śamīmaśvattha ārūḍhastatra puṁsavanaṁ kṛtam,
tadvai putrasya vedanaṁ tatstrīṣvā bharāmasi. AV. 6.11.1

[Meaning] When a horse like a strong husband should cohabit with a calm, tranquil wife, know that is named puṁsvana sanskāra. That act is for procreating a child. To procreate a child, we deposit sperm in women.

पुंसि वै रेतो भवति तत्स्त्रियामनु षिच्यते ।
तद्वै पुत्रस्य वेदनं तत्प्रजापतिरब्रवीत् ॥ अथर्व 6.11.2

puṁsi vai reto bhavati tatstriyāmanu ṣichyate;
tadvai putrasya vedanaṁ tatprajāpatirabravīt. AV. 6.11.2

[Meaning] Man possesses sperm; he discharges it in the woman's womb. It is a process of begetting a child. This act is called an act of prajāpati (procreating a child).

प्रजापतिरनुमतिः सिनीवाल्यचीक्लृपत् ।
स्रैषूयमन्यत्र दधत्पुमांसमु दधदिह ॥ अथर्व 6.11.3

prajāpatiranumatiḥ sinīvālyachīklṛpat,
sraiṣūyamanyatra dadhatpumāṁsamu dadhadiha. AV. 6.11.3

[Meaning] Father and compromising mother are competent to tend and foster the child in the womb. A female child is conceived in certain circumstances, but a male child is conceived under other conditions.

Here is the authority of the *Āśvalāyana Gṛhyasūtra* (1.13.5-6).

अथास्यै मण्डलागारच्छायायां दक्षिणस्या नासिकायामजीतामोषधीं नस्तः करोति ॥ आश्व.गृसू. 1.13.5

athāsyai   maṇḍalāgārachchhāyāyāṁ   dakṣiṇasyā
nāsikāyāmajītāmoṣadhīṁ nastaḥ karoti. Āśv.GS. 1.13.5

[Meaning] Afterwards, make the pregnant lady sit in circular shapped place under a shade and put the fresh herb in her nostrils.

प्रजावज्जीवपुत्राभ्यां हैके ॥ आश्व. 1.13.6

prajāvajjīvaputrābhyāṁ haike. Āśv. GS. 1.13.6

[Meaning] According to some Āchāryas, for want of a child, 'jīvaputra' named herbs is made to be smelled by the pregnant lady.

The husband, in the second or third month of pregnancy, makes his wife smell the hairy root and new leaves of the banyan tree through her right nostril, and other nourishing herbs like Coculus Cordicolius (Guḍichī) and Brāhmī should be given to her to eat. Similar is the authority of the *Pāraskara Gṛhyasūtra* (1.4.1.2).

अथ पुँसवनं पुरा स्पन्दत इति मासे द्वितीये तृतीये वा ॥ पारस्कर गृसू. 1.14.1

atha puṁsavanaṁ purā spandata iti māse dvitīye tṛtīye vā.

Pār.GS. 1.14.1

[Meaning] Before the foetus's movements are felt or before its heartbeat starts, in the second or third month, puṁsvana sanskāra should be performed.

There is evidence of the *Pāraskara Gṛhyasūtra*.

The Puṁsavana sanskāra is performed in the second and third months of pregnancy.

The same has been written in the *Gobhilīyā* and the *Śaunaka Gṛhya Sūtra*.

अथ पुंसवनविधिः
The Procedure of Puṁsvana Sanskāra

The priest and the host (Yajamāna) should do the procedure of 'Prayer', '*Svasti prakaraṇa*' and '*Śānti prakaraṇa*'. While praying with the Vedic mantras - *viśvāni deva.. etc.,* the host and the priest should pray to God, and the men there should meditate on God. They should afterwards recite the mantras of '*Svastivāchana*' and '*Śāntiprakaraṇa*' respectively. They should make all sorts of arrangements for the place of yajña, Yajñaśālā, Yajñakuṇḍa, YajñasaŚidhā, Yajñapātras and other utensils of Yajña. After that, perform the yajña with the mantras - *aym ta idhma.. and Om adite...etc.* They should give four oblations, four *āghārāvājyāhuti* oblations. four *vyāhṛti* oblations, two oblations with the mantras ओं

यदस्यकर्मणो० *(yadasyakarmaṇo..)* ओं प्रजापतये स्वाहा (*Oṁ prajāpataye svāhā*) । Thereafter they should offer the oblations of ghee with the following two mantras:

ओं आ ते गर्भो योनिमेतु पुमान् बाण इवेषुधिम् ।
आ वीरो जायतां पुत्रस्ते दशमास्यः स्वाहा ॥ आश्व० 1.13.6; अथर्व० 3.2.2

Oṁ ā te garbho yonimetu pumān bāṇa iveṣudhim |
ā vīro jāyatāṁ putraste daśamāsyaḥ svāhā ||

Āśv.GS. 1.13.6; AV. 3.2.2

[Meaning] O lady! May your vigorous embryo like arrow in its quiveer go to the womb and becoming ten-month-old may your strong child take birth smoothly and usually. Offer oblation for the fulfilment of the above wish.

ओं अग्निरैतु प्रथमो देवतानां सोऽस्यै प्रजां मुंचतु मृत्युपाशात् । तदयं राजा वरुणोऽनुमन्यतां यथेयं स्त्री पौत्रमघं न रोदात् स्वाहा ॥ आश्व० 1.13.6

Oṁ agniraitu prathamo devatānāṁ so'syai prajāṁ muṁchatu mṛtyupāsāt | tadayaṁ rājā varuṇo'numanyatāṁ yatheyaṁ strī pautramaghaṁ na rodāt svāhā. Āśv.GS. 1.13.6

[Meaning] Let God, the first among all the forces of creation, come to the protection of the womb and save the offspring of this lady from immature death. Let Varuṇa, the vital air, coordinate in this matter, and this lady may never wail for her child's grief. This oblation is offered for the fulfilment of the above wish.

After offering oblations with the above two mantras duly chanted, the husband should pronounce the following mantra, keeping his hand on his wife's heart in a lonely place.

ओ यत्ते सुसीमे हृदये हितवन्तः प्रजापतौ ।
मन्येऽहं मां तद्विद्वांसं माहं पौत्रमन्त्रियाम् ॥

O yatte susīme hṛdaye hitavantaḥ prajāpatau,

manye'ham mām tadvidvāmsam māham pautramanniyām.

[Meaning] O well-dressed lady! Whatever embryo is present in your child-protecting womb, I feel his presence. I pray to God that I should never be a bereaved father.

Afterwards, they should recite the Mahāvāmadevya-gāna, which has been given at the end of the chapter of Sāmānya Prakaraṇa (Common Procedure) and see off the men and women who came to attend this ceremony.

Then the husband should grind fresh leaves of banyan and Coculous Cordicolius (giloya). Sieving the same with a piece of cloth, and put it to the right nostril of the pregnant wife to inhale it. Thereafter the husband should chant these two mantras touching the womb of her wife:

हिरण्यगर्भः समवर्त्तताग्रे भूतस्य जातः पतिरेक आसीत्।
स दाधार पृथिवीं द्यामुतेमां कस्मै देवाय हविषा विधेम॥ यजु. 13.4

hiraṇyagarbhaḥ samavartatāgre bhūtasya jātaḥ patireka āsīt,
sa dādhāra pṛthivīm dyāmutemām kasmai devāya haviṣā
vidhema. YV. 13.4

[Meaning] Unto him, who, with energy in his womb, existed even before the origin of this visible universe; unto him, who was the single Master of all originated world; unto him who sustains this observer space and light space, do we offer worship, in love and through the practice of Yoga.

अद्भयः संभृतः पृथिव्यै रसाच्च विश्वकर्मणः समवर्त्तताग्रे।
तस्य त्वष्टा विदधद्रूपमेति तन्मर्त्यस्य देवत्वमाजानमग्रे॥ यजु. 31.17

adbhyaḥ sambhṛtaḥ pṛthivyai rasāchcha viśvakarmaṇaḥ
samavarttatāgre,
tasya tvaṣṭā vidadhadrūpameti tanmartyamsya
devatvamājānamagre. YV. 31.17

[Meaning] He existed prior to waters, the earth, the saps and the sun in His fullness. The Supreme Architect outlines His features. Thus, the godhood of the mortal one has been known for the first time.

सुपर्णोऽसि गुरुत्माँस्त्रिवृत्ते शिरा गायत्रं चक्षुर्बृहद्रथन्तरे पक्षौ ।
स्तोम ऽआत्मा छन्दाꣳस्यङ्गानि यजूꣳषि नाम ।
साम ते तनूर्वामदेव्यं यज्ञायज्ञियं पुच्छं धिष्ण्याः शफाः ।
सुपर्णोऽसि गरुत्मान्दिवं गच्छ स्वः पत ॥ यजु. 12.4

suparṇo'si gurutmāṁstrivṛtte śirā gāyatram chakṣurbṛhadrathantare pakṣau;
stoma 'ātmā chhandāṁsyaṅgāni yajūṁ ṣi nāma;
sāma te tanūrvāmadevyaṁ yajñāyajñiyaṁ puchchham dhiṣṇyāḥ śaphāḥ;
suparṇo'si garutmāndivaṁ gachchha svaḥ pata. YV. 12.4

[Meaning] O soul in a womb, you are like a fine-winged bird; your mind should engage in good karmas, meditating with God and acquiring spiritual knowledge. The teachings of the Gāyatī mantra should be your eye to guide you on the right path. The bṛ and rathantara sāmans are your wings. The stoma is your true self. The Vedic meters are your limbs. Yajuḥ is your name. Vāmadevya sāmans are your body. The material required for yajña should always follow you. Your legs take you to the highest places and positions. You are a fine-winged bird. You attain divinity and thereby a world of light (mokṣa).

इति पुंसवनसंस्कारविधिः समाप्तः ॥
iti puṁsavanasaṁskāravidhiḥ samāptaḥ.

Here ends the procedure of Puṁsvana Sanskāra.

सीमन्तोन्नयन संस्कार

Introduction to Sīmantonnayana Sanskāra

The Sīmantonnayana ceremony is performed in the fourth month of the pregnancy. According to Āśvalāyana Gṛhya Sūtra (1.14.1) had it as:

चतुर्थे मासि सीमन्तोन्नयनम् ।

That is, the Sīmantonnayana ceremony should be performed in the fourth month of pregnancy.

According to Ayurveda, all body parts are formed simultaneously during the third month.[1] The foetus attains the free flow of consciousness in his mind at the very time when the sense organs are manifested. Hence, their desire is transmitted through them. Due to this reason, it is not desirable to ignore the (desires of) foetus expressed through the mother. If the same are ignored, there may be destruction or morbidity (in the foetus). At this stage, the mother comes at par with the foetus for acquisition and maintenance regarding certain things. Therefore, the wise manage the pregnant lady with wholesome things like this.[2] So, Ayurveda advises that whatever the pregnant lady wants, should be provided to her except that damages the foetus.[3]

---

1. तृतीये मासि सर्वेन्द्रियाणि सर्वांगावयवाश्च यौगपद्येनाभिवर्तन्ते ।

चरकसंहिता, शारीरस्थान, 4.11

2. तस्य तत्कालमेव दन्द्रियाणि सन्तिष्ठनते, तत्कालमेव चेतसि वेदना निर्बन्धं प्रप्नोति; तस्मात्तदा-प्रभृति गर्भः स्पन्दते, प्रार्थयतेच जन्मान्तरानुभूतं यत् किंचित्, तद् द्वैहृदय्यमाचक्षते वृद्धाः । मातुजं चास्य हृदयं मातृहृदयेनाभिसम्बद्धं भवति रसवाहिनीभिः संवाहिनीभिः; तस्मात्तयोस्ताभिर्भक्तिः संस्पन्दन्ते । तच्चैव कारणमवेक्षमाणा न द्वैहृदय्यस्य विमानितं गर्भमिच्छन्ति कर्तुम् । विमानने ह्यस्य दृश्यते विनाशो विकृतिर्वा । समानयोगक्षेमा हि तदा भवति गर्भेण केषुचिदर्थेषु माता । तसमात् प्रियहिताभ्यां गर्भिणीं विशेषेणोपचरन्ति कुशलाः । चरकसंहिता, शारीरस्थान, 4.15

3 सा यद्यदिच्छेत् तत्तदस्यै दद्यादन्यत्र गर्भोपघातकरेभ्यो भावेभ्यः ।

Now, the purpose of Sīmantonayana Sanskāra can be understood easily. This Sanskāra is intended to take special care of the pregnant lady. When a pregnant lady undergoes the state of two hearts, one of the foetuses, and another of herself, she becomes one with the foetus. In this stage, the foetus expresses desire through the mother and whatever the mother does or thinks the same is impressed upon the foetus. It is the opportune time when the mother can impress the child with good Sanskāras. According to Dr Makoto Shichida, world-renowned founder of over 350 Child Academies in Japan, in his book "Right Brain Education in Infancy' says that the right brain is active during gestation, and cells are sensitive and can transmit subtle energy patterns to the brain; a child has an extrasensory perception in the womb. We have a historic example of Abhimanyu. He learnt the secret of entering the array of Ckakravyūha in his mother's womb. The following verses of Śārīra Sthāna (3.21-24) of Suśruta shed ample good light on the issue of transmission of the mother's Sanskāras into the infant.

येषु येषु इन्द्रियार्थेषु दौह्रदे वा विमानना ।
प्रजायते सुतस्यार्ति तस्मिन् तस्मिन्तथैन्द्रिये ॥ 21 ॥

yeṣu yeṣu indriyārtheṣu dauhṛde vā vimānanā;
prajāyate sutasyārti tasmin tasmintathaindriye. 21

[Meaning] If the pregnant women is disinclined to something, the foetus also becomes disinclined to the same thing.

राजः संदर्शने यस्याः दौह्रदं जायते स्त्रियाः ।
अर्थवन्तं महाभागं कुमारं सा प्रसूयते ॥ 22 ॥

चरकसंहिता, शारीरस्थान, 4.16

rājaḥ saṁdarśane yasyāḥ dauhṛdaṁ jāyate striyāḥ;
arthavantaṁ mahābhāgaṁ kumāraṁ sā prasūyate.22

[Meaning] If a pregnant women wants to see the king in the 4th month of her pregnancy, she delivers a child who is going to grow to be prosperous and rich person and holds a high position in life.

दुकूलपट्ट कौशेय भूषणादिषु दौहृदात् ।
प्रजायते सुतस्यार्ति तस्मिन् तस्मिन्तथैन्द्रिये ॥ 23 ॥

dukūlapaṭṭa kauśeya bhūṣaṇādiṣu dauhṛdāt;
prajāyate sutasyārti tasmin tasmintathaindriye. 23

[Meaning] If the pregnant women during 4th month of pregnancy longs for fine silks, clothes, ornaments etc., she delivers a child of aesthetic taste.

आश्रमे संयतात्मानं धर्मशीलं प्रसूयते ।
देवता प्रतिमायां तु प्रसूते पार्षदोपमम् ।
दर्शने व्यालजातीनां हिंसाशीलं प्रसूयते ॥ 24 ॥

āśrame saṁyatātmānam dharmaśīlaṁ prasūyate;
devatā pratimāyāṁ tu prasūte pārṣadopamam;
darśane vyālajātīnāṁ hiṁsāśīlaṁ prasūyate. 24

[Meaning] The birth of a pious and self-controlled child is indicated by its mother's longing for a visit to a hermitage. The desire of a pregnant woman to see a divine image or an idol predicts the birth of a child in her womb who would grace the council of an august assembly in life. Similarly, a desire to see a savage animal on the part of a pregnant woman signifies the presence of a child of savage and cruel temperament in her womb.

अतोऽनुक्तेषु या नारी समभिध्याति दौहर्दम् ।
शरीराचारशीलैः सा समानं जनयिष्यति ॥ 25 ॥

ato'nukteṣu yā nārī samabhidhyāti dauhardam;
śarīrāchāraśīlaiḥ sā samānaṁ janayiṣyati. 25

[Meaning] Whereas a desire on the part of a pregnant woman to see a particular animal, which has not been mentioned here, indicates that the child in the womb would be of such stature and would develop such traits of character in life as are peculiar to that animal.

आश्रमे संयतात्मानं धर्मशीलं प्रसूयते ।
देवता प्रतिमायां तु प्रसूते पार्षदोपमम् ।
दर्शने व्यालजातीनां हिंसाशीलं प्रसूयते ॥ 26 ॥

āśrame saṁyatātmānaṁ dharmaśīlaṁ prasūyate;
devatā pratimāyāṁ tu prasūte pārṣadopamam
darśane vyālajātīnāṁ hiṁsāśīlaṁ prasūyate. 24

[Meaning] a woman's desires during her pregnancy are determined by sanskaras of the previous birth of the child in the womb (that are to happen during the present life).

Since, it was a proved fact that the Sanskāras of mother during her pregnancy are going to influence the Sanskāras of the future child, so the Sīmantonnayana Sanskāra was prescribed to have a child of one's choice. In this regard Manu (9.9) says:

याटृशं भजते हि स्त्री सुतं सूते तथाविधम् ।
तस्मात् प्रजाविशुद्ध्यर्थं स्त्रियं रक्षेत् प्रयत्नतः ॥

yādṛśaṁ bhajate hi strī sutaṁ sūte tathāvidham,
tasmāt prajāviśuddhyarthaṁ striyaṁ rakṣet prayatnataḥ.

[Meaning] A pregnant woman gives birth to a child according to his mental status. So, let a pregnant woman be cared for properly to have the best offspring.

Thus, it is proved that during pregnancy, the Sanskāras of the mother need to be monitored carefully so that we may get a child endowed with high character and personality traits.

Gobhilīya Gṛhya Sūtra prescribes a ritual to be performed during Sīmantonayana Sanskāra. According to the ritual, the pregnant woman is asked to have a glimpse at a dish made of rice and lentils, popularly called 'Khichadi' mixed with ghee left of oblation for Yajña. The husband asks the wife-

किं पश्यसि?

kiṁ paśyasi?

[Meaning] What do you see?

The wife answers-

प्रजां पश्यामि । पशून् पश्यामि । सौभाग्यं पश्यामि । पत्युः दीर्घायुः पश्यामि ।

prajāṁ paśyāmi. paśūn paśyāmi | saubhāgyaṁ paśyāmi. patyuḥ dīrghāyuḥ paśyāmi.

[Meaning] I see a baby. I see prosperity. I see good fortune and a long life for my husband.

The Śāstra points out the types of thoughts required to be pondered over by the mother during pregnancy. A mother must enjoy the infant developing its own heart in the mother's womb. Till the child is born, the mother should keep dreaming of a child, prosperity, good fortune in the house and long life for her husband, and accordingly, she takes action. Good planning gives good results.

These three Sanskāras are pre-natal, i.e. performed befor the birth of a child. They are preparatory Sanskāras needed to plan a future child of once own choice. Rest of the 13 Sanskāras are post-natal. They are peformed after the birth of a child.

अथ सीमन्तोन्नयनम्

Sīmantonnayana Sanskāra

Now we tell you the third Sanskāra, called Sīmantonnayana through which the mind of pregnant woman be made satisfied and healthy, conception stable and of excellent quality to grow day by day, Now we provide here the authorities:

चतुर्थे गर्भमासे सीमन्तोन्नयनम् ॥ आश्वलायन गृसू 1.14.1

chaturthe garbhamāse sīmantonnayanam. Āśv.GS. 1.14.1

Sīmantonayana sanskāra should be conducted in the fourth month of pregnancy.

आपूर्यमाणपक्षे यदा पुंसा नक्षत्रेण चन्द्रमा युक्तः स्यात् ॥

आश्वलायन गृसू 1.14.2

āpūryamāṇapakṣe yadā puṁsā nakṣatreṇa chandramā yuktaḥ syāt. Āśv.GS. 1.14.2

[Meaning] Sīmantonayana sanskāra should be conducted in Śukla pakṣa (bright half) when moon is in conjuction with male constellations like Aśvinī, Bharaṇī, Puṣya, Āśleṣā, Maghā, Uttara Phalguni, Svāti, Jyeṣṭhā, Mūla, Pūrvāṣādhā, Uttarāṣādhā, Śravaṇa and Pūrva Bhādrapada.

अथास्यै युग्मेन शलालुग्रप्सेन त्रयेण्या च शलल्या त्रिभिश्च कुशपिंजूलैरूर्ध्वं सीमन्तं व्यूहति भूर्भुवः स्वरोमिति त्रिः । चतुर्वा । आश्व. गृसू 1.14.4-5

athāsyai yugmena śalālugrapsena trayeṇyā cha śalalyā tribhiścha kuśapiṁjūlairūrdhvaṁ sīmantaṁ vyūhati bhūrbhuvaḥ svaromiti triḥ, chaturvā. Āśv. GS. 1.14.4-5

[Meaning] Reciting the mantra '*bhur bhuvaḥ svarom*' comb upwards the hair of pregnant woman three times or four times with the comb made of two *Gular* fruits (cluster fig or the Ficus racemosa) or three porcupines' quill which has grown white at three places or three fresh straws of sacred Kusha grass.

पुंꣳसवनवत् ॥ पारस्कर गसू. 1.15.2

pumːsavanavat. Pār.GS. 1.15.2

प्रथमे गर्भे मासे षष्ठेऽष्टमे वा ॥ पारस्कर गसू. 1.15.3

prathame garbhe māse ṣaṣṭhe'ṣṭame vā. Pār.GS. 1.15.3

[Meaning] Or like the Punsavana sanskāra, this sanskāra may be conducted in the sixth or eighth month when moon is in conjuction with any of the male nakṣatras during the bright fortnight.

The Procedure of Sīmantonayana

After performing 'Prayer', 'Svastivāchana', 'Śantikaraṇa' and 'Sāmanya-prakaraṇa', the water should be sprinkled in the prescribed sides of the yajñavedī with the mantras of '*adite'numanyasva*' and with the following mantra on the four sides of the Vedī (fire-altar):

ओं देव सवितः प्रसुव यज्ञं प्रसुव यज्ञपतिं भगाय। दिव्यो गन्धर्व केतपूः केतन्नः पुनातु वाचस्पतिर्वाचं नः स्वदतु स्वाहा ॥ यजु॰ 11.7

Oṁ deva savitaḥ prasuva yajñaṁ prasuva yajñapatiṁ bhagāya, divyo gandharva ketapūḥ ketannaḥ punātu vāchaspatirvāchaṁ naḥ svadatu svāhā. YV. 11.7

First meaning in the context of Bhūtākāśa/Brahmāṇḍa: O energy, the material cause of creation, performs yajña of creation and stirs the creation-promoting elements towards transforming energy into matter particles. This energy, the material cause of creation, resides in dyauloka [Brahmākāśa] and sustains Bhūtākāśa. This energy impels intelligence into the universe. So, let it also sharpen our intelligence. May

God, the Governor of this cosmic energy, make good use of this energy in our interest.

The Second meaning in the context of Earth: O solar rays performs yajña of creation on Earth for prosperity and stirs the creation-promoting elements. This energy, causing creation on Earth, resides in dyauloka [sun] and sustains life on the Earth. This solar energy impels intelligence on the Earth. So, let it also sharpen our intelligence. May God, the Governor of the energy, make this energy for our good use.

ओं प्रजापतये त्वा जुष्टं निर्वपामि ॥

ओं प्रजापतये त्वा जुष्टं प्रोक्षामि ॥

Oṁ prajāpataye tvā juṣṭaṁ nirvapāmi.
Oṁ prajāpataye tvā juṣṭaṁ prokṣāmi.

After sprinkling the water on four sides of the yajñavedī the four oblations of Aghārāvājya-bhāgāhuti and four oblations of Vyāhriti āhutī (thus amounting to eight oblations in all should be offered according to the procedure mentioned in the Sāmānya Prakaraṇa (Common Procedure).

There after pronouncing the mantra ओं प्रजापतये त्वा जुष्टं प्रोक्षामि ॥ '*Oṁ prajāpataye tvā juṣṭaṁ nirvapāmi*' the host should take rice. Sesamum Indicum (*tila*) and moong dal (green gram) in equal quantity (about 6 gm. each) and wash it with water with Mantra '*Oṁ prajāpataye tvā juṣṭaṁ prokṣāmi*'. After washing the ingredients he should prepare khichari (name of dish) of them and after mixing sufficient ghee in the khichari, he should offer eight oblations of this with the following mantras:

ओं धाता ददातु दाशुषे प्राचीं जीवातुमुक्षितम्। वयं देवस्य धीमहि सुमतिं वाजिनीवति स्वाहा ॥ इदं धात्रे-इदन्न मम ॥ आश्व.गृसू. 1.14.13; अथर्व0 7.17

Oṁ dhātā dadātu dāśuṣe prāchīṁ jīvātumukṣitam, vayaṁ

devasya dhīmahi sumatiṁ vājinīvati svāhā. idaṁ dhātre-idanna mama. Āśv.GS. 1.14.13; AV. 7.17

[Meaning] O Lady of healthy progeny! May God who sustains the universe grant life-promoting juicy herbs for oblations. We concentrate our mind on the good knowledge of that mighty power. For the fulfilment of the above wish we offer this oblation. This oblation is meant only for Dhātā (God who sustains the universe) and it is not for me.

ओं धाता प्रजानामुत रायऽईशे धात्रेदं विश्वं भुवनं जनान। धाता कृष्टीरनिमिषाभिचष्टे धात्रऽइद्धव्यं घृतवज्जुहोत स्वाहा ॥ इदं धात्रे-इदन्न मम ॥

आश्व.गृसू. 1.14.3

Oṁ dhātā prajānāmuta rāya'īśe dhātredaṁ viśvaṁ bhuvanaṁ janāna, dhātā kṛṣṭīranimiṣābhichaṣṭe dhātra'iddhavyaṁ ghṛtavajjuhota svāhā. idaṁ dhātre-idanna mama. Āśv.GS. 1.14.3

[Meaning] The all-sustaining Lord is the master of all the creatures and wealth. This whole universe has come into being by his power and wisdom. He, the upholder of all, is watching every moment of all men's activities. O men! Offer the oblation full of ghee for obeying the instructions of the Lord, the sustainer of the universe. This oblation is intended for the fulfilment of the above wish. The oblation is meant only for Dhātā and not for me.

ओं राकामहं सुहवां सुष्टुती हुवे श्रृणोतु नः सुभगा बोधतु त्मना। सीव्यत्वपः सूच्या च्छिद्यमानया ददातु वीरं शतदायमुक्थ्यं स्वाहा ॥ इदं राकायै-इदन्न मम ॥

ऋ. 2.32.4

Oṁ rākāmahaṁ suhavāṁ suṣṭutī huve śṛṇotu naḥ subhagā bodhatu tmanā, sīvyatvapaḥ sūchyā chchhidyamānayā dadātu vīraṁ śatadāyamukthyaṁ svāhā. idaṁ rākāyai-idanna mama.

RV. 2.32.4

[Meaning] I, the husband, call my wife who is in her

full puberty like the full moon night with praiseful words, in all the functions of prayer and praise. Let the fortunate lady listen to my words and understand their intended sense. May she perform the functions of progeny in such a good way as she sews the clothes with the needle without her fingers being pricked. May she give me a brave child. The offered oblation is meant for Rākā (full moon night and wife full of puberty) and not for me.

यास्ते राके सुमतयः सुपेशसो याभिर्ददासि दाशुषे वसूनि । ताभिर्नो अद्य सुमना उपागहि सहस्रपोषं सुभगे रराणा स्वाहा ॥ इदं राकायै-इदन्न मम ॥ ऋ. 2.32.5

yāste rāke sumatayaḥ supeśaso yābhirdadāsi dāśuṣe vasūni,
tābhirno adya sumanā upāgahi sahasrapoṣaṁ subhage rarāṇā
svāhā. idaṁ rākāyai-idanna mama. RV. 2.32.5

[Meaning] O youthful lady like that of the full moon, come to me with delighted heart accompanied by your praise-worthy advice through which you give me various physical and spiritual wealth of munificent nature. O, lucky one! Come to me giving a thousand kinds of fortunes. This oblation is intended for the fulfilment of the above wish. This oblation is meant for Rākā (youthful wife) and not for me.

नेजमेष परा पत सुपुत्रः पुनरापत ।
अस्यै में पुत्रकामायै गर्भमा धेहि यः पुमान्स्वाहा ॥ ऋ.खिल. 34.1

nejameṣa parā pata suputraḥ punarāpata,
asyai meṁ putrakāmāyai garbhamā dhehi yaḥ pumānsvāhā.
RV.Kh. 34.1

[Meaning] My husband who is potentially vigorous has deposited the sperm in me, to beget a child. May my husband be free from all evils and reside with me with noble child.

यथेयं पृथिवी मह्युत्ताना गर्भमा दधे ।
एवं तं गर्भमा धेहि दशमे मासि सूतवे स्वाहा ॥ ऋ.खिल. 34.2

yatheyaṁ pṛthivī mahyuttānā garbhamā dadhe,
ēvaṁ taṁ garbhamā dhehi daśame māsi sūtave svāhā.

RV.Kh. 34.2

[Meaning] As this vast earth contains in her bosom the seeds of various things, so you do, O lucky lady. I desposit in you the sperm to give birth to a child in the tenth sidereal month.

विष्णोः श्रेष्ठेन रूपेणास्यां नार्यां गवीन्याम् ।

पुमासं पुत्राना धेहि दशमे मासि सूतवे स्वाहा ॥ आश्व० 1.14.3 ऋ० खिल 34.3

viṣṇoḥ śreṣṭhena rūpeṇāsyāṁ nāryāṁ gavīnyām;
pumāsaṁ putrānā dhehi daśame māsi sūtave svāhā.

Āśv.GS. 1.14.3; RV.Kh. 34.3

[Meaning] O man abiding the rules of household life! By God's best grace, you get a vigorous child in the tenth month from this lady who owns the wealth and animals like cows, etc.

Having offered the seven oblations of khichari (a dish made by mixing rice and lentils of black or green grams) with the above-quoted mantras, one should also offer eight oblations by the mantras प्रजापते न त्व० (*prajāpate na tva...*) etc. Again, one oblation of cooked rice should be offered with the mantra ओं प्रजापतये स्वाहा (*Oṁ prajāpataye svāhā...*). Afterwards, one oblation of khichari previously prepared should be offered by the mantra यदस्य कर्मणो० (*yadasya karmaṇo...*).

Thereafter offering eight oblations of ghee with the eight mantra beginning with त्वन्नो अग्रे० (*tvanno agne...*) etc. and four oblations of ghee with the four mantras of Vyāhṛti āhutī ओं भूरग्नये० (*Om bhūragnaye...*) the husband and wife should go to a lonely place and sit on a good seat in order that the seat of husband be in the back of the wife.

ओं सुमित्रिया न आप ओषधयः सन्तु । दुर्मित्रियास्तस्मै सन्तु योऽस्मान्द्वेष्टि यं

च वयं द्विष्मः ॥ यजु॰ 6.22

Oṁ sumitriyā na āpa Oṣadhayaḥ santu, durmitriyāstasmai santu yo'smāndvesṭi yaṁ cha vayaṁ dviṣmaḥ. YV. 6.22

[Meaning] May the waters and hersbs be friendly to us. May they be unfiendly or destructive to those diseases which harm us and whom we also dislike.

मूर्द्धानं दिवो अरतिं पृथिव्या वैश्वानरमृत आ जातमग्निम् ।
कविꣳ सम्राजमतिथिं जनानामासन्ना पात्रं जनयन्त देवाः ॥ यजु॰ 7.24

mūrddhānaṁ divo aratiṁ pṛthivyā vaiśvānaramṛta ā jātamagnim.
kaviṁ samrājamatithiṁ janānāmāsannā pātraṁ janayanta devāḥ. YV. 7.24

[Meaning] Let is produce a towering scholar who could top all scholars in knowledge and research; who would have news of all things hidden in the bosom of the earth; and would develop technology beneficial to all people; who would be a farsighted leader respected by all like a guest.

ओम् अयमूर्ज्जावतो वृक्ष ऊर्जीव फलिनी भव ।
पर्णं वनस्पते नु त्वा नु त्वा सूयताꣳ रयिः ॥ पारस्कर गृसू॰ 1.15.6; मन्त्र ब्रा. 1.5.6

Om ayamūrjjāvato vṛkṣa ūrjjīva phalinī bhava;
parṇaṁ vanaspate nu tvā nu tvā sūyatāṁ rayiḥ.
Pār. GS.1.15.6; Mantra Br. 1.5.6

[Meaning] O lady! As this tree of Ficus glomeraia (*udumbara*) is full of ripe fruits, so you become prolific with the arrival of good child. O proliferous lady! May be praising frequently your bud like child bring prosperity and happiness in my house with your co-operation.

ओं येनादितेः सीमानं नयति प्रजापतिर्महते सौभगाय ।
तेनाहमस्यै सीमानं नयामि प्रजामस्यै जरदष्टिं कृणोमि ॥ मन्त्र ब्रा. 1.5.2

Oṁ yenāditeḥ sīmānaṁ nayati prajāpatirmahate

saubhagāya;
tenāhamasyai sīmānaṁ nayāmi prajāmasyai jaradaṣṭiṁ
kṛṇomi. MBrā. 1.5.2

[Meaning] Just as Prajāpati delimits the boundaries of the stars for creating the universe, I, husband, also delimits the range of activites of my pregnant wife to beget a child, so that she may live full life span.

ओं राकामहः सुहवाः सुष्टुती हुवे श्रृणोतु नः सुभगा बोधतु त्मना। सीव्यत्वपः सूच्या छिद्यमानया ददातु वीरः शतदायुमुख्यम्॥ मन्त्र ब्रा. 1.5.3

Oṁ rākāmahaṁ suhavāṁ suṣṭutī huve śṛṇotu naḥ subhagā bodhatu tmanā, sīvyatvapaḥ sūchyā chhidyamānayā dadātu vīraṁ śatadāyumukhyam. MBrā. 1.5.3

[Meaning] I, the husband, call my wife in her full bloom like the full-moon night with praiseful words, in all the functions of prayer and praise. Let the fortunate lady listen to my words and understand their intended sense. May she perform the functions of progeny in such a good way as she sews the clothes with the needle without her fingers being pricked. May she give me a brave child. The offered oblation is meant for Rākā (full moon night and wife full of puberty) and not for me.

ओं यास्ते राके सुमतयः सुपेशसो याभिर्ददासि दाशुषे वसूनि।
ताभिर्नो अद्य सुमना उपागहि सहस्रपोषं सुभगे ररणा॥ मन्त्र ब्रा. 1.5.4

Oṁ yāste rāke sumatayaḥ supeśaso yābhirdadāsi dāśuṣe vasūni;
tābhirno adya sumanā upāgahi sahasrapoṣaṁ subhage raraṇā. MBrā. 1.5.4

[Meaning] O youthful lady like that of the full moon! Let you come to me with a delighted heart accompanied by your praise-worthy advice through which you give me munificent physical and spiritual wealth. O, lucky one! Come to me giving a thousand kinds of fortunes. This oblation is intended for the fulfilment of the above wish. This oblation is meant for Rākā (youthful wife) and not for me.

किं पश्यसि ?

kiṁ paśyasi ?

[Meaning] Husband asks, What do you see?

प्रजां पशून्त्सौभाग्यं मह्यं दीर्घायुष्ट्वं पत्युः ॥ मन्त्र ब्रा. 1.5.5

prajāṁ paśūntsaubhāgyaṁ mahyaṁ dīrghāyuṣṭvaṁ patyuḥ.
MBrā. 1.5.5

The wife answers:

[Meaning] I see a baby. I see prosperity. I see good fortune and a long life for my husband.

Chanting the above-cited seven mantras, the husband should drop fragrant oil in his wife's hair with his hand and dress the hair with a comb. Afterwards, he, taking the small smooth branch piece of *Arjuna* tree, or the grass of smooth Kuśā or the quills of porcupine, combed his wife's hair into two parts and arranged a coil of hair at the back. Afterwards, both should come to the yajñaśālā. At this time, musical instruments like Vīṇā, etc. should be played. Afterwards, the song of the Sāmaveda mantras given at the end of Sāmānya Prakaraṇa (Common Procedure) should be chanted. Chanting Sāmaveda mantras should be preceded by the following mantra:

ओं सोम एव नो राजेमा मानुषीः प्रजाः ।
अविमुक्तचक्र आसीरंस्तीरे तुभ्यम् असौ ॥ पारस्कर गृसू 1.15.8

Oṁ soma ēva no rājemā mānuṣīḥ prajāḥ,
avimuktachakra āsīraṁstīre tubhyam asau. Pār.GS. 1.15.8

[Meaning] May our King have peace and tranquillity, and may the human beings be blessed with happiness and prosperity. It is the river named.............(quote the name of the river) on the vast bank of which the people dwell.

Afterwards, the pregnant wife, pouring plenty of ghee in the *khichari* left out from the oblations, should see the reflection of her face in that ghee.

This time, the husband should ask, किं पश्यसि (*kiṁ paśyasi*)?—What do you see?)

The lady should reply- प्रजां पश्यामि (*prajāṁ paśyāmi*)— I see progeny.

After that, the old ladies of the family of pregnant lady whose husbands are alive, who have children, who are noble and educated sit together to chat and exchange pleasantries. The pregnant bride should eat that khichari dish, and old ladies sitting nearby should shower blessing on her in this manner:

ओं वीरसूस्त्वं भव, जीवसूस्त्वं भव, जीवपत्नी त्वं भव ॥ गो.गृसू. 2.7.12

Oṁ vīrasūstvaṁ bhava, jīvasūstvaṁ bhava, jīvapatnī tvaṁ bhava. Go.GS. 2.7.12

[Meaning] You give birth to a brave child, you give birth to a living child, your husband should not die before you.

They should speak these auspicious words. Afterwards, having accorded a warm welcome to the guests present in the function, ladies of the house should see off lady guests and gents to gents.

Here ends the procedure of Sīmantonayana.

अथ जातकर्मसंस्कारविधिः

Jātakarma Sanskāra

After the child's birth, the child is given a secret name, he is given a taste of honey & ghee, and the mother starts the first breastfeeding.

Following is the authority to suggest the time and procedure of this sanskāra:

सोष्यन्तीमद्भिरभ्युक्षति ॥ पारस्कर गृसू. 1.16.1

soṣyantīmadbhirabhyukṣati. Pār.GS.1.16.1

[Meaning] The persons concerned should sprinkle water on the mother of a child.

This authority is from Pāraskar Gṛhya Sūtra, and the same has been written in the Āśvalāyana, Gobhilīya and Śaunakīya Gṛhya Sūtras.

The Procedure of Jātakarma

When delivery time comes closer, sprinkle water on the pregnant woman with the following mantra:

ओम् एजतु दशमास्यो गर्भो जरायुणा सह ।

यथायं वायुरेजति यथा समुद्र एजति ।

एवायं दशमास्यो अस्रज्जरायुणा सह ॥ यजु० 8.28

Om ējatu daśamāsyo garbho jarāyuṇā saha,

yathāyaṁ vāyurejati yathā samudra ējati,

ēvāyaṁ daśamāsyo asrajjarāyuṇā saha. YV. 8.28

[Meaning] May the embryo of ten months move and grow with its membrane. As the wind moves without obstructions and the ocean remains undisturbed, this ten-month-old embryo takes birth without obstructions and any disturbance.

Note: Here, ten months are mentioned because, in

the Vedic period, Lunar Sidereal (Nākṣatra) Months were in currency. One Lunar Sidereal Month is around 27.2 days. Thus, Vedic Lunar Sidereal 10 months are equal to nine solar months.

After sprinkling the water, the following mantra should be recited in mind, and sprinkle water a second time.

ओम् अवैतु पृश्रिशेवलꣳशुने जराय्वत्तवे ।
नैव माꣳसेन पीवरीं न कसिं᳘मश्वनायतनमव जरायु पद्यताम् ॥

पारस्कर गृसू. 1.16.2

Om avaitu pṛśniśevalaṁśune jarāyvattave,

naiva māṁsena pīvarīṁ na kasiṁmaśchanāyatanamava jarāyu

padyatām. pāraskara gṛsū. 1.16.2

[Meaning] O birth giving woman! Let the membrane of the foetus which has many forms and is somewhat stiff come out for the purpose of devouring by dog etc. Let not the placenta separate from uterus, O strong Lady. By God's grace may you not experiecne uterine rupture causing life threat to the baby.

कुमारं जातं पुराऽन्यैरालम्भात् सर्पिर्मधुनी हिरण्यनिकाषं हिरण्येन प्राशयेत ॥

आश्व.गृसू. 1.15.1

kumāraṁ   jātaṁ   purā'nyairālambhāt   sarpirmadhunī
hiraṇyanikāṣaṁ hiraṇyena prāśayeta. āśva.gṛsū. 1.15.1

[Meaning] The father of the newly-born baby should make the baby suck the ghee and honey mixed in a golden pot and give it in the baby's mouth with the bar of gold before the newly born is taken away by others (in their laps).

When the child is born, the woman, like the nurse, should first remove the placenta and fetal membrane from the body of the baby after birth and clean at once the greasy deposits from its mouth, nose, ears, eyes, etc.

and should put the baby in the lap of its father after cleansing it with a smooth cloth and thus making the child clean and neat.

Then, the father of the newly born baby, sitting in a place where the wind and cold wind could not enter, should clamp it with a thread on the point about nine inches above from the root of this umbilical cord and cut it. He should carefully cut the part of it above the clamp. Afterwards, the baby should be bathed with lukewarm water and cleaned with a clean cloth. Dress the baby with new, clean clothes and come to the place of yajñakuṇḍa which should be prepared out of the house of maternity or the place where the yajñakuṇḍa made of copper has been arranged. He should arrange the samidhā (wood fuel) in the kuṇḍa according to the method prescribed previously in the Sāmānya Prakaraṇa (Common procedure). He should perform the procedure of Agnyādhāna and Samidādhāna as has been laid down in the Sāmānya-prakaraṇa. Afterwards, he should enkindle the fire, keeping the fragrant articles like ghee, etc., safely near the yajñavedī (fire altar). After washing hands and feet, he should arrange one seat for the priest on the southern side of the yajñavedī, and the priest (purohit) should sit on it, keeping his face northward.

Yajamāna, the father of the newly born baby, should take his seat stretched in the west of the vedī. He should wear a small cloth piece known as upvastra, keeping his face eastward. After everything is ready, he should ask the priest's consent to conduct the Jātakarma ceremony by pronouncing :

ओम् आ वसोः सदने सीद ॥

Om ā vasoḥ sadane sīda.

To give consent, the priest should speak - ओं सीदामि

(yes, I take a seat to conduct the ceremony) and take his seat.

After that, the priest should place samidhās of sandal wood in the Vedī reciting the four mantras prescribed in the Sāmānya Prakaraṇa, beginning with the Mantra अयं त इध्म॰ (*ayaṁ ta idhma...*). He should offer the four oblations of Aghārāvājya-bhāg-āhutis and four oblations of Vyāhṛti āhutis on the fire flamming in the vedī. Afterwards, two oblations of molten ghee should be offered by following two mantras:

ओं या तिरश्ची निपद्यते अहं विधरणी इति। तां त्वा घृतस्य धारया यजे सꣲराधनीमहम्। सꣲराधिन्यै देव्यै देष्ट्यै स्वाहा॥ इदं सराधिन्यै-इदन्न मम॥

मन्त्रब्राह्मण 1.5.6,7; गोभिलगृसू. 2.7.15

Oṁ yā tiraśchī nipadyate ahaṁ vidharaṇī iti, tāṁ tvā ghṛtasya dhārayā yaje saṁrādhanīmaham, saṁrādhinyai devyai deṣṭryai svāhā. idaṁ sarādhinyai-idanna mama.

Mantra Br. 1.5.6,7; Go.GS. 2.7.15

[Meaning] (Aham) I (yaje) greet (tām tvā) you, my wife, (ghṛtasya dhāryā) with the offering of ghee in the fire altar (yā) who (atiraśchi) agrees with me in all activities (vidharṇī); who is the custodian of all house-hold affairs. (aham) I (sanrādhinim) consider you an accomplisher of all domestic works. (Svāhā) I offer this oblation (sanrādhinyai, devyai, deṣṭrayai) for the devī who accomplishes all house-hold affairs. (idam) The oblation is meant (sanrādhinyai) for the devī who accomplishes all house-hold affairs (*idanna mam..*); it is not for me.

ओं विपश्चित्पुच्छमभरत्तद्धाता पुनराहरत्। परेहि त्वं विपश्चित्पुमानयं जनिष्यतेऽसौ नाम स्वाहा। इदं धात्रे-इदन्न मम॥ गोभिलगृसू. 2.7.16

Oṁ vipaśchitpuchchhamabharattaddhātā punarāharat, parehi tvaṁ vipaśchitpumānayaṁ janiṣyate'sau nāma svāhā, idaṁ dhātre-idanna mama. gobhilagṛsū. 2.7.16

[Meaning] (Vipaśchit) The wise men (abharat) take care of the progeny (puccham) as an honour of the family. (Dhātā punaḥ) God also (āharat) describes the child as an honour of the family. Therefore, (vipaśchit) O learned men! (tvam) You always (prehi) come to us happily and preach for our well being, (ayaṁ pumān) so that this my husband (asau nāma) who bears such a name (janiṣyate) may again produce a child endowed with all admirable qualities.

After offering these oblations with the above-cited two mantras, he should sing the Vāmadevya-gāna given at the end of Sāmānya prakaraṇa (Chapter on Common procedure) and perform the prayer of God as described in the beginning of Sāmānya prakaraṇa (Chapter on Common procedure). After that, the child's father should write 'Om' on the tongue of the child with the already prepared golden bar dipped in the ghee and honey appropriately mixed. Doing so, he should whisper वेदोऽसीति (your confidential name is Veda) in the right ear of the child and then, with the bar of the gold, make the child lick a small quantity of the mixed ghee and honey with the following Mantras:

ओं प्र ते ददामि मधुनो घृतस्य वेद सवित्रा प्रसूतं मघोनाम्। आयुष्मान् गुप्तो देवताभिः शतं जीव शरदो लोके अस्मिन् ॥ आश्व.गृसू. 1.15.1

Oṁ pra te dadāmi madhuno ghṛtasya veda savitrā prasūtaṁ maghonām, āyuṣmān gupto devatābhiḥ śataṁ jīva śarado loke asmin. Āśva.G.S. 1.15.1

[Meaning] O child! (te) for you (pra dadāmi) I give this (madhuno ghṛtasya) ghee and honey, (Veda) I know (prasūtam) that this ghee and honey has been produced by (savitrā) God (maghonām) who is the producer of all the wealth of the world, so you (devatābhiḥ guptaḥ) preserved and protected by learned mother, father and teacher (āyuṣmān) attain long life and (jīva) live (asmin loke) in this world (śaradaḥ śatam) for hundred autumns.

ओं भूस्त्वयि दधामि ॥

Oṁ bhūstvayi dadhāmi.

[Meaning] O Child! (dadhāmi) I establish (tvayi) in you the idea of (bhūḥ) God, Who is the giver of life.

ओं भुवस्त्वयि दधामि ॥

Oṁ bhuvastvayi dadhāmi.

[Meaning] (dadhāmi) I establish (tvayi) in you the idea of (bhuvaḥ) God who is all breatitude.

ओं स्वस्त्वयि दधामि ॥

Oṁ svastvayi dadhāmi.

[Meaning] (dadhāmi) I establish (tvayi) in you the idea of (svaḥ) God, Who is the source of all movements.

ओं भूर्भुवः स्वस्सर्वं त्वयि दधामि ॥ पारस्कर गृसू. 1.16.4

Oṁ bhūrbhuvaḥ svassarvaṁ tvayi dadhāmi. Pār.GS. 1.16.4

[Meaning] (dadhāmi) I establish (tvayi) in you the idea of (svaḥ sarvaṁ) God who is the life of all, all beatitude and the source of all movements.

ओं सदसस्पतिमद्भुतं प्रियमिन्द्रस्य काम्यम् ।
सनि मेधामयासिषꣳ स्वाहा ॥ यजु. 32.13

Oṁ sadasaspatimadbhutaṁ priyamindrasya kāmyam,
sani medhāmayāsiṣaṁꣳ svāhā ॥ YV. 32.13

[Meaning] May I attain Divinity (Sadasaspatim) who is the master of all the assembled masses of the world, (adbhutam) who is wondrous and (priyam) loved by all, (kāmyam) who is desired and attainable by (soul) embodied soul. May I also (ayāsiṣam) attain (sanim) discriminatory (medhām) intellectual power.

After giving the child ghee and honey six times with these above-cited six mantras, the rice and barley should be ground with water, and the liquid thus prepared should be sieved through a cloth piece and kept in a pot. The father of the child should touch a drop of this liquid in the mouth of the child with the thumb or ring finger taken together, pronouncing the following mantra:

ओम् इदमाज्यमिदमन्नमिदमायुरिदममृतम् ॥ मंत्रब्रा० 1.5 गोभिल गृसू. 2.7.20

Om idamājyamidamannamidamāyuridamamṛtam.

MBr 1.5; Go.GS. 2.7.20

[Meaning] This will add to your effulgence; this is eatable, prolongs life, and is nectarous (rasāyana).

It is the opinion of only Gobhilīya Gṛhya-sūtra, not of all others. Afterwards, the father of the baby should pronounce the following mantras in the right ear of the baby:

ओं मेधां ते देवः सविता मेधां देवी सरस्वती ।
मेधां ते अश्विनौ देवावाधत्तां पुष्करस्रजौ ॥ आश्व.गृसू.1.15.2

Oṁ medhāṁ te devaḥ savitā medhāṁ devī sarasvatī,
medhāṁ te aśvinau devāvādhattāṁ puṣkarasrajau ||1 ||

Āśv.GS. 1.15.2

[Meaning] O child! (Savitā deva) may God, the creator of all, (te) bless you (medhām) with wisdom; (devī sarasvatī) may Saraswati (teaching of the learned men) bless you with (medhām) wisdom; (aśvinau) may the prāṇa and apāna vāyus, i.e. prāṇāyāma (puṣkara sraja) originated from ākāśa enhance your wisdom.

ओम् अग्निरायुष्मान् स वनस्पतिभिरायुष्माँस्तेन त्वाऽऽयुषाऽऽयुष्मन्तं करोमि ॥

Om   agnirāyuṣmān   sa   vanaspatibhirāyuṣmāṁstena
tvā"yuṣā"yuṣmantaṁ karomi ||2 ||

[Meaning] (Agni) The fire (āyuṣmān) is the source of life, (āyuṣmān) you get oxygen (vanaspatibhiḥ) through plants and vegetation. (Āyuṣmantam karomi tvā) I make you attain long life, O child! (tena) with that source of life.

ओं सोमआयुष्मान् स ओषधीभिरायुष्माँस्तेन० ॥

Oṁ somaāyuṣmān sa Oṣadhībhirāyuṣmāṁstena..

[Meaning] (Soma) The moon (āyuṣmān) is the source of life. The polarized light of the moon provides taste and nutritional value to all the herbs, shrubs, and plants (Note: Here, the positive effect of polarized light on plants and their products, viz. fruits and vegetables, is cited). So, the moon is called the source of life.

ओं ब्रह्माऽऽआयुष्मत् तद् ब्राह्मणैरायुष्मत्तेन० ॥

Oṁ brahmā"āyuṣmat tad brāhmaṇairāyuṣmattena..

[Meaning] (Brahmā) The knowledge of Veda is (āyuṣmān) the source of life. (tad) The Vedic knowledge gives long life (brāhamaṇaih) when it is followed in life.

ओं देवा आयुष्मन्तस्तेऽमृतेनायुष्मन्तस्तेन० ॥

Oṁ devā āyuṣmantaste'mṛtenāyuṣmantastena..

[Meaning] (Devaḥ) The enlightened persons are (āyuṣmantaḥ) the source of long life; (te) they (āyuṣmantaḥ) give life (amṛtena) through their immortality advice.

ओम् ऋषय आयुष्मन्तस्ते व्रतैरायुष्मन्तस्तेन० ॥

Om ṛṣaya āyuṣmantaste vratairāyuṣmantastena..

[Meaning] (Ṛṣayaḥ) The seers are (āyuṣmantaḥ) the source of long life; (te) they (āyuṣmantaḥ) give life (vratena) through their vows, disciplinary life.

ओं पितर आयुष्मन्तस्ते स्वधाभिरायुष्मन्तस्तेन० ॥

Oṁ pitara āyuṣmantaste svadhābhirāyuṣmantastena..

[Meaning] (Pitara) The parents, grandfathers, etc. are

(āyuṣmantaḥ) the source of life; (te) they (āyuṣmantaḥ) give life (svadhābhiḥ) through their when they are taken care of and served with respect.

ओं यज्ञ आयुष्मान् स दक्षिणाभिरायुष्माँस्तेन० ॥

Oṁ yajña āyuṣmān sa dakṣiṇābhirāyuṣmāṁstena..

[Meaning] (Yajña) The Yajña is (āyuṣmān) the source of life. (Saḥ) It (āyuṣmān) gives benefit (dakṣiṇābhiḥ) when experts of yajña are honoured.

ओं समुद्र आयुष्मान् स स्रवन्तीभिरायुष्माँस्तेन त्वाऽऽयुषाऽऽयुष्मन्तं करोमि ॥

पार.गृसू. 1.16.6

Oṁ samudra āyuṣmān sa sravantībhirāyuṣmāṁstena tvā"yuṣā"yuṣmantaṁ karomi. Pār.GS. 1.16.6

[Meaning] (Samudra) The ocean (āyuṣmān) has a long life span. (Saḥ) it (āyuṣmān) gains life (sravantibhiḥ) by the rivers flowing down to it.

In a similar way, these nine mantras should again be recited in the left ear of the baby; thereafter, the father of the baby, putting his hand very gently on the shoulders of the baby without making it feel any load of his hand, should recite the following mantras:

ओम् इन्द्र श्रेष्ठानि द्रविणानि धेहि चित्तिं दक्षस्य सुभगत्वमस्मे। पोषं रयीणामरिष्टिं तनूनां स्वाद्मानं वाचः सुदिनत्वमह्णाम् ॥ ऋ० 2.21.6

Om indra śreṣṭhāni draviṇāni dhehi chittiṁ dakṣasya subhagatvamasme, poṣaṁ rayīṇāmariṣṭiṁ tanūnāṁ svādmānaṁ vāchaḥ sudinatvamahnām. RV. 2.21.6

[Meaning] O Lord Almighty! Please grant us excellent wealth and the capability to accomplish acts efficiently; give the fortune of good children. Grant us the nicety of speech and prosperity of the days.

अस्मे प्र यन्घि मघवन्नृजीषिन्निन्द्र रायो विश्वारस्य भूरेः। अस्मे शतं शरदो जीवसे धा अस्मे वीराञ्छश्वत इन्द्र शिप्रिन् ॥ ऋ. 3.36.10

asme pra yandhi maghavannṛjīṣinnindra rāyo viśvārasya bhūreḥ, asme śatam śarado jīvase dhā asme vīrāmchhaśvata indra śiprin. RV. 3.36.10

[Meaning] (Maghvan) O Lord Almighty! Grant us (bhure) all worldly wealth and the object aimed to attain by all. Kindly grant us the plentiful wealth to be desired by all. O Lord, give us a hundred autumns of life. O omniscient. All-powerful Lord! Please give us a large number of brave and strong men.

ओम् अश्मा भव परशुर्भव हिरण्यमस्तृतं भव ।
वेदो वै पुत्रनामासि स जीव शरदः शतम् ॥ अथर्व. 1.15.3

Om aśmā bhava paraśurbhava hiraṇyamastṛtam bhava,
vedo vai putranāmāsi sa jīva śaradaḥ śatam. AV. 1.15.3

[Meaning] O child! By God's grace, you become firm and strong like a rock, axe for wicked and bright in character and knowledge like gold. You are the son of mine and Veda by confidential name, so you live a hundred autumns.

Afterwards, he should chant the following Mantra thrice in mind.

त्र्यायुषं जमदग्नेः कश्यपस्य त्र्यायुषम् ।
यद्देवेषु त्र्यायुषं तन्नो अस्तु त्र्यायुषम् ॥ यजु० 3.62; पार.गृसू.1.16.7

trayāyuṣam jamadagneḥ kaśyapasya trayāyuṣam,
yaddeveṣu trayāyuṣam tanno astu trayāyuṣam.

YV. 3.62; Pār.GS.1.16.7

May by God's grace there be three times life of my eyes, three times life of my vital airs, three times life and may that three times life of learned persons be attained by us and may it be three times for us.

Thereafter, he should take off the hands from the shoulders of the child and go to the place where the child was born and should pronounce in mind the following Mantra.

ओं वेद ते भूमि हृदयं दिव चन्द्रमासि श्रितम् ।
वेदाहं तन्मां तद्विद्यात्पश्येम शरदः शतं जीवेम
शरदः शतꣳश्रृणुयाम शरदः शतम् ॥ पार.गृसू. 1.16.17

Oṁ veda te bhūmi hṛdayaṁ diva chandramāsi śritam,
vedāhaṁ tanmāṁ tadvidyātpaśyema śaradaḥ śataṁ jīvema
śaradaḥ śataṁśṛṇuyāma śaradaḥ śatam. Pār.GS. 1.16.17

[Meaning] O lady! (the ground of childbirth) I know your heart and mind, which got fixed in the moon in the heavenly region and let it know me. May you and I be able to see a hundred autumns. Live a hundred autumns and possess the audibility of ears for a hundred autumns.

The father of the child pronouncing the following Mantras should sprinkle fragrant water on the body of the lady who has delivered the child:

यत्ते सुसीमे हदयꣳ हितमन्तः प्रजापतौ ।
वेदाहं मन्ये तद्ब्रह्म माहं पौत्रमघं निगाम् ॥
सा.मन्त्रब्रा. 1.5.10; गोभिल गृसू० 2.8.4

yatte susīme hadayaṁ hitamantaḥ prajāpatau,
vedāhaṁ manye tadbrahma māhaṁ pautramaghaṁ nigām.
Sā.Mbr. 1.5.10; Go.GS. 2.8.4

[Meaning] O lady of attractive hair-bunch; I know that of your heart which is fixed in the Lord of the creatures, that is very generous, and I also realize this fact. May God be graceful to me so that I cannot be subjected to pain caused by the absence of progeny.

यत्पृथिव्या अनामृतं दिवि चन्द्रमसि श्रितम् ।
वेदामृतं दिवि चन्द्रमसि श्रितम् ।
वेदामृतस्याहं नाम माहं पौत्रमघꣳ रिषम् ॥11 ॥
सा.मन्त्रब्रा. 1.5.11; गोभिल गृसू० 2.8.5

yatpṛthivyā anāmṛtaṁ divi chandramasi śritam;
vedāmṛtaṁ divi chandramasi śritam;

vedāmṛtasyāhaṁ nāma māhaṁ pautramaghaṁ riṣam.

Sā.Mbr. 1.5.11; Go.GS. 2.8.5

[Meaning] O lady! I know that of your heart, which is the substantial product of the earth and is fixed on the moon in space. I know it is the means of immortality in this world. May I not be subjected to the pain caused by the absence of progeny.

इन्द्राग्नी शर्म यच्छतं प्रजायै मे प्रजापतिः ।
यथायं न प्रमीयते पुत्रो जनित्र्या अधि ॥12॥

सा.मन्त्रब्रा. 1.5.12; गोभिल गृसू० 2.8.6

indrāgnī śarma yachchhataṁ prajāyai me prajāpatiḥ;
yathāyaṁ na pramīyate putro janitrayā adhi.

Sā. Mbr. 1.5.12; Go.GS. 2.8.6

[Meaning] Let the fire and electricity which are the preserver of worldly subjects give us pleasure, in the way that this child in the lap of mother may not be subjected by immature death.

यददश्चन्द्रमसि कृष्ण पृथिव्या हदयꣳश्रितम् ।
तदहं विद्वꣳस्तत्पश्यन् माहं पौत्रमघꣳ रुदम् ॥13॥

सा.मन्त्रब्रा. 1.5.13; गोभिल गृसू० 2.8.7

yadadaśchandramasi kṛṣṇa pṛthivyā hadayaṁ śritam;
tadahaṁ vidvaṁstatpaśyan māhaṁ pautramaghaṁ rudam.

Sā.Mbr. 1.5.13; Go.GS. 2.8.7

[Meaning] I know that the blank substance of the earth fixed in the moon and carefully seeing it may not weep for the pain caused by the absence of progeny.

The father should bless the child with the following Mantras:

कोऽसि कतमोऽस्येषोऽस्यमृतोऽसि ।
आहस्पत्यं मासं प्रविशासौ ॥ सा.मन्त्रब्रा. 1.5.14; गोभिल गृसू० 2.8.13

ko'si katamo'syeṣo'syamṛto'si;
āhaspatyam māsaṁ praviśāsau. Sā. Mbr. 1.5.14; Go.GS. 2.8.13

[Meaning] O child! who are you? Amongst whomsoever are you? You are this one of our souls. You are immortal. May God grace you to enter the month which is produced by the sun.

स त्वाह्ने परिदाल्वहस्त्वा रात्र्यै परिददातु रात्रिस्त्वाहोरात्राभ्यां परिददाल्वहोरात्रौ त्वार्द्धमासेभ्यः परिदत्तामर्द्धमासास्त्वा मासेभ्यः परिददतु मासास्त्वर्तुभ्यः परिददत्वृतवस्त्वा संवत्सराय परिददतु संवत्सरस्त्वायुषे जरायै परिददाल्वसौ ॥

सा.मन्त्रब्रा. 1.5.15; गोभिल गृसू० 2.8.14

sa   tvāhne   paridātvahastvā   rātrayai   paridadātu rātristvāhorātrābhyāṁ paridadātvahorātrau tvārddhamāsebhyaḥ paridattāmarddhamāsāstvā   māsebhyaḥ   paridadatu māsāstvartubhyaḥ paridadatvṛtavastvā saṁvatsarāya paridadatu saṁvatsarastvāyuṣe jarāyai paridadātvasau.

Sā. Mbr. 1.5.15; Go.GS. 2.8.14

[Meaning] By God's grace, may the sun give you to the days, may the days give you for nights, may nights give you to day and night, O child! may day and night give you to half months. May half months give you to months, may the months give you to seasons, may seasons in their turn preserve you the whole year, may the full year preserve you for lite and timely maturity of age.

He again pronouncing the following Mantaras: should smell the head of the child. In the same manner, he should smell the head of the child when he (father) comes from the journey of outstations so that there grows more love between the son and parents.

अङ्गादङ्गात्सꣳस्रवसि हृदयादधिजायसे ।
प्राणं ते प्राणेन सं दधामि जीव मे यावदायुषम् ॥ सा.म.ब्रा. 1.5.16

aṅgādaṅgātsaṁsravasi hṛdayādadhijāyase,
prāṇaṁ te prāṇena saṁ dadhāmi jīva me yāvadāyuṣam.

Sāma.Br. 1.5.16

[Meaning] O child! You are born from every limb of

my body; you have come to exist from my heart. I preserve your vital airs with my vital airs; O child live up to the life span prescribed to live normally.

अङ्गादङ्गात्संभवसि हृदयादधिजायसे ।
वेदो वै पुत्रनामासि स जीव शरदः शतम् ॥ साम.ब्रा. 1.5.17

aṅgādaṅgātsaṁbhavasi hṛdayādadhijāyase;
vedo vai putranāmāsi sa jīva śaradaḥ śatam. Sāma. Br. 1.5.17

[Meaning] O child! You are born from every part of my body and have come to exist from my heart. You are my son, and you are Veda in your confidential identity.

अश्मा भव परशुर्भव हिरण्यमस्तृतं भव ।
आत्मासि पुत्र मा मृथाः स जीव शरदः शतम् ॥ साम.ब्रा. 1.5.18

aśmā bhava paraśurbhava hiraṇyamastṛtaṁ bhava;
ātmāsi putra mā mṛthāḥ sa jīva śaradaḥ śatam.

Sāma.Br. 1.5.18

[Meaning] May you become firm and strong like a rock, like an axe to destroy injustice, and as bright as gold with knowledge and action. O child, you are my soul and spirit. Die not an immature death and live a hundred autumns.

पशूनां त्वा हिङ्करेणाभिजिघ्राम्यसौ ॥ साम.ब्रा. 1.5.19

paśūnāṁ tvā hiṅkareṇābhijighrāmyasau ॥ Sāma.Br. 1.5.19

[Meaning] I smell your head with the lowing of animals.

Again, praying to God with the following Mantras restoring the lady to a delightful mood, the child's father should wash the lady's (the child's mother's) breasts with lukewarm, odoriferous water and wipe them;

ओम् इडासि मैत्रावरुणी वीरे वीरमजीजनथाः ।
सा त्वं वीरवती भव याऽस्मान्वीरवतोऽकरत् ॥ पार.गृसू.1.16.17

Om iḍāsi maitrāvaruṇī vīre vīramajījanathāḥ,

sā tvaṁ vīravatī bhava yā'smānvīravato'karat.

Pār.GS.1.16.17

[Meaning] O brave lady! You are like the Iḍā nāḍi (of left nostril) of two vital airs, the prāna and apāna; you have given birth to a brave child. May you, who have made us the possessors of a brave child, be the mother of the brave child.

The father of the child pronouncing the following Mantra should put the right breast of the child's mother into the mouth of child:

ओम् इमꣳ स्तनमूर्जꣳस्वन्तं धयापां प्रपीनमग्रे सरिरस्य मध्ये ।
उत्सं जुषस्व मधुमन्तमर्वन्त्समुद्रियꣳ सदनमा विंशस्व ॥ यजु० 17.87

Om imaṁ stanamūrjjaṁsvantaṁ dhayāpāṁ prapīnamagne sarirasya madhye;
utsam juṣasva madhumantamarvantsamudriyaṁ sadanamā viṁśasva. YV. 17.87

[Meaning] O child! You keeping yourself strong and sturdy amongst you men, suck the breast which has got fat with the flow of milk, you throughout your infancy, affectionately suck the breast full of palatable milk and thus enjoy the state of blooming strength you attain not only earthly knowledge but also the knowledge of mid sphere and space.

With the following mantras, he should put the left breast of the child's mother into the mouth of the child:

ओं यस्ते स्तनः शशयो यो मयोभूर्यो रत्नधा वसुविद्यः सुदत्रः ।
येन विश्वा पुष्यसि वार्याणि सरस्वति तमिह धातवे कः ॥

शब्रा.14.9.4.28; पार.गृसू. 1.16.21

Oṁ yaste stanaḥ śaśayo yo mayobhūryo ratnadhā vasuvidyaḥ sudatraḥ,
yena viśvā puṣyasi vāryāṇi sarasvati tamiha dhātave kaḥ.

Ś.Br. 14.9.4.28; Pār.GS. 1.16.21

[Meaning] O lady of knowledge and wisdom, you give to this child that of your breast which is in your body, which is the source of pleasure, by which you grow and strengthen all the limbs of the child, which has in it the qualities and effect of precious metals and intellectual strength and which gives strength and vigour to the child, to suck it.

Afterwards, a jug full of water should be put on the earth in the side where the lady having given birth to the child keeps her head, and thus, this jug should be kept there for ten nights. The lady who delivered the child should remain in the place of delivery for ten days. The Mantra with which the jug of water be kept there runs as follows:

ओम् आपो देवेषु जाग्रथ यथा देवेषु जाग्रथ।
एवमस्याꣳसूतिकायाꣳसपुत्रिकायां जाग्रथ ॥ पार.गृसू.1.16.22

Om āpo deveṣu jāgratha yathā deveṣu jāgratha,
ēvamasyāṁsūtikāyāṁ saputrikāyāṁ jāgratha.

Pār.GS.1.16.22

[Meaning] The water always remains effective amongst all the physical forces, as they remain activated in all the physical powers, so they remain effective and activated in the place of maternity where the child has been born.

With the following two Mantras, there should be offered in the fire the oblations of cooked rice mixed with mustard seeds up to ten days in the place where delivery took place each evening and morning when the night and day meet together.

ओं शण्डामर्का उपवीरः शौण्डिकेय उलूखलः।
मलिम्लुचो द्रोणासश्च्यवनो नश्यतादितः स्वाहा॥
इदं शण्डामर्काभ्यामुपवीराय शौण्डिकेयायोलूखलाय
मलिम्लुचाय द्रोणेभ्यश्च्यवनाय-इदन्न मम॥ पार.गृसू.1.16.23

Oṁ śaṇḍāmarkā upavīraḥ śauṇḍikeya ulūkhalaḥ,
malimlucho droṇasaśchyavano naśyatāditaḥ svāhā.
idaṁ śaṇḍāmarkābhyāmupavīrāya śauṇḍikeyāyolūkhalāya
malimluchāya droṇebhyaśchyavanāya-idanna mama.

Pār.GS. 1.16.23

[Meaning] Let the deadly diseases and diseases inflicting pain, creating discomfiture to the child, the diseases born of contact with pathogenic bacteria and dirty things, the diseases affecting ear, nose, and throat, the diseases creating general debility in the body flee away from this place by God's grace.

ओम् आलिखन्ननिमिषः किंवदन्त उपश्रुतिर्हर्यक्षः कुम्भीशत्रुः पात्रपाणिनृ मणिर्हन्त्रीमुखः सर्षपारुणश्च्यवनो नश्यतादितः स्वाहा ।
इदमालिखतेऽनिमिषाय किंवदद्भ्य उपश्रुतये हर्यक्षाय कुम्भीशत्रवे पात्रपाणये नृमणये हन्त्रीमुखाय सर्षपारुणाय च्यवनाय-इदन्न मम ॥ पार.गृसू.1.16.23

Om ālikhannanimiṣaḥ kiṁvadanta upaśrutirharyakṣaḥ
kumbhīśatruḥ patrapāṇirnṛ maṇirhantrīmukhaḥ
sarṣaparuṇaśchyavano naśyatāditaḥ svāhā,

idamālikhate'nimiṣāya kiṁvadadbhya upaśrutaye
haryakṣāya kumbhīśatrave pātrapāṇaye nṛmaṇaye
hantrīmukhāya sarṣaparuṇāya chyavanāya-idanna mama.

Pār.GS.1.16.23

[Meaning] Let the germs and pathogenic bacteria which constantly bite, making unintelligible sounds active in approaching the child, having yellow eyes, creating cough in the nose treating like enemies, whose hands are like pot, killing the man, having violent and voracious mouths, red like a mustard seed, causing decay, flee away from this place by God's grace. The oblations offered here are meant for these and are not for me.

After that, the highly learned, pious men subscribing to the Vedic religion standing outside and the father of the child remaining inside should delightfully pronounce the following Mantras of blessing:

मा नो हासिषु ऋषयो दैव्या ये तनूपा ये नस्तन्वस्तनूजाः ।
अमर्त्या मर्त्यां अभि नः सचध्वमायुर्धत्त प्रतरं जीवसे नः ॥ अथर्व 6.4.41

mā no hāsiṣu ṛṣayo daivyā ye tanūpā ye nastanvastanūjāḥ;
amartyā martyāṁ abhi naḥ sachadhvamāyurdhatta
prataraṁ jīvaseṁ naḥ. AV. 6.4.41

[Meaning] Let not the sense organs of our bodies leave us. Let not the immunity power of our body leave us; let not our children produced from our body leave us. Let there be no disconnect of enlightened beings from ordinary human beings, and let them provide us knowledge of a praiseworthy life.

इमं जीवेभ्यः परिधिं दधामि मैषां नु गादपरो अर्थंमेतम् ।
शतं जीवन्तः शरदः पुरूचीस्तिरो मृत्युं दधतां पर्वतेन ॥ अथर्व॰ 12.2.23

imaṁ jīvebhyaḥ paridhiṁ dadhāmi maiṣāṁ nu gādaparo
arthaṁmetam;
śataṁ jīvantaḥ śaradaḥ purūchīstiro mṛtyuṁ dadhatāṁ
parvatena. AV. 12.2.23

[Meaning] I (God) enjoin the guiding principle of life for all living creatures; let not anyone violate that principle; may all human beings live a life of hundred autumns acting upon in various ways, and may all of you hide your death (by Brahmacharya and leading a Vedic life) like a mountain hide the things.

विवस्वान्नो अभ्यं कृणोतु यः सुत्रामा जीरदानुः सुदानुः ।
इहेमे वीराः बहर्वो भवन्तु गोमदश्वन्मय्यस्तु पुष्टम् ॥ अथर्व 18.3.61

vivasvānno abhyaṁ kṛṇotu yaḥ sutrāmā jīradānuḥ sudānuḥ;
iheme vīrāḥ baharvo bhavantu gomadaśvanmayyastu
puṣṭam. AV. 18.3.61

[Meaning] May God, who throws away all ignorance and is an excellent protector, giver of everything and invigorator of energy, free us from fear. May there be many brave men in the world, and may I be endowed with the intellectual [gomat] and physical power [aśvavat].

Now here ends the procedure of the ceremony of a newly born child.

अथ नामकरणसंस्कारविधिं वक्ष्यामः

The Ceremony of Naming

अत्र प्रमाणम्—

atra pramāṇam—

The authority of scriptures on this subject—

नाम चास्मै दद्युः ॥

nāma chāsmai dadyuḥ.

[Meaning] They (the parent, Āchārya, etc.) give the child name.

घोषवदाद्यन्तरन्तःस्थमभिनिष्ठानान्तं द्व्यक्षरम् ॥

चतुरक्षरं वा ॥ आश्व० गृसू० 1.15.4-5

ghoṣavadādyantarantaḥsthamabhiniṣṭhānāntaṁ dvyakṣaram chaturakṣaraṁ vā. Āśv. GS. 1.15.4-5

The name should start with a voiced consonantal sound like (ga, gha, ja, jha, ḍa, ḍha, da, dha, ba, bha, ha aspirate sounds and include one of the semivowels (ya, ra, la, va) in the middle and voiceless pirant (:) in the end. The name should have two syllables or four syllables.

द्व्यक्षरं प्रतिष्ठाकामश्चतुरक्षरं ब्रह्मवर्चसकामः ॥आश्व० गृसू० 1.15.6

dvyakṣaraṁ pratiṣṭhākāmaśchaturakṣaraṁ brahmavarchasakāmaḥ. Āśv.GS. 1.15.6

[Meaning] Parents desiring their child to earn a name and fame should give him a name of two syllables; if they desire their child to be an intellectual, they should give him a name of four syllables.

युग्मानि त्वेव पुंसाम् ॥ आश्व० गृसू० 1.15.7

yugmāni tveva puṁsām. Āśv. GS. 1.15.7

[Meaning] The name of the male child should be of

even numbers of syllables, like 2, 4, 6...

अयुजानि स्त्रीणाम् ॥

ayujāni strīṇām.

The female child's name should be of odd numbers of syllables like 1, 3,5......

अभिवादनीयं च समीक्षेत तन्मातापितरौ विदध्यातामोपनयनात् ॥

आश्व० गृसू० 1.15.4-10

abhivādanīyaṁ   cha   samīkṣeta   tanmātāpitarau vidadhyātāmopanayanāt. Āśv.GS. 1.15.4-10

One name of the child be given by Āchārya so as it remains till the ceremony of sacred thread and this name be known by father and mother of the child.

It is from the Āśvalāyana Gṛhya Sūtra.

Now we quote Pāraskara Gṛhyasūtra.

दशम्यामुत्थाप्य पिता नाम करोति । द्व्यक्षरं चतुरक्षरं वा घोषवदाद्यन्तरन्तःस्थं दीर्घाभिनिष्ठानान्तं कृतं कुर्यान्न तद्धितम् । अयुजाक्षरमाकारान्तः स्त्रियै । शर्म ब्राह्मणस्य वर्म क्षत्रियस्यगुप्तेति वैश्यस्य ॥ पारस्कर गृसू० 1.17.1-4

daśamyāmutthāpya   pitā   nāma   karoti, dvyakṣaraṁ chaturakṣaraṁ   vā   ghoṣavadādyantarantaḥsthaṁ dīrghābhiniṣṭhānāntaṁ   kṛtaṁ   kuryānna   taddhitam, ayujākṣaramākārāntaṁ striyai, śarma brāhmaṇasya varma kṣatriyasyagupteti vaiśyasya. Pār.GS. 1.17.1-4

[Meaning] On the tenth day from the day of delivery of the child, the father takes the mother from the maternity place and performs the child's naming ceremony. The name should contain two or four syllables and a voiced consonant in the beginning, intervened by a semivowel and ending with a long vowel. In the end, it should have a kṛt pratyaya (primary suffix) and not taddhita pratyaya (secondary suffix). The name of the female child should be of odd syllables and ending with आकार, ईकार (ā and ī sounds. For example, Śrī, Hrī, Yaśodā, Sukhadā, Saubhāgypradā etc.[4] The name of the child endowed with the characteristics of an intellectual should be followed with the epithet of 'Sharman', e.g Devasharmā, and that of a child with characteristics of a Kṣatriya with 'Varman', e.g. Devavarmā and that of a child with trading or merchant tendency with 'Gupta', e.g. Devagupta; and a child having tendency of dullness, illiteracy with 'Dasa', e.g. Devadāsa.

Gobhilīya (2.8.8-18) and the Śaunaka Gṛhyasūtras तेद ब that an attractive name should be given to the child.

The time of Naming Ceremony

The name should be given to a child on the 11th day, ten days from the day of the birth, or the hundred-first day (101st day) or on the very day of the child's birth at the beginning of the second year.

On the day fixed for the child's naming ceremony, the guests, friends and well-wishers should be cordially invited, and the yajmāna (the father of the child) and the priests of the yajña should start the procedure of the ceremony.

---

[4] But female child should not be assigned the following names:

नक्षवृक्षनदीनाम्नीं नान्त्यपर्वतनामिकाम् ।
न पक्ष्यहिप्रेष्यनाम्नीं न च भीशणनामिकाम् ॥ मनु० 3.9

Names of stars- रोहिणी, रेवती etc., names of trees and plants like चम्पा, तुलसी etc., names oas: गंगा, यमुना, सरस्वती etc., names of unrespectful professions like चाण्डाली, names of mountains like विन्ध्याचला, हिमालय; names of birds like- कोकिला, हंसा etc., names of snake like सर्पिणी, नागी etc., names indicating servents like दासी, किङ्करी, चण्डिका etc., are prohibited.

The naming ceremony should be started with mantras for the prayer of God (Īśvara stuti), Svastivāchana, Śāntikaraṇa as prescribed in Sāmānya Prakaraṇa, and the complete procedure of Sāmānya prakaraṇa should be performed. Afterwards, four oblations of Āghārāvājyabhāgāhuti; four Vyāhṛiti oblations, eight oblations with eight mantras beginning with त्वन्नो अग्रे॰ as given in the Sāmānya Prakaraṇa, should be offered. These make a total of 16 oblations of ghee.

Afterwards, the child's mother should give him a bath with clean water and dress him in excellent, clean outfits. She should come to the place of yajñakuṇḍa and, passing behind the child's father, stand on the right side of him (the child's father). She should hand over the child to his father, keeping his head in the north, and she should, returning from the back side of her husband, take her seat in the north side, keeping her face in the east.

Afterwards, the father, keeping the child's head in the north direction and feet in the south direction, should hand over the child to his wife. Afterwards, they should perform the main procedure prescribed for the same sanskāra. Take a spoonful of ghee from the yajña sāmagri arranged for sanskāra. Yajmāna, the father of the child, should offer one oblation reciting the following mantra:

ओं प्रजापतये स्वाहा । गोभिल गृसू. 2.8.12

Oṁ prajāpataye svāhā. Go.GS. 2.8.12

After that, four oblations should be offered - one oblation with each in the name of Tithi, Nakṣatra, Tithi-devatā and Nakshatra-devatā. The oblations of ghee should be offered by pronouncing the names of Tithi, Nakṣatra, Tithi-devatā and Nakshatra-devatā in the fourth nominal case-ending. For example, if the birth of a child took place on Pratipadā (the first lunar tithi) and there was Aśvinī Nakṣatra, the oblations should be offered as:

ओं प्रतिपदे स्वाहा। ओं ब्रह्मणे स्वाहा। ओम् अश्विन्यै स्वाहा। ओम् अश्विभ्यां स्वाहा॥ गोभिल गृसू.० 2.8.12

Om pratipade svāhā, Om brahmaṇe svāhā, Om aśvinyai svāhā, Om aśvibhyāṁ svāhā. Go.GS. 2.8.12

Afterwards one oblation with the स्विष्टकृत मंत्र and four Vyāhṛti oblations should be offered totalling 5 oblations.

Then, the mother taking the child in her lap should sit on a comfortable seat, and the father of the child should recite the following mantras by feeling the breathing of the child:

कोऽसि कतमोऽसि कस्यासि को नामासि। यस्य ते नामामन्महि यं त्वा सोमेनातीतृपाम। भूर्भुवः स्वः सुप्रजाः प्रजाभिः स्याꣳ सुवीरो वीरैः सुपोषः पोषैः॥

यजु. 7.29

ko'si katamo'si kasyāsi ko nāmāsi; yasya te nāmāmanmahi yaṁ tvā somenātītṛpāma; bhūrbhuvaḥ svaḥ suprajāḥ prajābhiḥ syām̐ suvīro vīraiḥ supoṣaḥ poṣaiḥ. YV. 7.29

[Meaning] O Child! You are the source of pleasure and delight; you are the most delighting factor; you belong to God, the Lord of creatures. You have your own identity through which you are known to us. We have satisfied you with the nice sip of milk; may God bless you to make us satisfied; may God who is existent, conscious and all-blissful bless us all with good progeny, bless us with brave children and bless us with spiritual and material prosperity and with all the means of protection and preservation.

ओं कोऽसि कतमोऽस्येषोऽस्यमृतोऽसि।
आहस्पत्यं मासं प्रविशासौ॥ गोभिल गृसू. 2.8.13-14

Om ko'si katamo'syeṣo'syamṛto'si,
āhaspatyaṁ māsaṁ praviśāsau. Go. GS. 2.8.13-14

[Meaning] O Child! Who are you? Who do you belong to? Really, you are immortal, and you belong to

All-blissful God. May you enter into the months after months in the reign of God.

In place of the word असौ used at the end of the second mantra, the name given to the child (as per the manner prescribed above) should be pronounced.

The following mantras should be used to give blessings to the child.

ओं स त्वाह्ने परिददात्वहस्त्वा रात्रै परिददातु रात्रिस्त्वाहोरात्राभ्यां परिददात्वहोरात्रौ त्वार्द्धमासेभ्यः परिदत्तामर्द्धमासास्त्वा मासेभ्यः परिददतु मासास्त्वर्तुभ्यः परिददत्वृतवस्त्वा संवत्सराय परिददतु संवत्सरस्त्वायुषे जरायै परिददातु, असौ ॥ मंत्रब्रा. 1.5.15 गोभिल गृसू.० 2.8.15

Oṁ sa tvāhne paridadātvahastvā rātrayai paridadātu rātristvāhorātrābhyāṁ paridadātvahorātrau tvārddhamāsebhyaḥ paridattāmarddhamāsāstvā māsebhyaḥ paridadatu māsāstvarttubhyaḥ paridadatvṛtavastvā saṁvatsarāya paridadatu saṁvatsarastvāyuṣe jarāyai paridadātu, asau.

M.Br. 1.5.15 Go.GS. 2.8.15

[Meaning] By God's grace, may the sun give you to the days, may the days give you for nights, may nights give you to day and night, O child! may day and night give you to half months. May half months give you to months, may the months give you to seasons, may seasons in their turn preserve you the whole year, may the full year preserve you for lite and timely maturity of age.

Following the above procedure, a name should be given to the child, and the same should be announced to the people attending this ceremony. The ceremony should be concluded by reciting the Vāmadevya gāna quoted at the end of Sāmānya Prakaraṇa.

Afterwards, give a warm send-off to all the respected guests who graced the occasion with their presence. All people before departure should pray to God by reciting the prayer mantras prescribed for this purpose and give blessings to the child as follows:

हे बालक! त्वमायुष्मान् वर्च्चस्वी तेजस्वी श्रीमान् भूयाः ।

he bālaka! tvamāyuṣmān varchchasvī tejasvī śrīmān bhūyāḥ.

[Meaning] O Child! May you be long-lived, learned, pious, famous, perseverant, influential, philanthropic and prosperous.

इति नामकरणसंस्कारविधिः समाप्तः ॥

iti nāmakaraṇasaṁskāravidhiḥ samāptaḥ.

Here ends the procedure of the Naming Ceremony.

अथ निष्क्रमणसंस्कारविधिं वक्ष्यामः
Purpose and Period of Niṣkramaṇa Sanskāra

The Vedic seers propose this for two purposes: 1. The child is exposed to the pure air of the outside environment. 2. He is allowed to experience Brahman's creation, and the first source of creation is the sun. So, he is exposed and allowed to have a glimpse of the sunlight.

The Niṣkramaṇa Sanskāra is the name of sanskāra in which the child is exposed to the outside world. As per convenience, the parents should take the child outside for a round, or they should positively take him round in the fourth month. There are authorities in this regard:

चतुर्थे मासि निष्क्रमणिका। पार.गृसू. 1.17.5

chaturthe māsi niṣkramaṇikā. Pār.GS. 1.17.5

[Meaning] In the fourth month of the date of birth, a child should be exposed to the outside world.

सूर्यमुदीक्षयतितच्चक्षुरिति॥ पार.गृसू. 1.17.6

sūryamudīkṣayatitachchakṣuriti. Pār.GS. 1.17.6

[Meaning] The child should be exposed to the sun by chanting 'तच्चक्षुर्देवहितम्॰' (*tachchurdevahitam...*) mantra.

It is also in Gobhil Gṛhyasūtra (2.8.1)

जननाद्यस्तृतीयो ज्यौत्स्नस्तस्य तृतीयायाम्॥ गोभिलगृसू. 2.8.1

jananādyastṛtīyo jyautsnastasya tṛtīyāyām. Go.GS. 2.8.1

[Meaning] There are two alternatives regarding the time or ceremony of Niṣkramaṇa.

1. The first time is the third day of the third bright half of the Moon from the child's birth date.

2. The second time is the birth tithi of the child in the fourth month from the date of birth.

Procedure of of Niṣkramaṇa Sanskāra

On the day of this sanskāra, the parents should give a bath to the child in the morning after sunrise with clean water and dress him with a lovely formal outfit. Afterwards, the mother of the child should bring the child to the yajñaśālā, passing from the right side of her husband and coming in front of him; she should hand over the child to her husband, keeping the head of the child in the north. She should sit to the left of her husband, keeping her face eastward.

यत्ते सुसीमे हदयꣳ हितमन्तः प्रजापतौ ।
वेदाहं मन्ये तद्ब्रह्म माहं पौत्रमघं निगाम् ॥

सा.मन्त्रब्रा. 1.5.10; गोभिल गृसू० 2.8.4

yatte susīme hadayam̐ hitamantaḥ prajāpatau,
vedāham manye tadbrahma māham pautramagham nigām.

Sā. Mbr. 1.5.10; Go.GS. 2.8.4

[Meaning] O lady of attractive hair-bunch; I know that of your heart which is fixed in the Lord of the creatures, that is very generous, and I also realize this fact. May God be graceful to me so that I cannot be subjected to pain caused by the absence of progeny.

यत्पृथिव्या अनामृतं दिवि चन्द्रमसि श्रितम् ।
वेदामृतं दिवि चन्द्रमसि श्रितम् ।
वेदामृतस्याहं नाम माहं पौत्रमघꣳरिषम् ॥11 ॥

सा.मन्त्रब्रा. 1.5.11; गोभिल गृसू० 2.8.5

yatpṛthivyā anāmṛtam divi chandramasi śritam;
vedāmṛtam divi chandramasi śritam;
vedāmṛtasyāham nāma māham pautramagham̐ riṣam.

Sā. Mbr. 1.5.11; Go.GS. 2.8.5

[Meaning] O lady! I know that of your heart, which is

the substantial product of the earth and is fixed on the moon in space. I know it is the means of immortality in this world. May I not be subjected to the pain caused by the absence of progeny.

इन्द्राग्री शर्म यच्छतं प्रजायै मे प्रजापतिः ।
यथायं न प्रमीयते पुत्रो जनित्र्या अधि ॥12॥

सा.मन्त्रब्रा. 1.5.12; गोभिल गृसू॰ 2.8.6

indrāgnī śarma yachchhataṁ prajāyai me prajāpatiḥ;
yathāyaṁ na pramīyate putro janitrayā adhi.

Sā. Mbr. 1.5.12; Go.GS. 2.8.6

[Meaning] Let the solar radiations and geothermal energy, which are the preservers of life on the earth, give us pleasure so that this child in the mother's lap may not be subjected to immature death.

Praying God with these three mantras, as mentioned above, the procedure of prayer of God by eight mantras of Prayer, Svastivāchana (स्वस्तिवाचन) Śāntikaraṇa (शान्तिकरण) and complete Havan of Sāmānya Prakaraṇa should be performed. The father of the child holding the child touches the head of the child with the following three mantras.

ओम् अङ्गादङ्गात्सम्भवसि हृदयादविधजायसे ।
आत्मा वै पुत्रनामासि स जीव शरदः शतम् ॥ पार॰ गृसू॰ 1.18.2

Om aṅgādaṅgātsambhavasi hṛdayādavidhajāyase,
ātmā vai putranāmāsi sa jīva śaradaḥ śatam. Pār. GS. 1.18.2

[Meaning] O Child! You come into existence from all of the parts of my body (during orgasm, all body parts are stimulated) and take birth from my heart. You are my soul. May you not die before me, and may you enjoy the life of a hundred autumns.

ओं प्रजापतेष्ट्वा हिङ्कारेणावजिघ्रामि ।
सहस्रायुषाऽसौ जीव शरदः शतम् ॥ पार॰ गृसू॰ 1.18.3

Oṁ pujāpateṣṭvā hiṅkāreṇāvajighrāmi,
sahasrāyuṣā'sau jīva śaradaḥ śatam. Pār.GS. 1.18.3

[Meaning] O Child! (avajighrāmi) I smell your head (hiṅkāreṇa) with the affectionate words granted to me by (prajāpateḥ) God. (sahasrāyuṣā) May you attain a very long life and (jiva) live (śaradaḥ śatam) a hundred autumns.

गवां त्वा हिङ्करेणावजिघ्रामि।
सहस्रायुषाऽसौ जीव शरदः शतम् ॥ पार० गृसू० 1.18.4

gavāṁ tvā hiṅkareṇāvajighrāmi;
sahasrāyuṣā'sau jīva śaradaḥ śatam. Pār.GS. 1.18.4

[Meaning] O Child! (avajighrāmi) I smell (tvā) your head (hiṅkāreṇa) with affectionate sounds (gavām) of cows. (asau) May you attain (sahasrāyuṣā) a very long life and (jīva) live (śaradaḥ śatam) a hundred autumuns.

The father of the child should whisper the following mantra in the right ear of child:

अस्मे प्र यन्धि मघवन्नृजीषिन्निन्द्र रायो विश्वारस्य भूरेः ।
अस्मे शतः शरदो जीवसे धा अस्मे वीरांछश्वत इन्द्र शिप्रिन् ॥

ऋ० 3.36.10 । पार० गृसू० 1.18.4

asme pra yandhi maghavannṛjīṣinnindra rāyo viśvārasya
bhūreḥ;
asme śataṁ śarado jīvase dhā asme vīrāṁchhaśvata indra
śiprin. RV. 3.36.10; Pār.GS 1.18.4

[Meaning] (Maghvan) O Lord Almighty! Kindly grant us (bhureḥ rāyaḥ) abundant worldly wealth (viśvārasya) to be desired by all. O lord, give (asme) us (śataṁ śaradaḥ) a hundred autumns (jīvase) of life. (śiprin) O omniscient, (Indra) All-powerful Lord! Give (asme) us (śaśvat) a large number (vīrān) of brave and strong men.

The following Mantra should be whispered in the left ear of the child by his father:

इन्द्र श्रेष्ठानि द्रविणानि धेहि चित्तिं दक्षस्य सुभगत्वमस्मे ।
पोषं रयीणामरिष्टिं तनूनां स्वाद्मानं वाचः सुदिनत्वमह्नाम् ॥2॥

ऋ० 2.21.6 । पा० गृसू 1.18.5

*indra śreṣṭhāni draviṇāni dhehi chittiṁ dakṣasya
subhagatvamasme,*
*poṣaṁ rayīṇāmariṣṭiṁ tanūnāṁ svādmānaṁ vāchaḥ
sudinatvamahnām. RV. 2.21.6; Pār.GS.1.18.5*

[Meaning] O Lord Almighty! Please (dhehi) grant us (śreṣṭhāni draviṇāni) wealth earned through dharma [right means]; grant us (dakṣasya) capability to accomplish acts efficiently; give us the (ariṣṭim) fortune of (tanūnām) good children. Grant us (svādmānam) the nicety (vāchah) of speech and (ahnām sudinatvam) prosperity of the days.

The father, now, should pass over the child to the child's mother, keeping its head in the north and its feet in the south directions and silently touching his wife's head. Afterwards, he should expose the child to the sun chanting the following mantras:

ओं तच्चक्षुर्देवहितं पुरस्ताच्छुक्रमुच्चरत् । पश्येम शरदः शतं जीवेम शरदः शतꣳश्रृणुयाम शरदः शतं प्र ब्रवाम शरदः शतमदीनाः स्याम शरदः शतं भूयश्च शरदः शतात् । यजू० 36.24 ॥ पार गृसू० 1.17.6

*Oṁ tachchakṣurdevahitaṁ purastāchchhukramuchcharat,
paśyema śaradaḥ śataṁ jīvema śaradaḥ śataṁ śṛṇuyāma
śaradaḥ śataṁ pra bravāma śaradaḥ śatamadīnaḥ syāma śaradaḥ
śataṁ bhūyaścha śaradaḥ śatāt. YV.36.24; Pār.GS.1.17.6*

[Meaning] That sunlight is the eye of the universe. It embodies in itself all energy particles. This shining light energy rises in the east. Having endowed with energy, may we see for a hundred autumn seasons; may we hear Śāstras for a hundred autumn seasons; may we speak, teach and preach for a hundred autumn seasons; may we be unsubdued for a hundred autumn seasons; may we do so even more than a hundred autumn seasons.

Exposing the child to the fresh air in the sun, the father should bring the child to the yajñaśālā, and all people present over there should bless it (the child) with the following utterances:

लं जीव शरदः शतं वर्धमानः ॥

tvaṁ jīva śaradaḥ śataṁ vardhamānaḥ

[Meaning] O Child! You grow in health and strength and live for a hundred autumns.

Note: These mantras show that during the Vedic period, the year also started from the autumn season.

Afterwards, the mother and father of the child, paying due respect to the guests, should give a warm send-off to the ladies and gentlemen who attended the ceremony.

After that, at night, when the moon has risen, the mother of the child dressing the child in nice outfits should come in front of her husband from his right side and give the child to him, keeping the child's head in the north direction and feet in the south direction. The mother, taking a turn to the right of her husband, should come on his left, standing before the moon face to face with water filled in side and offer prayer to God with the following mantra:

ओं यददश्चन्द्रमसि कृष्णं पृथिव्या हृदयꣳ श्रितम्।
तदहं विद्वाꣳस्तत्पश्यन्माहं पौत्रमघꣳ रुदम्॥

मन्त्र ब्रा. 1.5.13 ॥ गोभिल गृ.सू. 2.8.6.7

Oṁ yadadaśchandramasi kṛṣṇaṁ pṛthivyā hṛdayaṁ śritam,
tadahaṁ vidvāṁ statpaśyanmāhaṁ pautramaghaṁ rudam.

Mantra Br. 1.5.13. Go.GS. 2.8.6.7

Performing the prayer of God by the mantra mentioned above, the mother should drop the water filled in her hands on the ground. Afterwards, she, passing from the back side of her husband and coming before him by his right side, should take the child from him and again passing behind the husband should come by his left and stand keeping the head of the child in the north direction and feet in the south direction. The father of the child, then taking water in his hands, perform the prayer of God with the mantra ॐ यददश्चन्द्रमसि० and drop water on the ground. Thus, both (the wife and husband) go home in a delightful mood.

इति निष्क्रमणसंस्कारविधिः समाप्तः ॥

iti niṣkramaṇasaṁskāravidhiḥ samāptaḥ.

Here ends the procedure of the Niṣkramaṇa Sanskāra.

अथान्नप्राशनविधिं वक्ष्यामः

Annaprāśana Sanskāra

This Annaprāśana ceremony should be performed when the child gains strength to digest cereals.

There is authority of Āśvalāyana Gṛhyasūtra.

षष्ठे मास्यन्नप्राशनम् ॥

ṣaṣṭhe māsyannaprāśanam.

[Meaning] In the six months from birth, a child should undergo the Annaprāśana ceremony

घृतौदनं तेजस्कामः ॥

ghṛtaudanaṁ tejaskāmaḥ.

दधिमघुघृतमिश्रितमन्नं प्राशयेत् ॥

dadhimaghughṛtamiśritamannaṁ prāśayet.

There are similar authorities of Paraskara Gṛhyasūtra, etc.

In the sixth month, the child should fed cereal. He who desires his child to be brilliant and famous should feed him cooked rice mixed with ghee or rice mixed with honey, curd and ghee according to the following procedure. That is, after having performed the complete procedure of Prayer of God, Svastivāchana, Śāntikaraṇa and complete Sāmānya Prakaraṇa, the person concerned should perform the Cereal feeding ceremony on the day on which the child was born. The rice should be prepared by the following method:

ओं प्राणाय त्वा जुष्टं प्रोक्षामि ।

Oṁ prāṇāya tvā juṣṭaṁ prokṣām.

ओम् अपानाय त्वा जुष्टं प्रोक्षामि ।

Om apānāya tvā juṣṭaṁ prokṣām.

ओं चक्षुषे त्वा जुष्टं प्रोक्षामि ।

Om chakṣuṣe tvā juṣṭaṁ prokṣām.

ओं श्रोत्राय त्वा जुष्टं प्रोक्षामि ।

Om śrotrāya tvā juṣṭaṁ prokṣām.

ओम् अग्रये स्विष्टकृते त्वा जुष्टं प्रोक्षामि ॥

Om agnaye sviṣṭakṛte tvā juṣṭaṁ prokṣām.

The purport of these above-cited mantras is that the rice be washed, cleaned, and cooked nicely, and ghee in proper quantity be mixed in the rice where it is in the cooking process. When this rice has been cooked properly and has become cold, it should be put in Homasthāli, the pot of Homa. He should then distribute some of the rice in the pots of yajamāna, the purohit and Ṛtvija, with the following five mantras.

ओं प्राणाय त्वा जुष्टं निर्वपामि । ओम् अपानाय त्वा० । ओं चक्षुषे त्वा० । ओं श्रोत्राय त्वा० । ओम् अग्रये स्विष्टकृते त्वा० ॥

Om prāṇāya tvā juṣṭaṁ nirvapāmi, Om apānāya tvā..., Om chakṣuṣe tvā.., Om śrotrāya tvā.., Om agnaye sviṣṭakṛte tvā...

After that, the Yajamāna should perform Agnyādhāna, Samidādhāna, etc. and then should offer eight oblations in total, that is, the four oblations of Āghārāvājyabhāgāhuti and four oblations of Vyāhṛti. Afterwards, the oblation of the cooked rice (kept in the pots of Purohita, etc.) should be offered with the following mantras:

देवीं वाचमजनयन्त देवास्तां विश्वरूपाः पशवो वदन्ति ।
सा नो मन्द्रेषमूर्जं दुहाना धेनुर्वागस्मानुप सुष्टुतैतु स्वाहा ॥
इदं वाचे-इदन्न मम ॥ ऋ. 8.100.11; पार. गृसू 1.19.2

devīṁ vāchamajanayanta devāstāṁ viśvarūpāḥ paśavo vadanti;

sā no mandreṣamūrjaṁ duhānā dhenurvāgasmānupa

suṣṭutaitu svāhā;
idaṁ vāche-idanna mama. RV. 8.100.11; Pār.GS. 1.19.2

[Meaning] At the beginning of creation, the seers received the divine speech (Veda vāk) which was later spoken by various beings. That speech spoken beautifully by us gave us the knowledge of energy and food, etc., like a milch cow. Whatever is uttered herein is accurate. The oblation offered is meant for vāk (speech), not for me.

वाजो नोऽअद्य प्र सुवाति दानं वाजो देवाँ ऋतुभिः कल्पयाति। वाजो हि मा सर्ववीरं जजान विश्वा आशा वाजपतिर्जयेयꣳस्वाहा ॥ इदं वाचे वाजाय-इदन्न मम ॥
यजु. 18.33; पार.गृसू. 1.19.3.1

vājo no'adya pra suvāti dānaṁ vājo devām̐ ṛtubhiḥ kalpayāti। vājo hi mā sarvaṁvīraṁ jajāna viśvā āśā vājapatirjayeyaṁsvāhā ॥ idaṁ vāche vājāya-idanna mama.
YV. 18.33; Pār.GS. 1.19.3.1

[Meaning] This food gives us the power of donating sperm; this also makes the learned man strong with seasons; this is the food which makes us possess children; may I possess food and conquer all the directions. The oblation offered for food, and it is not for me.

Thereafter, more ghee should be poured into this cooked rice, and the four oblations should be offered with the following mantras:

ओं प्राणेनान्नमशीय स्वाहा ॥ इदं प्राणाय-इदन्न मम ॥1 ॥
Oṁ prāṇenānnamaśīya svāh. idaṁ prāṇāya-idanna mama.

I, through prāṇa vāyu, take the food.

ओम् अपानेन गन्धानशीय स्वाहा ॥ इदमपानाय-इदन्न मम ॥
Om apānena gandhānaśīya svāhā. idamapānāya-idanna mama.

I, through apāna vāyu, take the things other than food.

ओं चक्षुषा रुपाण्यशीय स्वाहा ॥ इद्र चक्षुषे-इदन्न मम ॥3 ॥

Oṁ chakṣuṣā rupāṇyaśīya svāhā. idra chakṣuṣe-idanna mama.

I, through my eyes, see the colours and forms.

ओं श्रोत्रेण यशोऽशीय स्वाहा ॥ इद्र श्रोत्राय-इदन्न मम ॥

Oṁ śrotreṇa yaśo'śīya svāhā. idra śrotrāya-idanna mama.

I, through my ears, hear the words of fame.

Following which, one oblation of 'Sviṣṭakṛta' should be offered with the यदस्य कर्मणो॰ mantra as written in the Sāmānya Prakaraṇa. After that, giving four oblations of the vyāhṛti, eight obligations with ओं लं नो॰ etc. mantras should be offered, thus making it a total of 12 āhutis.

After that, the yajamāna should mix curd, honey and ghee in a small quantity in the rice left over after obligations and feed the child in a very minute quantity according to its capacity with the following mantra:

ओम् अन्नपतेऽन्नस्य नो देह्यनमीवस्य शुष्मिणः ।
प्रप्र दातारं तारिष ऊर्जं नो धेहि द्विपदे चतुष्पदे ॥ यजु॰ 11.83

Om annapate'nnasya no dehyanamīvasya śuṣmiṇaḥ,
prapra dātāraṁ tāriṣa ūrjjaṁ no dhehi dvipade chatuṣpade.

YV. 11.83

[Meaning] O Lord of food, grant us food devoid of infections and diseases, invigorating us. Give prosperity and pleasure to the cultivator of food. Grant us food for the maintenance of our quadrupeds and bipeds.

After feeding the child with the rice, his mouth should be washed and chant the Vāmadevyagāna as described at the end of Sāmānya Prakaraṇa. The parents and other old ladies and gentlemen pray God and bless the child with the following इड utterance:

त्वमन्त्रपतिरन्नादो वर्धमानो भूयाः ॥

tvamannapatirannādo vardhamāno bhūyāḥ.

[Meaning] O child! May you by God's grace become master of food, eater or consumer of food, growing in strength and life.

Finally, the father of the child should give a warm send-off to all gentlemen and ladies who attended the ceremony.

इत्यन्नप्राशनसंस्कारविधिः समाप्तः ॥

ityannaprāśanasaṁskāravidhiḥ samāptaḥ.

Here ends the procedure of Annaprāśana.

अथ चूडाकर्मसंस्कारविधि वक्ष्यामः

Chuḍākarma Sanskāra

This ceremony of tonsure or forming of the crest (choṭi) is the eighth one. It is also called the first haircut sanskāra. In this regard, the Āśvalāyana Gṛhyasūtra observes thus:

तृतीय वर्षे चौलम् ॥

उत्तरतोऽग्नेर्व्रीहियवमाषतिलानां शरावाणि निदधाति ॥ आश्व॰ गृसू॰ 1.17.1-2

tṛtīya varṣe chaulam ॥

uttarato'gnervrīhiyavamāṣatilānāṁ śarāvāṇi nidadhāti ॥

Āśva.GS. 1.17.1-2

[Meaning] the first hair-cut ceremony should occur in the third year. In the North of the fire-altar, place the pots of rice, barley, black gram and sesamum seed.

The *Pāraskara Gṛhyasūtra* also observes in the same manner:

सांवत्सरिकस्य चूडाकरणम् ॥ पार॰ 2.1.1

sāṁvatsarikasya chūḍākaraṇam. Pār.GS. 2.1.1

[Meaning] Crest forming ceremony (tonsure) should be done after the expiry of an year.

The *Gobhilīya Gṛhyasūtra* also has a similar view nonetheless.

This ceremony for forming a crest should be performed in the third or the first years from the date of the child's birth. On a happy day in the bright fortnight of the winter solstice, this ceremony should be performed.

The Procedure of Chūḍākarma Sanskāra

In the beginning, the rituals of Sāmānya Prakarṇa

should be performed. The four earthenware pots full of rice, barley, black gram, and sesamum seed should be placed in the north direction of the yajñavedi (fire altar). Afterwards, the procedure of sprinkling water on the four sides of the Vedi should be carried out with four prescribed mantras starting from ओं अदिते अनुमन्यस्व॰ (*Oṁ adite anumanyasva..*) and ending with ओं देव सवितः प्रसुव॰ (*Om deva savitaḥ prasuva..*). Afterwards, Agnyādhāna (placing fire) and Samidādhāna (samidhās/firewoods) kindle the fire in the yajña-kuṇḍa. Offer a total of 16 oblations, four of āghārāvājyābhāgāhuti, four of vyāhṛti āhutīs, and eight oblations of ājyāhuti with eight mantras- त्वन्नो अग्रे.. (*tvanno agne...*) etc. as described in the Sāmānya Prakaraṇa, should be offered. Afterwards four oblations of ghee with four mantras beginning with ओं भूर्भुवः स्वः। अग्न आयूंषि॰ (*Oṁ bhūrbhuvaḥ svaḥ. Agna āyumṣi..*) etc. be offered. Again, four vyāhṛti āhutīs (oblations) and one oblation of Sviṣṭkṛt with mantra यदस्य कर्मणो॰ (*yadasya karmaṇo...*) should be offered.

After performing the procedure mentioned above, the ceremony performer should meditate upon God and chant the following mantra with a gaze pointed at the barber.

ओम् आयमगन्त्सविता क्षुरेणोष्णेन वाय उदकेनेहिं। आदित्या रुद्रा वसव उन्दन्तु सचेतसः सोमस्य राज्ञो वपत प्रचेतसः ॥ अथर्व. 6.68.1

Om āyamagantsavitā kṣureṇoṣṇena vāya udakenehiṁ। *ādityā rudrā vasava undantu sachetasaḥ somasya rājño vapata prachetasaḥ* ॥ *AV. 6.68.1*

[Meaning] This intelligent barber has come here with a razor. O active person, come here with heated water. Let 12 Ādityas, 11 Rudras and 8 Vasus moisten the hair of the child. O learned persons, get this illustrious soma (child) shaved.

Afterwards, the father of the child sitting behind the child taking a little hot water in one pot and a little cold water in the other pot should mix the waters of both pots, pronouncing the mantra.

ओं उष्णेन वाय उदकेनेहि ॥

Oṁ uṣṇena vāya udakenehi.

[Meaning] Let the hot water be mixed with cold water.

Afterwards, take a little water, a little butter or the curd and moisten the hair of the child three times and recite the following mantras.:

ओम् अदितिः शमश्रु वपत्वाप उन्दन्तु वर्चसा ।
चिकित्सतु प्रजापतिदीर्घायुत्वाय चक्षसे ॥ अथर्व. 6.68.2

Om aditiḥ śamaśru vapatvāpa undantu varchasā,
chikitsatu prajāpatidīrghāyutvāya chakṣase. AV. 6.68.2

[Meaning] Let this sharp-edged razor shave the hair and let the water moisten it with its moistening power. May the Lord of the creatures (God) restore his health for watching this world for a long time.

ओ सवित्रा प्रसूता दैव्या आप उन्दन्तु ते तनूं दीर्घायुत्वाय वर्चसे ॥

पार० गृसू० 2.1.9

O savitrā prasūtā daivyā āpa undantu te tanūṁ dīrghāyutvāya varchase ॥ Pār.GS. 2.1.9

[Meaning] O child! Let the rainy waters created by radiation heating from the sun moisten your body to attain long life and divine glory.

Afterwards, the child's father combs the hair and holds it. After that, pronouncing the mantra.

ओं ओषधे त्रायस्वैनम् ॥ यजु. 6.15

Oṁ Oṣadhe trāyasvainam. (yaju. 6.15)

[Meaning] Let the herb protect this child.

Take three darbha-grass and slightly press the hair of the right side with these darbhas and have a glance at the razor, pronouncing the mantra:

ओं विष्णोर्दंष्ट्रोऽसि ॥ साम मन्त्र ब्रा॰ 1.6.4

Oṁ viṣṇordanṣṭro'si. Sāma MBr. 1.6.4

[Meaning] Razor is the means of performing this yajña of chuḍākarma.

Afterwards, he should hold the razor in his right hand, pronouncing the following mantra:

ओ शिवो नामासि स्वधितिस्ते पिता नमस्ते ऽअस्तु मा मा   हिꣳसीः ॥

यजु॰ 3.63; पार॰ गृसू॰ 2.1.11

O śivo nāmāsi svadhitiste pitā namaste 'astu mā mā himˣsīḥ. YV. 3.63; Par.GS. 2.1.11

[Meaning] This razor is for auspiciousness; the steel, which is so strong as vajra, is its producing material; let it be fit for cutting the hair and not cause pain anyhow.

After that the father of the child should bring the razor and the कुशा (kuśa grass) near the hair-bunch of the child, chanting the following Mantras:

ओं स्वधिते मैनꣳहिꣳसीः ॥ यजु॰ 4.1

Oṁ svadhite mainaṁ hiṁ sīḥ. YV. 4.1

[Meaning] Let not this steel razor inflict any harm to this child.

ओं निवर्त्तयाम्यायुषेऽन्नाद्याय प्रजननाय रायस्पोषाय सुप्रजास्त्वाय सुवीर्याय ॥

यजु॰ 3.63; पार॰ गृसू॰ 2.11

Oṁ nivarttayāmyāyuṣe'nnādyāya prajananāya rāyaspoṣāya suprajāstvāya suvīryāṁya. YV. 3.63; Pār.GS. 2.11

[Meaning] O Child! I perform this tuft-ceremony to give you a long life, constructive power, wealth, good progeny and strength.

Cut the hair of the baby with razor along with kuśa grass and pronounce the following mantra:

ओं येनावपत्सविता क्षुरेण सोमस्य राज्ञो वरुणस्य विद्वान् ।
तेन ब्रह्मणो वपतेदमस्य गोमानश्ववानयमस्तु प्रजावान् ।

अथर्व॰ 6.68.3; पारस्कर गृसू॰ 2.1.11

Oṁ yenāvapatsavitā kṣureṇa somasya rājño varuṇasya vidvān I
tena brahmaṇo vapatedamasya gomānaśvavānayamastu prajāvān I AV. 6.68.3; Pār. GS. 2.1.11

[Meaning] How the skilled barber has shaven with the razor, this illustrious child. May this child be the possessor of intellectual and physical power and progeny.

The hair cut by the razor or scissor, along with the kuśas should be collected in the leaves of the Śamī tree (Prosopis cineraria) arranged there previously in a pot for the same purpose. If any hair is scattered on the ground when cutting, it should be picked up through the cow dung and put in the pot already containing hair, leaves of Śamī tree and kuśas.

Afterwards, in the same manner, the second-time haircut ceremony should be performed on the other side and be kept in the pot chanting the following mantras:

ओं येन धाता वृहस्पतेरग्नेरिन्द्रस्य चायुषेऽवपत् ।
तेन त आयुषे वपामि सुश्लोक्याय स्वस्तये ॥ आश्व॰ 1.17.12

Oṁ yena dhātā vṛhaspateragnerindrasya chāyuṣe'vapat,
tena ta āyuṣe vapāmi suślokyāya svastaye. Āśv. GS. 1.17.12

[Meaning] O Baby! I cut your hair for your long life, fame and prosperity in the manner the All-sustaining

Power has given longevity to the cosmos, thermal energy and electric force to the universe.

In the same manner, the third time, the hair should be shaved by the following mantra:

ओं येन भूयश्च रात्र्यां ज्योक् च पश्याति सूर्यम् ।
तेन त आयुषे वपामि सुश्लोक्याय स्वस्तये ॥ आश्व० 1.17.12

Oṁ yena bhūyaścha rātrayāṁ jyok cha paśyāti sūryam,
tena ta āyuṣe vapāmi suślokyāya svastaye. Āśv.GS. 1.17.12

O Baby! I cut your hair for your long life, fame and prosperity so that you may see again and again the objects in the night and the sun for the whole lifetime.

Afterwards, with the three mantras mentioned above:

ओं येनावपत्०
Oṁ yenāvapat..

ओं येन धाता०
Oṁ yena dhātā..

ओं येन भूयश्च०
Oṁ yena bhūyaścha..

and the fourth mantra as it is being given below (ओं येन पूषा०), the hair of the baby should be cut for the fourth time in a similar manner as mentioned above:

ओं येन पूषा बृहस्पतेर्वायोरिन्द्रस्य चावपत् । तेन ते वपामि ब्रह्मणा जीवातवे जीवनाय दीर्घायुष्ट्वाय वर्चसे ॥ गोभिल, 2.9.11-16

Oṁ yena pūṣā bṛhaspatervāyorindrasya chāvapat, tena te vapāmi brahmaṇā jīvātave jīvanāya dīrghāyuṣṭvāya varchase.

Go. GS. 2.9.11-16

[Meaning] O Child! I cut your hair for your survival and long life in the manner by which the Pūṣā (life source of the universe) maintains the life of the cosmos, air and the electric force of the universe.

It is the procedure to be followed for cutting the right-side hair of the baby. Once this is completed, the same procedure will be applied to cut the left-side hair. After that, the hair of the hind and foreside of the head should be cut. However, while cutting the hair for the fourth time, the following mantra should be chanted instead of येन पूषा०.

ओं येन भूरिश्चरादिवं ज्योक् च पश्चाद्धि सूर्यम् । तेन ते वपामि ब्रह्मणा जीवातवे जीवनाय सुश्लोक्याय स्वस्तये ॥ पार० 2.1.16

Oṁ yena bhūriścharādivaṁ jyok cha paśchāddhi sūryam.
tena te vapāmi brahmaṇā jīvātave jīvanāya suślokyāya svastaye.
Pār.GS. 2.1.16

[Meaning] O Child! I move the razor on your head (to cut your hair) for your survival, life, prolonged age, fame, and prosperity in the way the air moves in the heavenly region from high pressure to low pressure created by the sun.

Afterwards, the hair on hind-side of the head once again be cut, pronouncing the following mantra:

ओं त्र्यायुषं जमदग्नेः कश्यपस्य त्र्यायुषम् ॥
यद्देवेषु त्र्यायुषं तन्नो अस्तु त्र्यायुषम् ॥ यजु० 3.62 पार० 2.1.14

Oṁ trayāyuṣaṁ jamadagneḥ kaśyapasya trayāyuṣam.
yaddeveṣu trayāyuṣaṁ tanno astu trayāyuṣam.
YV. 3.62; Pār. 2.1.14

[Meaning] May our jamadagni (eyes), kaśyapa (prāṇa) and other devaḥ (sense organs) attain three times the average age of human human beings (300 years of age), as is attained by enlightened persons/yogīs.

Afterwards, pronouncing the mantra ओं त्र्यायुषं०, the father of the child should touch the head of the baby starting from the hind part of the head, and when the mantra is concluded, he should give the razor to barber.

He should, then, chant the following mantra:

ओं यत्क्षुरेण मर्चयता सुपेशसा वप्ता वपसि केशान् ।
शुन्धि शिरो मास्यायुः प्रमोषीः ॥ आश्व० 1.17.15

Oṁ yatkṣureṇa marchayatā supeśasā vaptā vapasi keśān, śundhi śiro māsyāyuḥ pramoṣī. Āśv. GS. 1.17.15

[Meaning] O barber! You are the cutter of the hair; you cleanse the head of the child with the swift, soft razor by which you cut his hair and do not decrease his life.

After pronouncing this mantra as mentioned above, he (the father of the child) asks the barber to sharpen the razor on his stone and advises him (the barber) that he (the barber) nicely drench the child's head with hot and cold water very smoothly, do the shaving attentively with a smooth hand, and avoid any cut from the razor. Saying so, he takes the barber in the north direction of the yajña-kuṇḍa and seats the baby in his front, keeping the baby's face eastward and getting the baby shaved, leaving only the hair which he (the father of the child) does not want to get shaved. However, the hair should be kept unshaven on five sides or any one side or get it completely shaved for the first time as keeping tuft at the second time is best.

When the baby's shaving has been completed, the baby's father should gift the barbar whatever is worth gifting near the Yajñakuṇḍa. The barber should be honoured with some money and clothes. The barber be advised by the child's father to carry the hair, darbha-grass, leaves of Śamī tree and cow-dung in the jungle, dig a pit and burry all this therein, or he may burry all this in a pit near cow-shed, river-bank or bank of pond. Either he should advise the barber to do so or send someone with him to do the needful through the barber.

After shaving is complete, the baby's father, taking curd or butter in his hand and rubbing it on the head of the baby, should bathe her. After dressing the baby in a nice outfit, the father should keep the baby with him, sit on an excellent seat, keep his own face eastward, and perform the singing of Mahāvāmdeva Gāna. Afterwards, the baby's mother should give due respect to ladies, and the baby's father should give due respect to men and give them all a warm send-off. While leaving the house, all guests and parents of the baby should meditate upon God and bless the child with the sentence- "ओं त्वं जीव शरदः शतं वर्धमानः ॥" (That is, "O baby! you live hundred autumns growing in strength and vigour.)

Thus, all should go to their homes, and parents should keep themselves and the baby happy.

इति चूडाकर्मसंस्कारविधिः समाप्तः ॥

iti chūḍākarmasaṁskāravidhiḥ samāptaḥ.

Here ends the procedure of Chūḍākarma

अथ कर्णवेधसंस्कारविधिं वक्ष्यामः

Karṇavedha (Ear-piercing) Sanskāra

Now, we will relate the sanskāra of piercing the ears.

The Scriptural evidence in this regard is quoted here.

कर्णवेधो वर्षे तृतीये पंचमे वा ॥

karṇavedho varṣe tṛtīye paṁchame vā ॥

It is the statement of the Kātyāyana Gṛhyasūtra (1.2). The proper time of piercing the ear or nose of the child is the third or the fifth year from the date of birth.

On the day when the piercing of the ears or nose of the child is fixed, the mother of the child should take the child to the yajñaśālā (place of yajña) after giving him/her bath in the morning with clean water and getting him/her dressed with clothes and ornaments, the procedure of Sāmānya Prakaraṇa should be followed thoroughly. Afterwards, putting some eatables or toys before the child by an experienced physician who has specialized in the Charaka and Suśruta (books of medicine) and who can do the work of protecting arteries and veins, etc., should pierce the ears and nose; he should pierce the right ear first with the following mantra:

ओं भद्रं कर्णोभिः श्रृणुयाम देवा भद्रं पश्येमाक्षभिर्यजत्राः ।
स्थिरैरङ्गैस्तुष्टुवाꣳसस्तनूभिर्व्यशेमहि देवहितं यदायुः ॥ यजु० 25.21

Oṁ bhadraṁ karṇobhiḥ śṛṇuyāma devā bhadraṁ paśyemākṣabhiryajatrāḥ ।
sthirairaṅgaistuṣṭuvāṁ sastanūbhirvyaśemahi devahitaṁ yadāyuḥ ॥ YV. 25.21

[Meaning] O divine beings, may we, in your good company, hear with our ears only that which is truthful; may we, being sanctified, see with our eyes only that which is benevolent. Endowed with steady limbs and bodies, ever eulogising and contemplating the Supreme, may we enjoy the life-span as enjoyed by the scholars.

He should pierce the left ear with the following mantra:

वक्ष्यन्ती वेदा गनीगन्ति कर्ण प्रियꣳ सखायं परिषस्वजाना ।
योषेव शिङ्क्ते वितातधि धन्वंज्या इयꣳसमने पारयन्ती ॥

यजु॰ 29.40; पार॰ 1.17

vakṣayantī vedā ganīganti karṇa priyaṁ sakhāyaṁ parisasvajānā,
yoṣeva śiṅkte vitātādhi dhanvaṁjyā iyaṁ samane pārayantī॥ YV. 29.40; Pār. 1.17

[Meaning] These bows that protect us in combat; on being strained on the bow embraces his friend bow, and while being drawn up to ears, it whispers in the ear of the warrior like a woman in the ears of her husband.

After that, the same physician should put a bar or wire in the pierced holes so that the holes should not close, and he should apply medicine to the holes so that the ears may not get infected and heal soon.

इति कर्णवेधसंस्कारविधिः समाप्तः ॥

iti karṇavedhasaṁskāravidhiḥ samāptaḥ.

Here ends the procedure of the ceremony of piercing the ears.

अथोपनयन संस्कारविधिं वक्ष्यामः

Upanayana Sanskāra

अत्रप्रमाणानि-

atrapramāṇāni-

In this regard, scriptural authorities are cited below.

अष्टमे वर्षे ब्राह्मणमुपनयेत ॥ गर्भाष्टमे वा ॥
एकादशे क्षत्रियम् ॥ द्वादशे वैश्यम् ॥
आषोडशाद् ब्राह्मणस्यानतीतः कालः ॥
आद्वाविंशात्क्षत्रियस्य, आचतुर्विंशाद्वैश्यस्य,
अत ऊर्ध्वं पतितसावित्रीका भवन्ति ॥ आश्व.गृसू. 1.19.1-6

aṣṭame varṣe brāhmaṇamupanayeta ॥ garbhāṣṭame vā.
ēkādaśe kṣatriyam ॥ dvādaśe vaiśyam.
āṣoḍaśād brāhmaṇasyānatītaḥ kālaḥ.
ādvāviṁśātkṣatriyasya, āchaturviṁśādvaiśyasya,
ata ūrdhvaṁ patitasāvitrīkā bhavanti. Āśv.GS. 1.19.1-6

[Meaning] The child of Brāhmaṇa sanskāras should be initiated for studies in the eighth year from the date of birth or the date of conception; the child of Kṣatriya sanskāras should be initiated for studies in the eleventh year from the date of birth or from the date of conception; the child of Vaiśya sanskāras should be initiated for studies in the 12th year from the date of his birth or from the date of conception. Positively, the children of Brāhmaṇa, Kṣatriya and Vaiśya sanskāras should respectively be initiated for studies before the 16th, 22nd and 24th years of their age. If not initiated in these years, they will be treated as deprived of studentship.

Note: Here, an initiation of a child of Śudra sanskāras is not ordained because the children of Śudra sanskāras generally do not want to go for formal studies. They want to choose the job of labour or service sector as their profession. For that profession, no formal or skill education is required. Because the objective of human life is to achieve dharma, artha, kāma and mokṣa, all these life objectives cannot be attained without spiritual and material education. So, spiritual and material education was a must during the Vedic period.

The above-cited evidence is from the Āśvalāyana Gṛhyasūtra (1.19.1-6). Similar observations can be noted from the Pāraskara Gṛhyasūtra, etc. The meaning is given as follows:

Note: Brāhmaṇa means a spiritually empowered visionary person, enlightened person. Kṣatriya means a defence personnel, politician, administrator or judge. Vaiśya means a business person, a producer, or a person from the marketing field. Śudra means a labourer or service provider.

Below is quoted a statement from the Manusmṛti (2.37); accordingly, a student who is willing to attain Brahma-varchasva (spiritual aura) should be initiated into studies in the fifth year after his conception ears.

ब्रह्मवर्चसकामस्य कार्यं विप्रस्य पंचमे ।
राज्ञो बलार्थिनः षष्ठे वैश्यस्येहार्थिनोऽष्टमे ॥ मनु॰ 2.37

brahmavarchasakāmasya kāryaṁ viprasya paṁchame,
rājño balārthinaḥ ṣaṣṭhe vaiśyasyehārthino 'ṣṭam.

Manu, 2.37

[Meaning] A student willing to attain Brahma-varchasva (spiritual aura) should be initiated into studies in the fifth year after his conception. A student yearning for prowess should be initiated in the sixth year, and a student willing to be a business person in the eighth year after his conception.

Nevertheless, the above condition is possible only

when the child's parent has been married after having completed the strict discipline of Brahmacharya on their part. Only such parents can have excellent children who could be brilliant enough to start their studies early. (From experiments, it has been proved that all students cannot start their studies at an early age).

The time of yajñopavita (initiation into studies)

In this regard the Śatapatha Brāhmaṇa (2.1.3.5) observes as under:

वसन्ते ब्राह्मणमुपनयेत् । ग्रीष्मे राजन्यम् ।
शरदि वैश्यम् । सर्वकालमेके ॥

vasante brāhmaṇamupanayet, grīṣme rājanyam,
śaradi vaiśyam, sarvakālamek.

[Meaning] The child of Brāhmaṇa sanskāras should be initiated into formal education in the spring season; the child of Kṣatriya sanskāras should be initiated into formal education in the summer season; and the child of Vaiśya sanskāras should be initiated into formal education in the autumn season respectively, or all seasons are best for initiation into formal education.

Three or one day prior to the day of the initiation, students to be initiated should have three or one fasts.

पयोव्रतो ब्राह्मणो यवागूव्रतो राजन्य आमिक्षाव्रतो वैश्यः ॥

payovrato brāhmaṇo yavāgūvrato rājanya āmikṣāvrato
vaiśyaḥ.

[Meaning] During the time of fastings, the child of Brāhmaṇas sanskāras can take only milk once or many times; the child of Kṣatriya sanskāras can take barley gruel (by boiling barley in water and mixing it with sugar). The child of Vaiśya sanskāras should complete his fast by taking Āmikṣā.

Note: This Āmikṣā is sometimes called Śrikhaṇḍa or Sikhaṇḍa. It is prepared from curd (four parts), milk (one part), sugar in proportionate quantity and saffron. This preparation is made after straining curd, etc., through the cloth piece. The children of three varṇas (sanskāras), as described above, should eat only things prescribed for them when they feel hungry, and they should not eat or drink anything else.

The Procedure of Upanayana Sanskāra

The utensils to be used in the yajña, etc., should be collected and appropriately secured and cleaned the day before the initiation ceremony; on the day of the ceremony, everything as needed mentioned in the Sāmānya Prakaraṇa, should be arranged near the yajñakuṇḍa (yajña-place). The child to be initiated should be shaved and bathed with clean water and dressed in a nice outfit. Either the father of the child or the Āchārya, having fed the child with sweets, eatables, etc. seat him on a comfortable seat in the west of the yajñavedī keeping his face eastward, the father of the child and the priests of the ceremony who are mentioned in the Sāmānya Prakaraṇa, taking their respective seats in the previously described manner should properly perform rituals of the yajña like sipping of water etc.

Afterwards, the Āchārya conducting the ceremony should make the child utter the following sentence.

ब्रह्मचर्यमागाम्, ब्रह्मचार्यसानि ॥

brahmacharyamāgām, brahmachāryasāni.

[Meaning] May I enter the Brahmacharya Āśrama (student life), and thus may I be a Brahmachārī (student).

The Āchārya/Āchāryā chanting the following mantra should give the child a dress and invest him/her with an upanayana (thread).

ओं येनेन्द्राय बृहस्पतिर्वासः पर्यदधादमृतम् ।
तेन त्वा परिदधाम्यायुषे दीर्घायुत्वाय बलाय वर्चसे ॥ पार० गृ० 1.2.7

Oṁ yenendrāya bṛhaspatirvāsaḥ paryadadhādamṛtam,
tena tvā paridadhāmyāyuṣe dīrghāyutvāya balāya varchase.

Pār.GS. 1.2.7

[Meaning] O Child! [आयुषे] for your health, [दीर्घायुत्वाय] long-life, [बलाय] strength and [वर्चसे] auspicious aura, [परिदधामि] I give this outfit to wear [त्वा] to you, [येन] through the method by which [बृहस्पतिः] Āchārya Bṛhaspati gives [अमृतं वासः] strong and durable dress to his [इन्द्राय] disciple Indra.

Afterwards the child taking the upanayana (sacred thread) in his hand should sit in front of the Āchārya/Āchāryā, and the Āchārya/Āchāryā pronouncing the following mantras should invest with sacred thread which he/she puts on in such a manner that it could be on the left shoulder near the throat hanging below the right-hand side up to the belt and the head be in the middle:

ओं यज्ञोपवीतं परमं पवित्रं प्रजापतेर्यत्सहजं पुरस्तात् ।
आयुष्यमग्र्यं प्रतिमुंच शुभ्रं यज्ञोपवीतं बलमस्तु तेजः ॥1 ॥

Oṁ yajñopavītaṁ paramaṁ pavitraṁ prajāpateryatsahajaṁ purastāt,
āyuṣyamagryaṁ pratimuṁcha śubhraṁ yajñopavītaṁ balamastu tejaḥ ॥1 ॥

[Meaning] This sacred thread is very sacrosanct. It usually and naturally extends out before the yajña Prajāpati. The Brahma yajña (formal education in Śāstra) was performed for initiation into the Āśrama of Saṁnyāsa. I invest you with this white yajñopavita (sacred thread), which, being a main thing, is meant for strength and vigour.

यज्ञोपवीतमसि यज्ञस्य त्वा यज्ञोपवीतेनोपनह्यामि ॥2 ॥

yajñopavītamasi yajñasya tvā yajñopavītenopanahyāmi ||2 ||

[Meaning] This sacred thread is really a sacred thread. I invest you with this to perform Brahma-yajña (study of Vedas and Śāstras).

Afterwards, the Āchārya, making the child sit on the right of him, should perform the Svastivāchana, Śāntikaraṇa, Samidādhāna and Agnyādhāna. Afterwards, pouring water in the four sides of the yajña-kuṇḍa with the mantras beginning with ओम् आदितेऽनुमन्यस्व० etc. as per the prescribed procedure of the Sāmānya Prakaraṇa the preparation should be made to offer Ājyāhutīs.

Considering the woodfuel blazing and taking ghee in a spoon from the pot of ghee, he should offer sixteen oblations consisting of four oblations of Āghārāvājyābhāgāhuti. Four oblations of Vyāhṛti Āhutis and eight oblations of Aṣṭājyāhuti should be offered. After that, the oblations of principal Homa with the special oblations prepared for the purpose should be offered by the child himself with the following: ओं भूर्भुवः स्वः। अग्र आयूंषि० etc. four mantras. Thereafter, the five oblations be offered with the following five mantras:

ओं अग्रे व्रतपते व्रतं चरिष्यामि तत्ते प्रब्रवीमि तच्छकेयम्।

तेनर्ध्यासमिदमहमनृतात्सत्यमुपैमि स्वाहा ॥ इदमग्रये-इदन्न मम ॥ मंत्रा. 1.6.9

Oṁ agne vratapate vrataṁ chariṣyāmi tatte prabravīmi tachchhakeyam,
tenardhyāsamidamahamanṛtātsatyamupaimi svāhā.
idamagnaye-idanna mama. MBr. 1.6.9

[Meaning] O Self-refulgent God! You are the master of Vrata or Saṅkalpa; I will observe the Vrata/Saṅkalpa of Brahmacharya, I declare before you. May I observe my Vrata. May I prosper with that vrata (saṅkalpa) and attain the highest truth rising above from the untruth.

Whatever has been uttered herein is true. The oblation offered is meant for Agni, and it is not for me.

ओं वायो व्रतपते० स्वाहा ॥ इदं वायवे-इदन्न मम ॥ मंत्रा. 1.6.10

Oṁ vāyo vratapate.. svāhā. idaṁ vāyave-idanna mama.

MBr. 1.6.10

[Meaning] (वायो) O All Knowing and All-Moving God! You are the custodian of our saṅkalpa. The oblation offered is meant for All knowing God and it is not for me.

ओं सूर्य व्रतपते० स्वाहा ॥ इदं सूर्याय-इदन्न मम ॥ मंत्रा. 1.6.11

Oṁ sūrya vratapate.. svāhā. idaṁ sūryāya-idanna mama.

MBr. 1.6.11

[Meaning] (सूर्य) O Luminous God! You are the custodian of our saṅkalpa. The oblation offered is meant for Luminous God and it is not for me.

ओं चन्द्र व्रतपते० स्वाहा ॥ इदं चन्द्राय-इदन्न मम ॥ मंत्रा. 1.6.12

Oṁ chandra vratapate.. svāhā. idaṁ chandrāya-idanna mama. MBr. 1.6.12

[Meaning] (चन्द्र) O All Blissful God! You are the custodian of our saṅkalpa. The oblation offered for Blissful God and it is not for me.

ओं व्रतानां व्रतपते० स्वाहा ॥ इदमिन्द्राय व्रतपतये-इदन्न मम ॥ मंत्रा. 1.6.13

Oṁ vratānāṁ vratapate... svāhā. idamindrāya vratapataye-idanna mama. MBr. 1.6.13

[Meaning] O Custodian of all the vratas (saṅkalpas) and laws! The oblation offered is meant for the Indra, and it is not for me.

After that, the six oblations consisting of four oblations of Vyāhṛti Āhutis, one of Sviṣṭakṛt, and one of Prajāpati-āhuti should be offered.

All these fifteen oblations stated above (four oblations of अग्र आयूंषि॰ etc., four Mantras; five oblations of अग्रेव्रतपते॰ etc. Mantras; and six oblations of Vyāhṛti, Sviṣṭakṛt and Prajāpati) should be offered by the child himself who is being invested with the sacred thread.

Afterwards, the Āchārya should sit in the north of the Yajñakuṇḍa, keeping his face eastward, and the child should sit in front of the Āchārya, keeping his face westward.

Afterwards, the Āchārya looking at the child should chant the following mantra:

ओम् आगन्त्रा समगन्महि प्र सुमर्त्यं युयोतन ।
अरिष्टाः संचरेमहि स्वस्ति चरतादयम् ॥ मन्त्र ब्रा. 1.6.14 ॥ गोभिल 2-10-20

Om āgantrā samaganmahi pra sumartyaṁ yuyotana ।
ariṣṭāḥ saṁcharemahi svasti charatādayam ॥

MBr. 1.6.14; Go.GS. 2-10-20

O Self-refulgent God! We have (*samaganmahi*) entered into good terms with this boy (*āgantrā*) observing saṅkalpa of Brahmacharya. Kindly (*yuyotana*) bless this boy with the company of (*sumartyaṁ*) good persons and teachers. (*saṁcharemahi*) We take care of (*ariṣṭaḥ*) all the problems of this lad. May this lad (*chartāt*) walk on the earth (*savasti*) in a blessed manner.

माणवकवाक्यम्-ओं ब्रह्मचर्यमागामुप मा नयस्व ॥

मन्त्र ब्रा. 1.6.16; गोभिल 2.10.21

māṇavakavākyam-Oṁ brahmacharyamāgāmupa mā nayasva.

MBr. 1.6.16; Go.GS. 2.10.21

The student (child) says--"O teacher! I have observed Brahmacharya; now kindly admit me and invest me with the sacred thread."

आचार्योक्तिः — को नामासि ॥ मन्त्र ब्रा. 1.6.17; गोभिल 2.10.22

āchāryoktiḥ-ko nāmāsi. MBr. 1.6.17; Go.Br. 2.10.22

आचार्योक्तिः-एतन्नामास्मिं ॥ मन्त्र ब्रा. 1.6.1

āchāryoktiḥ-ētannāmāsmiṁ. MBr. 1.6.1

Āchārya says- What is your name? Replies the student -- Sir, My name is so and so. Or I bear such a name.

Afterwards, the Ācharya should fill up the right palm of the student with clean and pure water and pronounce the following mantras:

ओम् आपो हि ष्ठा मयोभुवस्ता न ऊर्जे दधातन। महे रणाय चक्षसे॥

ऋ 10.9.1; यजु. 11.50

Om āpo hi ṣṭhā mayobhuvastā na ūrje dadhātana |
mahe raṇāya chakṣase. RV. 10.9.1; YV. 11.50

[Meaning] The waters are the source of happiness. May they help us in attaining food and help us to have a wonderful glimpse.

यो वः शिवतमो रसस्तस्य भाजयतेह नः। उशतीरिव मातरः॥

ऋ 10.9.2; यजु. 11.51

yo vaḥ śivatamo rasastasya bhājayateha naḥ, uśatīriva mātaraḥ. RV. 10.9.2; YV. 11.51

[Meaning] Let the pleasant essence of water be helpful for us, like the mothers who feed their breasts to children for their well-being.

तस्मा अरं गमाम वो यस्य क्षयाय जिन्वथ। आपो जनयथा चनः॥

ऋ 10.9.3; यजु. 11.52

tasmā araṁ gamāma vo yasya kṣayāya jinvatha, āpo janayathā cha naḥ. RV. 10.9.3; YV. 11.52

[Meaning] [*āpaḥ*] Waters [*jinvatha*] make us delighted by [*kṣayāya*], the growth [*yasya*] of food grains and herbs. Let [*tasmai*] those waters responsible for the growth of herbs and food grains be [*araṁ*] immediately [*gamāma*] acquired by [*vaḥ*] you for the sufficient growth of food grains and herbs. Let them be helpful in the [*janayatha*] welfare of [*chanaḥ*] our progeny.

Afterwards, the Āchārya, taking water in his hand sprinkle it on the child, pronouncing the following mantras:

ओं तत्सवितुर्वृणीमहे वयं देवस्य भोजनम् ।
श्रेष्ठं सर्वधातमं । तुरं भगस्य धीमहि ॥ ऋ० 5.82.1

Oṁ tatsaviturvṛṇīmahe vayaṁ devasya bhojanam,
śreṣṭhaṁ sarvadhātamaṁ, turaṁ bhagasya dhīmahi.

RV. 5.82.1

[Meaning] We, for our maintenance, accept whatever good food has been provided by God who is the mighty power and creater of the world. We also accept the strength and might of all powerful God who maintains and preserves the existence of all the objects of creation.

Afterwards the Āchārya holding the hand of the child filled with water, including child's thumb, therewith make the child pour down the handful of water in a pot chanting the following Mantras:-

ओं देवस्य त्वा सवितुः प्रसवेऽश्विनोर्बाहुभ्यां पूष्णो हस्ताभ्यां हस्तं गृह्णाम्यसौ ॥
आश्व. गृसू. 1.20.4

Oṁ devasya tvā savituḥ prasave'śvinorbāhubhyāṁ pūṣṇo
hastābhyāṁ hastaṁ gṛhṇāmyasau. Āśv. GS. 1.20.4

[Meaning] O Child! I admit you in the life of Brahmacharya to make you attain the knowledge of creation and the creator. I hold your hand in my hand with the firmness of the sun holding the earth and with the firmness of Puṣan (prāṇa-vāyu) holding the life of a living being.

Similarly, again, for the second time, the Āchārya takes water in his hand, pours it into the palm of the child and holds the child's palm together with his thumb, making him pour the water into the pot. The Ācharya should chant the following sentence in doing so:

ओं सविता ते हस्तमग्रभीत्, असौ । आश्व० 1.20.2

Oṁ savitā te hastamagrabhīt, asau. Āśv.GS.

[Meaning] O Child! Your hand has been held by the teacher representing Savitā (Brahman, the Creator) and the source of all knowledge.

Again, for the third time, the Ācharya taking water in his own hand and pouring it into the palm of the child and holding his hand together with his thumb should make him pour water into the pot. In doing so, he should chant the following mantra:

ओं अग्निराचार्यस्तव, असौ ॥ आश्व० 1.20.5

Oṁ agnirāchāryastava, asau. Āśv. GS. 1.20.5

[Meaning] O Child! Āchārya acts as agni in the Brahmayajña (the student is soma).

Afterwards, Āchārya, going out and standing in front of the sun, should ask the child to have a look at the sun and recite the following two mantras complying with this procedure:

ओं देव सवितरेष ते ब्रह्मचारी ते गोपाय समामृत ॥ आश्व० 1.20.6

Oṁ deva savitareṣa te brahmachārī te gopāya samāmṛta.

Āśv.GS. 1.20.6

[Meaning] O Deva Savitā (Sun) symbolic of Brahman, this child is your Brahmachārī. Please protect and preserve him so he can perform his duties well.

After that, the Ācharya returns to the Yajña-maṇḍapa with the child and, sitting in the north of *yajñakuṇḍa*, should recite the following two mantras and the child should take a round of the Ācharya and sit before him.

ओं युवा सुवासाः परिवीत आगात स उ श्रेयान् भवति जायमानः ॥

ऋ. 3.8.4; आश्व० 1.20.8

Om yuvā suvāsāḥ parivīta āgāta sa u śreyān bhavati jāyamānaḥ. RV. 3.8.4; Āśv.GS. 1.20.8

[Meaning] This child possesses a strong physique, [*suvāsāḥ*] dressed in a nice outfit [*praivītaḥ*] wearing the sacred thread that comes before me. [*saḥ u*] He [*jāyamānaḥ*] taking the second birth in the domain of study [bhavati] becomes [*śreyān*] dignified.

ओं सूर्यस्यावृतमन्वावर्त्तस्व, असौ ॥ साम.मन्त्रब्रा.1.6.19; गोभिल 2.10.28

Om sūryasyāvṛtamanvāvarttasva, asau.

Sām.Mbrā. 1.6.19; Go.GS. 2.10.28

[Meaning] O Child! You circumambulate your Ācharya, who is the sun of knowledge.

After this, the Ācharya should touch the child's right shoulder with his right hand and, afterwards, cover his hand with a piece of cloth. Ācharya should pronounce the following mantra.

ओं प्राणानां ग्रन्थिरसि मा विस्रसोऽन्तक इदं ते परिददामि, अमुम् ॥

गो० 2.10.28

Om prāṇānāṁ granthirasi mā visraso'ntaka idaṁ te paridadāmi, asum. Go. GS. 2.10.28

[Meaning] Let not this navel which pools the prāṇas (vital airs) be displaced from its proper place, [*Antaka*] O Brahman (the Annihilator of all)! I, the Āchārya, [*paridadāmi*] give the custody [*amum*] of this child to [*te*] you. I declare this keeping this child in my mind.

Thereafter Āchārya pronouncing the following mantra should touch the belly of the child.

ओं अहुर इदं ते परिददामि, अमुम् ॥ साम मन्त्रब्रा. 1.6.21; गोभिल 2.10.58

Om ahura idaṁ te paridadāmi, amum.

Sām. MBr. 1.6.21; Go.GS. 2.10.58

[Meaning] O God! giver of motion to the prakṛti (in active energy) in the beginning of creation, I, the Āchārya ... etc.

Āchārya should touch child's heart and pronounce :-

ओं कृशन इदं ते परिददामि, अमुम् ॥ साम मन्त्रब्रा. 1.6.22; गोभिल 2.10.59

Oṁ kṛśana idaṁ te paridadāmi, amum.

Sām. MBr. 1.6.22; Go. GS. 2.10.59

[Meaning] O God! You are invigorator of the fire. I, the Āchārya ...etc.

The Āchārya should touch child's right shoulder and pronounce:

ओं प्रजापतये त्वा परिददामि, असौ ॥ साम मन्त्रब्रा. 1.6.23; गोभिल 2.10.60

Oṁ prajāpataye tvā paridadāmi, asau.

Sām. MBr. 1.6.23; Go.GS. 2.10.60

[Meaning] O Child! I appoint you to realize Brahman and follow his commands.

The Āchārya should touch child's left shoulder and should pronounce:

ओं देवाय त्वा सवित्रे परिददामि, असौ ॥ साम मन्त्रब्रा.1.6.24; गोभिल 2.10.61

Oṁ devāya tvā savitre paridadāmi, asau.

Sāma MBr. 1.6.24; Go.GS. 2.10.61

[Meaning] O Child! I appoint you to realize All-creating Brahman and obey His commands.

Thereafter, the Āchārya keeping his hand on the Child's breasts, should pronounce the following Mantra:

ओं तं धीरासः कवय उन्नयन्ति स्वाध्यो३ मनसा देवयन्तः ॥

ऋ० 3.8.4 ॥ आश्व० 1.20.9

Oṁ taṁ dhīrāsaḥ kavaya unnayanti svādhyo3 manasā devayantaḥ. RV. 3.8.4. Āśv. GS. 1.20.9

[Meaning] [*dhīrāsaḥ*] The yogīs who have [*kavayaḥ*] transcendental vision, [*svādhyaḥ*] who can observe samādhi, [*manasā devayantaḥ*] who aspire for the divinity (mokṣa) [*unnayanti*] raise this student to the high status of genius and character.

After that, the Āchārya keeping him in front of the child and putting his hand on the right side of the chest of the child should pronounce the following mantra of the sacred pledge:

ओं मम व्रते ते हृदयं दधामि मम चित्तमनुचित्तं ते अस्तु।
मम वाचमेकमना जुषस्व बृहस्पतिष्ट्वा नियुनक्तु मह्यम्॥ पार॰ 2.2.16

Oṁ   mama   vrate   te   hṛdayaṁ   dadhāmi   mama chittamanuchittaṁ te astu,
mama vāchamekamanā juṣasva bṛhaspatiṣṭvā niyunaktu mahyam. Pār.GS. 2.2.16

[Meaning] O disciple! I make your mind concordant with my saṅkalpa of leading you to divinity; let your mind be concordant with my mind constantly, you being fully attentive, grasp my words with affection and attain the meaning of these words and Brahman, Who is the master of Vedic speech, unite you with me in thought and act according to your saṅkalpa (vow) from this very day to day.

After that, Āchārya should ask the child to pronounce this mantra ओं मम व्रते॰ ॥ *Oṁ mama vrate.*

Similarly, the disciple should also request the Āchārya to take the saṅkalpa. I hold your mind and heart in me for that advancement of my study and learning and good action. May your mind be accordant with that of my mind. Please listen to my words with attention, and may God keep you constantly engaged in the task of my well-being.

Thus, both should complete the procedure of taking saṅkalpa.

आचार्योक्तिः — को नामाऽसि ॥

āchāryoktiḥ-ko nāmā'si ॥

Āchārya asks -- What is your name?

बालकोक्तिः — अहम्भोः ॥

bālakoktiḥ-ahambhoḥ ॥

Student replies- Sir, my name is so and so.

आचार्यः — कस्य ब्रह्मचार्य्यसि ॥

āchāryaḥ-kasya brahmachāryyasi ॥

Āchārya – Whose Brahmchārī are you?

बालकः — भवतः ॥

bālakaḥ-bhavataḥ.

Student - Yours, sir.

The Āchārya should pronounce the following mantra for the safety of the child:

इन्द्रस्य ब्रह्मचार्य्यस्यग्निराचार्यस्तवाहमाचार्यस्तव असौ ॥ पार. 2.2.31

indrasya   brahmachāryyasyagnirāchāryastavāhamāchāryas-tava asau. Pār.GS. 2.2.31

[Meaning] O Child! You are the Brahmachārī of Almighty Brahman. I, as your Āchārya, act as Agni for this Brahmayajña, you being the Soma in this yajña.

ओं कस्य ब्रह्मचार्य्यसि प्राणस्य ब्रह्मचार्यसि कस्त्वा कमुपनयते काय त्वा परिददामि ॥

Oṁ kasya brahmachāryyasi prāṇasya brahmachāryasi kastvā kamupanayate kāya tvā paridadāmi.

[Meaning] O Child! For what you have become Brahmachārī. I have become Brahmachārī to learn Prāṇa-vidyā (yoga). What gives you happiness? Brahman. So, I initiate you in Brahmacharya for realizing Brahman.

ओं प्रजापतये त्वा परिददामि। देवाय त्वा सवित्रे परिददामि। अद्भ्यस्त्वौषधीभ्यः परिददामि। द्यावापृथिवीभ्यां त्वा परिददामि। विश्वेभ्यस्त्वा भूतेभ्यः परिददाम्यरिष्ट्यै॥ पार० 2.2.21

Om prajāpataye tvā paridadāmi, devāya tvā savitre paridadāmi, adbhyastvauṣadhībhyaḥ paridadāmi, dyāvāpṛthivībhyāṁ tvā paridadāmi, viśvebhyastvā bhūtebhyaḥ paridadāmyariṣṭyai ‖ *Pār.GS. 2.2.21*

[Meaning] O Child! I initiate you in Brahmacharya to obey the command of Prajāpati; I initiate you realize Brahman, the efficient cause of creation; I initiate you for attaining the knowledge of (adbhyaḥ) prakṛti and its particles; I initiate you for achieving the understanding of Chidākāśa (space of Brahman) and Bhūtākāśa (space known to modern physics) [or sun and the earth] and for the wellbeing of all living beings.

After this Upanayana ceremony is finished, the father of the child and Āchārya, if they think fit, should hold the Vedārambha ceremony on the very day. If they feel about keeping Vedārambha on another day, they should sing Mahāvāmdevya gāna as has been prescribed at the end of Sāmānya Prakaraṇa. The mother of the child paying full respect to ladies sends them off, and the child's father gives respect to gentlemen and sends them off.

The mother and father of the child, the Ācharya, other relatives, friend etc, should say together.

ओं त्वं जीव शरदः शतं वर्द्धमानः।
आयुष्मान् तेजस्वी वर्चस्वी भूयाः॥

Om tvaṁ jīva śaradaḥ śataṁ varddhamānaḥ,
āyuṣmān tejasvī varchasvī bhūyāḥ.

[Meaning] O Child! You, growing in strength and vigour live hundred autumns. You become long-lived, brilliant and radiant.

इत्युपनयनसंस्कारविधिः समाप्तः ॥

ityupanayanasaṁskāravidhiḥ samāptaḥ ॥

Here ends the procedure of the Upanayana ceremony.

अथ वेदारम्भसंस्काराविधिर्विधीयते
Vedārambha Sanskāra

To undertake to observe the discipline and rules for studying the four Vedas with all their systems and ancillary sciences beginning from the Mantra of Gayatri - is called the Vedārambha.

Time- The day of the investiture of sacred thread is also the time of Vedārambha. If the same cannot be performed on the day of Upanayana or it is not desired to be done on the same day, it will be performed on the next day. If this next day is also not suitable, the ceremony of Vedārambha be performed on any day within one year (from the date of Upanayana performed).

Procedure of Vedārambha Sanskāra

On the day fixed for the Vedārambha ceremony, the performer of the ceremony, i.e., the father of the child or in the father's absence, the Āchārya should give a bath to the child with pure, clean water and dress him in a nice outfit. He should sit with the child on a comfortable seat west of the Yajña-vedi, keeping his face eastward.

Thereafter, the Iśvarastuti, Prārthanā-Upāsanā, Svasti-vāchana and Śāntikaraṇa mantras should be recited. Agnyādhāna with ओं भूर्भुवः स्व॰ Samidādhāna with ओम् अयन्त इध्म॰ etc. three mantras and the sprinkling of water on the four sides of the yajñakuṇḍa with ओम् अदिते..... ओं देव सवितः॰ etc.four mantras should be performed.

Thereafter the fire of the Yajñkuṇḍa should be kindled with ओम् उद्बुध्यस्वाग्रे॰ and on the enkindled samidhās (wood-fuel) for oblations of Āghārāvājyabhāgāhuti, four Vyāhṛti Āhutis, and eight

Ajyāhutīs with ओं त्वन्नो अग्रे..., etc. eight mantras) (all totalling 16) should be offered. Then principal homa should be performed (with the four mantras ओं भूर्भुवः स्वः..., etc. After that, four oblations of Vyāhṛti Āhutī (thus totalling six in all) should be offered from the hand of the child.

Afterwards, the fire of the Yajñakuṇḍa should be gathered in the Kuṇḍa with the following Mantra-

ओम् अग्रे सुश्रवः सुश्रवसं मा कुरु। ओं यथा त्वमग्रे सुश्रवः सौश्रवसं कुरु। ओं यथा त्वमग्रे देवानां यज्ञस्य निधिपा असि। ओम् एवमहं मनुष्याणां वेदस्य निधिपो भूयासम्॥ पार. गृसू. 2.4.2

Om agne suśravaḥ suśravasaṁ mā kuru, Oṁ yathā tvamagne suśravaḥ sauśravasaṁ kuru, Oṁ yathā tvamagne devānāṁ yajñasya nidhipā asi, Om ēvamahaṁ manuṣyāṇāṁ vedasya nidhipo bhūyāsam. Pār. GS. 2.4.2

[Meaning] O famous Āchārya! Please make me earn fame in the field of education. O Āchārya! As you enjoy prominence and are highly learned, you make me enjoy prominence and become highly learned. O Āchārya! As you, among the learned men, are the preserver of the treasure of knowledge, Yajña etc., so I become amongst the men, the preserver of the treasure of the Vedic knowledge and speech,

Afterwards, the child taking a round of the Yañakuṇḍa should sprinkle water around the Yajñakuṇḍa with the procedure and chanting of ओम् आदितेऽनुमन्यस्व etc. four mantras.

After that, the child standing on the south side of the Yajñakuṇḍa, keeping his face northward, should take one wood stick dipped in ghee and should offer it in the middle of the fire of the vedi after reciting the following mantra:

ओम् अग्नये समिधमाहार्षं बृहते जातवेदसे। यथा त्वमग्ने समिधा समिध्यस एवमहमायुषा मेधया वर्चसा प्रजया पशुभिर्ब्रह्मवर्चसेन समिन्धे जीवपुत्रो ममाचार्यो मेधाव्यहमसान्यनिराकरिष्णुर्यशस्वी तेजस्वी ब्रह्मवर्चस्यन्नादो भूयासꣳ स्वाहा ॥

पार.गृसू. 2.4.3

Om agnaye samidhamāhārṣaṁ bṛhate jātavedase, yathā tvamagne samidhā samidhyasa ēvamahamāyuṣā medhayā varchasā prajayā paśubhirbrahmavarchasena samindhe jīvaputro mamāchāryo medhāvyahamasānyanirākariṣṇuryaśasvī tejasvī brahmavarchasyannādo bhūyāsaꣳ svāhā. Pār.GS. 2.4.3

[Meaning] I have brought the wood fuel for enkindling the fire of Yajña, which is mighty and is present in all the created objects of the world. As this fire blazes with wood fuel, so I shine with long life, wisdom, vigour, progeny, animals and the knowledge of Veda and Brahman. May my Āchārya have his sons alive, and may I be enriched with high intellectual power. May I not be arrogant to anyone. I may be prominent, vigourous, possessed of divine merits and the producer of grain and food.

In the same manner, the second and third wood-stick should be offered. Thereafter, the fire of the vedi should be accumulated by chanting the mantra - ओम् अग्रे सुश्रवः सुश्रवसं॰ and water should be sprinkled in the four sides of the vedi with ओम् आदितेऽनुमन्यस्व॰ etc. four mantras. The child sitting in the west of the vedi, keeping his face in the east, slightly warming his palms and touching water should touch his mouth seven times with each of the following mantras likewise:

Here, the word likewise means that the procedure of warming palms and touching water with them should be repeated each time.

ओं तनूपा अग्नेऽपि तन्वं मे पाहि ॥

Om tanūpā agne'pi tanvaṁ me pāhi ॥

[Meaning] O Brahman! You are the protector of the bodies, also protect my body.

ओम् आयुर्दा अग्नेऽस्यायुर्मे देहि ॥

Om āyurdā agne'syāyurme dehi ॥2 ॥

[Meaning] O Brahman! You are the giver of life, grant me long life.

ओं वर्चोदा अग्नेऽसि वर्चो मे देहि ॥

Om varchodā agne'si varcho me dehi ॥3 ॥

[Meaning] O Brahman! You are the giver of Brahma varchasva (Spiritual Aura), give me Brahma varchasva (Spiritual Aura).

ओम् अग्ने यन्मे तन्वाऽऊनं तन्म आपृण ॥ यजु. 3.17

Om agne yanme tanvā'ūnaṁ tanma āpṛṇa. YV. 3.17

[Meaning] O Brahman! whatever is deficient in my body, make it up.

ओं मेधां मे देवः सविता आदधातु ॥

Om medhāṁ me devaḥ savitā ādadhātu ॥5 ॥

[Meaning] May the creator of the universe grant me wisdom.

ओं मेधां मे देवी सरस्वती आदधातु ॥

Om medhāṁ me devī sarasvatī ādadhātu ॥6 ॥

[Meaning] Let the all-flourshing knowledge give us wisdom.

ओं मेधाम अश्विनौ देवावाधात्तां पुष्करस्रजौ ॥ पार.गृसू. 2.4.8

Om medhāma aśvinau devāvādhāttāṁ puṣkarasrajau ॥
Pār.GS. 2.4.8

[Meaning] Let the (*aśvinau*) teacher and preacher honoured with the garlands lotus flowers give us knowledge

Afterwards the child should touch the parts of the body described in each Mantra by pronouncing the concerned following Mantras in the manner given below:

Touch the mouth by chanting the following mantra:

ओं वाक् च म आप्यायताम् ॥

Oṁ vāk cha ma āpyāyatām ॥

[Meaning] O Brahman! may I have powerful speech well developed organs of speech.

Touch the nose by chanting the following mantra:

ओं प्राणश्च म आप्यायताम् ॥

Oṁ prāṇaścha ma āpyāyatām ॥

[Meaning] O Brahman! may I have powerful smell and and well developed organ of smell.

Touch the eyes by chanting the following mantra

ओं चक्षुश्च म आप्यायताम् ॥

Oṁ chakṣuścha ma āpyāyatām ॥

[Meaning] O Brahman! may I have sound vision and well developed organ of sight.

Touch the ears by chanting the following mantra

ओं श्रोत्रं च म आप्यायताम् ॥

Oṁ śrotraṁcha ma āpyāyatām ॥

[Meaning] O Brahman! may I have powerful sense of sound and well-developed organs of sound.

Touch the both arms by chanting the following mantra:

ओं यशो बलं च म आप्यायताम् ॥

Oṁ yaśo balaṁcha ma āpyāyatām ॥

[Meaning] O Brahman! may I have name and fame and physical power in my arms.

The child should meditate upon Īśvara with the following Mantras:

ओं मयि मेधां मयि प्रजां मय्यग्निस्तेजो दधातु ।
मयि मेधां मयि प्रजां मयीन्द्र इन्द्रियं दधातु ।
मयि मेधां मयि प्रजां मयि सूर्यो भ्राजो दधातु ।
यत्ते अग्ने तेजस्तेनाहं तेजस्वी भूयासम् ।
यत्ते अग्ने वर्चस्तेनाहं वर्चस्वी भूयासम् ।
यत्ते अग्ने हरस्तेनाहं हरस्वी भूयासम् । आश्व० 1.21.4

Om mayi medhāṁ mayi prajāṁ mayyagnistejo dadhātu,
mayi medhāṁ mayi prajāṁ mayīndra indriyaṁ dadhātu,
mayi medhāṁ mayi prajāṁ mayi sūryo bhrājo dadhātu,
yatte agne tejastenāhaṁ tejasvī bhūyāsam,
yatte agne varchastenāhaṁ varchasvī bhūyāsam,
yatte agne harastenāhaṁ harasvī bhūyāsam. Āśv.G.S. 1.21.4

[Meaning] May Agni (Brahman who gives motion to the inactive energy in the beginning of creation) give me wisdom, progeny and strength. May Indra (the All-Powerful Brahman) bestow wisdom, progeny and powerful sense organs (receptors) upon me. May Sūrya (the All-Illuminating Brahman) grant me wisdom, progeny and brilliance. May I be effulgent with the effulgence you possess in you, my Lord! May I be powerful with the power you have in you, my Lord! May I be an overpowering force with the force wherewith you are endowed, my Lord!

Afterwards, the child walking to the north side of the Yajñakuṇḍa should sit on his knees, keeping his face in the east, and Āchārya should sit in front of the child, keeping his face westward.

बालकोक्तिः — अधीहि भूः सावित्रीं भो अनुब्रूहि ॥ आश्व० 1.21.4

bālakoktiḥ-adhīhi bhūḥ sāvitrīṁ bho anubrūhi.

Āśv. GS.1.21.4

Says the child— O Āchārya instruct me the Oṁ followed by three vyāhṛtis and Gāyatrī mantra, the subject matter of which is Savitā, the creator and the sun. Please teach me.

After that, the Āchārya puts a cloth piece on the shoulder of the child and his own shoulder, holds the fingers of both the hands of the child into his own hand and teaches the Gāyatrī mantra to the child thrice.

First time:

ओं भूर्भुवः स्व। तत्सवितुर्वरेण्यम् ॥

Oṁ bhūrbhuvaḥ sva; tatsaviturvareṇyam.

This part be got pronounced by the child word by word correctly.

Second time:

ओं भूर्भुवः स्वः। तत्सवितुर्वरेण्यं भर्गो देवस्य धीमहि।

Oṁ bhūrbhuvaḥ svaḥ; tatsaviturvareṇyaṁ bhārgo devasya dhīmahi.

This should be repeated by the child slowly and correctly word by word.

Third time:

ओं भूर्भुवः स्वः। तत्सवितुर्वरेण्यं भर्गो देवस्य धीमहि। धियो यो नः प्रचोदयात् ॥

Oṁ bhūrbhuvaḥ svaḥ, tatsaviturvareṇyaṁ bhargo devasya dhīmahi, dhiyo yo naḥ prachodayāt.

Āchārya makes the child repeat this and tells the child the short meaning of this mantra.

Meaning - Om is the prime name of Parameśvara in which all other names are contained; He is Bhūḥ because he is the life of life; He is Bhuvaḥ as He is the protector from all the pains; He is Svaḥ because he is all bliss and giver of bliss to His meditators. To that creator of all the worlds, the illuminator of all the stars like our sun etc; the giver of wisdom and wealth we establish in our heart as our worshipable Īśvara. We concentrate in our hearts the excellent attainable, thinkable quality and power of Brahman, who is desired by all and who is most predominating, pure, sanctimonious by nature and the destroyer of all sorts of pains. May he lead our intellects towards excellent quality, acts and temperaments. For this purpose, only the Lord of the universe should be eulogized, prayed and premeditated. None else but He should be treated as the object of worship, and none should be known as superior to Him.

Afterwards, the child and Āchārya should take a firm saṅkalpa (vow) as has been taken previously in the sacred thread ceremony with the following mantra:

ओं मम व्रते हृदयं ते दधामि मम चित्तमनुचित्तं ते अस्तु ।

मम वाचमेकव्रतो जुषस्व बृहस्पतिष्ट्वा नियुनक्तु मह्यम् ॥ पार.गृसू. 2.2.16

Oṁ mama vrate hṛdayaṁ te dadhāmi mama chittamanuchittaṁ te astu,
mama vāchamekavrato juṣasva bṛhaspatiṣṭvā niyunaktu mahyam. Pār. GS. 2.2.16

[Meaning] O disciple! I shape your mind and heart as per my saṅkalpa of imparting you knowledge, let your mind be concordant with my mind always, you being fully attentive grasp my words with affection and attain the meaning of these words and Brahman who is the master of Vedic speech, unite you with me in thought and action according to your pledge or saṅkalpa (vow) from this very day to day.

The Āchārya should tie the beautiful and smooth

gridle (मेखला) in waist of the child by chanting the following mantra:

ओम् इयं दुरुक्तं परिबाधमाना वर्णं पवित्रं पुनती म आगात् ।

प्राणापानाभ्यां बलमादधाना स्वसा देवी सुभगा मेखलेयम् ॥ पार०गृसू 2.2.8

Om iyam duruktam paribādhamānā varṇam pavitram punatī ma āgāt I

prāṇāpānābhyām balamādadhānā svasā devī subhagā mekhaleyam II Pār.GS. 2.2.8

[Meaning] This girdle is sacred and a betower of fortune like the sister; it leads to divinity. It obstructs evil from all sides and adds to Varṇa's sanctity. It gives strength by maintaining inhalation and exhalation. Let this girdle come into my possession.

The Āchārya pronouncing the following mantra should give the Brahmachārī (the child) two clean loin cloths (कोपीन), two waist cloths, one upper cloth and two lowers (कटिवस्त्र). Of these, one waist cloth (अंगोछा), one loincloth and one upper cloth should be put on by the child with the advice of Āchārya.

ओं युवा सुवासाः परिवीत आगात् स उ श्रेयान् भवति जायमानः ।

तं धीरासः कवय उन्नयन्ति स्वाध्यो३ मनसा देवयन्तः ॥

ऋ० 3.8.4 ॥ पार०गृसू. 2.29

Om yuvā suvāsāḥ parivīta āgāt sa u śreyān bhavati jāyamānaḥ I

tam dhīrāsaḥ kavaya unnayanti svādhyo3 manasā devayantaḥ II RV. 3.8.4; Pār. GS. 2.29

[Meaning] This child possessing strong physique, dressed in a nice outfit wearing the sacred thread, comes before me. He, taking the second birth in the domain of study, enjoys dignity. The enlightened persons well established in Samādhi raise this student to the high status of genius and character.

Afterwards, the Āchārya holding a stick in his hand should stand up before the child, and the child standing in front of the Āchārya with folded hand should take the stick from his hand and chant the following mantra.

ओं यो मे दण्डः परापतद्वै परापतद्वै हायसोऽधिभूम्याम् ।
तमहं पुनरादद आयुषे ब्रह्मणे ब्रह्मवर्चसाय ॥ पार.गृसू. 2.2.12

Oṁ yo me daṇḍaḥ parāpatadvai parāpatadvai hāyaso'dhibhūmyām,
tamahaṁ punarādada āyuṣe brahmaṇe brahmavarchasāya.

Pār.GS. 2.2.12

[Meaning] This stick which has come into my possession is based on the ground and looking up in the sky. I accept it mainly for attaining a long life, knowledge of the Veda and Brahmavarchasva (realizing Brahman).

Afterwards, the father should give a general information of Brahmacharya Āśrama to the child as follows:

ब्रह्मचार्यसि असौ ॥

brahmachāryasi asau

[Meaning] You have entered into Brahmacharya Āśrama from today on.

अपोऽशान ॥

apo'śāna.

[Meaning] You always sip potable, clean water before taking meals and performing daily prayers.

कर्म कुरु ॥

karma kuru.

[Meaning] Always be away from evil acts and follow acts of dharma.

दिवा मा स्वाप्सीः ॥

divā mā svāpsīḥ.

[Meaning] You do not ever sleep in day time.

आचार्याधीनो वेदमधीष्व ॥

āchāryādhīno vedamadhīṣva.

[Meaning] Under the worthy guidance and supervision of your Āchārya, always study the Veda and its auxiliary sciences.

द्वादश वर्षाणि प्रतिवेदं ब्रह्मचर्यं गृहाण वा ब्रह्मचर्यं चर ॥

dvādaśa varṣāṇi prativedaṁ brahmacharyaṁ gṛhāṇa vā brahmacharyaṁchara.

[Meaning] You lead the life of Brahmachārī throughout 48 years to devote 12 years each to study four Vedas or observe Brahmacharya without any failure unless you complete the study of four Vedas.

आचार्याधीनो भवान्यत्राधर्माचरणात् ॥

āchāryādhīno bhavānyatrādharmācharaṇāt.

[Meaning] You always follow dharma under your Āchārya, but you do not ever obey the advice of your Āchārya if he preaches you anything of adharma and desires you to act according to that.

क्रोधानृते वर्जय ॥

krodhānṛte varjaya.

[Meaning] Abstain from anger and telling a lie.

Always avoid the habit of the eight kinds of passionate acts like anger, greed, ego, attachment, etc.

मैथुनं वर्जय ॥ गो॰ गृ॰ 3.1.157

maithunaṁ varjaya. Go.GS. 3.1.157

[Meaning] Avoid sex.

उपरि शय्यां वर्जय ॥ गो० गृ० 3.1.158

upari śayyāṁ varjaya. Go.GS. 3.1.158

[Meaning] Do sleep only on ground, never sleep on a cot, etc.

कौशीलवगन्धांजनानि वर्जय ॥ गो० गृ० 3.1.159

kauśīlavagandhāṁjanāni varjaya. Go.GS. 3.1.159

[Meaning] Avoid singing, playing on musical instruments, dancing etc. Avoid use of perfumery and Añjana (collyrium)

अत्यन्तं स्नानं भोजनं निद्रां जागरणं निन्दां लोभमोहभयशोकान् वर्जय ॥

atyantaṁ snānaṁ bhojanaṁ nidrāṁ jāgaraṇaṁ nindāṁ lobhamohabhayaśokān varjaya.

[Meaning] Always avoid excessive bathing, eating, sleeping, waking, reproach, greed, undue indulgence, fear and grief.

प्रतिदिनं रात्रेः पश्चिमे यामे चोत्थायावश्यकं कृत्वा दन्तधावनस्नानसन्ध्योपासनेश्वरस्तुतिप्रार्थनोपासनायोगाभ्यासान्नित्य-माचर ॥

pratidinaṁ rātreḥ paśchime yāme chotthāyāvaśyakaṁ kṛtvā dantadhāvanasnānasandhyopāsaneśvarastutiprārthanopāsanāyog ābhyāsānnitya-māchara.

[Meaning] Rise on the fourth prahara of the night called Brahma-muhurta (3 AM); always do needful acts like going to the washroom, brushing the teeth, washing the mouth, taking a bath, two times Sandhyā, prayer and meditation upon Īśvara and the practice of Yogic exercises.

क्षुरकृत्यं वर्जय ॥

kṣurakṛtyaṁ varjaya.

[Meaning] Avoid shaving.

मांसरूक्षाहारं मद्यादिपानं च वर्जय ॥

māṁsarūkṣāhāraṁ madyādipānaṁ cha varjaya.

[Meaning] Do not eat meat, dry, coarse cereals and do not ever dring intoxicant drinks.

गवाश्वहस्त्युष्ट्रादियानं वर्जय ॥

gavāśchahastyuṣṭrādiyānaṁ varjaya.

[Meaning] Never ride on bullock, horses elephant, camel etc.

अन्तर्ग्रामनिवासोपानच्छत्रधारणं वर्जय ॥

antargrāmanivāsopānachchhatradhāraṇaṁ varjaya.

[Meaning] Never live in a village (except in Gurukula), and never use shoes and an umbrella.

अकामतः स्वयमिन्द्रियस्पर्शेन वीर्यस्खलनं विहाय वीर्यं शरीरे संरक्ष्योध्वरिताः सततं भव ॥

akāmataḥ svayasindriyasparśena vīryaskhalanaṁ vihāya vīryaṁ śarīre saṁrakṣayordhvaretāḥ satataṁ bhava.

[Meaning] Except in the case of urine discharge, never touch the organ of urine to cause the discharge of semen and restraining the semen in the body always try to become उध्वरिता (living in chastity.

तैलाभ्यङ्गमर्दनात्यम्लातितिक्तकषायक्षाररेचनद्रव्याणि मा सेवस्व ॥

tailābhyaṅgamardanātyamlātitiktakaṣāyakṣārarechanadravyā ṇi mā sevasva.

[Meaning] Avoid the use of massage with oil etc., do not use mustard-plaster for the beauty of the body, do not take ever the eatables which are very sour like tamarind etc. very pungent like red chillies etc. astringent like (हरड) Terminalia chebula; purgative like (जमालघोटा) Clerodendum Phlomoides acidic like more salty things.

नित्यं युक्ताहारविहारवान् विद्योपार्जने य यत्नवान् भव ॥

nityaṁ yuktāhāravihāravān vidyopārjane ya yatnavān bhava.

[Meaning] Daily do your work of taking meals and other dealings with great care and thought and be active in attaining knowledge.

सुशीलो मितभाषी सभ्यो भव ॥

suśīlo mitabhāṣī sabhyo bhava.

[Meaning] You should always possess good character, be not talkative and cultivate civilized behaviour in meetings and assemblies.

मेखलादण्डधारणभैक्ष्यचर्यसमिदाधानोदकस्पर्शनाचार्यप्रियाचरणप्रातः सायमभिवादनविद्यासंचयजितेन्द्रियत्वादीन्येते ते नित्यधर्माः ॥

mekhalādaṇḍadhāraṇabhaikṣayacharyasamidādhānodakaspa rśanāchāryapriyācharaṇaprātaḥsāyamabhivādanavidyāsaṁch ayajitendriyatvādīnyete te nityadharmāḥ ॥

[Meaning] You keep yourself bound by the duties of wearing a girdle, keeping the stick, mendicancy, performance of Agnihotra, bath, daily meditation upon Brahman, good sentiments for Āchārya and salutation to Āchārya every morning and evening. These are the deeds of your daily performance, and you should abstain from doing whatever has been prohibited.

As the father has completed his preaching, the child, having wished him 'Namaste', should say with folded hand, 'I would, no doubt, follow your preachings'.

Afterwards, the Brahmachārī circumambulating the Yajñakuṇḍa should stand in the west of it and ask for alms from mother, father, sister, brother, maternal uncle, mother's sister, uncle etc., who do not hesitate in giving alms and thus alms accumulated should be surrendered to Āchārya. Afterwards, Āchārya takes some-what cereal from that and returns the alms to the Brahmachārī, and he (Brahmachārī) should keep it safe for his own food.

Afterwards, seating the child on a decked seat, the song of Vāmdevya as has been prescribed in Sāmānya Prakaraṇa, should be chanted. After that, the child should eat the alms he kept for him.

Afterwards, there should be rest till evening and then (in the evening) Āchārya should make the prayer and meditation as described in Gṛhashāśrama Sanskāra, performed by the child with his own hands.

After that, the Āchārya with the Brahmachārī should sit in the west of the kuṇḍa keeping faces eastward and should prepare sthālīpāka (dish of barley or rice cooked in milk according to the method described in Sāmānya Prakaraṇa and sprinkling ghee on it should keep it safe there. They should perform samidhādāna and keep the samidhās burning. They should offer the four oblations of Āghārāvājyābhāgāhutis and four oblations of vyāhṛti āhutis totalling eight in number.

After that, the Brahmachārī standing up should offer three samidhās with the mantra ओम् अग्रे शुश्रव०

etc. Again, he should warm his hand-palms on the fire of the altar (agnikuṇḍa) should touch his body parts and mouth according to the procedure previously described in this Vedārambha Sanskāra. Afterwards, the child should hand over Āchārya, the previously prepared rice, for offering as oblations and taking as meals. Then Āchārya should take a proportion of it desired for offering oblations and sprinkling ghee on it, should offer three oblations with the following mantras:

ओं सदस्पतिमद्भूतं प्रियमिन्द्रस्य काम्यम् ।
सनि मेधामयासिष॰ स्वाहा ॥
इदं सदसस्पतये-इदन्न मम ॥ यजु॰ 32.13

Oṁ sadaspatimadbhūtaṁ priyamindrasya kāmyam;
sani medhāmayāsiṣa॰ svāhā;
idaṁ sadasaspataye-idanna mama. YV. 32.13

[Meaning] (*svāhā*) With oblations given in Brahmayajña, may I realize Brahman, who is the (*sadaspatim*) Governor of this universe, (*adbhutam*) wondrous, (*priyam*) dear to all, (*kāmyam*) desirable by (*indrasya*) souls. Through His realization, we are able to (*ayāsisam*) attain the (*sanim*) discriminatory (*medhām*) wisdom. The oblation offered is meant forthe Go evrnor of the Universe and it is not for me.

तत्सवितुर्वरेण्यं भर्गो देवस्य धीमहि ।
धियो यो नः प्रचोदयात् स्वाहा ॥
इदं सवित्रे-इदन्न मम ॥ यजु॰ 22.9

tatsaviturvareṇyaṁ bhargo devasya dhīmahi,
dhiyo yo naḥ prachodayāt svāhā.
idaṁ savitre-idanna mama. YV. 22.9

[Meaning] May we meditate upon the qualities of Creator Brahman which are worthy to be inculcated by us. May he guide our intellects on the path of dharma and Mokṣa. The oblation offered is meant for Creator Brahman and it is not for me.

ओम् ऋषिभ्यः स्वाहा ॥ इदं ऋषिभ्यः-इदन्न मम ॥ आश्व॰ 1.22.14

Om ṛṣibhyaḥ svāhā ॥ idaṁ ṛṣibhyaḥ-idanna mama,

Āśv.GS.1.22.14

[Meaning] We offer this oblation for Vedic Ṛṣis, who transmitted the knowledge of the Vedas to us. The oblation offered is meant for the Ṛṣis and not for me.

After having offered these three oblations mentioned above, the Āchārya should offer a fourth oblation with the mantra- ॐ यदस्य कर्मणो॰ etc. After that, he should offer four oblations of vyāhṛti Āhutis and eight oblations of ājyāhutis, totalling twelve in number. After that, the Brahamchārī sitting on a decked seat, keeping his face eastward, should do Vāmadevyagāna as has been described in Sāmānya Prakarṇa with the Āchārya. Then saying- अमुकगोत्रोत्पन्नोऽहं भो भवन्तमभिवादये (गोभिल॰ 2-10-25) 'I born in the geneology of so and so and wish you Namaste'— should say Namaste to the Āchārya.

Āchārya says-

आयुष्मान् विद्यावान् भव सौम्य ॥

āyuṣmān vidyāvān bhava saumya.

[Meaning] O Saumya (representing soma in the Brahmayajña)! May you be long-lived and celebrated with knowledge.

When Āchārya has given his blessing to the Brahmachārī, he should eat the cereals left out from yajña and also other sweets etc., with Āchārya sitting separately. Afterwards, washing hands and mouth, they entertain the people invited to grace the occasion with food according to their satisfaction. Afterwards, ladies should give a warm send-off to ladies and gents to gents. All the people leaving the place should give blessings to the child with the following Sanskrit sentence and go home.

हे बालक! त्वमीश्वरकृपया विद्वान् शरीरात्मबलयुक्तः कुशली वीर्यवानरोगः सर्वा विद्या अधीत्याऽस्मान् दिदृक्षुः सन्नागम्याः ॥

he bālaka! tvamīśvarakṛpayā vidvān śarīrātmabalayuktaḥ kuśalī vīryavānarogaḥ sarvā vidyā adhītyā'smān didṛkṣuḥ sannāgamyāḥ.

[Meaning] O child, by God's grace, you become learned, strong in body and be blessed with pleasure, vigour, health and having learnt all the branches of knowledge come from (Gurukula) to meet us.

Afterwards, the Brahmachārī (child) should sleep on the ground for three days. The Āchārya should make the Brahmachārī perform the procedure of three Samidhās with the mantra ओम् अग्रे सुश्रवः० etc. and the Aṅgasparśa procedure as has been laid down in the Vedārambha Sanskāra. He should also perform by the hand of Brahmachārī the four oblations of the sthālīpāka with the mantra सदसस्पति०. The Brahmachārī should take only the food free from acid and salt for three days.

Afterwards, he should go to Pāṭhaśālā and take the saṅkalpa of completing the education before Āchārya and his Āchārya also do so to give him education.

आचार्य उपनयमानो ब्रह्मचारिणं कृणुते गर्भमन्तः ।
तं रात्रीस्तिस्र उदरे बिभर्ति तं जातं द्रष्टुमभिसंयन्ति देवाः ॥ अथर्व० 11.5.3

āchārya upanayamāno brahmachāriṇaṁ kṛṇute garbhamantaḥ,
taṁ rātrīstisra udare bibhartti taṁ jātaṁ drraṣṭumabhisaṁyanti devāḥ. AV.11.5.3

[Meaning] On being invested with scared thread, the Āchārya/Āchāryā virtually takes Brahmachārī or Brahmachāriṇī into his/her womb for three days. When Brahmachārī or Brahmachāriṇī takes second birth from the womb of Āchārya or Āchāryā after completing education, all the enlightened scholars approach him/her collectively to have a glimpse.

इयं समित्पृथिवी द्यौर्द्वितीयोतान्तरिक्षं समिधा पृणाति ।
ब्रह्मचारी समिधा मेखलया श्रमेण लोकाँस्तपसा पिपर्ति ॥ अथर्व० 11.5.4

iyaṁ samitpṛthivī dyaurdvitīyotāntarikṣaṁ samidhā pṛṇāti,
brahmachārī samidhā mekhalayā śrameṇa lokāṁstapasā

piparti. AV. 11.5.4

[Meaning] The Brahmachārī/ Brahmachāriṇī at the time of Vedārambha offer three sticks in the fire of yajña, observing the saṅkalpa of Brahmacharya. These three sticks represent pṛthivī [Bhūtākāśa in the creation or earth in our solar system], antarikṣa [intervening space in creation or magnetosphere of the earth in our solar system] and dyau [Chidākāśa of creation or the sun of our solar system]. Brahmachārī/ Brahmachāriṇī, through the symbol of his/her girdle and sticks and his outstanding efforts and yoga, gains the knowledge of all the three worlds [pṛthivī, antarikṣa and dyau].

ब्रह्मचार्येति समिधा समिद्धः काष्र्णं वसानो दीक्षितो दीर्घश्मश्रुः ।

स सद्म एति पूर्वस्मादुत्तरं समुद्रं लोकान्त्संगृभ्य मुहुराचरिक्रत् ॥ अथर्व॰ 11.5.6

brahmachāryeti samidhā samiddhaḥ kārṣṇaṁ vasāno dīkṣito dīrghaśmaśruḥ, sa sadma ēti pūrvasmāduttaraṁ samudraṁ lokāntsaṁgṛbhya muhurācharikrat. AV. 11.5.6

[Meaning] The Brahmachārī/ Brahmachāriṇī, glittering with knowledge of pṛthivī, antarikṣa and dyau, wearing an attractive look, holding long beards, enters from Brahmacharya Āśrama called as pūrvasamudra (first ocean) to the Gṛhastha Āśrama (house-hold life) called as uttarsamudra (second ocean). He (*muhuḥ ācharikrat*) performs (lokān saṅgṛbhyaḥ) altruistic welfare activities.

ब्रह्मचर्येण तपसा राजा राष्ट्रं वि रक्षति ।

आचार्यो ब्रह्मचर्येण ब्रह्मचारिणमिच्छते ॥ अथर्व॰ 11.5.17

brahmacharyeṇa tapasā rājā rāṣṭraṁ vi rakṣati,
āchāryo brahmacharyeṇa brahmachāriṇamichchhate.

AV. 11.5.17

[Meaning] Only a king who has undergone Brahmacharya Āśrama and observed physical, mental and speech level austerity can rule a state or nation perfectly.

Similarly, an Āchārya who has observed strict Brahmacharya deserves to guide or supervise a Brahmachārī.

ब्रह्मचर्येण कन्या३ युवानं विन्दते पतिम् ॥ अथर्व॰ 11.5.18

brahmacharyeṇa kanyā3 yuvānaṁ vindate patim. AV.11.5.18

[Meaning] As a boy completing the life of perfect Brahmachārī wed to a girl, so the girls too, completing the life of Brahmacharya, should attain their soulmate in the full bloom of their youth.

ब्रह्मचारी ब्रह्म भ्राजद् बिभर्ति तस्मिन्देवा अधि विश्वे समोताः। प्राणापानौ जनयन्नाद व्यानं वाचं मनो हृदयं ब्रह्म मेधाम्॥ अथर्व॰ 11.5.24

brahmachārī brahma bhrājad bibharti tasmindevā adhi viśve samotāḥ। prāṇāpānau janayannāda vyānaṁ vācham mano hṛdayaṁ brahma medhām॥ AV. 11.5.24

[Meaning] When a Brahmachārī realizes Brahman (creation as His action and the four Vedas as the blueprint of creation in His mind), he shines forth. He becomes the dwelling place of all good qualities, and all learned scholars pay due respect to him. Such a Brahmachārī gains perfection in prāṇa, apāna and vyāna breathings, speech, control of mind, purity of conscience, and attains the intellect that imbibes the Vedas (blueprint of creation in the mind of Brahman).

ब्रह्मचर्यकालः

The period of Brahmacharya

Here is the authority of the *Chhāndogyopaniṣad* (3.16):

मातृमान् पितृमानाचार्य्यवान् पुरुषो वेद ॥ 14.6.10.2

mātṛmān pitṛmānāchāryyavān puruṣo veda॥ 14.6.10.2

Only those men and women are able to achieve Dharma, Arth, Kāma and Mokṣa who respectively have got the education and instructions till five years of age from mother, five to eight from father and eight to 48, 44, 40, 36, 30, 25 from Āchārya (in case of men) and 8, 16, 18, 22, 24 from Āchāryā (in case of women).

पुरुषो वाव यज्ञस्तस्य यानि चतुर्विंꣳशतिर्वर्षाणि तत् प्रातः सवनं चतुर्विꣳशतयक्षरा गायत्री गायत्रं प्रातःसवनं तदस्य वसवोऽन्वायत्ताः प्राणा वाव वसव एते हीदꣳ सर्व वासयन्ति ॥

puruṣo vāva yajñastasya yāni chaturviṁśatirvarṣāṇi tat prātaḥ savanaṁ chaturviṁśatayakṣarā gāyatrī gāyatraṁ prātaḥsavanaṁ tadasya vasavo'nvāyattāḥ prāṇā vāva vasava ēte hīdaṁ sarva vāsayanti.

A person is verily a yajña. 24 years of Brahmacharya is like morning offerings. Gāyatrī metre has 24 syllables. Morning offerings are made with mantras composed in Gāyatrī metre. The vasus (life-sustaining factors) are linked to this offering. Prāṇas (bio-energy of the body) are vasus because they sustain the entire metabolism of the body.

तच्चेदेतस्मिन् वयसि किञ्चिदुपतपेत्स ब्रूयात्प्राणा वसव इदं मे प्रातःसवनं माध्यन्दिनं सवनमनुसन्तनुतेति माहं प्राणानां वसूनां मध्ये यज्ञो विलोप्सीयेत्युद्धैव तत एत्यगदो ह भवति ॥२॥

tañ ced etasmin vayasi kiñcid upatapet. sa brūyāt prāṇā vasava. idaṁ me prātaḥ savanaṁ mādhyandinaṁ savanaṁ anu saṁ tanute ti. māhaṁ prāṇānāṁ vasūnāṁ madhye yajño vilopsīyeti. uddhaiva tat etyagado ha bhavati.

[Meaning] In this age, whoever treats himself in the fire of knowledge (endows him with knowledge), his bio-energy acts as Vasu (the support of his life) for him. Let this morning offering (24 years of Brahmacharya) continue to the midday offering (44 years of Brahmacharya). Let my life not be broken off in the midst. If this body is kept healthy, it will become invulnerable to various diseases.

Suppose anyone asks Brahmacharī to execute marriage or enjoy carnal pleasure before 25 years of age. In that case, he should reply to the man that he would not be able to observe the strict discipline of Brahmacharya of 44 years, the middle one, had he not made his prāṇās, mind and sense organs strong by adhering to Brahmacharya till 25 years. He should say. "The Brahmacharya of the first category make the ground for the Brahmacharya of the middle category. Am I a fool like you who would quickly destroy the body, which is the organization of prāṇās, mind and soul, the means of all good qualities, acts and good sanskāras, and deprive myself of the benefits of this human body? Why should I sink into the deep sea of great sufferings by breaking the sankalpa of Brahmacharya, which is the basis of all Aśramas and the most excellent act among all the acts and the leading cause of all virtues? He who observes the discipline of Brahmacharya in the first phase of 25 years becomes free from all diseases, attaining knowledge through the power of Brahmacharya. Therefore, I would not break the sankalpa of Brahmachārya under the influence of the exhortations of fools like you."

अथ यानि चतुश्चत्वारिꣳशद्वर्षाणि तन्माध्यन्दिनꣳसवनं चतुश्चत्वारिꣳशदक्षरा त्रिष्टुप् त्रैष्टुभं माध्यन्दिनꣳ सवनं तदस्य रुद्रा अन्वायत्ताः प्राणा वाव रुद्रा हीदꣳ सवꣳ रोदयन्ति ॥

atha yāni chatuṣchatvāriṁśadvarṣāṇi tanmādhyandinaṁsavanaṁ chatuśchatvāriṁṁśadakṣarā triṣṭup traiṣṭubham mādhyandinam savanam tadasya rudrā anvāyattāḥ prāṇā vāva rudrā hīdam savamm rodayanti.

[Meaning] The 44 years of Brahmacharya is like midday offering. Triṣṭup metre has 44 syllables. Midday offerings are made with mantras composed in the Triṣṭup metre. The rudras are linked to this offering. Prāṇas (bio-energy of the body) is verily the rudras, because people start weeping when they leave the body.

तं चेदेतस्मिन् वयसि किंचिदुपतपेत् स ब्रूयात् प्राणा रुद्रा इदं मे माध्यन्दिनꣳसवनं तृतीयसवनमनुसन्तनुतेति माहम्प्राणानाꣳ रुद्राणां मध्ये यज्ञो विलोत्सीयेत्युद्धै व तत एत्यगदो ह भवति ॥

tam chedetasmin vayasi kimchidupatapet sa brūyāt prāṇā rudrā idam me mādhyandinamsavanam tṛtīyasavanamanusantanuteti māhamprāṇānām rudrāṇām madhye yajño vilotsīyetyuddhai va tata ētyagado ha bhavati.

[Meaning] In this age, whoever treats himself in the fire of knowledge (endows himself with knowledge), (let him know that) his bio-energy is rudra that makes people weep while leaving the body. Let this midday offering (44 years of Brahmacharya) continue over to the third (evening) offering (48 years of Brahmacharya). Let my life not be broken off in the midst (in between). If this body is kept healthy, it will be invulnerable to various diseases.

Suppose anyone says to the Brahmachārī who will observe Brahmacharya of the middle category that he should leave Brahmacharya and enjoy married life. In that case, the answer is "Whatever pleasure can be obtained by married life, the Brahmacharya life gives more pleasure than that. If one does not observe Brahmacharya in his life, he cannot attain pleasure even in a dream without observing it. Only Brahmachārī can attain all material and spiritual happiness, and no one else. Therefore, I would achieve complete happiness enjoying wisdom, strength, long life and dharma without breaking the saṅkalpa of Brahmacharya, which is the excellent source of complete pleasure and happiness. I will not spoil myself and my family by doing marriage early, under the persuasion of you fools.

अथ यान्यष्टाचत्वारिꣳशद्वर्षाणि तत् तृतीयसवनमष्टाचत्वारिꣳशदक्षरा जगती जागतं तृतीयसवनं तदस्यादित्या अन्वायत्ताः प्राणा वावादित्या एते हीदꣳ सर्वमाददते ॥

atha yānyaṣṭāchatvāriṁśadvarṣāṇi tat tṛtīyasavanamaṣṭāchatvāriṁśadakṣarā jagatī jāgataṁ tṛtīyasavanaṁ tadasyādityā anvāyattāḥ prāṇā vāvādityā ēte hīdaṁ sarvamādadate.

[Meaning] The 48 years of Brahmacharya is like a third evening offering. Jagatī metre has 48 syllables. Evening offerings are made with mantras composed in Jagatī metre. The Ādityas are linked to this offering. Prāṇas (bio-energy of the body) are verily the Ādityas because they enable the body to receive all knowledge.

तं चेदेतस्मिन् वयसि किंचिदुपतपेत् स ब्रूयात् प्राणा आदित्या इदं मे तृतीयसवनमायुरनुसन्तनुतेति माहं प्राणा नामादित्यानां मध्ये यज्ञो विलोप्सीयेत्युद्धैव तत एत्यगदो हैव भवति ॥

taṁ chedetasmin vayasi kiṁchidupatapet sa brūyāt prāṇāādityā idaṁ me tṛtīyasavanamāyuranusantanuteti māhaṁ prāṇā nāmādityānāṁ madhye yajño vilopsīyetyuddhaiva tata ētyagado haiva bhavati.

[Meaning] In this age, whoever treats himself in the fire of knowledge (endows himself with knowledge), (let him know that) his bio-energy is called āditya. Let this third offering (48 years of Brahmacharya) continue over to the whole life. Let my life not be broken off in the midst (in between). If this body is kept healthy, it will be invulnerable to various diseases.

If anyone desires to deviate him from the path of supreme dharma, the Brahmachārī should reply saying, "O fool of the first waters! keep away from me. I always keep away from your foul words leading to downfall. I would never destroy this excellent Brahmacharya. I will complete it, becoming devoid of all diseases and be endowed with the all sciences, high qualities, good karmas, and best temperament. May God fulfill this auspicious saṅkalpa of mine through his kindness so that I could specifically make your children happy by preaching and educating you ignorants.

चतस्रोऽवस्थाः शरीरस्य वृद्धियौवनं संपूर्णता किंचित्परिहाणिश्चेति। तत्राषोडशाद् वृद्धिः। आपंचविंशते यौवनम्। आचत्वारिंशतस्सम्पूर्णता। ततः किंचत्परिहाणिश्चेति॥

chatasro'vasthāḥ śarīrasya vṛddhiyauvanaṁ saṁpūrṇatā kiṁchitparihāṇischeti, tatrāṣoḍaśād vṛddhiḥ, āpaṁchaviṁśate ryauvanam, āchatvāriṁśatassampūrṇatā, tataḥ kiṁchatparihāṇischeti.

There are four stages of this human body—growth, youth, maturity and decay. The growth stage begins at the age of 16 and is completed in the 25th year of age. If anyone spoils the dhatus (fundamental tissues) in the growth stage, he or she will destroy his or her physical and mental health like the axed tree and broken pot and repent on his/her act. He/she will not find any chance to undo his/her mistake. The stage of youth begins at the age of 25 years and finishes at 40 years. He who does not preserve this stage thoroughly would destroy his fortune. The third stage, called maturity, starts at the 40th year. Anyone who, after observing Brahmacharya, fails to cohabit with his wife in prescribed timings, or cohabit with others' wives, and do not follow the pledge of devotion to his own wife and fail to observe Brahmacharya for one year after the wife has become pregnant, would lose everything earned by him. The fourth stage begins from 40th year onward and continues till the time of production of semen in body cease to take place. Afterwards the stage of decay commences. Any one who will spoil his semen excessively would fall the victim of diseases like tubercuiosis and fistula. He who keeps himself well balanced and safe in these four stages, would enjoy hale and hearty life and contribute to the happiness of the world. There is authority from the Suśruta.

पंचविंशे ततो वर्षे पुमान्नारी तु षोडशे ।
समत्वागतवीर्यौ तौ जानीयात् कुशलो भिषक् ॥

paṁchaviṁśe tato varṣe pumānnārī tu ṣoḍaśe,
samatvāgatavīryau tau jānīyāt kuśalo bhiṣak.

[Meaning] A dextrous physician should know that a male in 25th year attains the same productive capability as a female in 16th year of her age.

Here, one should be aware that the periods of these four stages vary from males to females. Whatever productive capability is available in the body of male in the age of 25-years, the same is available in the female body in the age of sixteen years. If early marriage is required, it should not be before the male attaining the age of 25-years and the female of 16-years. The marriage solemnised in this age is called of inferior quality marriage.

The marriages solemnised between a female of 17 years and the male of 30 years, or between a female of 18 years and a male of 36 years, or a female of 19 and a male of 38 is treated as of middle quality marriage. The marriages between females of 20, 21, 22, 24 years and males respectively of 40, 42, 46, 48 years is called as of best quality marriage.

O Brahmachārī! you bear in mind all these factors, since they will be helpful in leading a good life in other Āśramas.

Those who want to promote their families, progenies, relatives and their countries should take stock of the following things:

श्रोत्रं त्वक् चक्षुषी जिह्वा नासिका चैव पंचमी ।
पायूपस्थं हस्तपादं वाक् चैव दशमी स्मृता ॥ मनु॰ 2.90

śrotram tvak chakṣuṣī jihvā nāsikā chaiva paṁchamī,
pāpūpastham hastapādaṁ vāk chaiva daśamī smṛtā.

Manu, 2.90

[Meaning] The ear, the skin, the eyes, the tongue, and the nose as the fifth, the anus, the organ of generation, hands and feet, and the (organ of) speech, named as the tenth.

बुद्धीन्द्रियाणि पंचैषां श्रेत्रादीन्यनुपूर्वशः ।
कर्मेन्द्रियाणि पंचैषां पाय्वादीनि प्रचक्षते ॥ मनु॰ 2.91

buddhīndriyāṇi paṁchaiṣāṁ śretrādīnyanupūrvaśaḥ,
karmendriyāṇi paṁchaiṣāṁ pāyvādīni prachakṣate.

Manu. 2.91

[Meaning] First five of them, starting from the ear to nose are called organs of sense, and rest five of them, starting from the anus to the organ of speech are called motor organs.

एकदशं मनो ज्ञेयं स्वगुणेनोभयात्मकम् ।
यस्मिन् जिते जितावेतौ भवतः पंचकौ गणौ ॥ मनु॰ 2.92

ēkadaśaṁ mano jñeyaṁ svaguṇenobhayātmakam,
yasmin jite jitāvetau bhavataḥ paṁchakau gaṇau.

Manu, 2.92

[Meaning] Manas (mind), the internal sense organ, is the eleventh, which by its quality of Saṅkalpa (accumulation of sanskāras) and Vikalpa (erasing of sanskāras) has attained nature of both; when that has been subdued, both those sets of five organs have been conquered.

इन्द्रियाणां विचरतां विषयेष्वपहारिषु ।
संयसे यत्नमातिष्ठेद्विद्वान् यन्तेव वाजिनाम् ॥ मनु॰ 2.88

indriyāṇāṁ vicharatāṁ viṣayeṣvapahāriṣu,
saṁyase yatnamātiṣṭhedvidvān yanteva vājinām. Manu, 2.88

[Meaning] A wise man should strive to restrain his sense organs running after their stimuli, like a charioteer his horses.

इन्द्रियाणां प्रसङ्गेन दोषमृच्छत्यसंषयम् ।
संनियम्य तु तान्येव ततः सिद्धि नियच्छति ॥ मनु॰ 2.93

indriyāṇāṁ prasaṅgena doṣamṛchchhatyasaṁśayam,
saṁniyamya tu tānyeva tataḥ siddhi niyachchhati.

Manu 2.93

[Meaning] Through the attachment of his sense organs to their stimuli a man doubtlessly will incur guilt; but if he keeps them under complete control, he will obtain success in his life.

वेदास्त्यागश्च यज्ञाश्च नियमाश्च तपांसि च ।
न विप्रभावदुष्टस्य सिद्धिं गच्छन्ति कर्हिचित् ॥ मनु॰ 2.97

vedāstyāgaścha yajñāścha niyamāścha tapāṁsi cha,
na viprabhāvaduṣṭasya siddhiṁ gachchhanti karhichit.

Manu, 2.97

[Meaning] Neither (the study of) the Vedas, nor renunciation, nor Yajñas, nor any niyama (purification of body and mind, contentment, penance, studies, and mediation), nor austerities, ever procure success to a man whose mind is responding to stimuli.

वशे कृत्वेन्द्रियग्रामं संयम्य च मनस्तथा।
सर्वान् संसाधयेदर्थानाक्षिण्वन् योगतस्तनुम् ॥ मनु॰ 2.100

vaśe kṛtvendriyagrāmam saṁyamya cha manastathā,
sarvān saṁsādhayedarthānākṣiṇvan yogatastanum.

Manu 2.100

[Meaning] One should perform all his works keeping all the sense organs as well as the mind in control with efforts without injuring his body.

यमान् सेवेत सततं न नियमान् केवलान् बुधः।
यमान् पतत्यकुर्वाणो नियमान् केवलान् भजन् ॥ मनु॰ 4.204

yamān seveta satatam na niyamān kevalān budhaḥ,
yamān patatyakurvāṇo niyamān kevalān bhajan.

Manu 4.204

[Meaning] A wise man should constantly follow (yamas) the social discipline, he may not follow (niyamas) self discipline always; for he who does not follow the yamas, while he obeys the niyamas alone, is down graded in the society.

अभिवादनशीलस्य नित्यं वृद्धोपसेविनः।
चत्वारि तस्य वर्द्धन्ते आयुर्विद्या यशो बलम् ॥ मनु॰ 2.121

abhivādanaśīlasya nityaṁ vṛddhopasevinaḥ,
chatvāri tasya varddhante āyurvidyā yaśo balam.

Manu 2.121

[Meaning] A student who is humble, well behaved and shows respect to scholars and elderly persons and always ready to offer his unstinted services to them gains in life span, knowledge, name, fame and strength.

अज्ञो भवति वै बालः पिता भवति मन्त्रदः।
अज्ञं हि बालमित्याहुः पितेत्येव तु मन्त्रदम् ॥ मनु॰ 2.153

ajño bhavati vai bālaḥ pitā bhavati mantradaḥ,
ajñaṁ hi bālamityāhuḥ pitetyeva tu mantradam.

Manu, 2.153

[Meaning] A person destitute of knowledge is indeed like a child, and he who imparts knowledge is like a father, so an ignorant is often called as child and the informed as father.

न हायनैर्न पलितैर्न वित्तेन न बन्धुभिः ।
ऋषश्चक्रिरे धर्मं योऽनूचानः स नो महान् ॥ मनु॰ 2.154

na hāyanairna palitairna vittena na bandhubhiḥ,
ṛṣaśchakrire dharmaṁ yo'nūchānaḥ sa no mahān.

Manu 2.154

[Meaning] Greatness comes neither with the passage of time, nor through white hairs, nor through wealth, nor through greatness of relatives. The seer have made a rule, "One who is devoted to learning is great".

न तेन वृद्धो भवति येनास्य पलितं शिरः ।
यो वै युवाऽप्यधीयानस्तं देवाः स्थविरं विदुः ॥ मनु॰ 2.156

na tena vṛddho bhavati yenāsya palitaṁ śiraḥ,
yo vai yuvā·pyadhīyānastaṁ devāḥ sthaviraṁ viduḥ.

Manu 2.156

[Meaning] A man is not therefore (considered) senior because his head is gray, but even young person who is devoted to learning is considered senior by experienced scholars.

यथा काष्ठमयो हस्ती यथा चर्ममयो मृगः ।
यश्च विप्रोऽनधीयानस्त्रयस्ते नाम बिभ्रति ॥ मनु॰ 2.157

yathā kāṣṭhamayo hastī yathā charmamayo mṛgaḥ,
yaścha vipro'nadhīyānastrayaste nāma bibhrati. *Manu 2.157*

[Meaning] As an elephant made of wood, as an antelope made of leather, such is an intellectual who has no dedication and devotion for learning; those three are essentially for nothing but bear such names.

सम्मानाद् ब्राह्मणो नित्यमुद्विजेत विषादिव ।
अमृतस्येव चाकाङ्क्षेदवमानस्य सर्वदा ॥ मनु॰ 2.162

sammānād brāhmaṇo nityamudvijeta viṣādiva,
amṛtasyeva chākānkṣedavamānasya sarvadā. manu0 2.162

[Meaning] That scholar alone is said to possess true knowledge of the Veda and God, who develops aversion for honours and awards as if it were poison, develops liking for dishonours or non-honours as if it were nectar.

वेदमेव सदाऽभ्यस्येत्तपस्तप्यन् द्विजोत्तमः ।
वेदाभ्यासो हि विप्रस्य तपः परमिहोच्यते ॥ मनु॰ 2.166

vedameva sadā·bhyasyettapastapyan dvijottamaḥ,
vedābhyāso hi viprasya tapaḥ paramihochyate. Manu, 2.166

[Meaning] Let a high profile student who desires to perform austerities, repeatedly practice the Veda; for the study of the Veda is declared to be the highest austerity for a student in this world.

योऽनधीत्य द्विजो वेदमन्यत्र कुरुते श्रमम् ।
स जीवन्नेव शूद्रत्वमाशु गच्छति सान्वयः ॥ मनु॰ 2.168

yo'nadhītya dvijo vedamanyatra kurute śramam,
sa jīvanneva śūdratvamāśu gachchhati sānvayaḥ.

Manu, 2.168

[Meaning] A educated person who abandons the study of Veda and applies his energies elsewhere, remains uneducated throughout his life and categorised as Śudra.

यथा खनन् खनित्रेण नरो वार्यधिगच्छति ।
तथा गुरुगतां विद्यां शुश्रूषुरधिगच्छति ॥ मनु॰ 2.218

yathā khanan khanitreṇa naro vāryadhigachchhati,
tathā gurugatāṁ vidyāṁ śuśrūṣuradhigachchhati.

Manu, 2.218

[Meaning] As the man who digs with a spade (into the ground) obtains water, even so an obedient (student) obtains the knowledge which lies (hidden) in his/her teacher.

श्रद्धानः शुभां विद्यामाददीतावरादपि ।
अन्यादपि परं धर्मं स्त्रीरत्नं दुष्कुलादपि ॥ मनु॰ 2.238

śraddadhānaḥ śubhāṁ vidyāmādadītāvarādapi,
anyādapi param dharmaṁ strīratnam duṣkulādapi.

Manu, 2.238

[Meaning] It is a matter of trust that one may receive good learning even from a junior; learn to be dutiful even from the outsider, and may get an excellent wife even from a corrupt or base family.

विषादप्यमृतं ग्राह्यं बालादपि सुभाषितम् ।
विविधानि च शिल्पानि समादेयानि सर्वतः ॥ मनु॰ 2.239

viṣādapyamṛtaṁ grāhyaṁ bālādapi subhāṣitam,
vividhāni cha śilpāni samādeyāni sarvataḥ. Manu, 2.239

[Meaning] Nectar may be taken even from poison, good advice even from a child, good conduct even from a foe, and gold even from an heap of rubbish.

These are the ślokas from Manusmriti.

यान्यनवद्यानि कर्माणि । तानि सेवितव्यानि । नो इतराणि । यान्यस्माकꣳ सुचरितानि । तानि त्वयोपास्यानि । नो इतराणि । एके चास्मच्छ्रेयाꣳसो ब्राह्मणाः । तेषां त्वयासनेन प्रश्वसितव्यम् ॥ तैत्तिरीय उप॰ 7.11

yānyanavadyāni karmāṇi, tāni sevitavyāni, no itarāṇi, yānyasmākaṁ sucharitāni, tāni tvayopāsyāni, no itarāṇi, ēke chāsmachchhreyāṁso brāhmaṇāḥ, teṣāṁ tvayāsanena prasvasitavyam. Taittirīya up. 7.11

[Meaning] O disciple! do you attend to and follow only those acts which are unblamable, not others. Follow our good   conducts only and not others. Only pay resepct to those scholars who are the best among us.

O disciple! do you attend to and follow only those acts which are unblamable, devoid of pāpa, i.e. devoid unust, adharma and fruaght with justice and dharma and do not follow the acts otherwise, i.e. faught with adharma. O disciple! do follow good actions full of dharma of your āchārya, mother and father. Never translate into action our wicked acts. O Brahmachārī! you do the company of those persons amongst us who abide by dharma, and known to have Brahma-realization, trust them what they say.

ऋतं तपः सत्यं तपः श्रुतं तपः शान्तं तपो दमस्तपश्शमस्तपो दानं तपो यज्ञस्तपो ब्रह्मभूर्भुवः सुवर्ब्रह्मै तदुपास्वैतत्तपः ॥ तैत्तिरीय उप० 10.8

ṛtaṁ tapaḥsatyaṁ tapaḥ śrutaṁ tapaḥ śāntaṁ tapo damastapaśśamastapo dānaṁ tapo yajñastapo brahmabhūrbhuvaḥ suvarbrahmai tadupāsvaitattapaḥ.

Taittirīya up. 10.8

[Meaning] Following eternal laws is tapas; following truth is tapas; study of the Vedas is tapas; to maintain composure of mind is tapas; to withdraw mind from external world is tapas; to have controle over senses is tapas; cherity is tapas; yajñais tapas; to worship Brahman by chanting Bhuḥ, Bhuvaḥ and Svaḥ is tapas.

O disciple! you accept only whatever is true and real, speak truth, study the true Śāstras like the Vedas; restrain your mind from attending to unrighteous conduct, control your sense organs like ears etc. from bad acts and employ them in good acts, become calm and quiet by renouncing anger etc. dissiminate good qualities like knowledge etc; enjoy the company of learned and perform Agnihotra etc; acquire the knoledge of all the objects found on the earth, in space and stars etc.; do practies of yoga, Prāṇāyāma and worship only one Brahman (Paramātman) who is second to none. Doing all such acts is called Tapas.

ऋतञ्च स्वाध्यायप्रवचने च। सत्यञ्च स्वाध्यायप्रवचने च। तपश्च स्वाध्या०। दमश्च स्वाध्या०। शमश्च स्वाध्या०। अग्नयश्च स्वाध्या०। अग्निहोत्रं च स्वाध्या०। सत्यमिति सत्यवचा राथीतरः। तप इति तपोनित्यः पौरुशिष्टिः। स्वाध्यायप्रवचने एवेति नाको मौद्गल्यः। तद्धि तपस्तद्धि तपः ॥ तैत्तिरीय उप० 7.9

ṛtaṁcha svādhyāyapravachane cha, satyaṁcha svādhyāyapravachane cha, tapaścha svādhyā.., damaścha svādhyā.., śamaścha svādhyā.., agnayaścha svādhyā..., agnihotraṁ cha svādhyā..., satyamiti satyavachā rāthītaraḥ, tapa iti taponityaḥ pauruśiṣṭiḥ, svādhyāyapravachane ēveti nāko maudgalyaḥ, taddhi tapastaddhi tapaḥ. Taittirīya up. 7.9

O Brahmachārī! do you accept truth, learn and teach others. Always preach truth, speak truth, learn and teach others. Get rid of the notion of pleasure and pain; practise yoga and prāṇāyāma, learn and teach others. Restrain your sense-organs from attending to bad things, empoly them in good acts, acquire knowledge and give it to others also. Withdraw your mind and soul from unjust actions, employ them in just actions. Persuade others to do good and just actions; learn and teach others. Learn and make others learn the science of Agni (energy). Learn and teach others performing Agnihotra. To be truthful is tapas, according to Āchārya Rāthitara. To suffer pain in following and conducting according to the justice is tapas, according to Āchārya Pauruśiṣṭi. To learn and teach others according to the dictates of dharma is tapas, is the opinion of Nāka Maudgalya. Know that other āchāryas too endorse whatever stated above is tapas.

These preachings should be imparted to the child within three days by the Āchārya or by the father of the child.

Afterwards, the child should be admitted to the Gurukula. Male chiled should be sent to the Gurukula of male students and female chiled should be sent to the Kanyā Gurukula.

If the children have not been taught the articulation of the alphabats, the male Āchārya to boy and female Āchārya to girl should teach Paṇini's Varṇochchāraṇa Śikṣā in the period of a month. Thereafter, the Aṣṭādhyāyi of Pāṇini should be taught with splitting padas and meaning within eight months or a year followed by the dhātupāṭha and derivation of conjugational forms of verbs in 10 lakāras as well as 10 types of derivations. Afterwards they should teach the liṅgānuśāsana of Pāṇini, Unādipāṭha and Gaṇapāṭha alongwith nominal derivations of -ण्वुल् (-ṇvul) and -तृच (-tṛch) ending forms within the period of six months. Then there should be the second reading of the Aṣṭādhyāyi specially with reference to meaning of padas, compounds, questions and answers, utsarga (general rules) and apavāda (exceptional rules) preceded by Anvaya (sequence of padas in a sūtra in resepct of their intended sense). Practice of Sanskrit speaking should be contnued simultaneously. This syllabus should be covered within 8 months.

Thereafter the Mahābhāṣya by Patañjali Muni, gloss or commentary on six treaises like Varṇochchāraṇa Śikṣā, Aṣṭādhyāyī Dhātupāṭha, Gaṇapāṭha, Unādigaṇa and Liṅgānuśāsana should be learnt and taught within 18 months i.e. one and a half year. Thus completing the study of Śikṣā and Grammar within three years and 5 months or 3 years and 9 month, or within four years, one should be able to understand the intricacies of Sanskrit language.

Afterwards having studied the *Nighaṇṭu* and *Nirukta* of Yāska, the *Koṣa* (Lexicon) of Kātyāyana Muni within one and half year, one should correctly know the meaning of Avyaya (indeclinables), and know the three types of words called yaugika (having an etymological meaning), yogarūḍha (having etymological and conventional meaning) and ruḍha (having conventional meaning) with reference to relation between subject and predicate delineated by Āptamuni. Afterwards student should study the Piṅgala sūtra by Piṅgalāchārya with its commentary within three months and next three months should devoted in learning the art of composition of ślokas. Thereafter the Kāvyālaṅkāra Sūtra of Yāska with Vātsyāyana's commentry with special reference to Ākāṅkṣā (mutual implication or expectancy), Yogyatā (consistency), Āsatti (proximity) and Tātparyārtha (intention) alongwith the Anavaya (sequence) should be studied. Manusmṛti, Vidurniti and 10 Sargas of any chapter of the Rāmāyaṇa of Vālmīki should also be studied within one year.

Another one year should be devoted to the study of Mathematics including Algebra, Geometry, Arithmatic from any Siddhānata text like the Sūryasiddhānta etc. Study of Vedāṅgas from Nighaṇṭu (Vedic Lexicon) to Jyotiṣa (Astronomy) should be completed within four years.

Afterwards the Pūrvamimānsā of Jaiminī with the commentary of Vyāsa muni, Vaiśeṣika sūtras of Kaṇāda with the commentary of Gotama known as Praśastapāda commentary; the Nyāyasūtra of Gotama with the commentary of Vātsyāyana Muni, the Yogasūtras of Patañjali with Vyāsa's commentary, the Sankhya Sūtras known as Sānkhya Śāstra by the Kapila Āchārya with the commentary of Bhāguri Muni and the Śārīraka sūtra of Vyāsa with the commentary of Jaiminī or Baudhāyana in addition to the Īśa, Kena, Katha, Praśna, Mundaka, Māndukya, Aitareya, Taittirīya, Chhāndogya and Brhadāranyaka etc. 10 Upanisads and Vedānta with the commentary of Vyāsa should be studied within next two years.

Thereafter, within the period of next three years one should study and teach the *Rgveda* with the specific knowledge of metres, accents, padapātha, anvaya, and gist with the help of grammar including Bahvrcha *Aitaraya Brāhmana* of Rgveda, the Śrauta and Grhya sūtras of Āśvalāyana known as Kalpa sūtras. In the same way, the *Yajurveda* with padapātha and *Satapatha Brāhmana* in two years; the *Sāmaveda* with padapātha, Sāmagānas and *Sāma Brāhmana* in two years; and the *Atharvaveda* with padapātha and the *Gopatha Brāhmana* within two years. Thus, four Vedas and all these texts should be studied and taught in nine years.

Thereafter the Ayurveda, the Upaveda of *Atharvaveda* known as the Śāstar of medical sciences, composed of the Ārsa (written by seers) texts like Suśruta, Nighantu of Dhanvantari and Charaka of Patanjali should be learnt within three years. The operational instruments given in the Suśruta should be manufactured and students of medicies should dissect dead bodies and examine the parts of body. They should learn carefully the sciences of anatomy etc. given in them.

Afterwards, the *Dhanurveda*, the Upaveda of the

Yajurveda known as the military science written by Aṅgirā and other seers not generally available now, should be learnt practically within three years.

Further, the student should be taught Gandharvaveda, the Upaveda of the *Sāmaveda*. It includes the Nārada Saṁhitā and other texts. The student should do the practice of Svara (musical note), Rāga (melody), Rāgiṇī (lyrics), Samaya (time), Vāditra (musical intrument), Grāma (tones), Tāla (rhythm) and Murchhanā (modulation) for three years.

Then, *Arthaveda*, the Upaveda of the *Ṛgveda* known as the Śilpasāstra (Engineering and Technology) which includes the various treatises composed of Viśvakarma. Tvaṣṭā and Maya should be studied within six years, and one should be familiar with the technology of Aeroplanes, telegraphy, geology, etc.

In this way, completing the syllabus beginning from Śikṣha and ending with Ayurveda, known as the 14 Arts and Sciences in 31 years, the student should be great scholar, so that he/she may contribute to the progress and prosperity of whole world apart from his/her own progress and prosperity.

इति वेदारम्भसंस्कारविधिः समाप्तः ॥

iti vedārambhasaṁskāravidhiḥ samāptaḥ.

Here ends the Vedārambha-Sanskāra.

अथ समावर्त्तनसंस्कारविधि वक्ष्यामः

Samāvarttana Sanskāra

Here we would prescribe the procedure of Samāvartana, the convocation or graduation ceremony.

In the Samāvartana sanskāra the student having completed the observance of Brahmacharya, the study of the Vedas alongwith their auxillary sciences and having attained knowledge of physical sciences, returns to the parental home from the Gurukula to enter into household life.

There are authorities:

वेदसमाप्तिं वाचयीत । आश्व.गृसू. 1.22.16

vedasamāptiṁ vāchayīta. Āśv.GS. 1.22.16

[Meaning] Samāvartana Sanskāra should be conducted after conclusion of the study of the Veda.

कल्याणैः सह सम्प्रयोगः । आश्व.गृसू. 1.23.20;

kalyāṇaiḥ saha samprayogaḥ. Āśv.GS. 1.23.20

[Meaning] Always deal with good persons who are your wellwishers.

स्नातकायोपस्थिताय । राज्ञे च । आचार्यश्वशुरपितृव्यमातुलानां च । दधनि मध्वानीय । सर्पिर्वा मध्वलाभे । विष्टरः पाद्यमर्ध्यमाचमनीयं मधुपर्कः ॥1 ॥

आश्व.गृसू. 1.24.2-7

snātakāyopasthitāya, rājñe cha, āchāryaśvaśurapitṛvyamātulānāṁ cha, dadhani madhvānīya, sarpirvā madhvalābhe, viṣṭaraḥ pādyamardhyamāchamanīyaṁ madhuparkaḥ ॥ Āśv.GS. 1.24.2-7

[Meaning] On the arrival of a student after graduation, king, Āchārya, father-in-law, uncle and maternal uncle, the water for washinig feet should be served first, followed by water for washing mouth and then water for sipping should be served to them and they be offered a nice seat to sit. They should be served curd mixed with honey; in case honey is not available, curd mixed with ghee should be served in a clean pot.

According to Paraskara Gṛhya Sūtra:

वेदꣳसमाप्य स्नायाद्। पार.गृसू. 2.6.1

veda ꣳsamāpya snāyād, Pāra. GS. 2.6.1

[Meaning] Having completed studies in Veda, a student should undergo graduation ceremony.

ब्रह्मचर्यं वाष्टचत्वारिꣳशकम्। पार.गृसू. 2.6.2

brahmacharyam vāṣṭachatvāri ꣳśakam. Pār.GS. 2.6.2

[Meaning] Or one can undergo graduation ceremony after completion of 48 years' saṅkalp of Brahmacharya.

त्रय एव स्नातका भवन्ति। पार.गृसू. 2.5.32

traya ēva snātakā bhavanti. Pār.GS. 2.5.32

[Meaning] Only three types of persons can undergo graduation ceremony.

विद्यास्नातको व्रतस्नातको विद्याव्रतस्नातकश्चेति ॥ पार.गृसू. 2.5.33-35

vidyāsnātako vratasnātako vidyāvratasnātakaścheti.

Pār.GS. 2.5.33-35

[Meaning] Vidyāsnātaka (a person who has completed study of the Vedas), Vrata snātaka (a person who has completed the saṅkalpa or vrata of Brahmacharya) and Vidyā-vrata-snātaka (a person who has completed both study of the Veda and vrata of Brahmacharya) can undergo the ceremony of graduation or Samāvartana Sanskāra.

The Samāvartana Sanskāra be performed when the study of the Vedas is finished. One should always deal with pious persons. When there come any of the following — a student after completing the study of the Veda or completing the vrata of Brahmacharya, a king, an Āchārya, father-in-law, uncle and maternal uncle— the water for washing feet should be served first, followed by water for washing the mouth, thereafter water for sipping should be served to them. They are given a nice seat to sit. Afterwards, honeymixed curd, if not available, the ghee mixed curd in a clean pot should be sserved to them. This is called madhuparka. There are three categories of Snātakas: the graduates of Gurukulas. These are Vidyāsnātaka, Vratasnātaka and Vidyā-vrata-snātaka. Therefore a student who has completed the studies of Veda and completed the vrata of Brahmacharya of 48 years should take the bath of Vidya-vrata (completion of study and Brahmacharya vrata).

तं प्रतीतं स्वधर्मेण धर्मदायहरं पितुः ।
स्रग्विणं तल्प आसीनमर्हयेत् प्रथमं गवा ॥ मनु॰ 3.3

tam pratītam svadharmeṇa dharmadāyaharam pituḥ,
sragviṇam talpa āsīnamarhayet prathamam gavā. Manu, 3.3

[Meaning] The Brahmachārī (student) who is the son of learned parent, should seat the Āchārya, who is like his father on a goot couch/sofa, garland him and give the gift of cow, the robes, money etc, to honour him as per his capability.

तानि कल्पद् ब्रह्मचारी सलिलस्य पृष्ठे तपोऽतिष्ठत्तप्यमानः समुद्रे। स स्नातो बभ्रुः पिङ्गल पृथिव्यां बहु रोचते ॥ अथर्व॰ 11.5.26

tāni kalpad brahmachārī salilasya pṛṣṭhe tapo'tiṣṭhattapyamānaḥ samudre। sa snāto babhruḥ piṅgala pṛthivyām bahu rochate. AV. 11.5.26

[Meaning] (ब्रह्मचारी) Vedic scholar (तानि कल्पत् अतिष्ठत्) for harnessing geothermal energy surveys (तपः तप्यमानः समुद्रे) the hottest sea spreading centres as well as (सलिलस्य पृष्ठे) the surface of oceans. (स्नातः) Having graduated (बभ्रुः) with robust physique and (पिंगलः) magmatic complexion, (सः) he has become (बहु) highly (रोचते) glorified on (पृथिव्याम्) the planet.

Period: The period of Samāvartana (graduation ceremony and marriage) ranges from 25 years of age to 48 years of age in case of males and 16 years of age to 24 years of age in case of females. Of these, 25 years (in case of males) and 16 years (in case of females) is considered to be the lowest period; 30 years to 36 years (in case of males) and 17 and 18 years (in case of females) is considerd to be the moderate period; 40, 42, 46 and 48 years (in case of males) and 20, 21, 22 and 24 years respectively (in case of females) is considered to be the best period for samāvartana (graduation) and marriage. But the man and woman should desire to enter into the life of house-hold only when they have completed the education, handicrafts, vrata of Brahmacharya. There are two places of conducting marriage ceremony. One is the home of the Āchārya and the other is one's own house. At any one of these places, marriage can be solemanized according to the procedure laid down for marriage after having completed the graduation ceremony.

The Procedure of Samāvarttan Sanskāra

On the day fixed for the Samāvartana (graduation) the yajña-kuṇḍa etc. prescribed in the Sāmānya Prakaraṇa should be arranged in the house of Āchārya. All the utensils required in the yajña should be collected and arranged one day before the program. The Sthālipāka having been prepared, ghee and pots should be kept safe in the yajñaśālā, near the yajñavedi (firealtar). The persons concerned with the yajña and sanskāra should take their respective seats according to the procedure prescribed on four sides of the yajñakuṇḍa and do prayer of Paramātman, Svastivāchana, Śāntikaraṇa and the men and women who have come to participate should concentrate their mind on the meditation of Brahman. Afterwards the procedure of Agnyādhāna (fire laying ceremony), samidhādāna (samidhā-laying) as prescribed in the Sāmānya Prakaraṇa should be performed followed by the sprinkling of water on four sides. The Āchārya takinig his seat in the west and keeping his face eastward should offer four Āghārāvājya-bhāgāhuti, four vyāhṛti āhutīs, one sviṣṭakṛt, one prajāpatya, eight ājyāhutīs totaling 18 in all. Afterwards, the Brahmachārī should keep together the fire in the middle of the kuṇḍa with the mantra; (ओमग्ने सुश्रयः०) He should laid down three samidhās with the mantra (ओं अग्रये समिध०). Thereafter he should touch his body parts in accordance with the procedure laid down in the chapter of Vedārambha. First he should touch his mouth with water taken in his hands after showing it to fire chanting the seven mantras starting with (ओं तनूपा०); Thereafter he should touch his body parts with the seven mantras starting with (ओं वाक् च म०) etc. Then taking one pot from the eight pots of water mixed with perfumes herbacious substances kept in the northside of the vedi, the Brahmachārī takes water from it chanting the follwing mantra:

ओं ये अप्स्वन्तरग्रयः प्रविष्टा गोह्य उपगोह्यो मयूषो मनोहास्खलो विरुजस्तनूदुषुरिन्द्रियहा तान् विजहामि यो रोचनस्तमिह गृह्णामि । पार० 2.6.10

Oṁ ye apsvantaragnayah praviṣṭā gohya upagohyo mayūṣo manohāskhalo virujastanūduṣurindriyahā tān vijahāmi yo rochanastamiha gṛhṇāmi. Pār.GS. 2.6.10

[Meaning] I renounce here the eight kinds of energies present in the waters and various activities. These are: energy that remains concealed, that heats the body, that distroys the strength, that reduces the power of mind, that brings out constipation etc., that creates various pains, that spoils the body and that kills the organs. I accept only that energy that is (*rochanaḥ*) beneficial to me.

He should take bath and chant the followiong mantra:

ओ तेन मामभिसिंचामि श्रियै यशसे ब्रह्मणे ब्रह्मवर्चसाय । पार० 2.6.11

O tena māmabhisimchāmi śriyai yaśase brahmaṇe brahmavarchasāya. Pār.GS. 2.6.11

[Meaning] I take bath with this water for the sake of glory, name and fame, propagation of Vedic knowledge and for the aura generated around body due to study of Vedas and performing Vedic karmas.

Afterwards the Brahmachārī reciting the mantra (ओं ये अप्स्वन्तर०) should take water into his water pot from the second pot of the above mentioned eight pots. Thereafter he should take bath and chant the following mantra:

ओं येन श्रियमकृणुतां येनावमृशताᳬसुराम् ।
येनक्ष्यावभ्यसिंचतां यद्वां तदश्विना यश: ॥ पार० 2.6.12

*Om yena śriyamakṛṇutām yenāvamṛśatāᳬsurām,
yenakṣayāvabhyasimchatām yadvām tadaśvinā yaśaḥ.*

Pār. GS. 2.6.12

[Meaning] May I attain by the fame of the Aśvinis, the surgeons and physicians whereby they add to the glory of enlightened persons, increase their comfort and keep their eyes always moistened.

Afterwards he should first chant the mantra (ओं ये अप्स्वन्तर०) and take water from three pots and should take bath chanting the mantras beginning with (ओम् आपो हिष्ठा०) written in the chapter of Upanayana sanskāra. Thereafter, he should take other three remaining pots of the eight pots and should take bath chanting in mind the three mantras (ओम् आपो हि०), etc.

Afterwards the Brahmachārī chanting the following mantra should relinquish his girdle and stick:

ओम् उदुत्तमं वरुण पाशमस्मदवाधमं वि मध्यमꣳ श्रथाय ।
अथा वयमादित्य व्रते तवानागसोऽअदितये स्याम ॥ यजु॰ 12.2

Om uduttamaṁ varuṇa pāśamasmadavādhamaṁ vi madhyama: śrathāya,
athā vayamāditya vrate tavānāgaso'aditaye syāma. YV. 12.2

[Meaning] O Prakṛti, the material cause of creation, you keep us away from your network of higher (Chidākāśa) space, the network of lower (Bhūtākāśa) space and the network of middle (intermediate) space. And thereafter may we be devoid of pāpa, O Āditya Brahmachārī, in thy vrata for undisturbed Brahmacharya (of 48 years), that is, we may not be instrumental behind in breaking of your vrata. That is why this oblation is offered. This offering is for Prakṛti, Āditya Brahmachārī, and for the undisturbed vrata of Brahmacharya and not for me.

NB: The mantra suggests that one can achieve Mokṣa by staying sway from natural attractions and observing the vrata of Āditya Brahmacharya, i.e living a celibate life of 48 years for attaining knowledge.

ओम् उद्यन् भ्राजभृष्णुरिन्द्रो मरुद्भिरस्थात् प्रातर्यावभिरस्थाद्दशसनिरसि दशसनिं मा कुर्वाविदन् मा गमय । उद्यन् भ्राजभृष्णुरिन्द्रो मरुद्भिरस्थाद्दिवा यावभिरस्थाच्छतसनिरसि शतसनिं मा कुर्वाविदन् मा गमय । उद्यन् भ्राजभृष्णुरिन्द्रोमरुद्भिरस्थात् सायंयावभिरस्थात् सहस्रसनिरसि सहस्रसिंनं कुर्वाविदन् मा गमय ॥ पार॰ 2.6.16

Om udyan bhrājabhṛṣṇurindro marudbhirasthāt prātaryāvabhirasthāddaśasanirasi daśasaniṁ mā kurvāvidan mā gamaya, udyan bhrājabhṛṣṇurindro marudbhirasthāddivā yāvabhirasthāchchhatasanirasi śatasaniṁ mā kurvāvidan mā gamaya, udyan bhrājabhṛṣṇurindromarudbhirasthāt sāyaṁyāvabhirasthāt sahasrasanirasi sahasrasiṁnam kurvāvidan mā gamaya. Pār.GS.2.6.16

[Meaning] O Brahman! you previal everywhere and shine like the sun; You are firm in your powers followed by the various physical forces; You are worshipped by all the men of sharp sightedness in the morning. You are pervading in ten directions. Make me able to serve the humankind abiding in all ten corners of the world. Give me power to realize you as you know my all acts.

The Snātaka Brahmachārī (graduate), then should eat curd and sesame seed (Sesamum Indicum Linn) and have his head and beared shaved, file his nails and should brush his teeth with the Udumbara (Ficus Glomerata) and doing so chant the following mantra:

ओम् अन्नाद्याय व्यूहध्वꣳ सोमो राजाऽयमागमत् ।
स मे मुखं प्रमार्क्ष्यते यशसा च भगेन च ॥ पार॰ 2.6.17

Om annādyāya vyūhadhvaꣳ somo rājā'yamāgamat,
sa me mukhaṁ pramārkṣayate yaśasā cha bhagena cha.

Pār.GS. 2.6.17

[Meaning] O men! brush your teeth to take food. This potable water has been brought to wash my teeth. This potable water will wash my mouth after I brush my teeth and thus would make me crowned with fame and property in the society.

Afterwards the Brahmachārī having smeared his body with perfumes and taken bath with clean potable water, should wear dhoti or yellow cloth and apply the sandal wood powder. He should then touch the eyes, mouth and nostrils with the following mantras:

ओम् प्राणापानौ मे तर्पय चक्षुर्मे तर्पय श्रोत्रं में तर्पय ॥ पार॰ 2.6.18

Om prāṇāpānau me tarpaya chakṣurme tarpaya śrotraṁ
meṁ tarpaya. Pār.GS. 2.6.18

[Meaning] O Almighty Brahman! make my prāṇa (inhalation) and apāna (exhalation) full of vitality, make my eyes full of sight, make my ears full of audibillity.

Thereafter, he taking water in his hands, moving a little in the left side and keeping his face southward should chant the following mantra and pour the water on the ground:

ओम् पितरः शुन्धध्वम् ॥ पार० 2.6.19

Om pitaraḥ śundhadhvam. Pār.GS. 2.6.19

[Meaning] Let the pitaraḥ, the preserving or protecting powers of the nature be firm, and pure.

Then the Brahmachārī moving a little right wishper in mind the following mantra:

ओं सुचक्षा अहमक्षीभ्यां भूयासꣳ सुवर्चा मुखेन।
सुश्रुत्कर्णाभ्यां भूयासम् ॥ पार० 2.6.19

Oṁ suchakṣā ahamakṣībhyāṁ bhūyāsaꣳ suvarchā mukhena, suśrutkarṇābhyāṁ bhūyāsam. Pār.GS. 2.6.19

[Meaning] O God! may I see good things with my eyes, may I have handsome face and may I have good audibility with my ears.

He then should put on a best outfit and chant the following mantras:

ओम् परिधास्यै यशोधास्यै दीर्घायुत्वाय जरदष्टिरस्मि।
शतं च जीवामि शरदः पुरूची रायस्पोषमभिसंव्ययिष्ये ॥ पार० 2.6.20

Om paridhāsyai yaśodhāsyai dīrghāyutvāya jaradaṣṭirasmi, śataṁ cha jīvāmi śaradaḥ purūchī rāyaspoṣamabhisaṁvyayiṣye. Pār.GS. 2.6.20

[Meaning] Just to cover my body, for my status, long life, material and spiritual prosperity, I put on clothes decently, because, having attained prosperity and progeny, I aspire to live the old age as a hale and hearty man. May God bless me to live a life of 100 years.

He should put on nice upavastra (upper outfits) chanting the following Mantra:

ओं यशसा मा द्यावापृथिवी यशसेन्द्राबृहस्पती ।
यशौ भगश्च मा विदद्यशो मा प्रतिपद्यताम् ॥ पार० 2.6.21

Oṁ yaśasā mā dyāvāpṛthivī yaśasendrābṛhaspatī,
yaśau bhagaścha mā vidadyaśo mā pratipadyatām.

Pār.GS. 2.6.21

[Meaning] O gentlemen! may I live between the earth and space with name and fame; may the prosperity and scholarship come to me with name and fame; may worshipable God bless me with name and fame. May all of you also bless me with name and fame.

The Brahmachārī should take a garland of flowers in his hand chanting the following mantra:

ओं या आहरज्जमदग्रिः श्रद्धायै मेधायै कामायेन्द्रियाय ।
ता अहं प्रतिगृह्णामि यशसा च भगेन च ॥ पार० 2.6.23

Oṁ yā āharajjamadagniḥ śraddhāyai medhāyai kāmāyendriyāya,
tā ahaṁ pratigṛhṇāmi yaśasā cha bhagena cha.

Pār.GS. 2.6.23

[Meaning] I accept these flowers for my fame and prosperity like the king, who protects the institutions of the yajña, takes hold of the flowers to add to the grace of spiritual people, to enhance the intellectual power, for the fulfilment of desires and for providing soothing experience and good feel to the sense oragns.

Thereafter he should pronounce the following mantras and wear the garland which he had previously taken in his hand:

ओं यद्यशोऽप्सरसामिन्दश्चकार विपुलं पृथु ।
तेन सङ्ग्रथिताः सुमनस आबध्नामि यशो मयि ॥ पार० 2.6.24

Oṁ yadyaśo'psarasāmindaśchakāra vipulaṁ pṛthu,
tena saṅgrathitāḥ sumanasa ābadhnāmi yaśo mayi.

Pār.GS. 2.6.24

[Meaning] Whatever great fame a king earns by using these flowers amongst his workers with that fame, I wear this garland which has asthetically been prepared.

Afterwards, holding in his hands a turban, shawl and cap or a crown, he should chant the mantra (ओं युवा सुवासा॰) quoted in the Upanayana sanskāra and put it on his head. Then, he should take an ornament in his hand and wear it with the following mantra:

ओम् अलङ्करणमसि भूयोऽलङ्करणं भूयात् ॥ पार॰ 2.6.26

Om alaṅkaraṇamasi bhūyo'laṅkaraṇaṁ bhūyāt.

Pār.GS. 2.6.26

[Meaning] You are an ornament, ornament me.

He should apply collyrium in the eyes with the following mantra:

ओं वृत्रस्यासि कनीनकश्चक्षुर्दा असि चक्षुर्मे देहि ॥ यजु॰ 4.3; पार॰ 2.6.27

Oṁ vṛtrasyāsi kanīnakaśchakṣurdā asi chakṣurme dehi ॥

YV.4.3; Pār. GS. 2.6.27

[Meaning] O Brahman! You are the producer of the clouds. You are the giver of eyes, so please bestow upon me with good eyesight.

He should see his face in the mirror and utter:

ओं रोचिष्णुरसि ॥ पार॰ 4.6.28

Oṁ rochiṣṇurasi. Pār.GS 4.6.28

[Meaning] This glass is transparent and beautiful.

Thereafter he should have umbrella and utter the following mantra:

ओम् बृहस्पतेश्छदिरसि पाप्मनो मामन्तर्धेहि तेजसो यशसो माऽन्तर्धेहि ॥

पार॰ 2.6.29

Om bṛhaspateśchhadirasi pāpmano māmantardhehi tejaso yaśaso mā'ntardhehi. Pār.GS.2.6.29

[Meaning] This umbrella is the cover of the kings, let it cover me from pāpa (acts causing downfall of a human being), and let it not cover me from the valour and fame.

He should, then put on shoes with the following mantra:

ओम् प्रतिष्ठे स्थो विश्वतो मा पातम्। पार॰ 2.6.30

Om pratiṣṭhe stho viśvato mā pātam. Pār.GS. 2.6.30

[Meaning] O shoes you are my stand and protect me from thorn etc. Protect me from all directions.

Afterwards he should hold a smooth stick of bamboo etc. uttering the following mantra:

ओं विश्वाभ्यो मा नाष्ट्राभ्यस्परिपाहि सर्वतः॥ पार॰ 2.6.31

Oṁ viśvābhyo mā nāṣṭrābhyasparipāhi sarvataḥ.

Pār.GS. 2.6.31

[Meaning] Let this stick protect me from all the wicked persons in all conditions.

The parents and other relatives of the Brahmachārī should receive him cordially when he comes from the house of Āchārya. They receive him with great affection and gaiety. On his coming to the house, the father, mother, brother and relatives entertain him by offering madhuparka.

Again the Brahmachārī/Brahmachāriṇi and his/her parents entertain the Āchārya and the other guests attending the sanskāra with delicious food and drinks. They should allow the Āchārya sit on a cmfortable chair and offer in his honour the madhuparka, garland, gift of clothes and cow according to their capability and capacity. They should laud the Āchārya for his merit before the others and express their gratefulness for the education he had imparted to the student. They should address the people in the following manner :

Hear, you gentlemen! This honourable Āchārya has done a great good to me. He has saved me from incivility and has transformed me into a celebrated scholar. I can never disown me from whatever he has done for me. For this I only offer many thanks to my Āchārya and with great respect salute him. I further pray him to make other students successful and accomplished as he had made me by imparting value education and instructions. As you have blessed me with good education and knowledge. I, in turn, would do the same to other students. O Āchārya, I can never forget the good you have done to me.

May Almighty Brahman, the Master of the universe bless all with civility, knowledge, good physique, spiritual power and make all long-lived, healthy, industrious and courageous in discharging the duries and fulfilling the task of philanthropy, so that, all of us in the creation of God follow his good qualities, acts and nature and redeem the objective of human life, i.e. dharma, artha, kāma, and mokṣa and always live a hale and hearty life.

इति समावर्त्तनसंकारविधिः समाप्तः ॥

iti samāvarttanasamkāravidhiḥ samāptaḥ.

Here ends the procedure of the graduation ceremony.

अथ विवाहसंस्कारविधिं वक्ष्यामः

Marriage Sanskāra

Here under we would deal with the the procedure of Marriage Ceremony.

Vivāha, the marriage ceremony is the procedure wherein the man and woman having completed their education in Brahmacharya Āśrama want to bind themselves in nuptial bond with a view to create a good progeny to discharge their duties of Gṛhasthāśrama.

There are following authorities in this regard.

उदगयन आपूर्यमाणपक्षे पुण्ये नक्षत्रे चौलकर्मोपनयनगोदानविवाहाः ॥

udagayana āpūryamāṇapakṣe puṇye nakṣatre chaulakarmopanayanagodānavivāhāḥ.

[Meaning] The tonsure, Upanayana, Godāna and Vivāha (marriage) ceremonies should be solemnized during Uttarāyāṇa in the bright half of moon on an auspicious Nakṣatra.

सार्वकालमेके विवाहम् ॥ आश्व॰ गृसू॰ 1.4.1-.2

sārvakālameke vivāham. Āśv. GS. 1.4.1-2

[Meaning] The marriage ceremony can be performed at anytime throughout the year.

आवसथ्याधानं दारकाले ॥ पारस्कर 1.2.1

āvasathyādhānaṁ dārakāle. Pār.GS. 1.2.1

The Āvasathya agni is set up at the time of marriage.

पुण्ये नक्षत्रे दारान् कुर्वीत ॥ गोभिल॰ गृसू॰ 2.5.1

puṇye nakṣatre dārān kurvīta. Go.GS. 2.5.1

[Meaning] The marriage should be done on an auspicous Nakṣatra (i.e. when everybody is cheerful).

लक्षणप्रशस्तान् कुशलेन ॥ गोभिल॰ गृसू॰ 2.5.2

lakṣaṇaprasastān kusalena. Go.GS.2.5.2

The marriage should be solemnized during Uttarāyāṇa in the bright half of moon on a good day when parties are cheerful. Many Āchāryas are of the view that the marriage ceremony can be performed at anytime throughout the year. The fire which is set up at the time of marriage is called Āvasathya.

The marriage should be done on the auspicious Nakṣtra, i.e. when everybody is cheerful.

Period: The time of the marriage ceremony is the same which has been described in the Vedārambha sanskāra in the context of the categories of Brahmacharya. The age, family, residing place, body and nature of the bride and bride-groom, should be matched carefully i.e. both are informed of marriage match. The age of the bride-groom should be one and half time more then the age of the bride, which is a minimum requirement but maximum age of the bride-groom should be double the age of bride. The authorities on this issue are as under:

वेदानधीत्य वेदौ वा वेदं वापि यथाक्रमम् ।

अविप्लुतब्रह्मचर्यो गृहस्थाश्रममावसेत् ॥ मनु॰ 3.2 ॥

vedānadhītyavedau vā vedaṁ vā'piyathākramam.
aviplutabrahmacharyogṛhasthāsramamāvaset. Manu 3.2

2. (A student) who has studied in due order the three Vedas, or two, or even one only, without breaking the (rules of) studentship, shall enter the Gṛhastha Aśrama.

तं प्रतीतंस्वधर्मेणब्रह्मदायहरंपितुः ।

स्रग्विणंतल्पआसीनमर्हयेत्प्रथमंगवा ॥ मनु॰ 3.3 ॥

taṁ pratītaṁsvadharmeṇabrahmadāyaharaṁpituḥ,

sragviṇaṁtalpaāsīnamarhayetprathamaṁgavā. Manu, 3.3

3. He who gladly performed his duties of a student and inherited the knowledge of the Veda from his father, shall be honoured, sitting on a couch/sofa and adorned with a garland, with the present of a cow.

गुरुणानुमतःस्नात्वासमावृत्तोयथाविधि ।
उद्वहेतद्द्विजोभार्यांसवर्णांलक्षणान्विताम् ॥ मनु० 3.4 ॥

guruṇānumataḥsnātvāsamāvṛttoyathāvidhi,
udvahetadvijobhāryāṁsavarṇāṁlakṣaṇānvitām. Manu, 3.4

4. Having bathed, with the permission of his teacher, and performed according to the rule the Samāvartana Sanskāra (the ceremony of returning home after graduation), a student shall marry a wife of equal merit, profession and temperament who is endowed with good character.

असपिण्डाचयामातुरसगोत्राचयापितुः ।
साप्रशस्ताद्द्विजातीनांदारकर्मणिमैथुने ॥ मनु० 3.5 ॥

asapiṇḍāchayāmāturasagotrāchayāpituḥ,
sāpraśastādvijātīnāṁdārakarmaṇimaithune. Manu, 3.5

5. A damsel who neither has Sapiṇḍa relationship on the mother's side (i.e. who doesn't not belong to the gotra of the mother, maternal grand mother and maternal great grand mother), nor does she belong to the gotra of the father, is recommended to a student for wedlock and conjugal union.

महान्त्यपिसमृद्धानिगोऽजाविधनधान्यतः ।
स्त्रीसम्बन्धेदशैतानिकुलानिपरिवर्जयेत् ॥ मनु० 3.6 ॥

mahāntyapisamṛddhānigo'jāvidhanadhānyataḥ,
strīsambandhedaśaitānikulāniparivarjayet. Manu, 3.6

6. In connecting himself with a wife, let him carefully avoid the ten families, be they ever so great, or rich in

kine, goats, sheep, grain, or (other) property.

हीनक्रियं निष्पुरुषं निश्छन्दो रोमशार्शसम् ।
क्षयामयाव्यपस्मारिश्चित्रिकुष्ठिकुलानिच ॥ मनु॰ 3.7 ॥

hīnakriyaṁ niṣaparuṣaṁ niśchhando romaśārśasa,
kṣayāmayāvyapasmāriśvitrikuṣṭhikulānicha.Manu, 3.7

7. The family that neglects spiritual acts and Vedic Sanskāras; that which is coward; that in which the Veda is not studied; that one the members of which have thick hair on the body; that which is subject to hereditary diseases like piles, tuberculosis, indigestion, epilepsy, or (श्चित्रि) white or (कुष्ठि) black leprosy.

नोद्वहेत्कपिलांकन्यांनाधिकाङ्गीनरोगिणीम् ।
नालोमिकांनातिलोमांनवाचाटां नपिङ्गलाम् ॥ मनु॰ 3.8 ॥

nodvahetkapilāṁkanyāṁnādhikāṅgīṁnaroginīm,
nālomikāṁnātilomāṁnavāchāṭāṁ napingalām. Manu, 3.8

8. Let him not marry a maiden (with) monkey coloured skin, nor one who has an extra limb, nor one who is sickly, nor one either with no hair or too much, nor one who talks nonesense or has yellow pigments on the body.

नऋक्षवृक्षनदीनाम्नींनान्त्यपर्वतनामिकाम् ।
नपक्ष्यहिप्रेष्यनाम्नींनचभीषणनामिकाम् ॥ मनु॰ 3.9 ॥

narkṣavṛkṣanadīnāmnīṁnāntyaparvatanāmikām,
napakṣayahipreṣyanāmnīṁnachabhīṣaṇanāmikām.Manu, 3.9

9. Nor one named after a constellation, a tree, or a river, nor one bearing the name symbolising a low or mean sense, or of a mountain, nor one named after a bird, a snake, nor one whose name denotes a sense of slavery, nor one whose name is terrifying.

अव्यङ्गाङ्गींसौम्यनाम्रींहंसवारणगामिनीम् ।
तनुलोमकेशदशनांमृद्वङ्गीमुद्वहेत्स्त्रियम् ॥ मनु॰ 3.10 ॥

avyaṅgāṅgīṁsaumyanāmnīṁhaṁsavāraṇagāminīm,
tanulomakeśadaśanāṁmṛdvaṅgīmudvahetstriyam.

Manu, 3.10

10. Let him wed a female free from deformities, who has a decent/graceful name, the (graceful) gait like that of a Haṁsa (goose) or of an elephant, a smooth and silky hair on the body and on the head, small teeth, and soft limbs.

ब्राह्मोदैवस्तथैवार्ष:प्राजापत्यस्तथाऽसुर: ।
गान्धर्वोराक्षसश्चैवपैशाचश्चाष्टमोऽधम: ॥ मनु० 3.21 ॥

brāhmodaivastathaivārṣaḥprajāpatyastathā'suraḥ,
gāndharvorākṣasaśchaivapaiśāchaśchāṣṭamo'dhamaḥ.

Manu, 3.21

21. The 8 types of marriages are: the Brāhma, the Daiva, the Ārṣa, the Prājāpatya, the Āsura, the Gāndharva, the Rākṣasa, and the 8th one and most inferior is the Paiśācha.

Note: The above eight types of marriages are inferior in order. The first one the most superior type. Everybody is expected to go by the first one. Since, all human beings cannot be superior by nature, temperament and merit, so other forms of marriages are also sanctioned.

आच्छाद्यचार्चयित्वाचश्रुतशीलवतेस्वयम् ।
आहूयदानंकन्यायाब्राह्मोधर्म:प्रकीर्तित: ॥ मनु० 3.27 ॥

Āchchhādyachārchayitvāchaśrutaśīlavatesvayam,
āhūyadānaṁkanyāyābrāhmodharmaḥprakīrtitaḥ. Manu, 3.27

27. Giving away the daughter, robbed in gracious attire with due honour, to a man (bridegroom) learned in the Veda and of high moral and ethical values, duly invited by the parents of the bride for the purpose of marriage, is called the Brāhma marriage.

यज्ञेतुविततेसम्यग्ऋद्ध्विजेकर्मकुर्वते ।

अलङ्कृत्यसुतादानंदैवंधर्मंप्रचक्षते ॥ मनु॰ 3.28 ॥

yajñetuvitatesamyagṛtvijekarmakurvate,
alaṅkṛtyasutādānaṁdaivaṁdharmaṁprachakṣate. Manu,3.28

28. Giving away the daughter who has been decked with ornaments, in a marriage ceremony duly conducted for the purpose to a bridegroom who excels in the performance of all duties and yajñas, is called the Daiva marriage.

एकं गोमिथुनं द्वेवावरादादायधर्मतः ।
कन्याप्रदानं विधिवदार्षोधर्मः स उच्यते ॥ मनु॰ 3.29 ॥

ēkaṁ gomithunaṁ dvevāvarādādāyadharmataḥ,
kanyāpradānaṁ vidhivadārṣodharmaḥ sa uchyate.Manu,3.29

29. When the daughter is given away to the bridegroom after receiving from him, a pair of cow and a bull or two pairs for the fulfilment of the dharma, that is named the Ārṣa marriage.

सहौभौचरतांधर्ममितिवाचाऽनुभाष्यच ।
कन्याप्रदानमभ्यर्च्यप्राजापत्योविधिःस्मृतः ॥ मनु॰ 3.30 ॥

sahaubhaucharatāṁdharmamitivāchā'nubhāṣyacha ।
kanyāpradānamabhyarchyaprājāpatyovidhiḥsmṛtaḥ

Manu, 3.30

30. Giving away the daughter with due honour to the bridegroom by the parents after consulting both the bride and bridegroom whethe they mutually agree to enter into Gṛhastha life and perform the duties thereof, is called the Prājāpatya marriage.

ज्ञातिभ्योद्रविणंदत्त्वाकन्यायैचैवशक्तितः ।
कन्याप्रदानंस्वाच्छन्द्यादासुरोधर्मउच्यते ॥ मनु॰ 3.31 ॥

jñātibhyodraviṇaṁdattvākanyāyaichaivaśaktitaḥ ।
kanyāpradānaṁsvāchchhandyādāsurodharmauchyate ॥

Manu, 3.31

31. When (the bridegroom) receives a bride, after having given as much wealth as he can afford, to the kinsmen of bride and to the bride herself, according to his own will, that is called the Āsura marriage.

इच्छयाऽन्योन्यसंयोगःकन्यायाश्चवरस्यच ।
गान्धर्वःसतुविज्ञेयोमैथुन्यःकामसम्भवः ॥ मनु॰ 3.32 ॥

ichchhayā'nyonyasaṁyogaḥkanyāyāśchavarasyacha,
gāndharvaḥsatuvijñeyomaithunyaḥkāmasambhavaḥ.

Manu, 3.32

32. The Gāndharva marriage is the voluntary union of a bride and bridegroom due to sexual urge.

हत्वाछित्त्वाचभित्त्वाचक्रोशन्तींरुदतींगृहात् ।
प्रसह्यकन्याहरणंराक्षसोविधिरुच्यते ॥ मनु॰ 3.33 ॥

hatvāchhittvāchabhittvāchakrośantīṁrudatīṁgṛhāt,
prasahyakanyāharaṇaṁrākṣasovidhiruchyate ॥ *Manu, 3.33*

33. The forcible abduction of a maiden from her home, while she cries out and weeps, after (her kinsmen) have been slain or wounded and (their houses) broken open, is called the Rākṣasa marriage.

सुप्तांमत्तांप्रमत्तांवारहोयत्रोपगच्छति ।
सपापिष्ठोविवाहानांपैशाचश्चाष्टमोऽधमः ॥ मनु॰ 3.34 ॥

suptāṁmattāṁpramattāṁvārahoyatropagachchhati,
sapāpiṣṭhovivāhānāṁpaiśāchaśchāṣṭamo'dhamaḥ ॥*Manu,3.34*

34. When (a man) sexualy assault a girl who is sleeping, intoxicated, located in deserted or secluded place or mentally challenged, that is the eighth, the most base and immoral type of marriage called the Paiśācha marriage.

ब्राह्मादिषुविवाहेषुचतुर्ष्वेवानुपूर्वशः ।
ब्रह्मवर्चस्विनः पुत्राजायन्तेशिष्टसम्मताः ॥ मनु॰ 3.39 ॥

brāhmādiṣuvivāheṣuchatursvevānupūrvaśaḥ,

brahmavarchasvinaḥ putrājāyanteśiṣṭasammatāḥ ||Manu, 3.39

39. From the first four conjugal relationship we often have progenies radiant with knowledge of the Veda and honoured by the good persons.

रूपसत्त्वगुणोपेताधनवन्तोयशस्विनः ।
पर्याप्तभोगाधर्मिष्ठाजीवन्तिचशतंसमाः ॥ मनु॰ 3.40 ॥

rūpasattvaguṇopetādhanavantoyaśasvinaḥ,
paryāptabhogādharmiṣṭhājīvantichaśatamsamāḥ ||Manu, 3.40

40. Endowded with the qualities of beauty and sattvaguṇa, possessing wealth and fame, gaining as many enjoyments as they wish and being most dharma-abiding, these progenies will live a hundred years.

इतरेषुतुशिष्टेषुनृशंसाऽनृतवादिनः ।
जायन्तेदुर्विवाहेषुब्रह्मधर्मद्विषःसुताः ॥ मनु॰ 3.41 ॥

itareṣutuśiṣṭeṣunṛśamsā'nṛtavādinaḥ,
jāyantedurvivāheṣubrahmadharmadviṣaḥsutāḥ || *Manu,3.41*

41. But progenies produced from the remaining (four) blamable marriages, are found often cruel and speakers of untruth, hating the Veda and Vedic dharma.

अनिन्दितैःस्त्रीविवाहैरनिन्द्याभवतिप्रजा ।
निन्दितैर्निन्दिता नृणां तस्मान्निन्द्यान् विवर्जयेत् ॥ मनु॰ 3.42 ॥

aninditaiḥstrīvivāhairanindyābhavatiprajā,
ninditairninditā nṛṇām tasmānnindyān vivarjayet.

Manu.3.42

42. In the blameless marriages, blameless children are born to men, in blamable (marriages), blamable (offspring) are born; one should therefore avoid the blamable (forms of marriages).

उत्कृष्टायाभिरूपाय वराय सदृशाय च ।

अप्राप्तामपि तां तस्मै कन्यां दद्याद्विचक्षणः ॥1 ॥

utkṛṣṭāyābhirūpāya varāya sadṛśāya cha,
aprāptāmapi tāṁ tasmai kanyāṁ dadyādvichakṣaṇaḥ ॥1 ॥

If parents desire the marriage of their daughter, they should prefer to select a bride-groom who is superior to her in merit, actions and nature and matches her in beauty and shape. In spite of her being within the six genealogical order of mother, she should be given to the sutable bridegroom only and to none else, so that the both of them delightfully promote the Gṛhastha-life and produce good progenies.

काममामरणात्तिष्ठेद् गृहे कन्यर्त्तुमत्यपि ।
न चैवैनां प्रयच्छेत्तु गुणहीनाय कर्हिचित् ॥2 ॥

kāmamāmaraṇāttiṣṭhed gṛhe kanyarttumatyapi,
na chaivaināṁ prayachchhettu guṇahīnāya karhichit ॥2 ॥

The parents of the girls should never marry their daughter to a man who is inferior, unmatched and wicked, she might stay in the house of her father unmarried till death and the same standard is applicable to a man that he should marry a bride compatible with him.

त्रीरिण वर्षाण्युदीक्षेत कुमार्यृतुमती सती ।
ऊर्ध्वन्तु कालादेतस्माद्विन्देत सदृशं पतिम् ॥3 ॥

trīriṇa varṣāṇyudīkṣeta kumāryṛtumatī satī,
ūrdhvantu kālādetasmādvindeta sadṛśaṁ patim ॥3 ॥

The marriage of girl, if desired, should be arranged in the fourth year leaving the three-year period from the day of menstruation.

Question: If it is so, what will be the applicability of the ślokas अष्टवर्षा भवेद् गौरी नववर्षा च रोहिणी (*aṣṭavarṣā bhaved gaurī navavarṣā cha rohiṇī*) etc.?

Answer: Nothing but they have miserable fate. Those who following these ślokas do the marriage of their children in immature age or child-hood will make them spoiled, ruined, diseased and short-lived, in reality, they destroy their famililes. If anyone desires to solemnize the marriage of his children earlier, he should follow the instructions of the Vedas and they should never do the marriage of girl before the minimum age of 16 years and of a boy before the minimum age of 25 years. Longer the period of marriage, greater will they benefit the bliss of life.

Questions: Should marriages be arranged in the near relatives or distant ones?

Answer: दुहिता दुहिता दूरे हिता भवतीति ॥

duhitā duhitā dūre hitā bhavatīti.

This is observation of the Nirukta. It says that marriage of a girl at distant place is more beneficial.

Question:- Why is marriage not permited in the same gotra or between brother and sister?

Answer: The first disadvantage of marriage in near blood relations is lack of love. In long relation marriages love becomes stronger. In near blood relation marriages, both the parteners are acquianted with their merits and demerits so they do not have any fear from each other. The second disadvantage is that in long relation marriages, the couples would have healthy offsprings. The third advantage of the distant marriage is that it results in the mutual love, progress and prosperity. The marriage in near relations does not give this benefit.

The Vedic evidence for the marriage at the age of maturity:

तमस्मेरा युवतयो युवानं ममृज्यमानाः परिं यन्त्यापः ।

स शुक्रेभिः शिक्वभी रेवदस्मेदीदायानिध्मो घृतनिर्णिगप्सु ॥ ऋ० 2.35.4

tamasmerā yuvatayo yuvānaṁ marmṛjyamānāḥ pariṁ yantyāpaḥ,
sa śukrebhiḥ śikvabhī revadasmedīdāyānidhmo ghṛtanirṇigapsu. RV. 2.35.4

The girls (of 20-24 years), having obtained good educations, marry, according to their choice, us (the bride-grooms) who are one and half-time or 2 times older than girls, well educated, endowed with merit and youthful, like the rivers approach the ocean. The Brahmachārī endowed with vigour etc., pure qualities attaining all sorts of praiseworthy things marry the girl in her prime youth. As the lightning or electricty in clouds purify the water vapours in clouds, similalry love, appearing dim from outside but keep blazing inside, is a purifying agent in the relation of the wife and husband that produced good progeny and happiness in their Gṛhastha life.

अस्मै तिस्रो अव्यथ्याय नारीर्देवाय देवीर्दिधिषन्त्यन्नम् ।
कृता इवोप हि प्रसर्स्रे अप्सु स पीयूषं धयति पूर्वसूनाम् ॥ ऋ० 2.35.5

asmai tisro avyathyāya nārīrdevāya devīrdighiṣantyannam,
kṛtā ivopa hi prasarsre apsu sa pīyūṣaṁ dhayati pūrvasūnām.
RV. 2.35.5

O women and men! As the learned ladies marry gents of high, medium and low profile to create progeny for the purpose of fulfilment of their kāma (mundane life desires). As the electricity in the clouds and causes the delivery of water vapours accumulated in the coulds on the earth in the form of rain, similarly, the husband and wife having a strong bond of love increase the prosperity and progeny in the Gṛhastha life.

अश्वस्यात्र जनिमास्य च स्वर्दुहो रिषः सम्पृचः पाहि सूरीन् ।
आमासु पूर्षु परो अप्रमृष्यं नारातयो वि नशन्नानृतानि ॥ ऋ० 2.35.6

aśvasyātra janimāsya cha svarduho riṣaḥ sampṛchaḥ pāhi sūrīn,
āmāsu pūrṣu paro apramṛṣyaṁ nārātayo vi naśannānṛtāni.

RV.2.35.6

The King and all other persons should impart good value education and instruction to the children in the cities and houses. Such values and education attained by the observance of Brahmacharya by the younger generation can never be destroyed even by an enemy. Younger generation receiving this type of value education is never afflicted by vices in their life. Therefore, O ladies and gents! Give all protection to the educated persons and education in the society. The house-hold life of the custodians of education continue to progress always.

वधूरियं पतिमिच्छन्त्येति य ईं वहाते महिषीमिषिराम् ।
आस्य श्रवस्याद्रथ आ च घोषात्पुरू सहस्रा परि वर्त्तयाते ॥ ऋ० 5.37.3

vadhūriyaṁ patimichchhantyeti ya īṁ vahāte mahiṣīmiṣirām,
āsya śravasyādratha ā cha ghoṣātpurū sahasrā pari varttayāte. RV. 5.37.3

O men! If a man in his prime youth finds his life partner in a woman who is educated, endowed with good qualities, good character, born in a noble family and aspires to find a suitable partner, such a couple prospers in the house-hold life with knowledge, wealth etc. from all sides. They can carry on the burden of house-hold life and accomplish many tasks.

उप व एषे वन्द्येभिः शूषैः प्र यह्वी दिवश्चितयद्भिरर्कैः ।
उषासानक्ता विदुषीव विश्वमा हा वहतो मर्त्याय यज्ञम् ॥ ऋ० 5.41.7

upa va ēṣe vandyebhiḥ śūṣaiḥ pra yahvī divaśchitayadbhirarkaiḥ,
uṣāsānaktā viduṣīva viśvamā hā vahato martyāya yajñam.

RV. 5.41.7

O men! If you bear children observing complete Brahmacharya, make them highly educated and solemnize their marriages according to their choice, they in return would give you all pleasure and happiness endowed with with the varous qualities, knowledge, various acts of good performances and different kinds of strength inclusive of physical and spiritual maturity. They can descharge satisfactorily the duties of household life. As the learned lady and man perform their tasks smoothly, similarly, they can perform their duty of Gṛhasth life properly. The above type of marriage is beneficial for all persons. The men and women of good nature, action and qualities can fulfill their desires nicely.

As the Veda sanctions the observance of Brahmancharya for girls, in the same manner the men should also observe Brahmacharya and attain perfect knowledge. He can go for a marriage with a female partner of equal, temperament, qualities and profession in his prime youth, if he so desires. This is the best marriage. Those who do not solemnize the marriage of girls or boys when they are matured enough, rather solemnize their their marriage in the young age without being so desired by them, they violate the rules of Brahman revealed in the Veda.

Question: Should marriage take place in one's own Varṇa (sanskāra, guṇa and conduct) or in other Varṇa also?

Answer: Marriage should take place in one's own Varṇa. However, the Varṇa system be based on sanskāra, guṇa (sattva, rajas, and tamas) and conduct and not on the birth-based caste. Those who who are well educated, learned, endowed with moral and ethical values, who have an attitude of helping the needy, observe self-restraint, devoid of evils like telling lie etc. and are ever ready in proliferation of knowledge and dharma (moral and ethical code of conduct, duties to family, society and nation), they will be called good Brāhamaṇas and Brāhmaṇīs. Those who are endowed with knowledge, physical prowess, valour and ever ready to grant justice are called best Kṣatriyas and kṣatriyās (female kṣatriya). Those who engage in the jobs of agriculture, domestication of animals, production, business and trade after attaining complete education and knowledge and have efficiency in the languages of various countries are considered to be the best Vaiśyas and Vaiśyās (female Vaiśya). Those who don't want to study at all or say uneducated are known as the Śudra (male Śudra) and Śudrā (female Śudra). As such, for happy married life, marriages should be solemnized of Brāhmaṇa (a boy of Brāhmṇa sanskāra, guṇa and conduct) with Brāhmaṇī (a girl of Brāhmaṇa sanskāra, guṇa and conduct); Kṣatriya (a boy of Kṣatriya sanskāra, guṇa and conduct) to a Kṣatriyā (a girl of Kṣatriya sanskāra, guṇa and conduct); a Vaiśhya (a boy of Vaiśya sanskāra, guṇa and conduct) to a Vaiśyā (a girl of Vaiśya sanskāra, guṇa and conduct); and a Śudra (a boy of Śudra sanskāra, guṇa and conduct) to a Śudrā (a girl of Śudra sanskāra, guṇa and conduct), otherwise the married life may become frought with problems.

There are following scriptural references in support of this type of Varṇa system (not the caste system):

धर्मचर्यया जघन्यो वर्णः पूर्वं पूर्वं वर्णमापद्यते जातिपरिवृत्तौ ॥1॥

अधर्मचर्यया पूर्वो वर्णो जघन्यं जघन्यं वर्णमापद्यते जातिपरिवृत्तौ ॥2॥

आपस्तम्ब

*dharmacharyayā   jaghanyo   varṇaḥ   pūrvaṁ   pūrvaṁ
varṇamāpadyate jātiparivṛttau ॥1॥*
adharmacharyayā pūrvo varṇo jaghanyaṁ jaghanyaṁ

varṇamāpadyate jātiparivṛttau ||2|| Āpastamba

[Meaning] By gaining knowledge, upgradation in sanskāras, guṇas and conduct an individual (male or female) of lower Varṇa rises to the higher Varṇas because of the upgradation in their sanskāras, and guṇas, consequently, he/she would have the right to perform the duties prescribed for the concerned higher Varṇa.

Similarly, due to abandoning the practice of the study of Śastras, degradation in sanskāras, guṇas and conduct, an individual (male or female) of high Varṇa falls to the lower Varṇa, because of the degradation in their sanskāras, guṇas and conduct, so they would lose the right to perform the duties of higher Varṇa, but would be bound to do the duties prescribed for the concerned lower Varṇa.

शूद्रो ब्राह्मणतामेति ब्राह्मणश्चैति शूद्रताम् ।
क्षत्रियाज्जातमेवन्तु विद्याद्वैश्यात्तथैव च ॥ मनुस्मृति

śūdro brāhmaṇatāmeti brāhmaṇaśchaiti śūdratām |
kṣatriyājjātamevantu vidyādvaiśyāttathaiva cha. manusmṛti

[Meaning] Through the education, higher guṇas, and conduct, a Śudra rises to the level of Vaiśya; Vaiśya to the level of Kṣatriya and Kṣatriya to the level of Brāhmaṇa. Similarly, due to low profil00e (low practice of study of Śastras, lowering of sanskāras, guṇas and conduct, a Brāhmaṇa is degraded to the level of Kśatriya; a Kṣatriya to the level of Vaiśya and a Vaiśya to the level of Śudra and so will lose his/her rights and duties.

This system is the mainstay of the social justice. Everyone has the right to reform himself/herself and try to maintain or rise to the higher levels. For the fear of being downgraded, the prople would stop committing evil acts. This paves the way of development and advancement of the world. Till the timings, this system was prevalent in the Āry0āvartta and men and women would marry after attaning complete knowledge and maturity, there was progress and advancement in all sectors and fields in the country. Application of this system is the ardent need of the hour, so that this Āryavartta can attain its past standard, pride and prosperity[5].

Examination of match— The following method or procedure may be followed to match the sanskāras, guṇas and conduct of bride and bridegroom.

1. Both should have similar sanskāras.

2. Both should have similar IQ (Intelligent quotient), EQ (Emotional quotient) and SQ (Spiritual Quotient).

3. Both should have similar habits.

4. Both should have equal physique.

5. Both should endow with similar values like non-voilence, truthfulness, sweat tonguedness, gratefulness, kindness, devoid of greed.

6. Both should have a nationalist attitude, i.e they should think of reforms and progress of the country.

7. They should always be eager and enthusiastic to attain more and more knowledge.

8. They should be fearless in speaking truth.

9. They should be devoid of the evils and vices of deception, envy, jealousy, sesual desires, anger, fraud, gambling, theft, addiction, non-vegetarianism, etc.

10. Both be equally efficient in domestic affairs.

---

[5] This shows the concerned of Swami Dayanand Saraswati regarding the pathetic condition of this country caused by the degradations of social valus and education system.

Whenever, coming f00rom distant places or at morning and evening they meet together, they should exchange (नमस्ते) **Namaste**. Thus both of them should enjoy the life by reciprocating affectionate speech, etc. The body of the wife should be slim as compared to the husband. She should be so tall as her head could reach upto the shoulder of her husband.

Thereafter, the internal examination should be carried out by women and men through mutual conversation etc.

ओम् ऋतमग्रे प्रथमं जज्ञे ऋते सत्यं प्रतिष्ठितम्। यदियं कुमार्य्यभिजाता तदियमिह प्रतिपद्यताम्। यत्सत्यं तद्दृश्यताम्॥ आश्व॰ 1.5.5

Om ṛtamagre prathamaṁ jajñe ṛte satyaṁ pratiṣṭhitam, yadiyaṁ kumāryyabhijātā tadiyamiha pratipadyatām, yatsatyaṁ taddṛśyatām. Āśv.GS. 1.5.5

[Meaning] (Ṛta) Motion came into being first. Prakṛti (inactive energy) was the base of ṛta (motion), i.e. motion made the prakṛti (inactive energy) active. Accept this bachelorette. Look for the truth.

When the time of marriage be fixed the girl should get intelligence about the bride-groom through the experts and exprerienced men and in the same manner the bride-groom shou0ld get the intelligence about the bride through expert and experienced ladies. Thereafter they shoud meet together in the presence of learned scholars and (the girl and the boy) should exchage their views with one another as under:

'O woman' or O man! ṛta (mahat-tattva that originated first from Prakṛti due to the union of Puruṣa and Prakṛti, according to the law of Sāṅkhya), which inherited in it satya (the imperishable Prakṛti constituted of three guṇas). As this universe has come into existence with the union of Prakṛti and Puruṣa, so we, the never married bachelors take the saṅkalpa to wed together. Let us accept each other, and have a firm courage to make this saṅkalpa a reality.

Procedure of Marriage Sanskāra

When the girl after discharge of monthly course comes to normalcy and on the day fixed for impregnation, all the necessary articles and material required for yajña should be arranged before hand. All the articles and yajña-material should be kept in safe custody after cleansing them; and yajñaśālā, vedi, yajña, priests of yajña, utensils required for yajña be settled and arranged as has been mentioned in the Sāmānya-prakaraṇa.

Thereafter, when one hour of night has passed, the bride and bride-groom should take bath with perfumed and clean water chanting the following mantras:

ओं काम वेद ते नाम मदो नामासि समानयामुꣵसुरा ते अभवत्।
परमत्र जन्माग्रे तपसो निर्मितोऽसि स्वाहा ॥1॥ साम॰ मन्त्र ब्रा॰ 1.1.2

Oṁ kāma veda te nāma mado nāmāsi samānayāmu ꣵ surā te abhavat,

paramatra janmāgne tapaso nirmito'si svāhā ॥ Sām.MBr. 1.1.2

[Meaning] O 00lord of sexual desire! Whole world knows you. You are famous as sexual urge. This girl has become a means of sexual urge. O sexual urge, you have your birth in the women folk. You have been created to carry on the duties of Gṛhasthāśrama.

ओं इमं त उपस्थं मधुना सꣵसृजामि प्रजापतेर्मुखमेतद् द्वितीयम्। तेन पुꣵसोभिभवासि सर्वानवशान्वशिन्यसि राज्ञि स्वाहा ॥ साम॰ मन्त्र ब्रा॰ 1.1.3

Oṁ imaṁ ta upasthaṁ madhunā sa ꣵ sṛjāmi prajāpatermukhametad dvitīyam, tena pu ꣵ sobhibhavāsi sarvānavaśānvaśinyasi rājñi svāhā. Sām.MBr. 1.1.3

[Meaning] O bride! Your reproductive organs have been created with sexual drive. This is the second outlet to enter into the Gṛhastha life. Through this organ you cast a spell on a person who could not be influenced by anybody. You are the subjugating entity and the mistress of the house.

ओम् अग्रि क्रव्यादमकृण्वन् गुहानाः स्त्रीणामुपस्थमृषयः पुराणाः।
तेनाज्यमकृण्वꣳ त्रैश्रृङ्गं त्वाष्ट्रं त्वयि तद्दधातु स्वाहा॥ गोपथ, 2.1.10

Om agni kravyādamakṛṇvan guhānāḥ strīṇāmupasthamṛṣayaḥ purāṇāḥ, tenājyamakṛṇvaꣳ traiśṛṅgaṁ tvāṣṭraṁ tvayi taddadhātu svāhā. Go.GS. 2.1.10

[Meaning] The philosophers and ancient seers call the reproductive organs of women as the kravyāda agni. They have also defined the semen, having productive power, ejected through the genitals of men as fluid like ghee. Let the man deposit the semen into your reproductive organ for getting progeny.

Therafter, the bride dressed in decorated outfits and ornaments should sit on a nice seat keeping her face eastwards.

Afterwards according to the procedure described in the Sāmānya Prakaraṇa, Īśvara-stuti, Prārthanā, Upāsana, Svastivāchana and0 Śānti mantars should be chaned. Thereafter, Agnyādhāna, Samidādhāna should be performed and cereals already prepared should be kept aside on the vedī. In the same manner the bride-groom also should put on nice dress and ornaments and sit on a decorated seat in the yajñaśālā keeping his face eastward. He should also perform the procedure of Īśvara-stuti, Prārthanā and Upāsana and get ready to go to the house of bride. Afterwards, the family members of bride and the family members of bride-groom lead bridegroom with respect to the house of bride. At the time when bride-groom enters into the house of bride, the bride and her family membrs should receive him by offering Madhuparka. The bride-groom on entering the house of bride should stand there keeping his face eastward and the bride and her family members should stand near bridegroom keeping their faces northwards. The bride and her family members should utter

ओं साधु भवानास्तामर्चयिष्यामो भवन्तम् ॥

Oṁ sādhu bhavānāstāmarchayiṣyāmo bhavantam.

[Meaning] Kindly stay here, we would receive you.

The bride-groom should say-

ओम् अर्चय ॥

Om archaya.

Thanks; please do.

Thereafter the bride should ask the bride-groom to take his seat, prepared for the purpose by saying-

ओं विष्टरो विष्टरो विष्टरः प्रतिगृह्यताम् ॥

Oṁ viṣṭaro viṣṭaro viṣṭaraḥ pratigṛhyatām.

Here is the seat, kindly accept it.

Bride-groom should thank her saying:

ओं प्रतिगृह्णामि ॥

Oṁ pratigṛhṇāmi.

Thanks.

The bride-groom should sit on the seat with his face eastward chanting the following mantra:

ओं वर्ष्मोऽस्मि समानानामुद्यतामिव सूर्यः ।

इमन्तमभितिष्ठामि यो मा कश्चाभिदासति ॥ पारस्कर गृसू. 1.3.8

Oṁ varṣmo'smi samānānāmudyatāmiva sūryaḥ,

imantamabhitiṣṭhāmi yo mā kaśchābhidāsati. Pār.GS. 1.3.8

[Meaning] I, at this juncture, hold superiority amongst my equal like the sun amongst stars (constellations). To him who tries to humiliate me, I will let down like this seat upon which I am sitting.

Men from bride's family should give a small pot full of water in the hand of bride and she should say:

ओं पाद्यं पाद्यं पाद्यं प्रतिगृह्यताम् ॥ पारस्कर गृसू. 1.3.9

Oṁ pādyaṁ pādyaṁ pādyaṁ pratigṛhyatām. Pār.GS. 1.3.9

[Meaning] Here is water to wash feet, kindly accept it.

Bride-groom replies-

ओं प्रतिगृह्णामि ॥

Oṁ pratigṛhṇāmi.

Thanks.

Bride-groom should take the pot of water from the hand of bride and wash his feet uttering the following mantra:

ओं विराजो दोहोऽसि विराजो दोहमशीय मयि पाद्यायै विराजो दोहः ॥

पारस्कर गृसू. 1.3.12

Oṁ virājo doho'si virājo dohamaśīya mayi pādyāyai virājo dohaḥ. Pār. GS. 1.3.12

[Meaning] O waters! you are the essence of various vegetations on the earth. May I obtain you, the essence of vegetations, for the removal of diseases. You, the essence of vegetations, are present here for protecting my feet.

Afterwards, family members of the bride should give another pot full of clean water to bride and she should say:

ओम् अर्घोर्घोऽर्घः प्रतिगृह्यताम् ॥

Om arghorgho'rghaḥ pratigṛhyatām.

[Meaning] Here is water to wash the face, kindly accept it. The bride-groom taking water from brides's hand replies:

ओं प्रतिगृह्णामि ॥

Oṁ pratigṛhṇāmi.

Thanks.

The bride-groom should wash his face and utter the following mantra.

ओम् आप स्थ युष्माभिः सर्वान्कामानवाप्नवानि ॥
ओं समुद्रं वः प्रहिणोमि स्वां योनिमभिगच्छत ।
अरिष्टास्माकं वीरा मा परासेचि मत्पयः ॥ पारस्कर गृसू. 1.3.13; 14

Om āpa stha yuṣmābhiḥ sarvānkāmānavāpnavāni.
Oṁ samudraṁ vaḥ prahiṇomi svāṁ yonimabhigachchhata,
ariṣṭāsmākaṁ vīrā mā parāsechi matpayaḥ. Pār.GS. 1.3.13; 14

[Meaning] O waters! you are the harbinger of health. Through you I obtain the health. You are drafted up the sky by the radiation heating of the sun, so that you may fall back to your source (oceaninc waters on the earth) in a potable sate. Our children enjoy health and pleasure by the grace of God. These waters may not leave us.

Afterwards, the bride-groom should take his seat in the west of the maṇḍapa keeping his face eastward. Bride's family members should give her a small pot full of clean and pure water with a sipping spoon in the pot and the bride should offer it to the bride-groom uttering the following mantra:

ओम् आचमनीयमाचमनीयमाचमनीयम्प्रतिगृह्यताम् ॥

Om āchamanīyamāchamanīyamāchamanīyampratigṛhyatām.

[Meaning] Please accept this water for sipping, kindly accept it.

The bridegroom taking the pot from bride, says:

ओं प्रतिगृह्णामि ॥

Oṁ pratigṛhṇāmi.

Thanks.

The bride-groom should take the pot of water from the bride and put it before him. Taking water in the palm of right hand the bride-groom should utter the following mantra and sip it. He should utter the mantra thrice and sip water accordingly,

ओम् आ मागन् यशसा सꣳसृज वर्चसा। तं मा कुरु प्रियं प्रजानामधिपतिं पशूनामरिष्टिं तनूनाम् ॥ पारस्कर गृसू. 1.3.15

Om ā māgan yaśasā saꣳsṛja varchasā, taṁ mā kuru priyaṁ prajānāmadhipatiṁ paśūnāmariṣṭiṁ tanūnām. Pār.GS.1.3.15

[Meaning] O God! Please come to us with your great splendour, make us accomplished with your effulgence. By your grace, may we be affectionate to our children; may we be the dometicator of animals like cow etc. and be the protector of our body and its parts.

Afterwards, bride's family members should give the pot of madhuparka to her and she should extend it towards the bride-groom saying:

ओम् मधुपर्को मधुपर्को मधुपर्कः प्रतिगृह्यताम् ॥

Om   madhuparko   madhuparko   madhuparkaḥ pratigṛhyatām.

Here is madhuparka (mixture of curd and honey) kindly accept it.

The bride-groom taking the pot of Madhuparka from the hand of bride replies:

ओम् प्रतिगृह्णामि ॥

Om pratigṛhṇāmi.

Thanks, I am happy to accept it.

The bride-groom should utter the following sentence and minutely look at Madhuparka

ओम् मित्रस्य त्वा चक्षुषा प्रतीक्षे ॥ पारस्कर गृसू. 1.3.16

Om mitrasya tvā chakṣuṣā pratīkṣe ॥ Pār.GS. 1.3.16

[Meaning] I glance at you with friendly eyes.

ओ देवस्य त्वा सवितुः प्रसवेऽश्विनोर्बाहुभ्यां पूष्णो हस्ताभ्यां प्रतिगृह्णामि ॥

यजु० 1.10; पारस्कर गृसू. 1.3.17

O devasya tvā savituḥ prasave'śvirnorbāhubhyāṁ pūṣṇo hastābhyāṁ pratigṛhṇāmi. YV. 1.10; Pār.GS. 1.3.17

[Meaning] I hold you with arms of Aśvinis and hands of Pūṣā under the domain of sun.

The bride-groom should utter the following three mantras and glance at the madhuparka carefully:

ओं भूर्भुवः स्वः। मधु वाता ऋतायते मधु क्षरन्ति सिन्धवः। माध्वीर्नः सन्त्वोषधीः ॥ यजु० 13.27

Om bhūrbhuvaḥ svaḥ, madhu vātā ṛtāyate madhu kṣaranti sindhavaḥ, mādhvīrnaḥ santvoṣadhīḥ. YV. 13.27

Om is existent, conscious and all-bliss. For us who strictly adhere to the laws of nature and dictates of Brahman, sweet breeze blows, sweet is the flow of rivers and herbs are full fo sweetness.

ओं भूर्भुवः स्वः। मधु नक्तमुतोषसो मधुमत्पार्थिवं रजः। मधु द्यौरस्तु नः पिता ॥ यजु० 13.28

Om bhūrbhuvaḥ svaḥ, madhu naktamutoṣaso madhumatpārthivaṁ rajaḥ, madhu dyauerastu naḥ pitā.

YV. 13.28

Oṁ is existent conscious and all-bliss. For us, night is sweet and so is the dawn. Sweet is the earth and sweet is the space which is the protector of all.

ओं भूर्भुवः स्वः। मधुमान्नो वनस्पतिर्मधुमाँ अस्तु सूर्यः। माध्वीर्गावो भवन्तु नः॥ यजु० 13.29

Oṁ   bhūrbhuvaḥ   svaḥ,   madhuāmānno vanaspatirmadhumāṁ astu sūryaḥ, mādhvīrgāvo bhavantu naḥ. YV. 13.29

Oṁ is existent, conscious and all bliss. The vegetables are sweet for us and so is the sun. Rays of sun are also sweet for us.

Thereafter, the bridegroom should mix the honey with curd thrice with the second finger and the thumb of the right hand and utter the following mantra:

ओं नमः श्यावास्यायान्नशने यत्ते आविद्धं तत्ते निष्कृन्तामि।

Oṁ namaḥ śyāvāsyāyānnaśane yatte āviddhaṁ tatte niṣkṛntāmi,

The madhuparka is food for the energizing the digestive system. I take away from it any thing uneatable that is mixed herein.

The bride-groom should churn the madhuparka three times with the second finger and the thumb of right hand chanting the above mantra. He should take a minute part of madhuparka and sprinkle it with the following mantras in all directions:

ओं वसवस्त्वा गायत्रेणच्छन्दसा भक्षयन्तु॥1॥

Oṁ vasavastvā gāyatreṇachchhandasā bhakṣayantu ॥1॥

[Meaning] Let Vasus (Brahmachārīs of 24 years of age) eat you uttering the Gāyatrī Chhanda.

Note: Gāyatrī Chhanda has 24 syllables, three pādas (quarters) of 8 (vasu) syllables each.

By this sprinkle in the East.

ओं रुद्रास्त्वा त्रैष्टुभेनच्छन्दसा भक्षयन्तु ॥2॥

Oṁ rudrāstvā traiṣṭubhenachchhandasā bhakṣayantu ॥2॥

[Meaning] Let Rudras (Brahmachārīs of 44 years of age) eat you uttering the Triṣṭup Chhanda.

Note: Triṣṭup Chhanda has 44 syllables, four pādas (quarters) of 11 (rudra) syllables each.

By this, sprinkle in the South.

ओम् आदित्यास्त्वा जागतेनच्छन्दसा भक्षयन्तु ॥3॥

Oṁ ādityāstvā jāgatenachchhandasā bhakṣayantu ॥3॥

[Meaning] Let Ādityas (Brahmachārīs of 48 years of age) eat you uttering the Jagati Chhanda.

Note: Jagati Chhanda has 48 syllables, four pādas (quarters) of 12 (āditya) syllables each.

By this, sprinkle in the West.

ओं विश्वे त्वा देवा आनुष्टभेनच्छन्दसा भक्षयन्तु ॥4॥

*Oṁ viśve tvā devā ānuṣṭabhenachchhandasā
bhakṣayantu ॥4॥*

[Meaning] Let all scholars eat you uttering the Anuṣṭup Chhanda.

Note: Anuṣṭup Chhanda has 32 syllables, four pādas (quarters) of 8 syllables each.

By this, sprinkle in the North.

ओं भूतेभ्यस्त्वा परिगृह्णामि ॥ आश्व० गृसू० 1.24.14-15

Oṁ bhūtebhyastvā parigṛhṇāmi. āśva0 gṛsū0 1.24.14-15

[Meaning] I accept you for all Bhūtās.

By this, in the above direction, three times.

Then, the bride-groom divides the madhuparka in

three parts, should put these parts in three bronze dishes separately. He should put these three dishes in front of him and utter the following mantra: he should eat a little or the whole of the madhuparka from each of the three dishes. The remaining part should be distributed among servants or be dropped in water:

ओं यन्मधुनो मधव्यं परमꣳरूपमन्नाद्यम्। तेनाहं मधुनो मधव्येन परमेण रूपेणान्नाद्येन परमो मधव्योऽन्नादोऽसानि॥ पार॰ 1.3

Oṁ yanmadhuno madhavyaṁ paramaꣳrūpamannādyam ǀ tenāhaṁ madhuno madhavyena paramena rūpeṇānnādyena paramo madhavyo'nnādo'sāni. Pār.GS. 1.3

[Meaning] O learned men! Pure honey procured from flowers is worthy to be eaten like all cereals. Let me be the consumer of the pure honey of flowers, eatable like all cereals.

Thereafter, the bride-groom should sip water twice by the following mantras one by each:

ओम् अमृतापिधानमसि स्वाहा॥ आश्व॰ गृसू॰ 1.24.21

Om amṛtāpidhānamasi svāhā. Āśv.GS. 1.24.21

[Meaning] O Immortalized energy [prakṛti], you act as the protective shield like that of a shawl. (First Sip)

ओं सत्यं यशः श्रीर्मयि श्रीः श्रयतां स्वाहा॥ आश्व॰ गृसू॰ 1.24.12

Om satyaṁ yaśaḥ śrīrmayi śrīḥ śrayatāṁ svāhā.

Āśv.GS. 1.24.12

[Meaning] May, the truth, fame and spiritual wealth and prosperity ever be with us. (second Sip)

After this, the bride-groom should touch his body parts like eyes etc. with water by the mantras prescribed for this purpose in the Havana.

Thereafter the bride should gift to the bride-groom cow and money etc. as per her capability uttering the following sentence:

ओं गौर्गौर्गौः प्रतिगृह्यताम् ॥

Om gaurgaurgauḥ pratigṛhyatām

[Meaning] Here is the cow or money, kindly accept it.

The bride-groom should accept it by uttering-

ओं प्रतिगृह्णामि ॥

Om pratigṛhṇāmi

Thanks, I accept it.

The person entrusted to accomplish the ceremonial work of the bride's party should take the bride-groom from (Sabhā-maṇḍpa-sthān) gathering hall or the place where madhiparka ceremony took place to the house and seat him keeping his face in the east direction and seat the bride before him (the bride-groom). He himself sit there keeping his face in the north direction and pronounce the following sentence:

ओम् अमुक गौत्रोत्पन्नामिमाममुकनाम्रीम्लङ्कृतां कन्यां प्रतिगृह्णातु भवान् ॥

Om amuka gautrotpannāmimāmamukanāmnīmlaṅkṛtāṁ kanyāṁ pratigṛhṇātu bhavān.

[Meaning] Kindly accept this girl named so and so, born in such and such family.

Note: In the place of ...... bride's name should be pronounced. In the place of .... the name of the bride should be pronounced in objective case.

Pronouncing the sentence ओम् अमुक गौत्रोत्पन्नाम् the concerned person from bride's party (parent or other relative) stretching right palm of the bride-groom put the palm of bride therein and then bride-groom say:

ओं प्रतिगृह्णामि ॥

Oṁ pratigṛhṇāmi.

Thanks, I accept her.

Thereafter the bride-groom should give to bride the best attires and (upavastra) upper clothing respectively with the following mantras:

ओं जरां गच्छ परिधत्स्व वासौ भवाकृष्टीनामभिशस्तिपावा। शतं च जीव शरदः सुवर्चा रयिं च पुत्राननुसंव्ययस्वायुष्मतीदं परिधत्स्व वासः ॥

पारस्कर गृसू. 1.4.12

Oṁ jarāṁ gachchha paridhatsva vāsau bhavākṛṣṭīnāmabhiśastipāvā, śataṁ cha jīva śaradaḥ suvarchā rayiṁ cha putrānanusaṁvyayasvāyuṣmatīdaṁ paridhatsva vāsaḥ.

Pār.GS.1.4.13

[Meaning] O bride! You attain the indefectible maturity of oldness with me, put on this cloth and be well-wisher of mankind, endowed with the resplendency of household life, acquire wealth, accompained by the boon of children; and O lady! blessed with long life, you put on this cloth.

ओं या अकृन्तन्नवयन् या अतन्वत याश्च देवीस्तन्तूनभितो ततन्थ। तास्त्वा देवीर्जरसे संव्ययस्वायुष्मतीदं परिधत्स्व वासः ॥ पार॰ गृसू॰ 1.4.13

Oṁ yā akṛntannavayan yā atanvata yāścha devīstantūnabhito tatantha, tāstvā devīrjarase saṁvyayasvāyuṣmatīdaṁ paridhatsva vāsaḥ. Pār.GS.1.4.13

[Meaning] O bride! Blessed with long life, put on also this upavastra (upper clothing). These ladies of my family who prepared fabrics, spun the thread and wove this cloth, and who in the process of weaving stretched and arranged the knot of warp and weft, may provide you the cloth till the attainment of indefectible maturity of oldness.

The bride-groom should dress himself with the vastra (lower outfit) and upavastra (upper outfit) respectively by the following mantras:

परिधास्यै यशोधास्यै दीर्घायुत्वाय जरदष्टिरस्मि।

शतं च जीवामि शरदः पुरूची रायस्पोषमभिसंव्ययिष्ये ॥ पार० 2.6.20

paridhāsyai yaśodhāsyai dīrghāyutvāya jaradaṣṭirasmi,
śataṁ cha jīvāmi śaradaḥ purūchī
rāyaspoṣamabhisaṁvyayiṣye. Pār.GS. 2.6.20

[Meaning] Just to cover my body, for my status, long life and material and spiritual prosperity, I put on clothes decently, because, having attained prosperity and progeny, I aspire to live the old age as a hale and hearty man. May God bless me a life of 100 years.

ओं यशसा मा द्यावापृथिवी यशसेन्द्राबृहस्पती।

यशो भगश्च मा विन्ददृशो मा प्रतिपद्यताम् ॥ पार० 2.6.21

Oṁ yaśasā mā dyāvāpṛthivī yaśasendrābṛhaspatī,
yaśo bhagaścha mā vindadyaśo mā pratipadyatām.

Pār.GS. 2.6.21

[Meaning] O gentlemen! May I live between the earth and sun with name and fame; may the prosperity and scholarship come to me with name and fame; may worshipable Brahman bless me with name and fame. May all of you also bless me with name and fame.

When the bride and bride-groom are engaged in changing their dresses, the preparation should be made and the following items should be arranged:

1. Wood-sticks for yajña should be kept reserved in sufficient quantity.

2. With Camphor or ghee the fire in the Kuṇḍa should be kindled.

3. Ghee should be molten and perfumed with the necessary yajña dravyas.

4. Spoon for offering oblations and other pots of yajña

should be arranged.

5. Havana Sāmagrī should be kept safe for the yajña.

6. One man from the party of bride-groom dressed neatly and cleanly, taking a jug full of water should circumambulate the yajña kuṇḍa and should sit in the south direction keeping his face in the north and having placed the jug in his front. He should sit there till the completion of marriage ceremony.

7. Similarly another person from the bride-groom's party taking a stick in his hand should sit in the south direction keeping his face in the north.

8. Bride's real brother or cousin brother or the son of maternal uncle, or the son of mother's sister as the case may be should sit there in the west direction of the vedī keeping four handful of roasted paddy for bride and bride-groom.

Afterwards escorted by the person entrusted with the ceremony, the bride should come before the bride-groom and both the bride and bride-groom should pronounce the following mantra:

ओं समंजन्तु विश्वे देवाः समापो हृदयानि नौ ।
सं मातरिश्वा सं धाता समुदेष्ट्री दधातु नौ ॥ ऋग्वेद 10.85.47

Oṁ samaṁjantu viśve devāḥ samāpo hṛdayāni nau,
saṁ mātariśvā saṁ dhātā samudeṣṭrī dadhātu nau ||1 ||

Ṛgveda 10.85.47

[Meaning] Let all the learned persons present here know that we are accepting each other voluntarily and pleasantly and our hearts are concordant and united like waters, let the air, Brahman, and the instructor keep us conjugated.

The bride-groom, taking the right hand of the bride into his own right hand and chanting the following mantra, should come to the yajñavedī:

ओं यदैषि मनसा दूरं दिशोऽनुपवमानो वा।
हिरण्यपर्णो वैकर्णः स त्वा मन्मनसां करोतु असौ ॥ पार॰ 1.4.15

Oṁ yadaiṣi manasā dūraṁ diśo'nupavamāno vā,
hiraṇyaparṇo vaikarṇaḥ sa tvā manmanasāṁ karotu asau.

Pār.GS. 1.4.15

The name of the bride should be uttered instead of असौ.

O bride or bride-groom! You voluntarily and mindfully approach one another like the wind and resplendent sun approach various directions from a great distance. May Brahman make both of us of concordant and united mind.

Afterwards the bride-groom should chant the following mantras:

ओं भूर्भुवः स्वः। अघोरचक्षुरपतिघ्येधि शिवा पशुभ्यः सुमनाः सुवर्चाः।
वीरसूर्देवकामा स्योना शन्नो भवद्विपदे शं चतुष्पदे ॥ ऋग्वेद 10.85.44

Oṁ bhūrbhuvaḥ svaḥ, aghorachakṣurapatighnyedhi śivā
paśubhyaḥ sumanāḥ suvarchāḥ, vīrasūrdevṛkāmā syonā śanno
bhavadvipade śaṁ chatuṣpade. Ṛgveda 10.85.44

[Meaning] O bride! By the grace of Brahman who is existent, conscious and all-bliss, you may not be ungenial in temperament and rigorous eyed towards husband. May you be benevolent to animals, and be conscientious, delighted at mind and possessed of gracious energy. May you be procreant of brave offsprings, desirous of divinity, and be bestower of happiness. May you be favourable to our bipends and kind to our quadrupeds.

ओं भूर्भुवः स्वः। स नः पूषा शिवतमामैरय सा न ऊरू उशती विहर।
यस्यामुशन्तः प्रहराम शेफं यस्यामु कामा बहवो विनिष्ठ्यै ॥ पारस्कर 1.4.16

Oṁ bhūrbhuvaḥ svaḥ, sa naḥ pūṣā śivatamāmairaya sā na

ūrū uśatī vihara, yasyāmuśantaḥ praharāma śephaṁ yasyāmu kāmā bahavo viniṣṭyai. Pār.GS. 1.4.16

[Meaning] May Brahman, the sustainer of creation, make this bride that ideal custodian of maternity who abiding with the sacrosanctity of the proceative function of the household life submits herself to her husband's impregnation and in whom are destined many desired ends of life.

Afterwards bride-groom and bride circumambulate the yajñakuṇḍa and take their seat at previously fixed place in such a manner as the bride, keeping her face in the east be in the right of the bride-groom and bride-groom on the left side of bride. The bride should chant the following mantra:

ओं प्र मे पतियानः पन्थाः कल्पताꣳशिवा अरिष्टा पतिलोकं गमेयम् ॥

साम मन्त्रब्रा॰ 1.1.8; गोभिल गृ.सू. 2.1.27

Oṁ pra me patiyānaḥ panthāḥ kalpatāꣳśivā ariṣṭā patilokaṁ gameyam. Sām.MBr. 1.1.8; Go.GS. 2.1.27

[Meaning] May this path of mine leading to husband-hood be auspicious and let me, unobstructed and free, go to husband's home.

The Main Homa of marriage ceremony: The following rites should be done in connection with the main homa of marriage ceremony.

Purohita: Priest to conduct the ceremony should be selected and appoined. He should take seat in the south of the vedī keeping his face in the north direction.

1. Āchamana (sipping of water) should be done with ओम्꣠ अमृतोपस्तरणमसि स्वाहा (*Om amṛtopastaraṇamasi svāhā*) etc. mantras.

2. Samidādhāna and agnyādhāna etc. should be done according to Sāmānya yajña procedure.

3. Sprinkling of water round the vedī with ओम् अदितेऽनुमन्यस्व *(Om adite'numanyasva)*, etc. four mantras.

4. आघारावाज्याभागाहुति *(Āghārāvājyābhagāhuti)*, व्याहृति *(vyāhṛti)*, आहुति *(āhuti)* and अष्टाज्याहुति *(aṣṭājyāhuti)* should be offered.

After performing all these above acts the bride should touch the right shoulder of bridegroom. Thereafter they should offer the four oblations of molten ghee with the four mantras - अग्न आयूंषि *(agna āyūṁṣi)* etc. They should offer the fifth oblation with the following mantra:

ओं भूर्भुवः स्वः । त्वमर्यमा भवसि यत्कनीनां नाम स्वधावनगुह्यं बिभर्षि । अंजन्ति मित्रं सुधितं न गोभिर्यद्दम्पती समनसा कृणोषि स्वाहा ॥ इदमग्रये-इदन्न मम ॥ ऋ० 5.3.2

Om bhūrbhuvaḥ svah, tvamaryamā bhavasi yatkanīnāṁ nāma svadhāvanguhyaṁ bibharṣi, aṁjanti mitraṁ sudhitaṁ na gobhiryaddampatī samanasā kṛṇoṣi svāhā. idamagnaye-idanna mama. RV. 5.3.2

Paramātmā is existent, conscious and all-bliss. This fire or heat which has its connection with girl is the most controlling power in the body. It consumes the oblations of cereal etc. and has a mysterious name- the Vaiśvānara.

Performers of yajñas keep this clandestine fire ablaze with ghee etc. like friend, as it makes the married couple of concordant mind.

The Ajyāhuti oblations should be offered in the fire of the vedī with the following twelve mantras:

ओम् ऋताषाड् ऋतधामाग्निर्गन्धर्वः । स न इदं ब्रह्म क्षत्रं पातु तस्मै स्वाहा वाट् ॥ इदमृताषाहे ऋतधाम्ने अग्रये गन्धर्वाय इदन्न मम ॥1॥

Om ṛtāṣāḍ ṛtadhāmāgnirgandharvah, sa na idaṁ brahma kṣatraṁ pātu tasmai svāhā vāṭ. idamṛtāṣāhe ṛtadhāmne agnaye gandharvāya idanna mama ॥1॥

[Meaning] (agni) Brahmachārī is of the form of Agni. (ṛtāṣāḍ) He Abides by the command of Brahman, and (ṛtdhāma) holds the effulgence of Brahman, (gandharvaḥ) He keeps his senses under control. May he be the (pātu) protector of Brāhma and Kṣātra power in our society or state. This oblation is meant for Brahmachārī who (ṛtāṣāha) obeys the command of Brahman, (ṛtadhāma) holds the effulgence of Brahman, and (gandharva) keeps his senses under control; it is it is not for me.

ओम् ऋतषाड् ऋतधामाग्निर्गन्धर्वस्तस्यौषधयोऽपृसरसो मुदो नाम। ताभ्यः स्वाहा॥ इदमोषधिभ्योऽप्सरोभ्यो मुद्भ्यः इदन्न मम ॥2॥

Om ṛtāṣāḍ ṛtadhāmāgnirgandharvastasyauṣadhayo'saraso mudo nāma, tābhyaḥ svāhā. idamoṣadhibhyo'psarobhyo mudbhyaḥ- idanna mama ॥2॥

[Meaning] (agni) Brahmachārī is of the form of Agni. (ṛtāṣād) He Abides by the command of Brahman, and (ṛtdhāma) holds the effulgence of Brahman, (gandharvaḥ) he keeps his senses under control. The herbs, waters and happiness are the necessities for him. This oblation is meant for them. It is for herbs, waters and happiness and not for me.

ओं सꣳहितो विश्वसामा सूर्यो गन्धर्वः। स न इदं ब्रह्म क्षत्रं पातु तस्मै स्वाहा वाट्॥ इदं सꣳहिताय विश्वसाम्ने सूर्याय गन्धर्वाय-इदन्न मम ॥3॥

Om saꣳhito viśvasāmā sūryo gandharvaḥ, sa na idaṃ brahma kṣatraṃ pātu tasmai svāhā vāṭ. idaṃ saꣳhitāya viśvasāmne sūryāya gandharvāya-idanna mama ॥3॥

[Meaning] (sūryaḥ) The sun (saṅhitaḥ) is the maker of twilight hours between day and night, (viśvasāmā) it gives peace to to the whole world, (gandharvaḥ) it sustains earth. May it (pātu) protect Brāhma and Kṣātra power in our society or state. It is meant for sun that makes twilight hours, gives peace in the world, and sustains earth and not for me.

ओं सꣳहितो विश्वसामा सूर्यो गन्धर्वस्तस्य मरीचयोऽप्सरसऽआयुवो नाम।
ताभ्यः स्वाहा॥ इदं मरीचिभ्योऽप्सरोभ्य आयुभ्यः-इदन्न मम॥4॥

Oṁ saꣳśito viśvasāmā sūryo gandharvastasya marīchayo'psarasa'āyuvo nāma, tābhyaḥ svāhā. idaṁ marīchibhyo'psarobhya āyubhyaḥ-idanna mama ॥4॥

[Meaning] (sūryaḥ) The sun (saṅhitaḥ) is the maker of twilight hours between day and night, (viśvasāmā) it gives peace to tó the whole world, (gandharvaḥ) it sustains earth. Its rays called apsarā gives life to all beings. Let me offer oblation for them. It is meant for rays of sun called apsarā that give life for all.

ओं सुषुम्णः सूर्यरश्मिश्चन्द्रमा गन्धर्वः। स न इदं ब्रह्म क्षत्रं पातु तस्मै स्वाहा
वाट्॥ इदं सुषुम्णाय सूर्यरश्मये चन्द्रमसे गन्धर्वाय-इदन्न मम॥5॥

Oṁ suṣumṇaḥ sūryaraśmiśchandramā gandharvaḥ, sa na idaṁ brahma kṣatram pātu tasmai svāhā vāṭ. idaṁ suṣumṇāya sūryaraśmaye chandramase gandharvāya-idanna mama ॥5॥

[Meaning] (sūryaraśmiḥ) Illuminated by the rays of sun the (suṣumṇaḥ) pleasent (chandramā) moon becomes gandharva (sustained by sun). May it (pātu) protect Brāhma and Kṣātra power in our society or state. This oblation is meant moon. It is for pleasent moon that draws its light from sun and not for me.

ओं सुषुम्णः सूर्यरश्मिश्चन्द्रमा गन्धर्वस्तस्य नक्षत्राण्यप्सरसो भेकुरयो नाम।
ताभ्यः स्वाहा॥ इदं नक्षत्रेभ्योऽप्सरोभ्यो भेकुरिभ्यः-इदन्न मम॥6॥

Oṁ suṣumṇaḥ sūryaraśmiśchandramā gandharvastasya nakṣatrāṇayapsaraso bhekurayo nāma, tābhyaḥ svāhā. idaṁ nakṣatrebhyo'psarobhyo bhekuribhyaḥ-idanna mama ॥6॥

Meaning] (suṣumṇaḥ) pleasent (chandramā) moon (sūryaraśmiḥ) draws its light from sun, so it is called gandharva (that holds the rays of sun). Constellations located in space are (bhekurayah) milestones for it. This oblation is offered to constellations. It is meant for constellations which act as milestones for moon loacted in space and not for me.

ओम् इषिरो विश्व्यचा वातो गन्धर्वः। स न इदं ब्रह्म क्षत्रं पातु तस्मै स्वाहा वाट्॥ इदमिषिराय विश्वव्यचसे वाताय गन्धर्वाय-इदन्न मम ॥7॥

Om iṣiro viśvyachā vāto gandharvaḥ, sa na idaṁ brahma kṣatraṁ pātu tasmai svāhā vāṭ. idamiṣirāya viśvavyachase vātāya gandharvāya-idanna mama ॥7॥

[Meaning] Moving and all-pervading air is the gandharva (sustainer of life). May it (pātu) protect Brāhma and Kṣātra power in our society or state. This oblation is meant it. It is for moving, all-pervading air and not for me.

ओम् इषिरो विश्व्यचा वातो गन्धर्वस्तस्यापोऽअप्सरसऽऊर्ज्जो नाम। ताभ्यः स्वाहा। इदमद्भ्योऽप्सरोभ्य ऊर्ग्भ्यः-इदन्न मम ॥8॥

Om iṣiro viśvyachā vāto gandharvastasyāpo'apsarasa'ūrjjo nāma, tābhyaḥ svāhā, idamadbhyo'psarobhya ūrgbhyaḥ-idanna mama ॥8॥

[Meaning] Moving and all-pervading air is the gandharva (sustainer of life). (āph) Air-particles known as urja (source of energy or power) have their abode in sky. The oblation is offered for them. This oblation is meant for air-particles, called urja, located in sky.

ओं भुज्युः सुपर्णो यज्ञो गन्धर्वः। स न इदं ब्रह्म क्षत्रं पातु तस्मै स्वाहा वाट्। इदं भुज्यवे सुपर्णाय यज्ञाय गन्धर्वाय इदन्न मम ॥9॥

Oṁ bhujyuḥ suparṇo yajño gandharvaḥ, sa na idaṁ brahma kṣatram pātu tasmai svāhā vāṭ, idaṁ bhujyave suparṇāya yajñāya gandharvāya idanna mama ॥9॥

[Meaning] Yajña is (bhujyuh) protector of creation, (gandharvah) sustainer of creation and (suparṇah) provides the ceation tree with beautiful leaves. May it (pātu) protect Brāhma and Kṣātra powers this creation. This oblation is offered to it. It is meant for meant for yajña that is (bhujyuḥ) protector of creation, (gandharvaḥ) sustainer of creation and (suparṇaḥ) provides the creation tree with beautiful leaves and not for me (oblation giver).

ओं भुज्युः सुपर्णो यज्ञो गन्धर्वःस्तस्य दक्षिणा अप्सरस स्तावा नाम। ताभ्यः स्वाहा॥ इदं दक्षिणाभ्योऽप्सरोभ्यः स्तावाभ्यः-इदन्न मम ॥10॥

Oṁ bhujyuḥ suparṇo yajño gandharvaḥstasya dakṣiṇā apsarasa stāvā nāma, tābhyaḥ svāhā. idaṁ dakṣiṇābhyo'psarobhyaḥ stāvābhyaḥ-idanna mama ॥10॥

[Meaning] Yajña is (bhujyuḥ) protector of all creatures, (gandharvaḥ) it is sustainer of creation and (suparṇaḥ) provides the earth with beautiful trees, plants and herbs. (tasya) Its (dakṣiṇā) fruit called (stāvā) thundering clouds is located in mid-sphere. This oblation is offered to them. It is meant for dakṣiṇa (fruit) of yajña called (stāvā) thundering clouds located in mid-sphere and not for me (oblation giver).

ओं प्रजापतिर्विश्वकर्मा मनो गन्धर्वः। स न इदं ब्रह्म क्षत्रं पातु तस्मै स्वाहा वाट्। इदं प्रजापतये विश्वकर्मणे मनसे गन्धर्वाय-इदन्न मम ॥11॥

Oṁ prajāpatirviśvakarmā mano gandharvaḥ, sa na idaṁ brahma kṣatraṁ pātu tasmai svāhā vāṭ, idaṁ prajāpataye viśvakarmaṇe manase gandharvāya-idanna mama ॥11॥

[Meaning] Mind is gandharva (sustainer) because it is master of all sense organs and plays a lead role in all actions. May this mind (pātu) protect Brāhma (intellectual) and Kṣātra (physical) powers of a human being. This oblation is offered to it. It is meant for gandharva mind, the master of all sense organs and playing a lead role in all actions. and not for me (oblation giver).

ओं प्रजापतिर्विश्वकर्मा मनो गन्धर्वस्तस्य ऋक्सामान्यप्सरस एष्टयो नाम।
ताभ्यः स्वाहा ॥ इदमृक्सामेभ्योऽप्सरोभ्य एष्टिभ्यः इदन्न मम ॥12॥

Oṁ prajāpatirviśvakarmā mano gandharvastasya ṛksāmānyapsarasa ēṣṭayo nāma, tābhyaḥ svāhā. idamṛksāmebhyo'psarobhya ēṣṭibhyaḥ-idanna mama ॥12॥

[Meaning] Mind is gandharva (sustainer) because it is master of all sense organs and plays a lead role in all actions. For mind, ṛchās (Ṛgveda mantras) and sāmans (Sāmaveda mantras) often known as (eṣṭayaḥ) means of prayer are located in space.

Note: In the beginning of creation, the Vedas existed in the form of vibrations, which were received by high profile seers in samādhi.

N.B. These oblations are called as Rāṣṭrabhṛta oblations. The security of Rāṣṭra is the main theme of them. Gṛhasthis are the pillar of nation. A Gṛhasthi is supposed to support the nationa and all three other Āśramas. So, Rāṣṭrabhṛta oblations have also been made the part of marriage ceremony to remind the wedded couple of their duty towards their nation in addtion to their family, society and environment around them. The security of a nation depends on the coordination of all the units of state. Household life is a small unit of society or state. House becomes an abode of bliss if there is coordination in the wife and husband. This is based on the firmess of conjugal coordination. Thus aiming at the security and safety of the state, great stress has been laid on the firmness of conjugal coordination through the education of permanent coordination of astronomical gandharva (sun) and apsarasas (sunrays). The married couple should learn a lesson from sun and its rays in maintaining close affinity between them.

With the following mantras oblations of Jaya homa

should be offered.

ओं चित्तं च स्वाहा ॥ इदं चित्ताय इदन्न मम ॥1॥

Oṁ chittaṁ cha svāhā. idaṁ chittāya-idanna mama ॥1॥

[Meaning] The oblation is offered to chitta (part of mind where information is stored). It is meant for chitta and not for me.

ओं चितिश्च स्वाहा ॥ इदं चित्त्यै-इदन्न मम ॥2॥

Oṁ chitiścha svāhā. idaṁ chittyai-idanna mama ॥2॥

[Meaning] This oblation is offered to chitti (information stored in mind). It is meant for chitti and not for me.

ओम् आकूतं च स्वाहा ॥ इदमाकूताय-इदन्न मम ॥3॥

Om ākūtaṁ cha svāhā. idamākūtāya-idanna mama ॥3॥

[Meaning] This oblation is offered to sense-organs. It is meant for akūta (sense organs) and not for me.

ओम् आकूतिश्च स्वाहा ॥ इदमाकूत्यै -इदन्न मम ॥4॥

Om ākūtiścha svāhā. idamākūtyai -idanna mama ॥4॥

[Meaning] This oblation offered to the objects of sense organs. It is meant for akūti (object of sense organs) and not for me.

ओं विज्ञातं च स्वाहा ॥ इदं विज्ञाताय-इदन्न मम ॥5॥

Oṁ vijñātaṁ cha svāhā. idaṁ vijñātāya-idanna mama ॥5॥

[Meaning] This oblation is offered to intellectual power. It is meant for vijñāta (intellectual power) and not for me.

ओं विज्ञातिश्च स्वाहा ॥ इदं विज्ञात्यै-इदन्न मम ॥6॥

Oṁ vijñātiścha svāhā. idaṁ vijñātyai-idanna mama ॥6॥

[Meaning] This oblation offered to what is obtained by intellectual power. It is meant for Vijñāti (what is obtained by intellectual power) and not for me.

ओं मनश्च स्वाहा ॥ इदं मनसे-इदन्न मम ॥7 ॥

Oṁ manaścha svāhā. idaṁ manase-idanna mama ॥7 ॥

[Meaning] This oblations is offered to manas (that part of mind which (saṅkalpa) gathers and (vikalpa) dispers information). It is meant for manas and not for me.

ओं शक्करीश्च स्वाहा ॥ इदं शक्करीभ्यः इदन्न मम ॥8 ॥

Oṁ śakvariścha svāhā. idaṁ śakvaribhyaḥ-idanna mama ॥8॥

[Meaning] This oblation is offered to the power of mind. It is meant for śakvari (power of mind) and not for me.

ओं दर्शश्च स्वाहा ॥ इदं दर्शाय-इदन्न मम ॥9 ॥

Oṁ darśaścha svāhā. idaṁ darśāya-idanna mama ॥9॥

[Meaning] This oblation is offered to new moon day. It is meant for darśa (new moon day) and not for me.

ओं पौर्णमासं च स्वाहा ॥ इदं पौर्णमासाय-इदन्न मम ॥10 ॥

Oṁ paurṇamāsaṁ cha svāhā. idaṁ paurṇamāsāya-idanna mama ॥10॥

[Meaning] This oblation is offered to full moon day. It is meant for Pūrṇamāsa (full moon day) and not for me.

ओं बृहच्च स्वाहा ॥ इदं बृहते-इदन्न मम ॥11 ॥

Oṁ bṛhachcha svāhā. idaṁ bṛhate-idanna mama ॥11॥

[Meaning] This oblation is offered to equinoctial days. It is meant for Bṛhat sāma (equinox) and not for me.

Note: Equator is called Bṛhat Sāma. Here Vernal are

Autumn Equinoxes and referred to.

ओं रथन्तरं च स्वाहा ॥ इदं रथन्तराय-इदन्न मम ॥ 12 ॥

Oṁ rathantaraṁcha svāhā. idaṁ rathantarāya-idanna mama ॥ 12 ॥

[Meaning] This oblation is offered to solstitial days. It is meant for Rathantara sāma (solstice) and not for me.

Note: Lines of Cancer and Capricorn are called Rathantara Sāma. Winter and Summer Solstices are referred to here.

ओं प्रजापतिर्जयानिन्द्राय वृष्णे प्रायच्छदुग्रः प्रतनाजयेषु। तस्मै विशः समनमन्त सर्वाः स उग्रः स इ हव्यो बभूव स्वाहा॥ इदं प्रजापतये जयानिन्द्राय-इदन्न मम ॥ 13 ॥ पारस्कर 1.5.8

Oṁ prajāpatirjayānindrāya vṛṣṇe prāyachchhadugraḥ pratanājayeṣu ı tasmai viśaḥ samanamanta sarvāḥ sa ugraḥ sa i havyo babhūva svāhā. idaṁ prajāpataye jayānindrāya-idanna mama ॥ 13 ॥ Pār.GS. 1.5.8

[Meaning] Brahman passed on Jaya mantras (mantras leading to victory in the battlefield of life) to particular souls, centre of life in the universe. Soul gains power to win over evil ideas with the help of Jaya mantras. That is why all the living beings subordinate them to soul. Soul is very powerful. It is worthy to receive mantars. The oblation offered is meant for Brahman, and the Jaya mantras passed on to Indra (soul) and not for me.

Afterwards the oblations of Abhyātana homa should be offered with the following mantras:

ओम् अग्निर्भूतानामधिपतिः स मावत्वस्मिन् ब्रह्मण्यस्मिन् क्षत्रेऽस्यामाशिष्यस्यां पुरोधायामस्मिन् कर्मण्यस्यां देवहूत्यांꣳ स्वाहा॥ इदमग्नये भूतानामधिपतये इदन्न मम ॥1॥

Om agnirbhūtānāmadhipatiḥ sa māvatvasmin brahmaṇyasmin kṣatre'syāmāśiṣyasyāṁ purodhāyāmasmin karmaṇyasyāṁ devahūtyāṁᵡ svāhā. idamagnaye bhūtānāmadhipataye-idanna mama ॥1॥

[Meaning] Agni (Jñānāgni) is the dominating power among the living beings. Let it be source of protection for us in our intellectual feats and let it be so in our administrative performances, let it be the source of protection in this auspicious act, let it be source of protection for this bride. Let it be source of protection in this marriage ceremony and let it be source of protection in this yajña wherein the oblations are offered for the natural powers and spiritual entities. The oblation offered is meant for Jñānāgni of living beings and not for me.

ओम् इन्द्रो ज्येष्ठानामधिपतिः स मावत्वस्मिन् ब्रह्मण्यस्मिन् क्षत्रेऽस्यामाशिष्यस्यां पुरोधायामस्मिन् कर्मण्यस्यां देवहूत्याᵡ स्वाहा ॥ इदमिन्द्राय ज्येष्ठानामधिपतये-इदन्न मम ॥2॥

Om indro jyeṣṭhānāmadhipatiḥ samāvatvasmin brahmaṇyasmin kṣatre'syāmāśiṣyasyāṁ purodhāyāmasmin karmaṇyasyāṁ devahūtyāᵡ svāhā. idamindrāya jyeṣṭhānāmadhipataye-idanna mama ॥2॥

[Meaning] Indra (mind) is the dominating power in all sense organs. Rest is like the previous one. The oblation offered is meant for the Jyeṣṭhādhipati Indra (mind dominating sense organs) and not for me.

ओं यमः पृथिव्याऽअधिपतिः स मावत्वस्मिन् ब्रह्मण्यस्मिन् क्षत्रेऽस्यामाशिष्यस्यां पुरोधायामस्मिन् कर्मण्यस्यां देवहूत्याᵡ स्वाहा ॥ इदं यमाय पृथिव्याअधिपतये-इदन्न मम ॥3॥

Oṁ yamaḥ pṛthivyā'dhipatiḥ sa māvatvasmin brahmaṇyasmin kṣatre'syāmāśiṣyasyāṁ purodhāyāmasmin karmaṇyasyāṁ devahūtyāᵡ svāhā. idaṁ yamāya pṛthivyāadhipataye-idanna mama ॥3॥

[Meaning-Social] Yama (discipline in state or society) is the mainstay on the earth. Rest is like the previous one. The oblation offered is meant for Prithvipati yama (discipline, the mainstay on the earth) and not for me.

[Meaning-Scientific] Yama (gravitationa pull of earth) is protector of life on earth. Rest is like the previous one. The oblation offered is meant for Prithvipati yama (gravitational pull of earth) and not for me.

ओं वायुरन्तरिक्षस्याधिपतिः स मावत्वस्मिन् ब्रह्मण्यस्मिन् क्षत्रेऽस्यामाशिष्यस्यां पुरोधायामस्मिन् कर्मण्यस्यां देवहूत्या॑ स्वाहा ॥ इदं यमाय पृथिव्याअधिपतये-इदन्न मम ॥4॥

Om vāyurantarikṣasyādhipatiḥ sa māvatvasmin brahmaṇyasmin kṣatre'syāmāśiṣyasyāṁ purodhāyāmasmin karmaṇyasyāṁ devahūtyā॑ svāhā. idaṁ yamāya pṛthivyāadhipataye-idanna mama ॥4॥

[Meaning] Vayu (air or magnetosphere of earth) is the protector of the atmosphere of earth. Rest is like previous one. The oblation offered is meant for antrikṣādhipati vayu (the protector of atmosphere of earth) and not for me.

ओं सूर्यो दिवोऽधिपतिः स मावत्वस्मिन् ब्रह्मण्यस्मिन क्षत्रेऽस्यामाशिष्यस्यां पुरोधायामस्मिन् कर्मण्यस्यां देवहूत्या॑ स्वाहा ॥ इदं सूर्याय दिवोऽधिपतये-इदन्न मम ॥5॥

Om sūryo divo'dhipatiḥ sa māvatvasmin brahmaṇyasmina kṣatre'syāmāśiṣyasyāṁ purodhāyāmasmin karmaṇyasyāṁ devahūtyā॑ svāhā. idaṁ sūryāya divo'dhipataye-idanna mama ॥5॥

[Meaning] Sūrya (the sun) is the lord of celestial region. Rest is like the previous one. The oblation offered is meant for (divo'dhipati Sūrya) the sun, the lord of celestial region and not for me.

ओं चन्द्रमा नक्षत्राणामधिपतिः स मावत्वस्मिन् ब्रह्मण्यस्मिन क्षत्रेऽस्यामाशिष्यस्यां पुरोधायामस्मिन् कर्मण्यस्यां देवहूत्या॑ स्वाहा ॥ इदं चन्द्रमसे

नक्षत्राणामधिपतये-इदन्न मम ॥6॥

Oṁ chandramā nakṣatrāṇāmadhipatiḥ sa māvatvasmin brahmaṇyasmin kṣatre'syāmāśiṣyasyāṁ purodhāyāmasmin karmaṇyasyāṁ devahūtyāꣳ svāhā. idaṁ chandramase nakṣatrāṇāmadhipataye-idanna mama ॥6॥

[Meaning] Chandramā (the moon) is the lord of stars. Rest is like the previous one. The oblation offered is meant for moon, the lord of stars and not for me.

ओं बृहस्पतिर्ब्रह्मणोऽधिपतिः स मावत्वस्मिन् ब्रह्मण्यस्मिन् क्षत्रेऽस्यामाशिष्यस्यां पुरोधायामस्मिन् कर्मण्यस्यां देवहूत्याꣳ स्वाहा ॥ इदं बृहस्पतये ब्रह्मणोऽधिपतये-इदन्न मम ॥7॥

Oṁ bṛhaspatirbrahmaṇo'dhipatiḥ sa māvatvasmin brahmaṇyasmin kṣatre'syāmāśiṣyasyāṁ purodhāyāmasmin karmaṇyasyāṁ devahūtyāꣳ svāhā. idaṁ bṛhaspataye brahmaṇo'dhipataye-idanna mama ॥7॥

[Meaning] Bṛhaspati (Brahman) is the lord of Brahmāṇḍa (universe). Rest is like the previous one. The oblation offered is meant for Brahman, the lord of universe and not for me.

ओं मित्रः सत्यानामधिपतिः स मावत्वस्मिन् ब्रह्मण्यस्मिन् क्षत्रेऽस्यामाशिष्यस्यां पुरोधायामस्मिन् कर्मण्यस्यां देवहूत्याꣳ स्वाहा ॥ इदं मित्राय सत्यानामधिपतये-इदन्न मम ॥8॥

Oṁ mitraḥ satyānāmadhipatiḥ sa māvatvasmin brahmaṇyasmin kṣatre'syāmāśiṣyasyāṁ purodhāyāmasmin karmaṇyasyāṁ devahūtyāꣳ svāhā. idaṁ mitrāya satyānāmadhipataye-idanna mama ॥8॥

[Meaning] (Mitra) Inactive energy (called prakṛti) particle is lord of (satya) prakṛti or inactive energy. Rest is like the previous one. The oblation offered is meant for (satyādhipati mitra) inactive energy particle, the lord of inactive energy and not for me.

Note: Prakṛti or inactive energy or non-baryonic energy is made of mitra (particles), when energy is activated, it is called baryonic energy, its particle is called varuṇa. Before comemncement of creation, Prakṛti (energy) remains in inactive state, it is activated by the will of Brahman. As such the particle of inactive energy is called mitra and active energy is called varuṇa. So, mitra is called lord of inactive energy.

ओं वरुणोऽपामधिपतिः स मावत्वस्मिन् ब्रह्मण्यस्मिन् क्षत्रेऽस्यामाशिष्यस्यां पुरोधायामस्मिन् कर्मण्यस्यां देवहूत्याꣳ स्वाहा। इदं वरुणायापामधिपतये-इदन्न मम ॥9॥

Oṁ varuṇo'pāmadhipatiḥ sa māvatvasmin brahmaṇyasmin kṣatre'syāmāśiṣyasyāṁ purodhāyāmasmin karmaṇyasyāṁ devahūtyāꣳ svāhā, idaṁ varuṇāyāpāmadhipataye-idanna mama ॥9॥

[Meaning] (Varuṇa) Active energy called vikṛti) particle is the lord of (apāṁ) active energy or baryonic energy. Rest is like the previous one. The oblation offered is meant for (apāmadhipati varuṇa) active energy particles and not for me.

ओं समुद्रः स्रोत्यानामधिपतिः स मावत्वस्मिन् ब्रह्मण्यस्मिन् क्षत्रेऽस्यामाशिष्यस्यां पुरोधायामस्मिन् कर्मण्यस्यां देवहूत्याꣳ स्वाहा॥ इदं समुद्राय स्रोत्यानामधिपतये-इदन्न मम ॥10॥

Oṁ samudraḥ srotyānāmadhipatiḥ sa māvatvasmin brahmaṇyasmin kṣatre'syāmāśiṣyasyāṁ purodhāyāmasmin karmaṇyasyāṁ devahūtyāꣳ svāhā. idaṁ samudrāya srotyānāmadhipataye-idanna mama ॥10॥

[Meaning] (Samudraḥ) The atmospheric ocean is the lord of waters on earth. Rest a like the previous one. The oblation offered is meant for (srotyādhipati samudra) atmopheric ocean and not for me.

ओं अन्नꣳ साम्राज्यानामधिपतिः तन्मावत्वस्मिन् ब्रह्मण्यस्मिन्

क्षत्रेऽस्यामाशिष्यस्यां पुरोधायामस्मिन् कर्मण्यस्यां देवहूत्याꣳ स्वाहा ॥ इदमन्नाय साम्राज्यानामधिपतये-इदन्न मम ॥11 ॥

Oṁ annaꣳ sāmrājyānāmadhipatiḥ tanmāvatvasmin brahmaṇyasmin kṣatre'syāmāśiṣyasyāṁ purodhāyāmasmin karmaṇyasyāṁ devahūtyāꣳ svāhā. idamannāya sāmrājyānāmadhipataye-idanna mama ॥11 ॥

[Meaning] (Annaṁ) Agricultural products are the backbone of empires. Rest is lake the previous one. The oblations offered is meant for (sāmrājyādhipati anna) agricultural products that are backbone of empires and not for me.

ओं सोमऽओषधीनामधिपतिः स मावत्वस्मिन् ब्रह्मण्यस्मिन् क्षत्रेऽस्यामाशिष्यस्यां पुरोधायामस्मिन् कर्मण्यस्यां देवहूत्याꣳ स्वाहा ॥ इदं सोमाय ओषधीनामधिपतये-इदन्न मम ॥12 ॥

Oṁ soma'Oṣadhīnāmadhipatiḥ sa māvatvasmin brahmaṇyasmin kṣatre'syāmāśiṣyasyāṁ purodhāyāmasmin karmaṇyasyāṁ devahūtyāꣳ svāhā. idaṁ somāya Oṣadhīnāmadhipataye-idanna mama.

[Meaning] (Soma) Moon is the lord of herbs on the earth. Rest is like the previous one. The oblation offered is meant for (oṣdhyādhipati soma) moon that is lord of herbs and not for me.

Note: The Vedic seers know the positive effect of the polarized light of the moon on herbs and plants.

The moon's light is polarized. Polarization is a property of light waves that depicts the direction of their oscillations. A polarized light vibrates or oscillates in only one direction. It stands in contrast to a non-polarized light that vibrates in many directions.

ओं सविता प्रसवानामधिपतिः स मावत्वस्मिन् ब्रह्मण्यस्मिन् क्षत्रेऽस्यामाशिष्यस्यां पुरोधायामस्मिन् कर्मण्यस्यां देवहूत्याꣳ स्वाहा ॥ इद्र सवित्रे

प्रसवानामधिपतये-इदन्न मम ॥13 ॥

Oṁ savitā prasavānāmadhipatiḥ sa māvatvasmin brahmaṇyasmin kṣatre'syāmāśiṣyasyāṁ purodhāyāmasmin karmaṇyasyāṁ devahūtyāꣳ svāhā. idra savitre prasavānāmadhipataye-idanna mama.

[Meaning] (Savitā) The creative power of the sun is the leader of (prasavānām) those that give birth or cause origin in the universe. Rest is like the previous one. The oblation offered is meant for (prasavādhipati savitā) sun who is the leader of birth-givers and not for me.

ओं रुद्रः पशूनामधिपतिः स मावत्वस्मिन् ब्रह्मण्यस्मिन् क्षत्रेऽस्यामाशिष्यस्यां पुरोधायामस्मिन् कर्मण्यस्यां देवहूत्याꣳ स्वाहा ॥ इदं रुद्राय पशूनामधिपतये-इदन्न मम ॥14 ॥

Oṁ rudraḥ paśūnāmadhipatiḥ sa māvatvasmin brahmaṇyasmin kṣatre'syāmāśiṣyasyāṁ purodhāyāmasmin karmaṇyasyāṁ devahūtyāꣳ svāhā. idaṁ rudrāya paśūnāmadhipataye-idanna mama.

[Meaning] (Rudraḥ) Prāṇa-vāyu or life-forces are the lord of all (paśu) creatures. Rest is like the previous one. The oblation offered is meant for (paśvadhipati rudra) life force of living beings and not for me.

ओं त्वष्टा रूपाणामधिपतिः स मावत्वस्मिन् ब्रह्मण्यस्मिन् क्षत्रेऽस्यामाशिष्यस्यां पुरोधायामस्मिन् कर्मण्यस्यां देवहूत्याꣳ स्वाहा ॥ इदं त्वष्ट्रे रूपाणामधिपतये-इदन्न मम ॥15 ॥

Oṁ tvaṣṭā rūpāṇāmadhipatiḥ sa māvatvasmin brahmaṇyasmin kṣatre'syāmāśiṣyasyāṁ purodhāyāmasmin karmaṇyasyāṁ devahūtyāꣳ svāhā. idaṁ tvaṣṭre rūpāṇāmadhipataye-idanna mama.

[Meaning] (Tvaṣṭā) Electromagnetic radiation is the lord of (rūpānām) colours. Rest is like the previous one. The oblation offered is meant for (rupādhipati tvaṣṭā) electromegnetic radiation, lord of colours and not for me.

ओं विष्णुः पर्वतानामधिपतिः स मावत्वस्मिन् ब्रह्मण्यस्मिन् क्षत्रेऽस्यामाशिष्यस्यां पुरोधायामस्मिन् कर्मण्यस्यां देवहूत्याꣳ स्वाहा ॥ इदं विष्णवे पर्वतानामधिपतये-इदन्न मम ॥16॥

Oṁ viṣṇuḥ parvatānāmadhipatiḥ sa māvatvasmin brahmaṇyasmin kṣatre'syāmāśiṣyasyāṁ purodhāyāmasmin karmaṇyasyāṁ devahūtyāꣳ svāhā. idaṁ viṣṇave parvatānāmadhipataye-idanna mama.

[Meaning] (Viṣṇuḥ) Radiation heating of the sun is the lord of clouds. Rest is like the previous one. The oblation offered is meant for (parvatādhipati viṣṇu) radiation heating from sun causing clouds and not for me.

ओं मरुतो गणानामधिपतयस्ते मावन्त्वस्मिन् ब्रह्मण्यस्मिन् क्षत्रेऽस्यामाशिष्यस्यां पुरोधायामस्मिन् कर्मण्यस्यां देवहूत्याꣳ स्वाहा ॥ इदं मरुद्ध्यो गणानामधिपतिभ्यः- इदन्न मम ॥17॥

Oṁ maruto gaṇānāmadhipatayaste māvantvasmin brahmaṇyasmin kṣatre'syāmāśiṣyasyāṁ purodhāyāmasmin karmaṇyasyāṁ devahūtyāꣳ svāhā. idaṁ marudbhyo gaṇānāmadhipatibhyaḥ-idanna mama.

[Meaning] (Marutaḥ) The forty-nine pressure belts in atmosphere are the lord of all gaṇas (groups). Rest is like the previous one. The olbation offered is meant for (gaṇādhipati marutas) pressure belts of atmosphere that are lord of all groups and not for me.

Note: Groups are known for their power and pressures. Marutas are 49 pressure belts of atmosphere. So, they are known as lord of all pressure exerting groups.

ओं पितरः पितामहाः परेश्वरे ततास्ततामहाः इह मावन्त्वस्मिन् ब्रह्मण्यस्मिन् क्षत्रेऽस्यामाशिष्यस्यां पुरोधायामस्मिन् कर्मण्यस्यां देवहूत्याꣳ स्वाहा ॥ इदं पितृभ्यः

पितामहेभ्यः परेभ्योऽवरेभ्यस्ततेभ्यस्ततामहेभ्यश्च इदन्न मम ॥18॥ पारस्कर 1.5.10

Oṁ pitaraḥ pitāmahāḥ pare'vare tatāstatāmahāḥ iha māvantvasmin brahmaṇyasmin kṣatre'syāmāśiṣyasyāṁ purodhāyāmasmin karmaṇyasyāṁ devahūtyā꙳ svāhā. idaṁ pitṛbhyaḥ pitāmahebhyaḥ parebhyo'varebhyastateīyastatāmahebhyaścha-idanna mama.

Pār.GS. 1.5.10

[Meaning] (Pitaraḥ) Our seniors [pitāmahāḥ] and seniors of seniors [pare avare] both low qualified and highly qualified [tattāḥ] other extended family members [tatāmahāḥ] and those are respected among the extended family members be our saviours in untellectual feats etc. Rest is like the previous one. The oblation offered is mean for (pitaraḥ, pitamāhāḥ, para-avara tataḥ tatāmahāḥ) senior, senior to seniors, exteded family members and respectable among extended family members and not for me.

Further the oblations should be offered with the following mantas :

ओम् अग्निरैतु प्रथमो देवताना꙳ सोऽस्यै प्रजां मुंचतु मृत्युपाशात्। तद꙳ राजा वरुणोऽनुमन्यतां यथेय꙳ स्त्री पौत्रमघं न रोदात् स्वाहा ॥ इदमग्नये-इदन्न मम ॥1॥

आश्व.गृसू. 1.13.6

Om agniraitu prathamo devatānā꙳ so'syai prajāṁ muṁchatu mṛtyupāśāt, tada꙳ rājā varuṇo'numanyatāṁ yatheya꙳ strī pautramaghaṁ na rodāt svāhā. idamagnaye-idanna mama. Āśv. GS. 1.13..6

[Meaning] (Agni) Enegy is the base of all natural forces. Let it reach, by grace of God, the bride for her protection and saving her offspring from immature death. Varuṇa, the energy particles may co-ordinate it in this matter and this bride may not ever wail for the grief of her child. I offer oblation for agni (energy). The oblation offered is meant for agni and it is not for me.

ओम् इमामग्निस्त्रायतां गार्हपत्यः प्रजामस्यै नयतु दीर्घमायुः। अशून्योपस्था जीवतामस्तु माता पौत्रमानन्दमभिविबुध्यतामियꣳ स्वाहा॥ इदमग्रये-इदन्न मम ॥2॥

Om imāmagnistrāyatāṁ gārhapatyaḥ prajāmasyai nayatu dīrghamāyuḥ, aśūnyopasthā jīvatāmastu mātā pautramānandamabhivibudhyatāmiya⸱ svāhā. idamagnaye-idanna mama.

[Meaning] May the (Gārhapatya Agni) family genes/sanskāras come to the safety of this bride and it lead her offspring to long life. May she be free from all defects of barrenness and be the mother of living children. May she ever be consicous of the pleasure of grand-children. I offer oblation for (gārhapatya agni) family genes or sanskāras. The oblation offered is meant for (gārhaptya agni) family sanskāras and not for me.

ओं स्वस्ति नोऽग्ने दिवा पृथिव्या विश्वानि धेह्ययथा यजत्र। यदस्यां मयि दिवि जातं प्रशस्तं तदस्मासु द्रविणं धेहि चित्रꣳ स्वाहा॥ इदमग्रये-इदन्न मम ॥3॥

Oṁ svasti no'gne divā pṛthivyā viśvāni dhehyayathā yajatra, yadasyāṁ mayi divi jātaṁ praśastaṁ tadasmāsu draviṇaṁ dhehi chitra⸱ svāhā. idamagnaye-idanna mama.

[Meaning] May (Agni) the genes/sanskāras inherited through family line by us, the married couple, protect our Gṛhastha yajña and modify our wrong genes/sanskāras for the benefit of our family line. Whatever good on this earth or sky be given to me. May we be given the various material means produced in earth to pull on our family life. I offer oblation for (agni) family genes/sanskāras. The oblation offered is meant for (agni) family sanskāras and not for me.

ओं सुगन्नु पन्थां प्रदिशं न एहि ज्योतिष्मध्ये ह्यजरं न आयुः। अपैतु मृत्युरमृतं म आगाद्वैवस्वतो नो अभयं कृणोतु स्वाहा॥ इदं वैवस्वताय इदन्न मम ॥4॥

Oṁ sugannu panthāṁ pradiśaṁ na ehi jyotiṣmadhye

hyajaraṁ na āyuḥ, apaitu mṛtyuramṛtaṁ ma āgādvaivasvato no abhayaṁ kṛṇotu svāhā. idaṁ vaivasvatāya-idanna mama.

[Meaning] (Vaivasvata) O Parmātman! Come to guide us to the easily approachable path of presperity, bless us with the life full of enlightenment and free from the problems of oldness, death may not hunt us, immortality by attained by us and by your blessing the time make us fearless. I offer oblation for Paramātman. The oblation offered is meant for Vatvasvata Paramātman and not for me.

ओं परं मृत्यो अनुपरेहि पन्थां यत्र नोऽन्य इतरो देवयानात् । चक्षुष्मते शृण्वते ते ब्रवीमि मा नः प्रजाꣳरीरिषो मोत वीरान्त्स्वाहा ॥ इदं मृत्यवे-इदन्न मम ॥5॥

Oṁ paraṁ mṛtyo anuparehi panthāṁ yatra no'anya itaro devayānāt, chakṣuṣmate śṛṇavate te bravīmi mā naḥ prajāꣳrīriṣo mota vīrāntsvāhā. idaṁ mṛtyave-idanna mama.

[Meaning] (Mṛtyu) O Paramātman, the presiding Deva of death! Take us beyond the path of death, which is a path different from devayāna, a path traveresed by enlightened persons. I pray Paramātman Who sees and hears everything not to destroy our offspring and brave men. I offer this oblation to (mṛtyu) presiding Deva of death. The oblations offered here is meant for (mṛtyu) presiding Deva of death and not for me.

ओं द्यौस्ते पृष्ठꣳ रक्षतु वायुरूरू अश्विनौ च । स्तनन्धयस्ते पुत्रान्त्सविताभिरक्षत्वावाससः परिधानाद् बृहस्पतिर्विश्वे देवा अभिरक्षन्तु पश्चात् स्वाहा ॥ इदं विश्वेभ्यो देवेभ्यः इदन्न मम ॥6॥

Oṁ dyauste pṛṣṭhaꣳ rakṣatu vāyururū aśvinau cha, stanandhayaste putrāntsavitābhirakṣatvāvāsasaḥ paridhānād bṛhaspatirviśve devā abhirakṣantu paśchāt svāhā. idaṁ viśvebhyo devebhyaḥ-idanna mama.

[Meaning] O bride! Let the Sun protect you from back, let the prāṇa and apāna and air protect your waist and lower limbs of the body, let (savitā) creative power of sun protect your children who are feed on breasts breastfed babies till the time they start wearing civilzed dresses and afterwards let (Bṛhaspati) Āchārya of Gurukua and other enlightened persons protect them. I offer oblation to all elightened persons. The oblation offered is meant for (viśvedevāḥ) all enlightened persons and not for me.

ओं मा ते गृहेषु निशि घोष उत्थादन्यत्र त्वद्रुदत्यः संविशन्तु। मा त्वꣳ रुदत्युरऽआवधिष्ठा जीवपत्नी पतिलोके विराज पश्यन्ती प्रजाꣳ सुमनस्यमानाꣳ स्वाहा॥ इदमग्नये इदन्न मम॥7॥

Oṁ mā te gṛheṣu niśi ghoṣa utthādanyatra tvadrudatyaḥ saṁviśantu, mā tvaꣳ rudatyura'āvadhiṣṭhā jīvapatnī patiloke virāja paśyantī prajāꣳ sumanasyamānāꣳ svāhā. idamagnaye idanna mama.

[Meaning] O bride! let there not be bewailing sound of any kind in your home in the night time, let not the weeping women also enter your house. Let you not punish your attendents in your house when in grief, let you live gracefully in your husband's house having your husband alive and seeing your children delightful and prosper. I offer oblation to (Gārhapatya Agni) fire representing household life. The oblation offered is meant for (Gārhapatya Agni) fire representing household life and not for me.

ओम् अप्रजस्यं पौत्रमर्त्यं पाप्मानमुत वाऽअघम्। शीर्ष्णः स्रजमिवोन्मुच्य द्विषꣳद्भ्यः प्रतिमुंचामि पाशꣳ स्वाहा॥ इदमग्नये इदन्न मम॥8॥

Om aprajasyaṁ pautramartyaṁ pāpmānamuta vā'adham, śīrṣṇaḥ srajamivonmuchya dviṣadbhyaḥ pratimuṁchāmi pāśaꣳ svāhā. idamagnaye-ida0nna mama.

[Meaning] O bride! like a garland from the head, I remove from you the evils of barrenness, affliction of child's death, evil conduct responsible for your downgradation and any bondage caused by your enemies. I offer oblation to (Gārhapatya Agni) fire representing household life. The oblation offered is meant for (Gārhapatya Agni) fire representing household life and not for me..

After this the four oblations should be offered with mantras - भूरग्नये स्वाहा (*bhūragnaye svāhā*)- etc.

The bride-groom standing in front of the bride sitting with her face in the east direction should keep his face in the west direction and lift up the bride by taking her right palm into his left hand. While grasping the lifted right-hand palm of the bride by his right hand, he should pronounce the following six mantras applied for Pāṇigrahaṇa (holding the hand of the bride):

ओं गृभ्णामि ते सौभगत्वाय हस्तं मया पत्या जरदष्टिर्यथासः ।
भगो अर्यमा सविता पुरन्धिर्मह्यं त्वादुर्गाहपत्याय देवा ॥   ऋ० 10.85.36

Oṁ gṛbhṇāmi te saubhagatvāya hastaṁ mayā patyā jaradaṣṭiryathāsaḥ,
bhago aryamā savitā purandhirmahyaṁ tvādurgāhapatyāya devā. RV. 10.85.36

[Meaning] I, the bride-groom, hold your hand unto mine for success in house-hold life. May you attain the old age, hale and hearty, with me as your husband. Paramātman, (bhagaḥ) Who is endowed with glory, (aryamā) the admmin—istrator of justice, (savitā) the creator and (purandhiḥ) sustainer of the universe and all the enlightened persons present here are giving you to me for the fulfilment of house-hold life's duty.

ओं भगस्ते हस्तमग्रभीत् सविता हस्तमग्रभीत् ।
पत्नी त्वमसि धर्मणाहं गृहपतिस्तव ॥

Oṁ bhagaste hastamagrabhīt savitā hastamagrabhīt,
patnī tvamasi dharmaṇāhaṁ gṛhapatisva.

[Meaning] Let (bhagaḥ) virtues and prosperity (agrabhīt) grasp (te) your (hastam) hand. Let (savitā) power of procreation hold your hand. You are my wife by virtue of Gṛhastha dharma and I am custodian of your house.

Note: In Sanskrit, there is a dictum, गृहिणी गृहमुच्यते ।
(gṛhiṇī gṛham uchyate) That is, wife is called house. As such gṛhapati (husband) is the custodian of house.

ममेयमस्तु पोष्या मह्यं त्वादाद् बृहस्पतिः ।
मया पत्या प्रजावति शं जीव शरदः शतम् ॥

mameyamastu poṣyā mahyaṁ tvādād bṛhaspatiḥ,
mayā patyā prajāvati śaṁ jīva śaradaḥ śatam.

[Meaning] O bride! (Bṛhaspati) the creator of Brahmāṇḍa (Universe) gave you to me. Let you be supported and nourished by me. O mother of my children, may you live hundred years delightfully with me as your husband.

Note: From this mantra, it is known that by that time year used to be started from Autumn season (22nd August) or Autumn eqinox (23rd September).

त्वष्टा वासो व्यदधाच्छुभे कं बृहस्पतेः प्रशिषा कवीनाम् ।
तेनेमां नारी सविता भगश्च सूर्यामिव परि धत्तां प्रजया ॥

tvaṣṭā vāso vyadadhāchchhubhe kaṁ bṛhaspateḥ praśiṣā kavīnām,
tenemāṁ nārī savitā bhagaścha sūryāmiva pari dhattāṁ prajayā.

[Meaning] (Śubhe) O auspicious bride! In the creation (bṛhaspateḥ) of Paramātman, (praśiṣā) following the teachings (kavīnām) of enlightened persons, may you (vyadadhāt) wear (vāsaḥ) ornaments and dresses shining like (tvaṣṭā) electromagnetic radiation (kaṁ) for the sake of my pleasure. May all-creating and glorious Brahman beautify this lady with offspring like the sunrays.

इन्द्राग्री द्यावापृथिवी मातरिश्वा मित्रावरुणा भगो अश्विनोभा ।
बृहस्पतिर्मरुतो ब्रह्म सोम इमां नारी प्रजया वर्धयन्तु ॥

indrāgnī dyāvāpṛthivī mātariśvā mitrāvaruṇā bhago aśvinobhā,
bṛhaspatirmaruto brahma soma imāṁ nārī prajayā vardhayantu.

[Meaning] Atmospheric electricity and geothermal energy, sun and earth, air, oxygen and hydrogen, (bhaga) good fortune, both aśvins (prāṇa and apāna), Governor of the universe, pressure belts, expanding universe, and moon may prosper this lady with offspring.

अहं वि ष्यामि मयि रूपमस्या वेददित्पश्यन्मनसः कुलायम् ।
न स्तेयमद्मि मनसोदमुच्ये स्वयं श्रथ्नानो वरुणस्य पाशन् ॥ अथर्व० 14.1.58

ahaṁ vi ṣyāmi mayi rūpamasyā vedaditpaśyanmanasaḥ kulāyam,
na steyamadmi manasodamuchye svayaṁ śrathnāno varuṇasya pāśan. AV. 14.1.58

[Meaning] I, bridegroom, have (viṣyāmi) fixed (mayi) into me (rūpam) the beauty (asyā) of this bride. (vedat) I know and (paśyan) see in her (kulāyam) the seat (manasaḥ) of my heart. I (na) will not (admi) eat anything (steyam) alone (but share with her). (śrathanānaḥ) Having freed myself from the (pāśan) attractions (varṇasya) of prakṛti (material world), I feel (manasā) mentally (uda muchye) relieved.

The saṅkalpa of hand-grasping should also be taken by the bride. Afterwards the bride-groom accompanied by the bride should circumambulate the agnikuṇḍa and the person who was sitting near the pot full of water and placed in the south direction, carrying the pot should follow the bride-groom and bride. After the circumambulation being finished both of them should take oath with the following mantra:

ओम् अमोऽहमस्मि सा त्वꣳ सा त्वमस्यमोहम्। सामाहमस्मि ऋक्त्वं द्यौरहं पृथिवी त्वं तावेव विवहावहै सह रेतो दधावहै। प्रजां प्रजनयावहै पुत्रान् विन्दावहे बहून्। ते सन्तु जरदष्टयः सं प्रियौ रोचिष्णू सुमनस्यमानौ। पश्येम शरदः शतं जीवेम शरदः शतꣳ श‍ृणुयाम शरदः शतम ॥ पार॰ 1.6.3

Om amo'ham00asmi sā tvaꣳ sā tvamasyamoham ǀ sāmāhamasmi ṛktvaṁ dyauraham pṛthivī tvaṁ tāveva vivahāvahai saha reto dadhāvahai, prajāṁ prajanayāvahai putrān vindāvahe bahūn, te santu jaradaṣṭayaḥ saṁ priyau rochiṣṇū sumanasyamānau, paśyema śaradaḥ śataṁ jīvema śaradaḥ śataꣳ śṛṇuyāma śaradaḥ śatama. Pār.GS. 1.6.3

[Meaning] O bride! I have (amaḥ) chosen you intentionally and voluntarily, and you have also (sā) chosen me deliberately and voluntarily as I accept you intentionally and voluntarily, so you do take me. I am like Sāma (mantra of Śāmaveda) and you are like Ṛk (mantra of Ṛgveda), I am like (dyau) the Sun and you are like (pṛthivī) the earth. Let us both marry each other pleasantly, and put our semen together, let us procreate children, let us have many children and let these children live till the expiry of old age. Both of us loving each other, admiring each other and keeping each other in good humour see hundreds of autumns or years, live hundreds of autumns and hear hundreds of autumns.

Thereafter, the bride-groom from behind the bride going near her and standing in the south direction keeping his face in the north, should hold the right palm of the bride in his right palm and thus both should stand. The man carryin0g the pot full of water should take his previously occupied seat south of the yajña vedī. Thereafter the mother or brother of the bride taking the roasted pady or maize kept in the winnowing basket in her or his left hand should lift the right foot of bride and should make her mount on the small slab of stone. At this time the bride-groom should pronounce the folowing mantra.

ओम् आरोहेममश्मानमश्मेव त्व॰ स्थिरा भव।
अभितिष्ठ पृतन्यतोऽवबाधस्व पृतनायतः ॥ पार॰ 1.7.1

Om ārohem0amaśmānamaśmeva tva॰ sthirā bhava,
abhitiṣṭha pṛtanyato'vabādhasva pṛtanāyataḥ. Pār.GS. 1.7.1

[Meaning] O bride! ascend this stone be firm like rock. Humiliate foes, overcome quarrelsome persons.

Thereafter the bride and bride-groom should stand near the yajñakuṇḍa keeping their faces in the east direction. In this performance the bride keeping herself in the south should place her folded palms on the folded palms of the bride-groom. After this the mother or brother of bride, as the case may be, should place the winnowing basket on the ground or give to some one else and sprinkle pure ghee on the coupled handpalms of the bride and bride-groom. In this performance the añjali (coupled handpalms) of the bride should be above the añjali of bride-groom. The mother or brother of bride after this should take two handful of roasted paddy or maize from the winnowing basket with her or his right hand, should drop in the coupled añjali (coupled handpalms) of the bride and bride-groom and should sprinkle a little pure ghee again on the roasted paddy or maize contained in the añjali of the bride and bride-groom. Then, the bride bending her own añjali with that of bride-groom should drop three oblations on the blazing fire, oOne by each, dividinig the roasted paddy in three euqal parts, with the following mantras:

ओम् अर्यमणं देवं कन्या अग्निमयक्षत। स नोऽअर्यमा देवः प्रेतो मुंचतु मा पतेः स्वाहा ॥ इदमर्यम्णे अग्रये-इदन्न मम ॥

Om aryamaṇaṁ devaṁ kanyā agnimayakṣata, sa no'aryamā devaḥ preto muṁchatu mā pateḥ svāhā. idamaryamṇe agnaye-idanna mama.

[Meaning] (Kanyā) The bride (agnim ayakṣat) offers the oblation in the fire of yajña, that (aryamaṇam) controls pathogenic bacteria. May that fire, controller of pathogenic b00acteria, be the source of separating me from parental family, but it should not keep me separate from my husband. I offer oblatio to aryamā agni (agni, the controller of pathogenic bacteria). the oblation offered is meant for aryamā agni, and not for me.

ओम् इयं नार्युपब्रूते लाजानावपन्तिका। आयुष्मानस्तु मे पतिरेधन्तां ज्ञातयो मम स्वाहा ॥ इदमग्नये-इदन्न मम ॥

Om iyaṁ nāryupabrūte lājānāvapantikā, āyuṣmānastu me patiredhantāṁ jñātayo mama svāhā. idamagnaye-idanna mama.

[Meaning] This lady offering the oblation of roasted paddy in the fire of yajña prays. May my husband attain long life and the members of the family and relations prosper. I offer oblation to agni (fire of yajña). The oblation offered is meant for Agni and not for me.

ओम् इमाँल्लाजानावपाम्यग्नौ समृद्धिकरणं तव। मम तुभ्यं च संवननं तदग्निरनुमन्यतामियꣳ स्वाहा ॥ इदमग्नये-इदन्न मम ॥

Om imāṁllājānāvapāmyagnau samṛddhikaraṇaṁ tava, mama tubhyaṁ cha saṁvananaṁ tadagniranumanyatāmiyaꣳ svāhā. idamagnaye-idanna mama.

[Meaning] O bride-groom! I drop these grains of roasted paddy in the fire for your prosperity and progress, may there be great affection between you and me for each other. This fire of yajña be the source of support for. I offer oblation to agni (fire of yajña). The oblation offered is meant for agni and not for me.

Thereafter the bride-groom should pronounce the

following mantra:

ओं सरस्वति प्रेदमव सुभगे वाजिनीवति ।
यान्त्वा विश्वस्य भूतस्य प्रजायामस्याग्रतः ।
यस्यां भूतᳵसमभवद्यस्यां विश्वमिदं जगत् ।
तामद्य गाथां गास्यामि या स्त्रीणामुत्तमं यशः ॥ पार॰ 1.7.2

Oṁ sarasvati predamava subhage vājinīvati,
yāntvā viśvasya bhūtasya prajāyāmasyāgrataḥ,
yasyaṁ bhūtᳵsamabhavadyasyāṁ viśvamidaṁ jagat,
tāmadya gāthāṁ gāsyāmi yā strīṇāmuttamaṁ yaśaḥ.

Pār.GS. 1.7.2

[Meaning] (subhage) Endowed with excellent power, and (vājinīvati) material resources, (sarasvati) O Prakṛti (pra ava) protect (idam) this married life. (yām tvā) You are called to have existed (agrataḥ) before (viśvasya asya bhūtasya) all this material creation and (prajāyām) living creation, (yasyām) from you (bhūtam) this material creation (samabhavat) took place, (yasyām) from you (idam) this (viśvam) whole (jagat) world was created. (gāsyāmi) I will sing (tām) that (gathām) story of prakṛti (yā) which involves (uttam) the most excellent (yaśaḥ) glory (strīṇām) of women.

Afterwards the bride-groom holding the right palm of bride into his own right palm pronounce the following mantras and circum-ambulate the yajñakuṇḍa:

ओं तुभ्यमग्रे पर्यवहन्त्सूर्यां वहतुना सह ।
पुनः पतिभ्यो जायां दा अग्रे प्रजया सह ॥ ऋ॰ 10.85.38 पार॰ 1.2.4

Oṁ tubhyamagre paryavahantsūryāṁ vahatunā saha,
punaḥ patibhyo jāyāṁ dā agne prajayā saha.

RV. 10.85.38; Pār.GS. 1.2.4

[Meaning] (Agne) O Agni of marriage sanskāra, parents of bride (agre) first (pari-avahan) give (sūryām) bride, luminous like sun-rays (tubhyam) to you (saha) with (vahatunā) her husband who is going to own her responsibility. Now you (punaḥ) again (dā) hand over (jāyām) this bride (patibhyaḥ) to her husband and his family members (prajaya saha) blessed with progeny.

ॐ कन्यला पितृभ्यः पतिलोकं यतीयमप दीक्षामयष्ट ।

कन्या उत त्वया वयं धारा उदन्या इवातिगाहेमहि द्विषः ॥ पार॰ 1.3.5

Oṁ kanyalā pitṛbhyaḥ patilokaṁ yatīyamapa dīkṣāmayaṣṭa, kanyā uta tvayā vayaṁ dhārā udanyā ivātigāhemahi dviṣaḥ.

Pār.GS. 1.3.5

[Meaning] (*kanyalā iyam*) This girl (*pitṛbhyaḥ apa*) leaving her parents house (*yati*) going to join (*patilokam*) the husband's family and (*ayaṣṭa*) accepted (*dikṣām*) rules of marriage. (*ut*) Now (*tvayā*) you as a husband should accept (*kanyā*) this girl as your wife. (*vayam*) We would dip deen in happiness like me as her husband. We would dip deep in joy like the streams of water crushing and overcoming the obstacles and jealousies.

After this the bride and bride-groom should stand for a little in the west of the yajñakuṇḍa keeping there faces eastward. Thereafter, they both should circumambulate the yajñakuṇḍa twice.

Thus completing the procedure three times in total, for the fourth time the bride and bride-groom should stand in the west of the vedī keeping their faces in the east direction. As the case may be, the mother or the brother of the bride, bending obliquely the winnowing basket should drop the remaining roasted pady in the añjali (hand-palms) of the bride. Then, the bride uttering the following mantra should offer one oblation of that in the blazing fire of the vedī.

ॐ भगाय स्वाहा ॥ इदं भगाय इदन्न मम ॥

Oṁ bhagāya svāhā. idaṁ bhagāya-idanna mama.

[Meaning] I offer this oblation for the (bhaga) good

fartune. The oblation offered is meant for (bhaga) good fortune and not for me.

Afterwards bridegroom should sit in the west, keeping his face in the east direction and having the bride seated in his right-side. They should offer one oblation of molten ghee by the spoon with the under-mentioned mantra:

ओं प्रजापतये स्वाहा ॥ इदं प्रजापतये इदन्न मम ॥ पार० 1.7.6

Oṁ prajāpataye svāhā. idaṁ prajāpataye-idanna mama.

Pār.GS. 1.7.6

[Meaning] We offer this oblation for (Prajāpati) creator of the world. The oblation offered is meant for Prajāpati and not for me.

Thereafter going to a private room the bridegroom should loosen the tied hair of bride with the follwing mantras:

प्र त्वा मुंचामि वरुणस्य पाशाद्येन त्वाबध्नात्सविता सुशेवः ।
ऋतस्य योनौ सुकृतस्य लोकेऽरिष्टान्त्वा सह पत्या दधामि ॥ ऋ० 10.85.24

pra tvā muṁchāmi varuṇasya pāśādyena tvābadhnātsavitā suśevaḥ,

ṛtasya yonau sukṛtasya loke'riṣṭāntvā saha patyā dadhāmi.

RV. 10.85.24

[Meaning] O bride! I (muñchāmi) free (tvā) you (pāśat) from the network (varuṇasya) of the material world in which (savitā) creator hitherto (abadhnāt) bound (tvā) you. (ṛtasya yonau) In the matter of yajña (sukṛtasya loke) and other good actions, I (dadhāmi) promise (tvām) you to be (saha) with me (patyā) as your husband.

प्रेतो मुंचामि नामुतः सुबद्धाममुतस्करम् ।
यथेयमिन्द्र मीढ्वः सुपुत्रा सुभगासति ॥ ऋ० 10.85.25

preto muṁchāmi nāmutaḥ subaddhāmamutaskaram,

yatheyamindra mīḍhvaḥ suputrā subhagāsati. RV. 10.85.25

[Meaning] I free this bride from the obligations of her father's family, of course, not from her obligations of husband's family where she stands (subaddhām) duty bound, so that she, with her (mīḍhvaḥ) valiant (Indra) Indra like husband might have good luck and noble progeny.

After this the bride and bride-groom should come in the Śabhā-maṇḍapa (meeting hall) and begin the procedure of (Sapta-padi) seven steps ceremony. At this juncture the shawl of bride should be tied with the upvastra (uuper cloth) of the bride-groom. this is called the conjugal tie of couple. Leaving their seats the bride and bride-groom both should stand up. Then the baidegroom holding the right hand palm of the bride in his own right hand and taking her with him should go in the north side of the yajñakuṇḍa (fire-altar). Both of them should stand near keeping their faces in the north directions but in this pose the bride-groom should put his right hand on the right shoulder of the bride. The bride-groom uttering the under mentioned mantra should ask the bride to walk by raising her right foot:

मा सव्येन दक्षिणमतिक्राम ॥

mā savyena dakṣiṇamatikrāma.

[Meaning] Let not your right foot be overstepped by the left foot.

In order to let her realize the importance of consistency and constancy in the life, bride-groom says to bride "Let not your left foot surpass your right foot." Afterwards the bride-groom taking the bride with him should walk and also make her to walk one step in the (Īśāna) north east direction with the following mantra.

Saptapadi

ओम् इष एकपदी भव सा मामनुव्रता भव विष्णुस्त्वा नयतु पुत्रान् विन्दावहै बहूँस्ते सन्तु जरदष्टयः ॥1॥

Om iṣa ēkapadī bhava sā māmanuvratā bhava viṣṇustvā nayatu putrān vindāvahai bahūm̐ste santu jaradaṣṭayaḥ.

[Meaning] O bride! take the first step for the sake of (iśa) agri0cultural products. Follow me in my saṅkalpa. May (Viṣṇu) all-pervading Brahman be your (nayatu) guide. May we both get children. Let your progeny be numerous and longlived.

The second to seven steps should be taken with the following mantra:

ओम् ऊर्जे द्विपदी भव० ॥2॥

Om ūrjje dvipadī bhava...

[Meaning] Take second step for (urja) good health. Follow me etc. etc.

ओं रायस्पोषाय त्रिपदी भव० ॥3॥

Oṁ rāyaspoṣāya tripadī bhava...

[Meaning] Take third step for wealth and knowledge. Follow me etc. etc.

ओं मयोभवाय चतुष्पदी भव० ॥4॥

Oṁ mayobhavāya chatuṣpadī bhava...

[Meaning] Take the fourth step for spiritual happiness. Follow me etc. etc.

ओं प्रजाभ्यः पंचपदी भव ॥5॥

Oṁ prajābhyaḥ paṁchapadī bhava.

[Mea0ning] Take the fifth step for progeny. Follow me etc. etc.

ओम् ऋतुभ्यः षद्दी भव० ॥6॥

Om ṛtubhyaḥ ṣaṭpadī bhava...

[Meaning] Take the sixth step for seasonal appropriate behaviour. Follow me etc. etc.

ओं सखे सप्तपदी भव ॥7॥

Oṁ sakhe saptapadī bhava.

[Meaning] Take the seventh step for friendship. Follow me etc. etc.

Note: Here it may be noted that rtual of Saptapadi associated with marriage ceremony is based upon astronomical phenomenon. Sun meets earth (sun is perpendicular on earth) at seven tropical points in a year. For example,

On Dec. 22nd, it meets earth at 23.5^0 south

On Jan. 21st, it meets earth at 20^0 south

On Feb. 18th, it meets earth at 12^0 south

On March 21st, it meets earth at 0^0

On April 21st, it meets earth at 12^0 north

On May 22nd, it meets earth at 20^0 north

On June 21st, it meets earth at 23.5^0 north

On July 22nd, it meets earth at 20^0 north

On August 21st, it meets earth at 12^0 north

On Sept. 22nd, it meets earth at 0^0

On Oct. 21st, it meets earth at 12^0 south

On Nov. 21st, it meets earth at 20^0 south

Thus, from the above table it is proved that during the 12 months of year, sun and earth walks 7 steps together. In other words, we can say that the astronomical friendship between earth and sun takes place walking seven steps together. The same thing holds true about the friendship of good human beings. Kalidasa in Kumar Sambhava says:

सतां संगतं साप्तपदीनमुच्यते ।

satāṁ saṁgataṁ sāptapadīnamuchyate.

[Meaning] Gentleman become friends after walking seven steps together.

Marriage is the friendship of two persons for life time. That is why the provision of Saptapadi has been made in marriage sanskāra.

Completing the procidure of (Saptapadi) seven-step-ceremony the bride-groom and bride, their knot having got tied, should take their previous seats. Thereafter the man who was sitting in the south of yajñakuṇḍa (firealtar) with the pot full of water, should carry that perviously placed pot near bride-groom. The bride taking a little water from that pot should sprinkle it on the bride-groom and he should pronounce the following four mantras at that time:

ओम् आपो हि ष्ठा मयोभुवस्ता न ऊर्जे दधातन ।
महे रणाय चक्षसे ॥ ऋ० 10.9.1

Om āpo hi ṣṭhā mayobhuvastā na ūrjje dadhātana,
mahe raṇāya chakṣase. RV.10.9.1

[Meaning] (āpaḥ) The waters (hi sṭha) are (mayaḥ bhuvaḥ) the source of happiness, may they be helpful for us in (dadhātana) attaining (ūrje) food and energy, so that (chakṣase) we may see or realize (mahe) mighty (raṇāya) splendour of divinity.

यो वः शिवतमो रसस्तस्य भाजयते ह नः । उशतीरिव मातरः ॥ ऋ० 10.9.2

yo vaḥ śivatamo rasastasya bhājayate ha naḥ,
uśatīriva mātaraḥ. RV 10.9.2

[Meaning] O waters (ha naḥ) allow us (bhājayate) to enjoy (yaḥ) that (rasaḥ) essence (vaḥ) of yours which is (śivatamaḥ) nectarous. Be like (mātaraḥ) the mothers (uśati) wishing for the well-being of their children.

तस्मा अरं गमाम वो यस्य क्षयाय जिन्वथ ।
आपो जनयथा च नः ॥ ऋ० 10.9.3

tasmā araṅ gamāma vo yasya kṣayāya jinvatha,
āpo janayathā cha naḥ. RV. 10.9.3

[Meaning] O waters, (yasya) let us (gamāma) acquire you (araṁ) in the sufficient quantity (tasmai) for thsoe agricultural products (yasya kṣayāya) for the growth of which (jinvatha) your presence is required. (āpaḥ) These waters are essential (naḥ) for us in (janayathā) production of various agricultural products.

ओम् आपः शिवाः शिवतमाः शान्ताः शान्ततमास्तास्ते कृण्वन्तु भेषजम् ॥
पार० 1.85-86

Om āpaḥ śivāḥ śivatamāḥ śāntāḥ śāntatamāstāste kṛṇvantu bheṣajam ॥ Pār.GS. 1.85-86

[Meaning] O bride! (āpaḥ) These are (śivāḥ) source of wellbeing and (śivatamāḥ) prosperity. They are (śāntatamāḥ) most advantageous. (tāḥ) Let them (kṛṇvantu) make you (bheṣajam) free from all sort of diseases.

After this the bride and bride-groom have a glimpse at the sun with the following mantra if marriage is being conducted in the day time.

ओं तच्चक्षुर्देवहितं पुरस्ताच्छुक्रमुच्चरत् । पश्येम शरदः शतं जीवेम शरदः शत꣢ श्रृणुयाम शरदः शतं प्र ब्रवाम शरदः शतमदीनाः स्याम शरदः शतं भूयश्च शरदः शतात् ॥ यजु० 36.24 पार० 1.8.7

Om tachchakṣurdevahitaṁ purastāchchhukramuchcharat,
paśyema śaradaḥ śataṁ jīvema śaradaḥ śataꣳ śṛṇuyāma śaradaḥ śataṁ pra bravāma śaradaḥ śatamadīnāḥ syāma śaradaḥ śataṁ

bhūyaścha śaradah śatāt. YV. 36.24; Pār.GS.1.8.7

[Meaning] O, God! You are the lighthouse for seekers. Let us see for hundred years, live for hundred years, hear for hundred years chanting your divine name. Let us not live in misery in the life span of hundred years. Let us live for another hundred years in the next life.

NB: During the Vedic period, the year also commenced with the Śarada Ṛtu i.e. the winter season. That is why the mantra uses the words '*Śaradah Śatam*' which literally means 'till hundred winter seasons'.

Afterward the bride-groom putting his right hand on right shoulder of bride touch her heart by the same hand and should utter the following mantra.

ओं मम व्रते ते हृदयं दधामि मम चित्तमनु चित्तं ते अस्तु।
मम वाचमेकमना जुषस्व प्रजापतिष्ट्वा नियुनक्तु मह्यम् ॥ पार० 1.8.8

Oṁ mama vrate te hṛdayaṁ dadhāmi mama chittamanu chittaṁ te astu,
mama vāchamekamanā juṣasva prajāpatiṣṭvā niyunaktu mahyam. Pār.GS. 1.8.8

[Meaning] I invite your attention to my vrata. Let my mind be concordant with thy mind. Follow my words with concentrated mind. Let (Prajāpati) creator of universe join thee with me.

Here in the similar manner the bride should also touch the heart of the bride-groom with her right hand and should pronounce the mantra मम व्रते ते हृदयं दधामि (*mama vrate te hṛdayaṁ dadhāmi*) etc. etc.

Afterwards, the bride-groom should put his right hand on the forehead of the bride and should look at the people gathered there on this occasion uttering the following mantra-

सुमङ्गलीरियं वधूरिमां समेत पश्यत।
सौभाग्यमस्यै दत्त्वायाथास्तं वि परेतन ॥ ऋ० 10.85.3 पारस्कर 1.8.9

sumangalīriyaṁ vadhūrimāṁ sameta paśyata,
saubhāgyamasyai dattvāyāthāstaṁ vi paretana.

RV. 10.85.3; Pār.GS. 1.8.9

[Meaning] This bride is my lucky wife. Come ye and see. Bless her before you go to your house. Be not unfriendly to her.

At this juncture the people gathered to grace the occasion, should bless with the following sentences:

ओं सौभाग्यमस्तु; ओं शुभं भवतु ॥

Oṁ saubhāgyamastu, Oṁ śubhaṁ bhavatu ॥

[Meaning] Let fortune attend you. Let everything be auspicious.

Thereafter, the oblation with the Sviṣṭakṛta mantra यदस्य कर्मणो॰ (*yadasya karmaṇo*) etc. etc. should be offered and further ājyāhutis with four mantras - भूरग्रये स्वाहा (*bhūragnaye svāhā*) etc. etc. should be offered, and thus पूर्वविधि (the first main fuction) of the marriage ceremony comes to an end.

After a short interval the second function of the marriage ceremony should be performed in the following manner:

1. Agnyādhāna - with ओं भूभूवः (*Oṁ bhūrbhūvaḥ*) etc. etc.

2. Samidādhāna - with अयन्त इध्म॰ (*ayanta idhma..*) etc.

3. Āghārāvājyāhutis with ओम् अग्रये स्वाहा (*Om agnaye svāhā*) etc.

4. Vyāhṛti āhutis - with ओं भूरग्रये स्वाहा (*Oṁ bhūragnaye svāhā*) etc.

Afterwards main part of the homa should be performed by offering oblations with the following mantras:

ओं लेखासन्धिषु पक्ष्मस्वारोकेषु च यानि ते ।
तानि ते पूर्णाहुत्या सर्वाणि शमयाम्यहं स्वाहा ॥ इदं कन्यायै-इदन्न मम ॥1 ॥

Oṁ lekhāsandhiṣu pakṣamasvārokeṣu cha yāni te,
tāni te pūrṇāhutyā sarvāṇi śamayāmyahaṁ svāhā. idaṁ
kanyāyai-idanna mama.

[Meaning] O Girl. whatever defects are seen in the streaks of your forehead and whatever are in the hair of eye-lids and the cavaties of naval etc. I allay with the pūrṇāhuti, (accomplished oblations). I offer oblation to kanyā. The oblations offered is for kanyā (girl) and not for me.

ओं कशेषु यच्च पापकमीक्षिते रुदिते च यत् । तानि॰ ॥2 ॥

Oṁ kaśeṣu yachcha pāpakamīkṣite rudite cha yat. tāni...

[Meaning] Whatever defect has made its place in hair, in sight and wailing etc. I allay with this pūrṇāhuti. Rest is like previous one.

ओं शीलेषु यच्च पापकं भाषिते हसिते च यत् । तानि॰ ॥3 ॥

Oṁ śīleṣu yachcha pāpakaṁ bhāṣite hasite cha yat. tāni...

[Meaning] Whatever defect has got its roots in ettiquette etc. I allay with the pūrṇāhuti. Rest is like previous one.

ओम् आरोकेषु च दन्तेषु हस्तयोः पादयोश्च यत् ॥ तानि॰ ॥4 ॥

Om ārokeṣu cha danteṣu hastayoḥ pādayoścha yat. tāni...

[Meaning] Whatever defect has made its place in tooth-wholes, in teeth, in hands and legs, I allay with the pūrṇāhuti. Rest is like previous one.

ओम् ऊर्वोरुपस्थे जङ्घयोः सन्धानेषु च यानि ते । तानि॰ ॥5 ॥

Om ūrvorupasthe jaṅghayoḥ sandhāneṣu cha yāni te. tāni..

[Meaning] Whatever defect has taken its place in thighs, genitals, crus, and bone-joints, I allay with this purṇāhuti. Rest is like previous one.

ओं यानि कानि च घोराणि सर्वाङ्गेषु तवाभवन् ।
पूर्णाहुतिभिराज्यस्य सर्वाणि तान्यशीशमं स्वाहा ॥ इदं कन्यायै-इदन्न मम ॥6 ॥

Oṁ yāni kāni cha ghorāṇi sarvāṅgeṣu tavābhavan,
pūrṇāhutibhirājyasya sarvāṇi tānyaśīśamaṁ svāhā. idaṁ
kanyāyai-idanna mama.

[Meaning] O bride! whatever are the serious defects in your other parts of the body, I allay them with these purṇāhutis of the ghee. I offer oblation to kanyā (girl) The oblation offered is meant for kanyā (girl) and not for me.

Afterwards, four oblations should be offered with the mantras भूरग्नये स्वाहा (*Oṁ bhūragnaye svāhā*) etc. etc.

Thereafter, the bride and the bride-groom should go out of the marriage hall to the north direction. And the bride-groom should make the bride to have a glimpse of (ध्रुव) Pole star, in case the marriage is being solemnised) in night. The procedure of this is as follows:

The bride-groom pointing out at the Pole-star says:

ध्रुवं पश्य (*dhruvaṁ paśya*) ॥

O bride! look at the Pole-star.

The bride replies - पश्यामि *(paśyāmi)* ॥

Yes, I see,

She further declares:

ओं ध्रुवमसि ध्रुवाहं पतिकुले भूयासम् (अमुष्य असौ) ॥ गोभिल॰ 2.3.8

Oṁ dhruvamasi dhruvāhaṁ patikule bhūyāsam (amuṣya
asau). Go.GS. 2.3.8

[Meaning] The Pole-star is (dhruva) stable, May I be (dhruva) stable in my husband's family.

The bride-groom says -

अरुन्धतीं पश्य ॥ गोभिल० 2.3.9

arundhatīṁ paśya. Go.GS. 2.3.9

[Meaning] O bride! look at the Arundhati, the star adjacent to Vasiṣṭha in Saptarṣis (See fig. below)

The bride replies : पश्यामि (*paśyāmi*) ॥

Yes, I see. Bride declares -

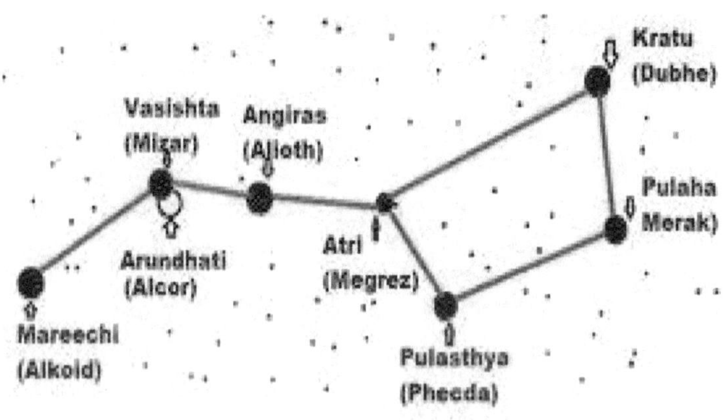

ओम् अरुन्धत्यसि रुद्धाहमस्मि (अमुष्य असौ) ॥ गो० 2.3.1.0

Om arundhatyasi ruddhāhamasmi (amuṣya asau).

Go.GS. 2.3.1.0

[Meaning] Just as Arundhati star is always bound to stay with Vasiṣṭha in the cluster of Saptarṣis, similarly, I named .... (bride should pronounce her name) am bound to stay with .... (bride should utter the name of bride-groom) as my husband.

N.B. Here in the place of असौ, the name of bride

should be uttered and in the place of अमुष्य the name of husband should be uttered by bride, but it should be in possessive case.

Thereafter the bride-groom looking at the bride should place his right hand on her forehead and should utter the following two mantras.

ओ धु वा द्यौर्धुवा पृथिवी धु वं विश्वमिदं जगत्‌।
धु वासः पर्वता इमे ध्रुवा स्री पतिकुले इयम्‌ ॥1 ॥

O dhru vā dyaurdhruvā pṛthivī dhru vaṁ viśvamidaṁ jagat,
dhru vāsaḥ parvatā ime dhruvā strī patikule iyam.

[Meaning] Stable is the heavenly region stable is this earth. stable is this universe, stable are these mountains and stable is this woman in the husband's house.

ओं ध्रुवमसि धु वन्त्वा पश्यामि ध्रुवैधि पोष्ये मयि।
मह्यं त्वादाद बृहस्पतिर्मया पत्या प्रजावती संजीव शरदः शतम्‌ ॥

Oṁ dhruvamasi dhru vantvā paśyāmi dhruvaidhi poṣye mayi,
mahyaṁ tvādāda bṛhaspatirmayā patyā prajāvatī saṁjīva śaradaḥ śatam.

[Meaning] O bride! stable are you and may I always see you stable. Be you stable near me who is your supporter. God has given you to me and having good progeny you may live hundred autumns (years) with me as your husband.

This second mantra should be interpreted on bride's part also.

Afterwards the bride and bride-groom should take their seats in the west of yajñakuṇḍa (firealtar) keeping their faces in the east. They should perform three āchamans (sipping of water) pronouncing ओम्‌ अमृतोपस्तरणमसि स्वाहा (*Om amṛtopastaraṇamasi svāhā*) ॥

Afterwards they should perform the yajña procedure:

1. Āchamana (Sipping of water).

2. Agnyādhāna (Kindling fire)

3. Samidādhāna (Placing samidhās)

4. Āghārāvājyāhutis (Ghee offerings)

5. Vyāhṛti Ahutis (Vyāhṛti offerings)

Afterwards the cooked rice in a small quantity should be kept in a pot and ghee should be sprinkled on it. ghee and rice should be mixed. The bride and bridegroom should take very little part of that rice in their right hands and offer oblation with the following mantras:

ओम् अग्नये स्वाहा ॥ इदमग्नये इदन्न मम ॥ गो॰ 2.3.117

Om agnaye svāhā. idamagnaye idanna mama. Go.GS. 2.3.117

[Meaning] We offer the oblation for Agni. The oblation offered is meant for Agni and not for me.

ओं प्रजापतये स्वाहा ॥ इदं प्रजापतये इदन्न मम ॥ गो॰ 2.3.118

Oṁ prajāpataye svāhā. idaṁ prajāpataye idanna mama.
                                            Go. GS. 2.3.118

[Meaning] We offer this oblation for Prajāpati. The oblation offered is meant for Prajāpati and not for me

ओं विश्वेभ्यो देवेभ्यः स्वाहा ॥ इदं विश्वेभ्यो देवेभ्यः इदन्न मम ॥
                                            गो॰ 2.3.119

Oṁ viśvebhyo devebhyaḥ svāhā. idaṁ viśvebhyo devebhyaḥ idanna mama. Go.GS. 2.3.119

[Meaning] We offer this oblation for Viśvedevās (all natural forces). The oblation offered is meant for Viśvedevas and it is not for me.

ओम् अनुमतये स्वाहा ॥ इदमनुमतये-इदन्न मम ॥ गो॰ 2.3.121

Om anumataye svāhā. idamanumataye-idanna mama.

Go.GS. 2.3.121

[Meaning] We offer this oblation for (Anumati) Full Moon Day. The oblation offered is meant for Full Moon day and not for me.

Thereafter, following āhutis should be offered

1. One Sviṣṭakṛt Āhui

2. Four Vyāhṛti Āhutis

3. Eight Ājyāhutis

Afterwards, the remaining cooked rice should be put in a pot and ghee should be mixed in it. The bride-groom keeping his right hand on it, should wishper the following mantras in mind and should eat a little of that cooked rice:

ओम् अन्नपाशेन मणिना प्राणसूत्रेण पृश्निना ।
बध्नामि सत्यग्रन्थिना मनश्च हृदयं च ते ॥1॥

Om annapāśena maṇinā prāṇasūtreṇa pṛśninā,
badhnāmi satyagranthinā manaścha hṛdayaṁ cha te.

[Meaning] O bride or bride-groom! I tie your heart and mind with the knot of truth, like the food is tied with prāṇa (life), beads with thread and food and prāṇa with space.

ओं यदेतद्धृदयं तव तदस्तु हृदयं मम ।
यदिदꣳ हृदयं मम तदस्तु हृदयं तव ॥2॥

Oṁ yadetaddhṛdayaṁ tava tadastu hṛdayaṁ mama,
yadidaꣳ hṛdayaṁ mama tadastu hṛdayaṁ tava.

[Meaning] O bride or bride-groom! that which is your heart be my heart and that which is my heart be your heart.

ओम् अन्नं प्राणस्य षड्विꣳशस्तेन बध्नामि त्वा असौ ॥3॥

Om annaṁ prāṇasya ṣaḍvi-śastena badhnāmi tvā asau.

[Meaning] O bride! I tie you with the anna (food) which is the 26th element supporting life.

In the place of असौ (*asau*) in the last mantra the name of the bride should be used in vocative case.

Remaining part of the cooked rice of which the small part was eaten by bride-groom, should be given to bride by the bride-groom. When bride has eatn it, the bride and bride-groom should take their seats in the yajñamandapa (yajña pavilion) keeping their faces in the east. They should perform the Mahāvāmdevya gāna of Sāmaveda.

Afterwards, performing, Stuti-prārthanā, Upāsanā, Svasti-vāchana and Śānti-karaṇa according as given in the Sāmānya-prakaraṇa, the bride and bride-groom should take meal free from salt and alkalinity and enriched with sweet, milk and ghee.

Thereafter, the priest, dhārmika persons, and the persons who are the participants of the ceremony should be entertained with nice food and then the male guests be given a cordial send off by men and ladies by ladies.

Then, on passing of four hours of night the bride-groom and bride arranging their separate beddings on the ground should sleep observing Brahmacharya vrata for three nights continualty. They should eat such a meal as may not cause nightfall. Then in the night of fourth day they should systematically perform the ceremony of impregnation. If there is, say any problem on the fourth day, they should perform it on another day according so their desire, but they should observe Brahmacharya firmly in doing so. They can perform the sanskāra of (garbhādhāna) impregnation with systematic procedure on the night that has been mentioned previously in the

Garbhādhāna sanskāra.

Thereafter, on the second or third day the people from the bride-groom family should take the bring bride and bride-groom to their home.

If the bride's eyes filled with tears when leaving the house of her parents, the following Mantra should be uttered:

जीवं रुदन्ति वि मयन्ते अध्वरे दीर्घमनु प्रसितिं दीधिर्युर्नरः ।
वामं पितृभ्यो य इदं समेरिरे मयः पतिभ्यो जनयः परिष्वजे ॥ ऋ० 10.40.10

jīvaṁ rudanti vi mayante adhvare dīrghāmanu prasitiṁ dīdhiryurnaraḥ,

vāmaṁ pitṛbhyo ya idaṁ samerire mayaḥ patibhyo janayaḥ pariṣvaje ‖ *RV. 10.40.10*

[Meaning] O learned persons! women embrace those men as their husbands to attain benefit of married life, who accept Gṛhastha Āśrama to take all trouble to give happiness and comforts to their wives, inspire them for participating in the yajña, obey the laws of the household life and strengthen the bond of love for the continuity of the family line of their parents.

The bride-groom sitting in the vehicle, keep the bride sitting by his right side and should utter the following mantras and make the vehicle move:

पूषा त्वेतो नयतु हस्तगृह्याश्विना त्वा प्र वहतां रथेन ।
गृहानगच्छ गृहपत्नी पथासो वशिनी त्वं विदथमा वदासि ॥1 ॥

pūṣā tveto nayatu hastagṛhyaśvinā tvā pra vahatāṁ rathena, gṛhāngachchha gṛhapatnī pathāso vaśinī tvaṁ vidathamā vadāsi.

[Meaning] O girl! your husband who has grasped the hand and has all means to support you, would bring you home, Let this fast moving vehicle carry you comfortably and you reach the home of your husband safely. Like a mistress of the house you have your husband under your command and supervise the establishment of your husband.

सुकिंशुकं शल्मलिं विश्वरूपं हिरण्यवर्णं सुवृतं सुचक्रम् ।
आ रोह सूर्ये अमृतस्य लोकं स्योनं पत्ये वहतुं कृणुष्व ॥2 ॥ ऋ० 10.85.20

sukiṁśukaṁ śalmaliṁ viśvarūpaṁ hiraṇyavarṇaṁ suvṛtaṁ suchakram,
ā roha sūrye amṛtasya lokaṁ syonaṁ patye vahatuṁ kṛṇuṣva. RV. 10.85.20

[Meaning] O Sun like refulgent bride! you ride this vehicle of Gṛhasthāśram which is made of wood of Śalmali and Palāśa (Bombax Heptaphylium); which has various colours and decorated with ornaments and which has quick moving wheels. You turn this married life into paradisal bliss of immortal joy for your husband and his family.

If there arises a need for the bride to ride a boat or ship while reaching her husband's house, the following mantra be chanted prior to embark the boat or ship.

अश्मन्वती रीयते सं रभध्वमुत्तिष्ठत प्र तरता सखाय ।

aśmanvatī rīyate saṁ rabhadhvamuttiṣṭhata pra taratā sakhāya.

[Meaning] O worldly people! if you have to cross the river of married life which is full of stones (challenges) and has risky currents, you invite all your courage, keep your feet firm and cross it.

In disembarking the boat, the following mantra be pronounced:

अत्रा जहाम ये असन्नशेवाः शिवान्वयमुत्तरेमाभि वाजान् ॥ ऋ० 10.53.8

atrā jahāma ye asannaśevāḥ śivānvayamuttaremābhi vājān.
RV. 10.53.8

[Meaning] We leave all the inauspicious things in the boat and get out from it to obtain the auspicious wealth like grain etc.

If on the way there happen to be crossroads, river, fear of wild beasts, thief etc., fearful places, uneven roads full of pits, grove of tall trees and cremation ground, the bride-groom should utter the following mantras:

मा विदन् परिपन्थिनो य आसीदन्ति दम्पती ।
सुगेभिर्दुर्गमतीतामप द्रान्त्वरातयः ॥ ऋ० 10.85.32

mā vidan paripanthino ya āsīdanti dampatī,
sugebhirdurgamatītāmapa drāntvarātayaḥ. RV. 10.85.32

[Meaning] Let not the (pari-panthinaḥ) wicked persons (ā sīdanti) come on the way of (dampatī) this couple. Let (arātayaḥ) enemies (ati) crossing over (durgam) unpassable paths and (itam) travelling (sugebhiḥ) on the easy paths (ap drāntu) stay away.

If on the way the vehicle breaks down or any unexpected calamity occurs, the couple may stay at any good place. They should offer the four oblations of ghee with the vyāhṛti mantras mentioned in the Sāmānya-Prakaraṇa. Afterwards, they would chant Mahāvāmdevya Gāna, as described in the Sāmānya Prakarṇa.

When the vehicle carrying the bride and bride-groom reaches at the front of the house of the bride-groom, a lady having good civic sense or a lady from the family who has been blessed with a child should receive bride and get her down the vehicle holding her hands alongwith the bride-groom and take her to sabhāmaṇḍapa (congregation hall) with her. The bride-groom reaching at the door of the sabhāmaṇḍapa should have a glance at the people who have come for this purpose and pronounce the following mantra:

सुमङ्गलीरियं वधुरिमां समेत पश्यत ।
सौभाग्यमस्यै दत्त्वायाथास्तं वि परेतन ॥ ऋ० 10.86.33

sumaṅgalīriyaṁ vadhurimāṁ sameta paśyata,
saubhāgyamasyai dattvāyāthāstaṁ vi paretana. RV. 10.86.33

[Meaning] This bride is my lucky wife. Come ye and see. Bless her before you go to your house. Be not unfriendly to her.

The guests should bless the bride uttering

ओं सौभाग्यमस्तु । ओं शुभं भवतु ॥
Oṁ saubhāgyamastu, oṁ śubhaṁ bhavatu.

[Meaning] Let fortune attend you. Let everything be auspicious.

Afterwards, the bride-groom take the bride into the sabhāmaṇḍapa having pronounced the following mantra:

इह प्रियं प्रजया ते समृध्यतामस्मिनगृहे गार्हपत्याय जागृहि ।
एना पत्या तन्वं सं सृजस्वाधा जिव्रीं विदथमा वदाथः ॥ ऋ० 10.85.27
iha priyaṁ prajayā te samṛdhyatāmasmingṛhe gārhapatyāya jāgṛhi,
ēnā patyā tanvaṁ saṁ sṛjasvādhā jivrīṁ vidathamā vadāthaḥ. RV. 10.85.27

[Meaning] May your family flourish here in this home. O bride! may you always be ready to play the role of mistress of this house. You do have physical meeting only with this husband of yours till attaining the old age. O bride and bride-groom you both appreciate each other.

Afterwards the bride and bride-groom should come near the Kuṇḍa (firealtar) which has been previously prepared. Al this time the bride-groom uttering the following mantra should seat the bride on the wood seat or the seat made of grass in the west of the Kuṇḍa (firealtar) on his right keeping her face eastward:

ओम् इह गावः प्रजायध्वमिहाश्वा इह पूरुषाः ।
इह सहस्रदक्षिणोऽपि पूषा नि षीदतु ॥ अ. 20.127.12

Om iha gāvaḥ prajāyadhvamihāśvā iha pūruṣāḥ,
iha sahasradakṣiṇo'pi pūṣā ni ṣīdatu. AV. 20.127.12

[Meaning] May the cows grow in numbers in this house, may here grow innumerable horses and also increase the number of men. May I the supporter of the house remain here well maintained donating in thousand numbers.

Afterwards, both of them should do three āchamanas (water sippings) with the mantras ओम् अमृतोपस्तरणमसि॰ (*Om amṛtopastaraṇamasi svāhā*) etc. One āchamana be done with the mantra only.

Subsequently, according to the procedure prescribed in the Sāmānya Prakaraṇa, the samidhā in the kuṇḍa be arranged and Agnyādhāna (fire-kindling ritual) be performed. When the fire is kindled in the kuṇḍa, ghee should be warmed and pured on it. Afterwards, the procedure of samidhādhāna (placing samidhās) be performed followed by four āghārāvājyābhāgāhutis, four vyāhṛti āhutis and eight ājayāhutis totalling 16 in numbers, should be offered. These oblations be offered by bride and bride-groom. Afterwards, they should preform the main homa by the following mantras, one oblation by each matra, total eight in all, be offered.

ओम् इह धृतिः स्वाहा ॥ इदमिह धृत्यै-इदन्न मम ॥1॥
Om iha dhṛtiḥ svāhā. idamiha dhṛtyai-idanna mama.

[Meaning] I offer this oblation for patience and tolerance to reign here in this house. The oblation offered is meant for dhṛti (patience) in this house and not for me

ओम् इह स्वधृतिः स्वाहा ॥ इदमिह स्वधृत्यै-इदन्न मम ॥2 ॥

Om iha svadhṛtiḥ svāhā. idamiha svadhṛtyai-idanna mama.

[Meaning] I offer this oblation for unity in my family. The oblation offered is meant for unity in my family and not for me.

ओम् इह रन्तिः स्वाहा ॥ इदमिह रन्त्यै-इदन्न मम ॥3 ॥

Om iha rantiḥ svāhā. idamiha rantyai-idanna mama.

[Meaning] I offer this oblation for the reign of enjoyment here in this house. The oblation offered is meant for enjoyment in this house and not for me.

ओम् इह रमस्व स्वाहा ॥ इदमिह रमाय इदन्न मम ॥4 ॥

Om iha ramasva svāhā. idamiha ramāya-idanna mama.

[Meaning] I offer this oblation for the happiness of bride in this house. The oblation offered is meant for happiness of bride this house and not for me.

ओं मयि धृतिः स्वाहा ॥ इदं मयि धृत्यै-इदन्न मम ॥5 ॥

Oṁ mayi dhṛtiḥ svāhā. idaṁ mayi dhṛtyai-idanna mama.

[Meaning] I offer this oblation for tolerance and firmness in me. The oblation offered is meant for tolerance and firmness in me and not for me.

ओं मयि स्वधृतिः स्वाहा ॥ इदं मयि स्वधृत्यै-इदन्न मम ॥6 ॥

Oṁ mayi svadhṛtiḥ svāhā. idaṁ mayi svadhṛtyai-idanna mama.

[Meaning] I offer this oblation for tolerance in me for my family. The oblation offered is meant for tolerance in me for my family and not for me.

ओं मयि रमः स्वाहा ॥ इदं मयि रमाय-इदन्न मम ॥7 ॥

Oṁ mayi ramaḥ svāhā. idaṁ mayi ramāya-idanna mama.

May there reign pleasure and enjoyment in me.

ओं मयि रमस्व स्वाहा ॥ इदं मयि रमाय-इदन्न मम ॥8 ॥

Oṁ mayi ramasva svāhā. idaṁ mayi ramāya-idanna mama.

[Meaning] I offer this oblation for my own happiness. The oblation offered is meant for my own happiness and not for other purpose.

Afterwards, the four oblations, one by each mantra, should be offered with the following mantras:

ओम् आ नः प्रजां जनयतु प्रजापतिराजरसाय समनत्त्वर्यया। अदुर्मङ्गलीः पतिलोकमा विश शं नो भव द्विपदे शं चतुष्पदे स्वाहा॥ इदं सूर्यायै सावित्रयै इदन्न मम ॥1॥

Om ā naḥ prajāṁ janayatu prajāpatirājarasāya samanaktvaryayā, adurbhaṅgalīḥ patilokamā viśa śaṁ no bhava dvipade śaṁ chatuṣpade svāhā. idaṁ sūryāyai sāvitrayai-idanna mama.

[Meaning] O bride! May God who is just and merciful, make our children endowed with good sanskāras, guṇas and conduct, so that we may attain great happiness till our old age. Let all ladies of the house keep whole family happy. You (bride) attain pleasure and enjoyment in the family of your husband. May you be source of happiness to our bipeds and our quadrupeds. This oblation is offered for bride refulgent like sun. The oblation offered is meant for Sūryā Sāvitri (bride) and not for me.

ओम् अघोरचक्षुरपतिघ्न्येधि शिवा पशुभ्यः सुमनाः सुवर्चाः वीरसूर्देवृकामा स्योना शन्नो भव द्विपदे शं चतुष्पदे स्वाहा॥ इदं सूर्यायै सावित्रयै-इदन्न मम ॥2॥

Om aghorachakṣur apatighnyedhi śivā paśubhyaḥ sumanāḥ suvarchāḥ vīrasūrdevṛkāmā syonā śanno bhava dvipade śaṁ chatuṣpade svāhā. idaṁ sūryāyai sāvitrayai-idanna mama.

[Meaning] O bride! By the grace of Brahman who is existent, conscious and all-bliss, you may not be ungenial in temperament and rigorous eyed towards husband. May you be benevolent to animals, and be conscientious, delighted at mind and possessed of gracious energy. May you be procreant of brave offsprings, desirous of divinity, and be bestower of happiness. May you be favourable to our bipends and kind to our quadrupeds.

ओम् इमां त्वमिन्द्र मीढ्वः सुपुत्रां सुभगां कृणु। दशास्यां पुत्राना धेहि पतिमेकादशं कृधि स्वाहा॥ इदं सूर्यायै सावित्रयै इदन्न मम॥3॥

Om imāṁ tvamindra mīḍhvaḥ suputrāṁ subhagāṁ kṛṇu, daśāsyāṁ putrānā dhehi patimekādaśaṁ kṛdhi svāhā, idaṁ sūryāyai sāvitrayai idanna mama.

[Meaning] O strong and mighty bride-groom! you are enriched with virile power and make this bride happy and bearing offsprings. You can have only up to ten chidren in your wife, not more. O bride! you also do not desire more children than ten and be content with them counting the husband as eleventh.

If you desire progeny beyond this number, you would produce children of short life and deprived of genius and you would also become short-lived and diseased. Therefore you do not procreate more progeny.

The meaning of sentence पतिमेकादशं कृधि (*patimekādaśaṁ kṛdhi*) will be different in the context of Niyoga. As God has given commandment for a husband to produce maximum ten children in his married wife. In the same manner, He has given the commandment for a married lady to have maximum ten children with the married husband or the husband of Niyoga after becoming widow. One woman should marry only one man at a time and one man only one women at a time and this is the injunction (of Śāstra). As a widowed women can have progeny through the tradition of Niyoga so a widowed man can also have children through Niyoga.

ओं सम्राज्ञी श्वशुरे भव सम्राज्ञी श्वश्वां भव। ननान्दरि सम्राज्ञी भव सम्राज्ञी

अधि देवृषु स्वाहा ॥ इदं सूर्यायै सावित्र्यै-इदन्न मम ॥ ऋ० 10.43.46

Oṁ samrājñī śvaśure bhava samrājñī śvaśrvāṁ bhava, nanāndari samrājñīṁ bhava samrājñī adhi devṛṣu svāhā. idaṁ sūryāyai sāvitrayai-idanna mama. RV. 10.43.46

[Meaning] I offer this oblation for you, O bride, to enjoy the status of empress in the hearts of your father-in-law, your mother-in-law, your sister-in-law, your brothers-in-law, to have an impartial affection for all. The oblation offered is meant for sun like refugent bride and not for me.

Afterwards one oblation of sviṣṭakṛt, four oblations of vyāhṛti āhutīs, and one oblation of prajāpatyāhuti should be offered, as is prescribed in the Sāmānya Prakaraṇa.

The bride-groom and bride should eat curd uttering the following mantra:

समंजन्तु विश्वे देवाः समापो हृदयानि नौ ।
सं मातरिश्वा सं धाता समु देष्ट्री दधातु नौ ॥ ऋ० 10.85.47

samaṁjantu viśve devāḥ samāpo hṛdayāni nau,
sam mātariśvā sam dhātā samu deṣṭrī dadhātu nau.

RV. 10.85.47

[Meaning] Let all the learned persons present here know that we are accepting each other voluntarily and pleasantly and our hearts are concordant and united like waters, let the air, Brahman, and the instructor keep us conjugated.

Afterwards the bride-groom and bride should offer their obeisance to father and mother of the bride-groom, and old people saying :

अहं भो अभिवादयामि ॥ गोभि० 2.4.11
ahaṁ bho abhivādayāmi. Go. GS. 2.4.11

[Meaning] I wish you namaste.

Thereafter, having dressed in nice outfit, let them sit on the decorated seat and chant Vāmdevyagāna. They should chant the stuti mantras as given in the Sāmānya Prakarṇa. At that time the ladies and gents who have come to grace the occasion should meditate upon Brahman with concentrated mind and the bride and bride-groom ask the parents and the Āchārya to chant svasti.

ओं स्वस्ति भवन्तो ब्रुवन्तु ॥ आश्व॰ गृ॰ 1.8.15

Oṁ svasti bhavanto bruvantu. Āśv.GS.1.8.15

[Meaning] Kindly you all say, 'svasti, svasti'.

Afterwards, father, āchārya and purohita, if they are learned, or if none of them is available, bride and bride-groom both, if they are learned or the knower of Veda, should chant 'Svastivāchana mantras' given in the Sāmānya Prakaraṇa. After the chanting is finished, the men and women who have come to participate in the function should say:

ओं स्वस्ति, ओं स्वस्ति, ओं स्वस्ति ॥

Oṁ svasti, Oṁ svasti, Oṁ svasti.

Thereafter, the hosts from bride-groom's family — father, uncle, brother etc. should give a warm send off to the gents and mother, aunt, etc to ladies.

In case, if due to some unavoidable circumstances, the impreganation ceremony could not take place in the house of the bride, the bride and bride-groom staying away from the saltish food, carnal desires and observing the vrata of Brahmacharya, should hold impregnation ceremony on the fourth day from the date of marriage according to the procedure laid down in Garbhādhāna Sanskāra.

Finally, the husband, mother-in-law, father-in-law,

sister-in-law, brother-in-law, wife of elder brother-in-law and other members of the family should greet the bride. They should always treat each other affectionately and exchange pleasantries. They should keep the bride in god humour by providing her with outfits and ornaments and the bride also should keep them delighted and pleased with her good conduct. The bride-groom should carry out in letter and spirit his Patnivarta dharma (one wife one husband) and wife should also carry out her Pativarta (one husband one wife) dharma. The bride-groom should always take care of the needs and pleasure of his wife and wife always should be obedient to her husband with her fair conduct and dealings.

इति विवाहसंस्कारविधिः समाप्तः ॥

iti vivāhasaṁskāravidhiḥ samāptaḥ

Thus ends here procedure of the Marriage Ceremony.

अथन्त्येष्टिकर्मविधिं वक्ष्यामः

Last Rites

The last rites of the dead body are called the Antyeṣṭi Sanskāra. There is no other Sanskāra, thereafter for this body. This is also called by the names of Naramedha, Puruṣmedha, Narayāga and Puruṣayāga.

भस्मान्तꣳ शरीरम् ॥ यजु॰ 40.15

bhasmāntaꣳ śarīram // YV. 40.15

[Meaning] The sanskāra or the last rite prescribed for the body implies upto the time of reducing dead body to ashes.

निषेकादिश्मशानान्तो मन्त्रैर्यस्योदितो विधिः ॥ मनु॰ ॥ 2.16

niṣekādiśmaśānānto mantrairyasyodito vidhiḥ //

Manu. 2.16

[Meaning] The beginning of the body implies the ceremony of impregnation and end of it implies the cremation i.e., the consignment of body to fire to reduce it to ashes.

Question: Are the rites like Daśagātra Ekādaśāha, Dvādaśāḥ, Sapiṇḍkarma, monthly or annual Gayā Śrāddha mentioned in the *Garuḍapurāṇa* and other texts false?

Answer: Yes, surely false as there is no injunction for such things in the Vedas and therefore, they should not be done. The soul departing from the body has neither any connection or relation at all with the previous relatives nor these living relatives have any connection with it. The soul has to take birth according its own karmas.

Q. Where does this soul go after death?

A. To the realm of Yama.

Q. What is the realm of Yama?

A. The realm of (vāyu) air.

Q. What is the realm of vāyu?

A. The space or the void.

Q. Is the yamaloka mentioned in the Garuḍapurāṇa and other texts false?

A. Certainly, it is false.

Q. Why then people of the world believe therein?

A. Due to the absence of knowledge and teaching of the Vedas. The story of Yama is entirely false as the term 'Yama' stands to mean the names of following things:

षळिद्यमा ऋषयो देवजा इति ॥ ऋ० 1.164.15

ṣaḷidyamā ṛṣayo devajā iti || RV 1.164.15

[Meaning] There are (ṣat) six seasons (yamāḥ) made of two monhs each (devajā) created by the sun.

Here the yamas are the names of seasons.

शकेम वाजिनो यमम् ॥ ऋ० 2.5.1

śakema vājino yamam || RV. 2.5.1

[Meaning] (vājinaḥ) Endowed with knowledge and exprience (śkema) we are able to know (yama) Brahman.

Here the yama is the name of Brahman.

यमाय जुहुता हविः । यमं ह यज्ञो गच्छत्यग्निदूतो अरंकृतः ॥ ऋ० 10.14.13
yamāya juhutā haviḥ | yamaṁ ha yajño gachchhatyagnidūto araṁkṛtaḥ || RV. 10.14.13

[Meaning] (juhutā) Offer (haviḥ) oblation (yamāya) for Agni, (yajña) this yajña (agnidūtaḥ) conducted with agni, as messenger of oblations, (gachchati) reaches (yamam) air (araṅkṛtaḥ) with all its beauty.

Here yama is the name of Agni.

यमः सूयमानो विष्णुः सम्भ्रियमाणो वायुः पूयमानः ॥ यजु॰ 8.57

*yamaḥ sūyamāno viṣṇuḥ sambhriyamāṇo vāyuḥ
pūyamānaḥ ॥ YV. 8.47*

[Meaning] (sūyamānaḥ) Rising sun is called (yamaḥ) yama (sambhriyamāṇaḥ), when collecting water vapours through its radiation heating it is called viṣṇu and when purifies the atmosphere, it is called vāyu.

Here, air, radiation heating and the sun are known as yama.

वाजिनं यमम् ॥ ऋ॰ 8.24.22

vājinaṁ yamam ॥ RV. 8.24.22

[Meaning] Swiftly moving air is yama.

Here also the yama is the name of vayu, as it moves swiftly.

यमं मातरिश्वनमाहुः ॥ ऋ॰ 1.164.46

śyamaṁ mātariśvanamāhuḥ ॥ RV. 1.164.46

[Meaning] Iśvara is known by the name of yama (supreme controller) and (mātṛśvā) first mover.

Here yama is the name of Īśvara.

All the above cited objects are called yama and therefore, all the fables and fancies of Purāṇas etc. are false.

Procedure of Last Rites

The dead, if male, should be given bath by men and if female should be given bath by women. Hair of the dead should be removed before giving bath to it. Paste of the sandal-wood should be applied on the body and it should be dressed with new clothes.

Ghee should be equal to the weight of the dead person. Well-to-do persons can use more ghee, but even if in the case of the poor the ghee should not be less than 17.5 kg (half maund). It should be arranged by a wealthy person or a the Pañchāyata (state) or by the contribution from the people. Well to do persons should mix in ghee the following things in the proportion described against each:

Kesar (saffron) - One māṣā (1 gm) in each one kg of ghee.

Kasturi (Musk) - One ratti (1 gm) in each one kg of ghee.

Agar (Acquilaria Malaccensis) - One kg in each one maund (35 kg)

Tagar (Veleriana Walichili) - One kg gm) in each one maund (35 kg).

Sandal-wood powder - One kg in each one maund (35 kg).

Comphor - as the circumstances permit.

Well-to-do persons should arrange for one maund (35 kg) sandal-wood, Twelve maunds (418 kg) fuel wood and sāmagri two times of the weight of the dead body.

All these things should be carried to the cremation ground.

If there is permanent Vedī in the cremation ground for the purpose of cremation, it should be used, if not, the new one should be made.

संस्थिते भूमिभागं खानयेद्दक्षिणपूर्वस्यां दिशि दक्षिणापरस्यां वा ॥1 ॥

vidhi-saṁsthite bhūmibhāgaṁ khānayeddakṣiṇapūrvasyāṁ diśi dakṣiṇāparasyāṁ vā ॥1 ॥

[Meaning] After death of a person, a portion of earth should be dug up either in south east or south west.

Cremation ground should be located to the south, south east or south west of the dwelling place of the people.

दक्षिणाप्रवणं प्राग्दक्षिणाप्रवणं वा प्रत्यग्दक्षिणाप्रवणमित्येके ॥2॥

dakṣiṇāpravaṇaṁ prāgdakṣiṇāpravaṇaṁ vā
pratyagdakṣiṇāpravaṇamityeke ॥2॥

[Meaning] Cremation pit should be dug in a way that its southern, southeastern or southwestern side should be deeper in the opinion of some experts.

The dimension of vedī should be as per the following measurements :

यावानुद्बाहुकः पुरुषस्तावदायामम् ॥3॥

yāvānudbāhukaḥ puruṣastāvadāyāmam ॥3॥

Length should be equal to the length of a man standing with his hands raising up.

व्याममात्रं तिर्यक् ॥4॥

vyāmamātraṁ tiryak ॥4॥

[Meaning] Breadth should be equal to two extended arms.

Breadth should be equal to the breadth of a person sleeping with his two hands stretched, i.e. it should be broader than 1 and 1/2 yards.

वितस्त्यर्वाक् ॥5॥

vitastyarvāk ॥5॥

[Meaning] Depth should be equal to the measure of 12 aṅgulas (fingers)

Depth should be equal to the heights of a man's

chest. The bottom should be of a yard in breadth.

केशश्मश्रुलोमनखानीत्युक्तं पुरस्तात् ॥6॥

keśaśmaśrulomanakhānītyuktaṁ purastāt ॥6॥

[Meaning] Already it has been suggested that hair, beard, nails, moustaches of a dead person should be removed.

द्विगुल्फं बर्हिराज्यं च ॥7॥

dvigulkaṁ barhirājyaṁ cha ॥7॥

[Meaning] Ghee and kuśa grass is required in abundant quatity.

दधन्यत्र सर्पिरानयन्त्येतत् पित्र्यं पृषदाज्यम् ॥8॥

dadhanyatra sarpirānayantyetat pitrayaṁ pṛṣadājyam ॥8॥

[Meaning] In the last rites, ghee is mixed with curd, this become pṛṣadājya (ghee mixed with coagulated milk) for the dead person.

अथैतां दिशमग्नीन्नयन्ति यज्ञपात्राणि च ॥9॥

athaitāṁ diśamagnīnnayanti yajñapātrāṇi cha ॥9॥

[Meaning] Fire and yajña pots should be carried to the southern direction of the Vedī

The dead-body should be laid on the pyre with its legs placed in south, south-east or south-west direction. Head should be placed in north, north-east or north-west direction. Dead body should be lowered down from side of legs as compared to the side of head.

Vedī should be sprinkled with water, and if cow-dung, is available, it should be purified by applying that.

Fuel wood should be piled in half of the Vedī from bottom just as the bricks are arranged in the wall. Wood logs thus piled should be intervened by camphor.

Afterwards, the logs of sandalwood and Palāśa should be piled till the height of 12 aṅgulas above Vedī.

Ghee should be molten and mixed with musk etc. fragrant substances. Big spoons made up either of wood, silver, gold or steel should be fixed or tied firmly in long sticks for offering oblations in the fire of the Vedī. They should be four. Four persons should offer Āhutīs at a time. Spoons should have such capacities that each of them could contain ghee equal to the quantitiy not more than one chhaṭānk (58 gm) and not less than half of a chhaṭānk (24 gm).

Lamp of ghee should be lighted. A man should enkindle a piece of camphor from the lamp and should light the pyre. In lighting the pyre, he should first begin from the hand and end at the feet. Thus, whole pyre should be lighted.

Afterwards the oblatins should be offered in the fire of the Vedī with the following mantras.

ओमग्नये स्वाहा ॥1॥

Omagnaye svāhā ॥1॥

[Meaning] This oblation is offered for agni.

ओं सोमाय स्वाहा ॥2॥

oṁ somāya svāhā ॥2॥

[Meaning] This oblation is offered for soma.

ओं लोकाय स्वाहा ॥3॥

oṁ lokāya svāhā ॥3॥

[Meaning] This oblation is offered for this universe.

ओमनुमतये स्वाहा ॥4॥

omanumataye svāhā ॥4॥

[Meaning] This oblation is offered for anumati (earth).

ओं स्वर्गाय लोकाय स्वाहा ॥5॥

oṁ svargāya lokāya svāhā ॥5॥

[Meaning] This oblation is offered for sun.

Offering the oblations with these five mantras, let the fire should be kindled and afterwards four persons standing separately should offer oblations with the Vedic mantras. They should drop the oblation in the fire at the sound of Svāhā.

अथ वेदमन्त्राः

Veda Mantras

सूर्यं चक्षुर्गच्छतु वातमात्मा द्यां च गच्छ पृथिवी च धर्मणा।
अपो वा गच्छ यदि तत्र ते हितमोषधीषु प्रतितिष्ठा शरीरैः स्वाहा ॥ ऋ.10.16.3

sūryaṁ chakṣurgachchhatu vātamātmā dyāṁ cha gachchha pṛthivī cha dharmaṇā ।
apo vā gachchha yadi tatra te hitamoṣadhīṣu pratitiṣṭhā śarīraiḥ svāhā ॥ RV. 10.16.3

[Meaning] O embodied soul! After death, the power of your sight be absored in the sun, may your (ātmā) soul go to (dyām) mokṣa or (vātam) to the amosphere (to take a rebirth), may you occupy the bodies of earthly creatures or divine people by (dharmavā) the merit of your actions; may you be born as aquatic animals or herbs and plants (pratitiṣṭhā) to stay (śariraiḥ) in mere body form, if it be (*te hitam*) thy lot.

अजो भागस्तपसा तं तपस्व तं ते शोचिस्तपतु ते अर्चिः।
यास्ते शिवास्तन्वो जातवेदस्ताभिर्वहैनं सुकृतामु लोकं स्वाहा ॥ ऋ.10.16.4

ajo bhāgastapasā taṁ tapasva taṁ te śochistapatu te archiḥ ।
yāste śivāstanvo jātavedastābhirvahainaṁ sukṛtāmu lokaṁ

svāhā || RV. 10.16.4

Here the instructions have been given to jīva (embodied soul) to uplift itself to higher state in order to achieve mokṣa.

[Meaning] (Jātavedaḥ) O jiva (embodied soul)! (te) your (bhāgaḥ) own original part, i.e. the soul is (ajaḥ) unborn and eternal by nature. (tapasva) Purify and (tapatu) season (tam) it to its (śochiḥ) original purity (tapasā) by the heat of austerity [yoga]. Whatever is (te) your remaining part, i.e. body, the mortal one, let (tam) that (tapatu) is burnt by (archiḥ) fire [after your death]. (yāḥ) Whatever (śivāḥ) good (tanvaḥ) bodies, Brahman has granted (te) to you [at the time of birth], (tābhiḥ) through these bodies do good karmas and (vaha) carry (enam) this soul to (sukṛtām loke) to those bodies that are occupied by divine beings.

अवसृज पुरग्रे पितृभ्यो यस्त आहुतश्चरति स्वधाभिः ।
आयुर्वसान उप वेतु शेषः संगच्छतां तन्वा जातवेदः स्वाहा ॥ ऋ.10.16.5

avasṛja puragne pitṛbhyo yasta āhutaścharati svadhābhiḥ |
āyurvasāna upa vetu śeṣaḥ samgachchhatām tanvā jātavedaḥ
svāhā || RV. 10.16.5

[Meaning] (Agne) O Brahman! (yaḥ) the dead body of which jīva (āhutaḥ) has been consigned to flame, and has been (charati) surrounded with (svadhābhiḥ) ghee etc. on all the sides, (ava) protect that jīva. (sṛja) Create this jīva (punaḥ) again (pitṛbhyaḥ) for taking care of its new parents. (śeṣaḥ jātavedaḥ) The surviving soul after its body having been consigned to flame, (āyuḥ vasānaḥ) assume a new life (upa vetu) received (tanvā) by a new body (sam gachchhatām) for doing its karmic business as usual.

अग्नेर्वर्म परि गोभिर्व्ययस्व सम्प्रोर्णुष्व पीवसा मेदसा च ।
नेत्वा धृष्णुर्हरसा जर्हृषाणो दधृग्विधक्ष्यन्पर्यङ्क्याते स्वाहा ॥ ऋ.10.16.7

*agnervarma   parigobhirvyayasva   samprornusva   pīvasā
medasā cha |*
*nettvā   dhṛṣṇurharasā   jarhṛṣāṇo   dadhṛgvidhakṣaya-
nparyankhayāte svāhā || RV. 10.16.7*

[Meaning] This soul gets its (varma) old body shield (pari vyayasva) burnt into ashes perfectly (agneḥ) in fire (gobhiḥ) with ghee etc., the products of cow, and (samprornusva) gets new body cover possessed with (pīvasā) sufficient flesh, and (medasā cha) fat etc. In the series of rebirth, let the soul acquire such proof or immunity from life and birth through yoga and austerities (na it) that its body (pari ankhyāte) is not burnt again and again by the (harasā dhṛṣṇu) overpowering (dadhṛk) bold fire, (vi dhakṣyan) capable of bruning the body, (jarhṛṣāṇaḥ) kindled by ghee etc.

यं त्वमग्ने समदहस्तमु निर्वापया पुनः ।
कियाम्ब्वत्र रोहतु पाकदूर्वा व्याल्कशा स्वाहा ॥ ऋ० 10.16.13

*yaṁ tvamagne samadahastamu nirvāpayā punaḥ |
kiyāmbvatra rohatu pākadarvā vyālkaśā svāhā ||5 ||*

RV. 10.16.13

[Meaning] (Agne) O fire, (tam) let that place be (nirvāpayā) cool (punaḥ) again (yaṁ) where (tvam) you (sam adahḥ) scorched and burnt the dead body. (atra) Let there (rohatu) grow (kiyāmbu) watery dūrvā grass (vyalkaśā) of different kinds.

Note: Dūrvā grass is also known as panic grass or durb grass.

परेयिवांसं प्रवतो महीरनु बहुभ्यः पन्थामनुपस्पशानम् ।
वैवस्वतं सङ्गमनं जनानां यमं राजानं हविषा दुवस्य स्वाहा ॥ ऋ० 10.14.1

*pareyivāṁsam   pravato   mahīranu   bahubhyaḥ
panthāmanupaspaśānam |*
vaivasvataṁ saṅgamanaṁ janānāṁ yamaṁ rājānaṁ haviṣā

duvasya svāhā || RV. 10.14.1

[Meaning] O jīva! you always (duvasya) lead (rājānam) glorious (yamam) time (vaivasvatam) born of sun (haviṣā) with the oblations of good karmas, as this time is the (saṅgamanam) ultimate end or destination of all (janānam) that are born. It (pareyivānsam anu) leads, after death, (pravataḥ) people performing various karmas or of various sanskāras (mahīḥ) to the species on this earth suitable for reaping the fruits of their karmas. (bahubhyaḥ) For many who want to enjoy spiritual bliss, the time (anupaspaśānam) clears (panthām) the path of happiness.

यमो नो गातुं प्रथमो विवेद नैषा गव्यूतिरपभर्तवा उ ।
यत्रा नः पूर्वे पितरः परेयुरेना जज्ञानाः पथ्या अनुस्वाः स्वाहा ॥ ऋ० 10.14.2

yamo no gātuṁ prathamo viveda naiṣā gavyūtirapabhartavā u /
yatrā naḥ pūrve pitaraḥ pareyurenā jajñānāḥ pathyā
anusvāḥ svāhā || RV. 10.14.2

[Meaning] (prathamaḥ yamaḥ) The first-born time (viveda) has registered (gātum) good and bad karmas (naḥ) of our life. (eṣā gavyuti) This course of good and bad karmas (na) cannot be (apabhartavā u) abandoned. (naḥ) Our (pūrve pitaraḥ) forefathers (preyuḥ) reaped the fruits of their karmas (yatrā) travelling on the same path of time. (enā jajñānāḥ) All living beings take birth following the same path of time. (anu) Following the same path, we are also bound (svāḥ pathyā) to reap the fruits of our karmas.

मातली कव्यैर्यमो अङ्गिरोभिर्बृहस्पतिऋक्वभिर्वावृधानः ।
यांश्च देवा वावृधुर्ये च देवान्त्स्वाहान्ये स्वधयान्ये मदन्ति स्वाहा ॥ ऋ० 10.14.3

mātalī   kavyairyamo   aṅgirobhirbṛhaspati-
rrkvabhirvāvṛdhānaḥ /
yāṁścha devā vāvṛdhurye cha devāntsvāhānye svadhayānye
madanti svāhā || RV. 10.14.3

[Meaning] (mātalī) The mind, which is called the charioteer of soul, (vvṛdhānaḥ) grows (kavyaḥ) with food; (yamaḥ) the life span of a human being grows (aṅgirobhiḥ) with practice of prāṇāyāma; (bṛhaspatiḥ) intellecual power of a human being grows (ṛkvabhiḥ) by gaining knowledge of Vedas and Śāstras; (cha) and (devāḥ) Natural forces (vvṛdhuḥ) give prosperity (yān) to those (ye) who replenish (devān) them [natural forces]. (anye) Natural forces (madanti) give prosperity to human beings by (svadhayā) providing them with food and natural resources and (anye) human beings (madanti) replenish natural forces (svahā) by offering oblations into yajña for them.

Note: This is the mutual contribution. Human beings should replenish natural forces and natural forces will give prosperity to human beings. Following śloka of Bhagvad Gītā also points out to the same thing.

देवान्भावयतानेन ते देवा भावयन्तु व: ।
परस्परं भावयन्त: श्रेय: परमवाप्स्यथ ॥ गीता ३.११ ॥

devānbhāvayatānena te devā bhāvayantu vaḥ,
parasparaṁ bhāvayantaḥ śreyaḥ paramavāpsyatha. Gītā, 3.11

[Meaning] Nourish the devas [natural forces] by performing yajña/havana and eco-friendly activities on the earth, and the natural forces will nourish you. Thus, by nourishing one another, you may attain the supreme good.

इमं यम प्रस्तरमा हि सीदाङ्गिरोभि: पितृभि: संविदान: ।
आ त्वा मन्त्रा कविशस्ता वहन्त्वेना राजन्हविषा मादयस्व स्वाहा ॥ ऋ० 10.14.4

imaṁ yama prastaramā hi sīdāṅgirobhiḥ pitṛbhiḥ saṁvidānaḥ ।
ā tvā mantrā kaviśastā vahantvenā rājanhaviṣā mādayasva svāhā ॥ RV.10.14.4

[Meaning] O (yama) life span of jīva! you (ā sid)

come to (imam) this (prastaram) body with (angirobhiḥ) with vital forces [prāṇas] (saṁvidānaḥ) harmonising with (pitṛbhiḥ) the protective energies of nature. (kaviśastāḥ mantraḥ) Let the mantras revealed to the seers (tvā ā vahantu) be your life force you in this body [a person should live a Vedic life] and then (rajan) shining and ruling in body (mādayasva) nourish this nature (haviṣā) with the oblations of yajña.

अङ्गिरोभिरागहि यज्ञियेभिर्यम वेरूपैरिह मादयस्व ।
विवस्वन्तं हुवे यः पिता तेऽस्मिन्यज्ञे बर्हिष्या निषद्य स्वाहा ॥ ऋ० 10.14.5

angirobhirāgahi yajñiyeiiāryama verūpairiha mādayasva /
vivasvantaṁ huve yaḥ pitā te'sminyajñe barhirṣyā niṣadya
svāhā // RV. 10.14.5

[Meaning] (yama) O life span of a jīva! you (āgahi) occupy this body (angirobhiḥ) with prāṇas (verūpaiḥ) and various (yajñiyebhiḥ) other means necessary for running this body (mādayasva) and make this body lively. Let me (huve) invoke (vivasvantam) the sun (yaḥ) who is (te pitā) the protector of this creation. The sun (ā niṣadya) participates (asmin) in this (yajñe) creation.

प्रेहि प्रेहि पथिभिः पूर्व्येभिर्यत्रा नः पूर्वे पितरः परेयुः ।
उभा राजाना स्वधया मदन्ता यमं पश्यासि वरुणं च देवं स्वाहा ॥ ऋ० 10.14.7

prehi prehi pathibhiḥ pūrvyebhiryatrā naḥ pūrve pitaraḥ
pareyuḥ /
ubhā rājānā svadhyā madantā yamaṁ paśyāsi varuṇaṁ cha
devaṁ svāhā // RV.10.14.7

[Meaning] O jīvas! (prehi prehi) you should tread (pūrvyebhiḥ) the old (pathibhiḥ) path (yatra) which (nah) our (pūrve pitaraḥ) fore-fathers (pareyuḥ) have trodden since eternity. (paśyāsi) You should (madantā) identify the real nature of (ubhā) both (rājānā yamam) the effulgent Brahman (cha) and (varuṇaṁ devam) the soul (svadhayā) through this material body.

संं गच्छस्व पितृभिः संं यमेनेष्टापूर्तेन परमे व्योमन् ।
हित्वायावद्यं पुनरस्तमेहि संं गच्छस्व तन्वा सुवर्चाः स्वाहा ॥ ऋ॰ 10.14.8

sam gachchhasva pitṛbhiḥ sam yameneṣṭāpūrtena parame vyoman /
hitvāyāvadyam punarastamehi sam gachchhasva tanvā suvarchāḥ svāhā // RV. 10.14.8

[Meaning] O jīva! by identifying your true nature and that of Brahman, you will (sam gachchhasva) reach (parame vyoman) space of Brahman called chidākāśa or mokṣa. Or by doing (iṣṭa-āpūrtena) actions of yajña, dāna and tapa prescribed in Śrauta [Vedic texts] and Smārta texts [Dharmaśātras], and (avadyam hitvā) by abandoning the actions leading to your downfall to lower species, you will attain (yamena) life span in human species and (punar ehi) will come back (astam) to this world with (suvarchā) divine (tanvā) body to join (pitṛbhiḥ) your friends and relatives of past lives.

अपेत वीत वि च सर्पतातोऽस्मा एतं पितरो लोकमक्रन् ।
अहोभिरद्भिरक्तुभिर्व्यक्तं यमो ददात्यवसानमस्मै स्वाहा ॥ ऋ॰ 10.14.9

apeta vīta vi cha sarpatāto'smā ētam pitaro lokamakran /
ahobhiradbhiraktubhivaryaktam yamo dadātyavasānamasmai svāhā // RV.14.9

[Meaning] (pitaraḥ) The sunrays (akran) have made (etam lokam) this earth habitat (asmai) for the jīva. These sunrays (apeta) come, (vīta) diverge and (visarpata) and spread (ataḥ) on earth. (yamaḥ) The sun dadāti) has made this earth (avasānam) resting place (asmai) for this jīva by (vyaktam) creating days, nights and water on it

यमाय सोमं सुनुत यमाय जुहुता हविः ।
यमं ह यज्ञो गच्छत्यग्निदूतो अरङ्कृतः स्वाहा ॥ ऋ॰ 10.14.13

yamāya somam sunuta yamāya juhutā haviḥ /
yamam ha yajño gachchhatyagnidūto araṅkṛtaḥ svāhā //
RV.10. 14.13

[Meaning] (somam) This earth was (sunuta) made, (yamāya) so that sunrays come on it and the yajña of creation may be accomplished here. (haviḥ) This havi or oblation is (juhutā) given to the yajña (yamāya) so that it may reach sun. Whatever is offered in (yajñaḥ) the yajña (gachchhati) goes to (yamam) the sun (agnidutaḥ) transported by fire (araṅkṛtaḥ) in an amazing way.

यमाय घृतवद्धविर्जुहोत प्र च तिष्ठत् ।
स नो देवेष्वा यमद्दीर्घमायुः प्र जीवसे स्वाहा ॥ ऋ० 10.14.14

yamāya ghṛtavaddhavirjuhota pra cha tiṣṭhat /
sa no deveṣvā yamaddīrghamāyuḥ pra jīvase svāhā //

RV.10.14.14

[Meaning] O jīvas! You always (juhota) perform yajñas (ghṛtavat) with oblation of ghee etc. (yamāya) for sun (pratiṣṭhat cha) to purify atmosphere and attain your highest goal of life. (saḥ) The sun has (dīrgham āyuḥ) long life (deveṣu) amongst all the heavenly bodies in our solar system. Let it (prāyamat) prolong (naḥ) our (jīvase) life on this earth.

यमाय मधुमत्तमं राज्ञे हव्यं जुहोतन ।
इदं नम ऋषिभ्यः पूर्वजेभ्यः पूर्वेभ्यः पथिकृद्भ्यः स्वाहा ॥ ऋ० 10.14.15

yamāya madhumattamaṁ rājñe havyaṁ juhotana /
idaṁ nama ṛṣibhyaḥ pūrvajebhyaḥ pūrvebhyaḥ
pathikṛdbhyaḥ svāhā // RV. 10.14.15

[Meaning] O jīvas! you (juhotana) offer the (madhumattamam) sweet oblations (yamāya rājñe) for sun, the king of solar sytem. Let (idam) this (nama) obeisance be due to (ṛṣibhyaḥ) seers, (pūrvajebhyaḥ pūrvebhyaḥ) our seniors (pathikṛdbhyaḥ) who made the path for us.

कृष्णः श्वेतोऽरुषो यामो अस्य ब्रघ्न ऋज्र उत शोणो यशस्वान् ।
हिरण्यरूपं जनिता जजान स्वाहा ॥ ऋ० 10.20.9

kṛṣṇaḥ śveto'ruṣo yāmo asya braghna ṛjra uta śoṇo yaśasvān /
hiraṇyarūpaṁ janitā jajāna svāhā // RV. 10.20.9

[Meaning] O jīvas! (yāmaḥ) The time (asya) of this sun is (kṛṣṇaḥ) black [during night], (śvetaḥ) white [during midday, (śoṇaḥ) red [during twilight hours. (aruṣaḥ) The bright sunlight moves (ṛjraḥ) in straight line. It has (bradhnaḥ) wide expanse (ut) and (yaśasvān) provides food and vegetations on earth. (janitā) Brahman (jajāna) has made it (hiraṇyarūpa) of golden hue. [Colour of energy is golden].

Note: Yama is sun, so yāma is both time created by sun and sunlight. Yāma is also called prahara, a time period of 3 hours. There is total 8 yāmas [praharas] in a day.

The four persons should offer seventeen oblations of ghee with the above-mentioned mantras, and thereafter offer oblations in the same manner with the following mantras:

प्राणेभ्यः साधिपतिकेभ्यः स्वाहा ॥1॥

prāṇobhyaḥ sādhipatikebhyaḥ svāhā ॥1॥

[Meaning] This oblation is for prāṇas with their strength

पृथिव्यै स्वाहा ॥2॥   अग्नये स्वाहा ॥3॥

pṛthivyai svāhā ॥2॥   *agnaye svāhā ॥3॥*

[Meaning] This oblation is for earth and agni

अन्तरिक्षाय स्वाहा ॥4॥   वायवे स्वाहा ॥5॥

antarikṣāya svāhā ॥4॥   *vāyave svāhā ॥5॥*

[Meaning] This oblation is for midsphere and air

दिवे स्वाहा ॥6॥   सूर्याय स्वाहा ॥7॥

dive svāhā //6 //   *sūryāya svāhā //7 //*

[Meaning] This oblation is for celestial sphere and sun

दिग्भ्यः स्वाहा ॥8 ॥   चन्द्राय स्वाहा ॥9 ॥

digbhyaḥ svāhā //8 //   *chandrāya svāhā //9 //*

[Meaning] This oblation is for directions and moon

नक्षत्रेभ्यः स्वाहा ॥10 ॥   अद्भ्यः स्वाहा ॥11 ॥

nakṣatrebhyaḥ svāhā //10 // adbhyaḥ svāhā //11 //

[Meaning] This oblation is for constellations and waters.

वरुणाय स्वाहा ॥12 ॥   नाभ्यै स्वाहा ॥13 ॥

varuṇāya svāhā //12 //   *nābhyai svāhā //13 //*

[Meaning] This oblation is for waters and navel.

पूताय स्वाहा ॥14 ॥   वाचे स्वाहा ॥15 ॥

pūtāya svāhā //14 //   *vāche svāhā //15 //*

[Meaning] This oblation is for cleanliness and speech.

प्राणाय स्वाहा ॥16 ॥   प्राणाय स्वाहा ॥17 ॥

prāṇāya svāhā //16 //   *prāṇāya svāhā //17 //*

[Meaning] This oblation is for prāṇas

चक्षुषे स्वाहा ॥18 ॥   चक्षुषे स्वाहा ॥19 ॥

chakṣuṣe svāhā //18 //   *chakṣuṣe svāhā //19 //*

[Meaning] This oblation is for eyes.

श्रोत्राय स्वाहा ॥20 ॥   श्रोत्राय स्वाहा ॥21 ॥

śrotrāya svāhā //20 //   *rotrāya svāhā //21 //*

[Meaning] This oblation is for ears.

लोमभ्यः स्वाहा ॥22 ॥   लोमभ्यः स्वाहा ॥23 ॥

lomabhyaḥ svāhā ||22 || *lomabhyaḥ svāhā ||23 ||*

[Meaning] This oblation is for hair.

त्वचे स्वाहा ||24 || त्वचे स्वाहा ||25 ||

tvache svāhā ||24 || *tvache svāhā ||25 ||*

[Meaning] This oblation is for skin.

लोहिताय स्वाहा ||26 || लोहिताय स्वाहा ||27 ||

lohitāya svāhā ||26 || *lohitāya svāhā ||27 ||*

[Meaning] This oblation is for blood.

मेदोभ्यः स्वाहा ||28 || मेदोभ्यः स्वाहा ||29 ||

[Meaning] This oblation is for fat.

medobhyaḥ svāhā ||28 || *medobhyaḥ svāhā ||29 ||*

माꣳसेभ्यः स्वाहा ||30 || माꣳसेभ्यः स्वाहा ||31 ||

māꣳsebhyaḥ svāhā ||30 || *māꣳsebhyaḥ svāhā ||31 ||*

[Meaning] This oblation is for flesh.

स्नावभ्यः स्वाहा ||32 || स्नावभ्यः स्वाहा ||33 ||

snāvabhyaḥ svāhā ||32 || *snāvabhyaḥ svāhā ||33 ||*

[Meaning] This oblation is for sinews.

अस्थभ्यः स्वाहा ||34 || अस्थभ्य स्वाहा ||35 ||

asthabhyaḥ svāhā ||34 || *asthabhyaḥ svāhā ||35 ||*

[Meaning] This oblation is for bones.

मज्जभ्यः स्वाहा ||36 || मज्जभ्यः स्वाहा ||37 ||

majjabhyaḥ svāhā ||36 || *majjabhyaḥ svāhā ||37 ||*

[Meaning] This oblation is for marrow.

रेतसे स्वाहा ||38 || पायवे स्वाहा ||39 ||

retase svāhā ||38 || *pāyave svāhā ||39 ||*

[Meaning] This oblation is for seamen and anus.

आयासाय स्वाहा ॥40॥   प्रायासाय स्वाहा ॥41॥

āyāsāya svāhā ॥40॥   *prāyāsāya svāhā ॥41॥*

[Meaning] This oblation is for perseverance and genuine efforts.

संयासाय स्वाहा ॥42॥   वियासाय स्वाहा ॥43॥

saṁyāsāya svāhā ॥42॥   *viyāsāya svāhā ॥43॥*

[Meaning] This oblation is for activities and upliftment.

उद्यासाय स्वाहा ॥44॥   शुचे स्वाहा ॥45॥

udyāsāya svāhā ॥44॥   *śuche svāhā ॥45॥*

[Meaning] This oblation is for efforts and purity.

शोचते स्वाहा ॥46॥   शोचमानाय स्वाहा ॥47॥

śochate svāhā ॥46॥   *śochamānāya svāhā ॥47॥*

[Meaning] This oblation is for that who mourns and who is being mourned.

शोकाय स्वाहा ॥48॥   तपसे स्वाहा ॥49॥

śokāya svāhā ॥48॥   *tapase svāhā ॥49॥*

[Meaning] This oblation is for grief and austerity.

तप्यते स्वाहा ॥50॥   तायमानाय स्वाहा ॥51॥

tapyate svāhā ॥50॥   *tapyamānāya svāhā ॥51॥*

[Meaning] This oblation is for that which gets heated up and agency of heat

तप्ताय स्वाहा ॥52॥   घर्माय स्वाहा ॥53॥

taptāya svāhā ॥52॥   *gharmāya svāhā ॥53॥*

[Meaning] This oblation is for heat and sunlight.

निष्कृत्यै स्वाहा ॥ 54 ॥   प्रायश्चित्यै स्वाहा ॥55 ॥

niṣkṛtyai svāhā ॥ 54 ॥   prāyaśchityai svāhā ॥55 ॥

[Meaning] This oblation is for vengeance, repentence.

भेषजाय स्वाहा ॥56 ॥   यमाय स्वाहा ॥57 ॥

bheṣajāya svāhā ॥56 ॥   yamāya svāhā ॥57 ॥

[Meaning] This oblation is for medicine and Yama

अन्तकाय स्वाहा ॥58 ॥   मृत्यवे स्वाहा ॥59 ॥

antakāya svāhā ॥58 ॥   mṛtyave svāhā ॥59 ॥

[Meaning] This oblation is for time and death.

ब्रह्मणे स्वाहा ॥60 ॥   ब्रह्महत्यायै स्वाहा ॥61 ॥

brahmaṇe svāhā ॥60 ॥   brahmahatyāyai svāhā ॥61 ॥

[Meaning] This oblation is for Brahman and disobedience of the command of Brahman.

विश्वेभ्योदेवेभ्यःस्वाहा ॥62 ॥

viśvebhyodevebhyaḥsvāhā ॥62 ॥

[Meaning] This oblation is for all natural forces

द्यावापृथिवीभ्याꣳस्वाहा ॥63 ॥ यजु॰ 39

dyāvāpṛthivībhyāꣳsvāhā ॥63 ॥ YV. 39

[Meaning] This oblation is for earth and sun

After offering the 63 seperate oblations with the above-mentioned sixty-three mantras, further oblations be offered with the following mantras:

सूर्यं चक्षुषा गच्छ वातमात्मना दिवं च गच्छ पृथिवीं च धर्मभिः ।
अपो वा गच्छ यदि तत्र ते हितमोषधीषु प्रतितिष्ठा शरीरैः स्वाहा ॥ अ. 18.2.7

*sūryaṁ chakṣuṣā gachchha vātamātmanā divaṁ cha gachchha pṛthivīṁ cha dhamabhiḥ ।
apo vā gachchha yadi tatra te hitamoṣadhīṣu pratitiṣṭhā*

śarīraiḥ svāhā || AV. 18.2.7

[Meaning] O embodied soul! After death, (chakṣuṣā) the power of your sight (gachchha) be absored (sūryam) in the sun, may your (ātmā) soul go to (divam) Mokṣa [space of Brahman] or (vātam) to the amosphere [to take a rebirth], may you occupy the (pṛthivīm) bodies of earthly creatures or divine people by (dharmabhiḥ) the merit of your actions; may you (gachchha) be born as (apaḥ) aquatic animals or (oṣadhiṣu) herbs and plants (pratitiṣṭhā) to stay (śariraiḥ) in material body, if it be (te hitam) thy lot.

सोम एकेभ्यः पवते घृतमेक उपासते ।
येभ्यो मधु प्रधावति तांश्चिदेवापि गच्छतात् स्वाहा ॥ अ. 18.2.14

soma ēkebhyaḥ pavate ghṛtameka upāsate |
yebhyo madhu pradhāvati tāṁśchidevāpi gachchhatāt
svāhā || AV. 18.2.14

[Meaning] (ekebhyaḥ) For vāta dominated people (soma) liquid foods or tila-oil (pavate) are purifying agents; (eke) pitta dominated people (upa āsate) should take (ghṛtam) ghee [for pacifying pitta]. (yebhyaḥ) For those who are afflicted by kapha, (madhu) honey (pradhāvati) works wonder. So, a person (gachchhatāt) should go (tān eva) for the same agent [watery food or tila-oil, ghee or honey] (chit) which is required for him as per vāta, pitta and kapha dominance.

ये चित्पूर्व ऋतसाता ऋतजाता ऋतावृधः ।
ऋषीन् तपस्वतो यम तपोजाँ अपि गच्छतात् स्वाहा ॥ अ. 18.2.15

ye chitpūrva ṛtasātā ṛtajātā ṛtāvṛdhaḥ |
ṛṣīn tapasvato yama tapojāṁ api gachchhatāt svāhā ||

AV. 18.2.15

[Meaning] O yama! (jīva bound with the laws of karmas) you (gachchhatāt) attain (ṛṣīn) species (tapojān) as per your sanskāras (tapasvataḥ) accumulated by you (pūrve) in your previous lives. (ye) All these species (chit) certainly (ṛtasātā) follow the law of ṛta [motion], (ṛtajātā) born as per law of ṛta [motion] and (ṛtāvṛdhaḥ) and grow as per law of ṛta [motion].

तपसा ये अनाधृष्यास्तपसा ये स्व ⌈र्ययुः ।
तपो ये चक्रिरे महस्तांश्चिदेवापि गच्छतात् स्वाहा ॥ अ. 18.2.16

tapasā ye anādhṛṣyāstapasā ye sva ryayuḥ /
tapo ye chakrire mahastāṁśchidevāpi gachchhatāt svāhā //
AV. 18.2.16

[Meaning] O jīva! you (gachchhatāt) attain the status of even those persons, (ye) who have become (anādhṛṣyāḥ) unsurmountable by (tapasā) yoga and austerity and (ye) those who (yayuḥ) have gained (svaḥ) the state of bliss (tapasā) through yoga and austerity. May you have those as your spiritual Gurus who have (mahaḥ tapaḥ) observed strict disciplines of yoga and austerity.

ये युध्यन्ते प्रधनेषु शूरासो ये तनूत्यजः ।
ये वा सहस्रदक्षिणास्तांश्चिदेवापि गच्छतात् स्वाहा ॥ अ. 18.2.17

ye yudhyante pradhaneṣu śūrāso ye tanūtyajaḥ /
ye vā sahasradakṣiṇāstāṁśchidevāpi gachchhatāt svāhā // AV. 18.2.17

[Meaning] O jīva! you (gachchhatāt) attain the status of those (devāḥ api) divine souls (ye śūrāsaḥ) who are brave and (yudhyante) fight (pradhaneṣu) in the tremendous battles for establishing dharma, (ye) who (tanustyajaḥ) are ready to sacrifice their lives for a good cause, (vā) and (ye) who (sahsra-dakṣiṇāḥ) give away thousands of rupees in charity.

स्योनास्मै भव पृथिव्यनृक्षरा निवेशनी ।
यच्छास्मै शर्म सप्रथाः स्वाहा ॥ अ. 18.2.19

syonāsmai bhava pṛthivyanṛkṣarā niveśanī /
yachchhāsmai śarma saprathāḥ svāhā // AV. 18.2.19

[Meaning] (pṛthvī) May this earth (bhava) be (syonā)

comfortable and (anṛkṣarā) free from thorny difficulties (asmai) for this departing soul (in its next life). May (saprathāḥ) this expansive earth be (niveśanī) inhabitable for him. May it (yachha) give him (śarma) peace, progress and happiness.

अपेमं जीवा अरुधन् गृहेभ्यस्तन्निर्वहत परि ग्रामादितः ।
मृत्युर्यमस्यासीद्दूतः प्रचेता असून् पितृभ्यो गमयां चकार स्वाहा ॥ अ. 18.2.27

apemaṁ jīvā arudhan gṛhebhyastannirvahata pari grāmāditaḥ |
mṛtyuryamasyāsīddūtaḥ prachetā asūn pitṛbhyo gamayāṁchakāra svāhā || AV. 18.2.27

[Meaning] (imam) This person was (ap arundhan) detained by (jivaḥ) family members (gṛhebhyaḥ) for household duty. Since now he has died, take (tam) him (itaḥ grāmāt) from the residential area to the crematorium located (pari nirvahat) at a distant place. (mṛtyuḥ) Death (āsīt) is the (dūta) heraldor (yamasya) of the end-of-life span of a person in the current birth. The death has made (asūn) the prāṇās or vital airs of the living body (gamayāṁ chakāra) leave body and go to (pitṛbhyaḥ) the atmosphere or rays of the moon. (prachetāḥ) Take care of yourself, do not bereave.

यमः परोऽवरो विवस्वान् ततः परं नाति पश्यामि किंचन ।
यमे अध्वरो अधि मे निविष्टो भुवो विवस्वानन्वाततान् स्वाहा ॥ अ. 18.2.32

yamaḥ paro'varo vivasvān tataḥ paraṁ nāti paśyāmi kiṁchana |
yame adhvaro adhi me niviṣṭo bhuvo vivasvānanvātatān svāhā || AV. 18.2.32

[Meaning] (yamaḥ) Time existed in avyakta or incalculable form (paraḥ) before every thing. (vivasvān) This sun, the creator of vyakta or calculable form of time, came into being (avaraḥ) later. (na ati paśyāmi) I do not see anything beyond the avyakta [incalculable] form of time. (adhvaraḥ) This creation (me) of ours (niviṣṭaḥ) is taking place (yame adhi) under this time as instrumental cause. (vivasvān) The sun (anvātatāna) has expanded its (bhuvaḥ) magnetic field.

अपागूहन्नमृतां मर्त्येभ्यः कृत्वा सवर्णामदधुर्विवस्वते ।
उताश्विनावभरद् यत्तदासीदजहादु द्वा मिथुना सरण्यूः स्वाहा ॥ अ. 18.2.33

apāgūhannamṛtāṁ   martyebhyaḥ   kṛtvāsavarṇāmadadhu-
rvivasvate |
utāśvināvabharad yattadāsīdajahādu dvā mithunā saraṇyūḥ
svāhā || AV. 18.2.33

[Spiritual Meaning] (amṛtām) Immortaliy (apāgūhan) is hidden for (martyebhyaḥ) mortals [It is for divine beings]. (savarṇām kṛtvā adadhuḥ) The same immortality can be established for (vivasvate) enlightened person. (yat) When (saraṇyūḥ) breathing excercises (āsīt) are done (tat) the same (uta abharat) would involve (āśvinau) two nostrils [prāṇa and apāna] which (ajahāt) gives birth (dvā mithunā) to chandra [iḍā] and sūrya [piṅgalā] svaras.

[Scientific Meaning] (amṛtām) Chidākāśa, the abode of inactive energy (apāgūhan) is hidden for (martyebhyaḥ) bhūtākāśa, the abode of active energy. (vivasvate) For the origin of bhūtākāśa, (savarṇām kṛtvā adadhuḥ) the same inactive energy was made active [by the saṅkalpa of Brahman] and established in bhūtākāśa. (Uta) Afterwards (yat saraṇyūḥ) whatever active energy (āsīt) was (tat) there, it (abharat) conceived (āśvinau) two aśvins [charges-negative and positive] and (ajahāt) released (dvā mithunā) twin-particles [particle called yama and anti-particle called yamī].

इमौ युनज्मि ते वह्नी असुनीताय वोढवे ।
ताभ्यां यमस्य सादनं समितिश्चाव गच्छतात् स्वाहा ॥ अ. 18.2.56

imau yunajmi te vahnī asunītāya voḍhave |

*tābhyāṁ yamasya sādanaṁ samitiśchāva gachchhatāt
svāhā || AV. 18.2.56*

[Meaning] O jīva! Let me (Brahman) (yunajmi) unite (te) your (asunītāya) subtle body devoid of prāṇās with (imau vahnī) prāṇa and apāna (voḍhve) to carry it to the next body. (tābhyām) With the help of these two, you (ava gachchhatāt) attain (yamasya sādanam) your new life span (samitiścha) and species prescribed for you according to your kārmika sanskāras.

After offering ten oblations with the above-mentioned ten mantras, the further oblation be offered with the following mantras:

अग्नये रयिमते स्वाहा ॥1 ॥

agnaye rayimate svāhā ||1 ||

[Meaning] (svāhā) This oblation for (agni) geothermal energy (rayimate) which is the producer of all the metallurgical wealth.

पुरुषस्य सयावर्यपेदघानि मृज्महे ।
यथा नो अत्र नापरः पुरा जरस आयति स्वाहा ॥2 ॥

*puruṣasya sayāvaryapedaghāni mṛjmahe /
yathā no atra nāparaḥ purā jarasa āyati tvāhā ||2 ||*

[Meaning] (sayāvari) The sanskāras travel with (puruṣasya) subtle body of soul. So let us (apet) remove (aghāni) sanskāras leading to our downgradation to lower species and (mṛjmahe) and purify our habits and actions. We should lead life (yathā) in such a way that (atra) in this world (na) no (aparaḥ) bad sanskāra (āyati) is accumulated (purā) before we reach (jarasa) the old age.

य एतस्य पथो गोप्तारस्तेभ्यः स्वाहा ॥3 ॥

ya ētasya patho goptārastebhyaḥ svāhā ||3 ||

[Meaning] (svāhā) This oblation is for the rays of the moon and air (goptārāḥ) which protect (pathaḥ) the path (etasya) of this jīva departing from body.

य एतस्य पथो रक्षितारस्तेभ्यः स्वाहा ॥4॥

ya ētasya patho rakṣitārastebhyaḥ svāhā ॥4॥

[Meaning] (svāha) This oblation is (tebhyaḥ) for those (goptāraḥ) who protect (pathaḥ) the path (etasya) of this jīva departing from the body.

य एतस्य पथोऽभिरक्षितारस्तेभ्यः स्वाहा ॥5॥

ya ētasya patho'bhirakṣitārastebhyaḥ svāhā ॥5॥

[Meaning] (svāhā) This oblation is (tebhyaḥ) for those (abhirakṣitāraḥ) who guard (pathaḥ) the path (etasya) of this jīva departing from the body.

ख्यात्रे स्वाहा ॥6॥

khyātre svāhā ॥6॥

[Meaning] (svāhā) This oblation is (khyātre) for that which promotes name and fame.

अपाख्यात्रे स्वाहा ॥7॥

apākhyātre svāhā ॥7॥

[Meaning] (svāhā) This oblation is (apākhyātre) for knowing that which defames us.

अभिलालपते स्वाहा ॥8॥

abhilālapate svāhā ॥8॥

[Meaning] (svāhā) This oblation is (abhilālapate) for explaining good deeds.

अपलालपते स्वाहा ॥9॥

apalālapate svāhā ॥9॥

[Meaning] (svāhā) This oblation is (apalālapate) for explaining bad deeds.

अग्नये कर्मकृते स्वाहा ॥10॥

agnaye karmakṛte svāhā ॥10॥

[Meaning] (svāhā) This oblation is for (agni) fire of

yajñavedī (karmakṛte) which accomplishes the task of yajñas like Agnhotra and so on.

यमत्र नाधीमस्तस्मै स्वाहा ॥11 ॥ तैआ. 6.2

yamatra nādhīmastasmai svāhā ॥11 ॥ TĀr. 6.2

[Meaning] (svāhā) This oblation is for (yam) that which is (na) not (adimaḥ) remembered (atra) here.

अग्रये वैश्वानराय सुवर्गाय लोकाय स्वाहा ॥12 ॥ तैआ. 6.3

agnaye veśvānarāya suvargāya lokāya svāhā ॥12 ॥ TĀr.6.3

[Meaning] This oblation is for (Agni Vaiśvānara) sun that lights up the whole universe and (suvarga loka) celestial sphere.

आयातु देव सुमनाभिरूतिभिर्यमो ह वेह प्रयताभिरक्ता ।

आसीदताꣳसुप्रयते ह बर्हिष्यूर्जाय जात्यै मम शत्रुहत्यै स्वाहा ॥13 ॥ तैआ. 6.5

āyātu devaḥ sumanābhir ūtibhiryamo ha veha prayatābhiraktā । āsīdatāꣳsuprayate ha barhiṣyūrjāya jātyai mama śatruhatyai svāvahā ॥13 ॥ TĀr. 6.5

[Meaning] May (ā yātu) I attain (devaḥ yamaḥ ha) divine life span (sumanābhiḥ ūtibhiḥ) due to my good karmas (vā iha) in this birth, (aktā) may our time (pra yatābhiḥ) pass in attaining the knowledge of Vedas. Let men and women (āsīdatām) participate and take seat in (mama barhiṣi) our vast yajñas (su pra yate) performed with good efforts (ūrjāya) for the purpose of attaining spiritual energy (jātyai), superior species (śatruhatyai) and dispelling of enemies like, covetousness, passion, aversion etc.

योऽस्य कौछ्य जगतः पार्थिवस्यैक इद्वशी ।

यमं भङ्ग्यश्रवो गाय यो राजाऽनपरोध्यः स्वाहा ॥14 ॥ तैआ. 6.5

yo'sya koṣṭhya jagataḥ pārthivasyaika idvaśī । yamaṁ bhaṅgyaśravo gāya yo rājā'naparodhyaḥ svāhā ॥14 ॥

TĀr. 6.10

[Spiritual Meaning] O jīvas! (gāya) you sing (bhaṅgya-śravaḥ) with the artistic method the prayer of (yamam) all ordaining Brahman (yaḥ) who is the (it ekaḥ vaśī) lone governor (asya) of this (pārthivaḥ jagataḥ) material expanse. (yaḥ) He is (anaparodhyaḥ) the unobstructed (rājā) king of all this.

[Scientific Meaning] O jīvas! (gāya bhaṅgya-śravaḥ) appreciate properly (yamam) the matter particle (yaḥ) that is (it ekaḥ vaśī) the lone controller (asya) of this (pārthivaḥ jagataḥ) material expanse. (yaḥ) This matter particle is (anaparodhyaḥ) the unobstructed (rājā) king of all this.

यमं गाय भङ्ग्यश्रवो यो राजाऽनपरोध्यः ।
येनाऽऽपो नद्य धन्वानि येन द्यौःपृथिवी दृढा स्वाहा ॥15॥ तैआ. 6.5

yamaṁ gāya bhaṅgyaśravo yo rājā'naparodhyaḥ /
yenā"po nadya dhanvāni yena dyauḥpṛthivī dṛḍhā
svāhā //15 // TĀr. 6.5

[Spiritual Meaning] O jīvas! (gāya) Sing (bhaṅgya-śravaḥ) with artistic method the prayer (yama) of ordainer Brahman (yaḥ) who is (anaparodhyaḥ) the unobstructed (rājā) king of all and (yena) who (dṛḍhā) has held firm the (āpaḥ) waters, (nadya) rivers, (dhanvāni) deserts (dyauḥ) stars and (pṛthivī) planets.

[Scientific Meaning] O jīvas! (gāya bhaṅgya-śravaḥ) Appreciate properly the contribution (yama) of matter particle (yaḥ) which is (anaparodhyaḥ) the unobstructed (rājā) king of this material expanse and (yena) which (dṛḍhā) has materialised (āpaḥ) waters, (nadya) rivers, (dhanvāni) deserts (dyauḥ) stars and (pṛthivī) planets.

हिरण्यकक्ष्यान्त्सुधुरान् हिरण्याक्षानयःशफान् ।
अश्वाननशशतो दानं यमो राजाभितिष्ठति स्वाहा ॥16॥ तैआ. 6.5

hiraṇyakakṣayāntsudhurān hiraṇyākṣānayaḥśaphān /
aśvānanaśśato dānaṁ yamo rājābhitiṣṭhati svāhā //16 //

TĀr. 6.5

[Meaning] (yamah rājā) Sun, the king of our solar system (hiranyakakṣyān) having golden orbit around the Galaxy (sudhurān) powerful axis (hiranyākṣa) looking golden (ayah śaphān) having steel like unbreakable disc (aśvan anaśśatah) and thousands of rays (abhitiṣṭhati) exists here (dānam) to give us life.

यमो दाधार पृथिवीं यमो विश्वमिदं जगत् ।
यमाय सर्वमित्तस्थे यत् प्राणद्वायुरक्षितं स्वाहा ॥17॥ तैआ. 6.5

yamo dādhāra pṛthivīṁ yamo viśvamidaṁ jagat l
yamāya sarvamittasthe yat prāṇadvāyurakṣitaṁ svāhā ll17 ll

TĀr. 6.5

[Meaning] (yamah) The sun (dādhāra) sustains (pṛthivīm) earth (yamah), it sustains (idam viśvam jagat) the whole life in our universe. (sarvam) Everything (yat) that is (rakṣitam) maintained by (prāṇat) breath or (vāyu) air (tasthe) exists (it) here (yamāya) because of sun.

यथा पंच यथा षड् यथा पंचदशर्षयः ।
यमं यो विद्यात् स ब्रूयाद्यथैक ऋषिर्विजानते स्वाहा ॥18॥ तैआ. 6.5

yathā paṁcha yathā ṣaḍ yathā paṁchadaśarṣayaḥ l
yamaṁ yo vidyāt sa brūyādyathaika ṛṣirvijānate svāhā ll18 ll

TĀr. 6.5

[Meaning] (yah) He who (vidyāt) knows (yamam) formation of sun, (sah) he can (ekah) alone (brūyāt) say that (vijānate) he knows (yathā) how (pañcha) the five evolutes of prakṛti called gross elements formed, (yathā ṣaḍ) how the six seasons formed (yathā pañchadaśa), how the 15 tithis [lunar days] formed and (ṛṣayah) how the other stars in the celestial sphere formed.

Note: In Yogadarśana also Patañjali says: सूर्ये संयमात् ब्रह्माण्ड ज्ञानम् (sūrye sañymāt brahmāṇḍa jñānam). That is when a yogī conducts sañyama in sun, he is able to know the formation of the whole universe.

त्रिकद्रुकेभिः पतति षड्डूर्वीरिकमिद् बृहत् ।
गायत्रीत्रिष्टुप्छन्दाꣳसि सर्वा ता यम आहिता स्वाहा ॥19॥ तैआ. 6.5

trikadrukebhiḥ patati ṣaḍūrvīrekam id bṛhat /
gāyatrītriṣṭupchhandāꣳsi sarvātāyama āhitā svāhā // TĀr. 6.5

[Meaning] (tri-kadrukebhiḥ) Through its three strides on earth- line of capricorn, line of cancer and equator, (yama) the sun [sunrays] (patati) fall perpendicular on in 12 months of a year at (ūrvīḥ) at six tropical lines plus (ekam bṛhat) one line with greatest diameter on earth, i.e. equator. (gāyatrī, triṣṭup chhandānsi sarvā tā) Gāyati, Triṣṭup etc. all chhandas are (yame āhitā) also based upon sun.

Note: Six plus one (seven) tropical places of earth where sunrays fall perpendicular in a year are:

On 21 Dec. 23.5^0 South of equator

On 21 Jan. 20^0 South of equator

On 18 Feb. 12^0 South of equator

On 21 March 0^0 equator (with greatest diameter)

On 21 April 12^0 North of equator

On 21 May 20^0 North of equator

On 21 June 23.5^0 North of equator (so on and so forth)

On 21 July 20^0 North of equator

On 22 August 12^0 North of equator

On 23 Sept. 0^0 equator (with greatest diameter)

On 21 Oct. 12^0 South of equator

On 21 Nov. 20^0 South of equator

On 21 Dec. 23.5^0 South of equator

अहरहर्नयमानो गामश्वं पुरुषं जगत् ।
वैवस्वतो न तृप्यति पंचभिर्मानवैर्यमः स्वाहा ॥20॥ तैआ. 6.5

aharaharnayamānau gāmaśvaṁ puruṣaṁ jagat I
vaivasvato na tṛpyati paṁchabhirmānavairyamaḥ
svāhā ॥20॥ TĀr. 6.5

[Meaning] (vaivasvataḥ yamaḥ) Galactic Sun (nayamānaḥ) taking along with it (gām) planets, satellites (aśvam), animals (puṛsam) and human beings (pañchabhiḥ mānavaḥ) made up of five bhūtas (jagat) goes around the Galaxy (ahar ahar) everyday and (na) never (tṛpyati) gets tired or stops.

वैवस्वते विविच्यन्ते यमे राजनि ते जनाः ।
ये चेह सत्येनेच्छन्ते य उ चानृत्वादिनः स्वाहा ॥21॥ तैआ. 6.5

vaivasvate vivichyante yame rājani te janāḥ I
ye cheha satyenechchhante ya u chānṛtvādinaḥ svāhā ॥21॥
TĀr. 6.5

[Meaning] (vaivasvate yame rājani) In the domain of the Galactic sun, which is the king of our universe, (vivichyante) a rational discrimination can be made between (ye) the men (satyena ichhante) who have attachment with eternal things (iha) in this world (u cha) and (ye) those (anṛtavādinaḥ) who have attachment with material things.

Note: Persons attached with eternal soul or Brahman rise up to divinity and finally attain mokṣa and those attached with material things are downgraded to lower species.

ते राजन्निह विविच्यन्तेऽथा यन्ति त्वामुप ।
देवांश्च ये नमस्यन्ति ब्राह्मणांश्चापचित्यति स्वाहा ॥22॥ तैआ. 6.5

te rājanniha vivichyante'thā yanti tvāmupa I
devāṁścha ye namasyanti brāhmaṇāṁśchāpachityani
svāhā ॥22॥ TĀr. 6.5

[Meaning] O Galactic sun! (iha) In this world, (atha upayānti tvām) at the time of death are discriminated the persons on two basis (ye) who (namasyanti) follow the path of (devāścha) enlightened beings (cha) and (apachityati) who follow the path of yajña, dāna and tapa [austerity].

Note: Those follow the path of enlightened beings attain mokṣa and those follow the path of yajña, dāna and tapa attain spiritual happiness in their next life.

यस्मिन्वृक्षे सुपलाशे देवैः संपिबते यमः ।
अत्रा नो विश्पतिः पिता पुराणा अनुवेनति स्वाहा ॥23॥ तैआ. 6.5

yasminvṛkṣe supalāśe devaiḥ saṁpibate yamaḥ |
atrā no viśpatiḥ pitā purāṇā anuvenati svāhā ॥23॥ TĀr. 6.5

[Meaning] (yamaḥ) The Brahman (saṁpibate) is realised properly (yasmin vṛkṣe supalāśe) on this Palāśa-tree of earth decked with worthless beautiful leaves (devaiḥ) by the enlightened persons. (viśpati) Brahman, who is lord of universe and (naḥ pitā) protects us like father (anuvenati) conducts (atra) here everything (purāṇāḥ) since time immemorial.

उत्ते तभ्नोमि पृथिवीं त्वत्परीमं लोकं निदधन्मो अहᳵ रिषम् । एताᳵ स्थूणां पितरो धारयन्तु तेऽत्रा यमः सादानात्ते मिनोतु स्वाहा ॥24॥ तैआ. 6.7

utte tabhnomi pṛthivīṁ tvatparīmaṁ lokaṁ nidadhanmo ahaᳵ riṣam | ētāᳵ sthūṇāṁ pitaro dhārayantu te'trā yamaḥ sādānātte minotu svāhā ॥24॥ TĀr. 6.7

[Meaning] O jīvas! I, Brahman, (ut tabhnomi) created (pṛthivīm) the earth (te) for you. O earth! (nidadhan) I have created (imam lokam) these creatures on you. (aham) I (mo) never (riṣām) give pain to anyone. Let the (pitaraḥ) men of wisdom amongst you (dhārayantu) maintain (etām) this (sthūṇām) earth. Let the (yamaḥ) sun or the king of universe (minotu) make this earth worthy of (te) your (sādanāt) abode.

यथाऽहान्यनुपूर्वं भवन्ति यथर्त्तव ऋतुभिर्यन्ति क्लृप्ताः ।
यथा न पूर्वमपरो जहात्येवा धातरायूꣳषि कल्पयैषां स्वाहा ॥25॥ तैआ. 6.10

*yathā'hānyanupūrvaṁ bhavanti yatharttava ṛtubhiryanti
klṛptāḥ /*
*yathā na pūrvamaparo jahātyevā dhātarāyū ṣi kalpayaiṣāṁ
svāhā ॥25॥ TĀr. 6.10*

[Meaning] (yathā) As (ahāni) the days (anpūrvam)
pass one after another, (yathā) as (ṛtavaḥ) the seasons
(kḷptāḥ yanti) linked with (ṛtubhiḥ) each other come and
go, (yathā) as (aparaḥ) the latter (na) does not (jahāti)
leave (pūrvam) former, (eva) in the same manner,
(kalpaya) manage (āyunṣi) the lives of (jñātayaḥ) these
living beings, (Dhātaḥ) O my Lord!

नहि ते अग्रे तनुवै क्रूरं चकार मर्त्यः । कपिर्बभस्ति तेजनं पुनर्जरायु गौरिव ।
अप नः शोशुचदघमग्रे शुशुध्या रयिम् । अपः नः शोशुचदघं मृत्यवे स्वाहा ॥26॥

तैआ. 6.10

*nahi te agne tanuvai krūraṁ chakāra martyaḥ /
kapirbabhasti tejanaṁ punarjarāyugauriva /   apa naḥ
śośuchadaghamagne śuśudhyā ryim / apaḥ naḥ śośuchadaghaṁ
mṛtyave svāhā ॥26॥ TĀr. 6.10*

[Meaning] O Brahman! Let (nahi martyaḥ) nobody
(chakāra) does (krūram) acts of cruelty (tanuvai) for the
maintenace of his/her body (te) in your creation. Let a
rajogūṇa dominant human being (kapiḥ) acting like
monkey (tejanam babhasti) sharpen and protect his/her
skills such as a cow protect its womb through
membrane. (Agne) O Brahman, (apa śośuchat) burn
(naḥ) our (agham) bad sanskāras and (śuśudhyā) purify
our (rayim) spiritual wealth. Once more (apaśośuchat)
burn (naḥ) our (agham) bad or tāmasika sanskāras. This
last oblation is for the death that separates a person from

his/her near and dear ones.

The 26 oblations with these above mantras be offered, thus there are one hundred twenty-one oblations in all, from 'अग्नये स्वाहाः *(agnaye svāhāḥ)*' to 'मृत्यवे स्वाहा *(mṛtyave svāhā)*'।

If four persons are engaged in offering oblations, the number of oblations thus becomes four hundred eighty-four and if only two persons give oblations, then they become two hundred forty-two oblations. If there is more ghee, more oblations can be offered again with these one hundred twenty-one mantras. These be repeated as long as the body is completerly burnt into ashes.

When the deadbody turns into ashes, all the survivors of the dead person should wash their clothes, take bath and wash-clean the house. They should then offer the oblations of ghee mixed with odiferous substances chaning the mantras of Svastivāchana and Śāntikaraṇa adding the word स्वाहा *(svāhā)* at the end of each mantra, so that the air of the dead person is replaced by fresh air keeping the survivors' mind hale and hearty. If cremation is followed by night, same oblations can be offered on the following day.

On the third day from the date of the cremation, any relative of the dead person should go to the cremation ground, pick up the burnt bones from the pyre and put them at any separate place into cremation ground meant for that purpose. Besides this, there remains nothing to be done for the dead, as it has been previously proved by the mantra of the *Yajurveda* 'भस्मान्तꣳ शरीरम्' *(bhasmāntaꣳ śarīram)* that there is no rite to be done for the dead except consigning the mortal remains to the flame and picking up the burnt bones (from the pyre and securing them somewhere in the cremation ground meant for that purpose). Yes, should a person belong to a well-to-do family, he/she in his lifetime or his/her survivors after his/her death may donate money for the proleferation of Vedic knowledge, or propagation of Vedic dharma, and or supporting an orphanage, nothing better than this.

इति मृतकसंस्कारविधिः समाप्तः ॥

iti mṛtakasaṁskāravidhiḥ samāptaḥ ॥

Here ends the procedure of the rite of the dead.

इति श्रीमत्परमहंसपरिव्राजकाचार्याणां श्रीयुतविरजानन्दसरस्वतीस्वामिनां महाविदुषां शिष्यस्य वेदविहिताचारधर्मनिरूपकस्य श्रीमद्दयानन्दसरस्वतीस्वामिनः कृतौ संस्कारविधिर्ग्रन्थः पूर्तिमगात् ॥

iti śrīmatparamahaṁsaparivrājakāchāryāṇāṁ

śrīyutavirajānandasarasvatīsvāmināṁ mahāviduṣāṁ

śiṣyasya vedavihitāchāradharmanirūpakasya

śrīmaddayānandasarasvatīsvāminaḥ kṛtau

saṁskāravidhirgranthaḥ pūrtimagāt ॥